T0342109

The Studios after the Studios

Post 45

Florence Dore and Michael Szalay, Editors
Post•45 Group, Editorial Committee

The Studios after the Studios

Neoclassical Hollywood (1970–2010)

J. D. Connor

Stanford University Press
Stanford, California

Stanford University Press
Stanford, California

This book has been published with the assistance of the Frederick W. Hilles Publication Fund of Yale University.

Printed in the United States of America on acid-free, archival-quality paper

Library of Congress Cataloging-in-Publication Data

Connor, J. D., author.
  The studios after the studios : neoclassical Hollywood (1970-2010) / J.D. Connor.
      pages cm -- (Post 45)
  Includes bibliographical references and index.
  ISBN 978-0-8047-9077-2 (cloth : alk. paper)
  1. Motion picture studios--California--Los Angeles--History. 2. Motion picture industry--California--Los Angeles--History. 3. Motion pictures--California--Los Angeles--History.
  4. Hollywood (Los Angeles, Calif.)--History. I. Title. II. Series: Post 45.
  PN1993.5.U65C626 2015
  384'.80979494--dc23
                              2014045954
  ISBN 978-0-8047-9474-9 (electronic)

Typeset by Bruce Lundquist in 10/15 Minion

Table of Contents

Acknowledgments

A book this long in the works incurs debts far too numerous to be repaid, but some of them are long-standing enough to have been forgiven. The first is owed to Stanley Cavell, who taught me how to watch movies and encouraged me to go to Johns Hopkins. The second is to Michael Rogin, who *told* me to go to Hopkins and who edited my first important piece of film writing. At Hopkins, my reading, writing, and teaching were shaped by Neil Hertz, Walter Benn Michaels, Kirstie McClure, Michael Fried, and Richard Macksey. This book in particular originated as an argument for and with Jerry Christensen's remarkable account of Hollywood filmmaking. His counsel has been invaluable.

My colleagues at Harvard, notably David Rodowick and Despina Kakoudaki, kept me afloat. Marjorie Garber gave me my shot. Tom Conley was a constant prod to read more deeply. Jim Engell provided crucial encouragement at an early stage of the project. Louis Menand was a model of humane mentoring and crystalline writing. My time there was leavened by visiting colleagues Haidee Wasson, Charles Acland, and Jim Hoberman, and Super TFs Dan Reynolds and Ally Field. Robb Moss was a perpetual reminder of the importance of our work, particularly our teaching. He also introduced me to production designer Rick Carter. Rick is as fascinated by the interplay of art and industry in Hollywood as I am and has been an essential interlocutor over the years.

At Yale my chairs, Alex Nemerov, David Joselit, and Ned Cooke in history of art, and Dudley Andrew and John MacKay in film studies, have been unflagging supporters. The collegiality in both programs has been a boon, and I want to thank in particular Carol Armstrong, Tim Barringer, Craig Buckley, Francesco Casetti, Milette Gaifman, Aaron Gerow, Ron Gregg, Erica James, Jackie Jung, Joost Keizer, Youn-mi Kim, Diana Kleiner, Kobena Mercer, Charles Musser, Rob Nelson, Brigitte Peucker, Kishwar Rizvi, Tamara Sears, Chris Wood, Mimi Yiengpruskawan, and Sebastian Zeidler.

I first encountered real editing in the work of Josh Glenn, Tom Frank, and Meghan O'Rourke. They believed that if I would only get out of the way of my prose, I actually had something to say. I hope I have, and I hope they are right.

As large as this book is, it stands upon an archive of hundreds of other readings done by absolutely superb undergraduates at Harvard and Yale and upon a monumental archive of financial data compiled in part by Carrie Andersen. I have also benefited from librarians in the special collections at the Margaret Herrick Library and the Baker Business Library at Harvard.

The Post•45 Series editors, Florence Dore and Michael Szalay, are the most dedicated commenters I have ever known. They and the other members of the Post•45 Steering Committee—Mary Esteve, Andy Hoberek, Amy Hungerford, Sean McCann, Deak Nabers, and Debbie Nelson—have suffered with this book almost as much as I have; they are true friends. Debbie also provided a comprehensive reading of the manuscript at a late stage. Over the years, Post•45 conferences have brought dozens of scholars together to discuss their work and, occasionally, mine. Those intimate, intense gatherings are the best warrant for the profession's continued productivity I know. Thomas Elsaesser, Richard Godden, Cathy Jurca, and Mark McGurl are great readers. They have posed questions that never stop nagging, and at various times I have attempted to ventriloquize and then answer them.

Emily-Jane Cohen went to bat for this first book, and for Post•45, and I cannot thank her enough. She and her team at Stanford University Press have been patient and accommodating as I figured out what the book was and what it wasn't. Friederike Sundaram was a sure hand through the production process. Cynthia Lindlof provided stellar copyediting. I would also like to thank the anonymous reader for the press, who offered essential late comments.

Part of Chapter 1 appeared in different form in "The Projections: Allegories of Industrial Crisis in Neoclassical Hollywood," *Representations* 71 (Summer 2000). Part of Chapter 7 appeared as "*U-571*: Breaking a Studio's Code," *The Baffler* 15 (February 2003). And part of Chapter 8 appeared as "The Anxious Epic," *Boston Globe*, November 28, 2004. I thank them for permission to reprint.

Finally, none of this would have been possible without the love and support of my wife, Lisa. She and our children, Henry and Margaret, make even the worst movies a treat.

The Studios after the Studios

Introduction

"Like every Hollywood movie, on some level it was about the business," Peter Biskind says about *Greystoke: The Legend of Tarzan, Lord of the Apes* (Hugh Hudson, Warner Bros., 1984).[1] It sounds like hyperbole—*every* Hollywood movie?—but Biskind explains that *Greystoke* is "about" the business because Tarzan represents "defenseless screenwriter" Robert Towne, threatened by "ferocious carnivores" in the industry. He leaves it at that, and if "every Hollywood movie" were about the business in that general way, we could leave it at that as well. We would not need to attend to the economic and institutional details of a film's production in order to understand it. But if it turns out that Hollywood movies are fundamentally about the business, then we have been doing the business of criticism wrong. We have failed to take our hyperbole to heart. While critics find it easy enough to demonstrate that movies are about many things, and while historians have done prodigious work tracing the operations of the business itself, with very few exceptions we have not explored Hollywood's peculiar sort of self-representation in sufficient detail, and we have not committed ourselves to reading films as corporate and industrial allegories as deeply as we should. As a consequence, and despite nearly a century of sustained effort, criticism has only barely begun to come to terms with the actual significance of Hollywood movies. We know that movies are at the center of the culture, or very near it; we know that years of labor and millions of dollars go into making and marketing them; we know that they solicit and often reward extreme levels of attention; yet somehow we don't quite know how labor and capital are transmogrified into story and style—or, how *this* labor and *this* capital become *this* story spun *this* way. And whenever we do discover a path that leads from the production to the narrative, or from the story to the backstory, that path seems contingent and willful, a desperate mark left by a "defenseless" individual protesting a "ferocious" institution.

Where Biskind suggests that movies are about the business because they capture the experience of particular individuals working in it, I propose that movies (Hollywood movies, in this era) are about the business more intensely—both more personally and more collectively. They are representations of experience, yes, but they can be much besides: scenarios, strategies, suggestions, pleas, business plans—there is no ruling out the role of the motion picture in the lives or careers or histories of its creators. The pressures that individuals, groups, guilds, professions, and corporations face can be channeled through their collective work on films. The balance between competing potential authors can be worked out on the page, on set, and on the screen far more precisely than criticism typically admits. Working out the correct balance among differing accounts of the system and the individual's role within it required the efforts of highly talented participants. And in the period I am discussing, from about 1970 to about 2010, those participants were guided by the conventions of their crafts and the imperatives of their industry toward classical values of necessity, continuity, and complementarity even when elements in the writing, or design, or effects were riotously excessive. Against those forces that would dissipate individual or corporate identity, Hollywood neoclassicism was in large part an effort to brand movies and their studios, and in the cases of the major franchises, it succeeded. In the process, movies became more intensely "about the business" than ever.

As a hypothesis, this yields immediate results. To return to Biskind's example, *Greystoke*'s allegory of contemporary screenwriting is fuller than he implies. In Towne's 1977 script, Tarzan masters speech and becomes something of a killer for hire, doing away with a man-eating lion in exchange for his passage to England. There, he inherits a title (authorship) and an estate (studio), but, new to the civilized world, he nearly dies of a childhood disease. When he recovers, he returns, again, to the jungle. To stay? The script is ambiguous—it trails off in outline form; certainly Towne would have changed much of the ending.[2] As allegory, though, it captures the fundamental late-seventies quandary of the screenwriter-auteur: Is he the proper heir of the great studio heads? (Jack Warner had only left the studio in the early seventies.) Will the foundling writer take his "rightful place" in the empire, or will he head off into the jungle? Towne didn't know, couldn't have known. He hadn't seen what direction the project would take.

If the script was open-ended, Towne hoped to work it out by directing it himself. But his plans were dashed when he ran over budget on his debut, *Personal Best*, and was compelled to sell *Greystoke* outright to Warners.[3] The studio made drastic changes to the story, reshuffling its timeline and rebalancing the narrative. Towne pulled his name from it and substituted that of his dog, P. H. Vazak. (The dog was nominated for an Oscar but lost.) Yet the screenplay did not become "less" about the business as a result of these changes. Like Towne, Warner Bros. didn't quite know how the story would end. It did know that "the old boy" (as director Hugh Hudson calls the elder Greystoke) was on his way out, and it certainly knew that turning the place over to some half-wild screenwriter (like Towne) was crazy. At the same time the studio also knew that the emotional turmoil generated by the conflict between dependence and autonomy was useful to it. Warners, in other words, knew that it needed screenwriters, and when it took control of *Greystoke*, it continued to build on Towne's allegorical foundation, reconfiguring it as a think piece on studio control. The hired-killer aspects were cut, and the tale of the lone screenwriter fighting off a band of angry carnivores became, more or less, Act I, just as Towne's struggles were Act I in the allegory of the film's production. At this point in the new narrative, the industry arrives, as literally as possible: A British expedition comes chugging down the river on the *Lucy Fisher*, shooting almost randomly (an evil version of cinematographer John Alcott), slaughtering apes in the name of science, inflating their carcasses with a bicycle pump in order to take more realistic pictures of them (an evil version of creature-crafter Rick Baker). As Hudson explained, the boat was "named after the executive Lucy Fisher at Warner Bros. at the time, [who] looked after the production of the film from the studio point of view."[4] The production had reason to feel fondly toward its producer. She had worked on Hudson's *Chariots of Fire* (Fox, 1981), and when she moved to Warners, she brought Hudson, some of the crew, and several actors along for *Greystoke*.

The identification of the studio with British imperial aristocracy was enticing. For the filmmakers, the decision to shoot the jungle scenes in Cameroon made them cinematic "pioneers," just like the members of the expedition. The

Figure I.1. The industry arrives in the form of the *Lucy Fisher*. *Greystoke* (Hugh Hudson, Warner Bros., 1984)

mapping of historical context onto production context proved irresistible, and in their DVD commentary Hudson and his line producer cannot help themselves, effortlessly slipping back and forth between descriptions of British imperial adventures and their own. But the movie takes its imperialism seriously throughout. The film delays its credits until after a jungle prologue. Only then do we see the Warners logo, followed by "Warner Bros. Presents" over a long shot of the Greystoke manor. It looks like a studio, and it functions like one—it sends out expeditions (productions), it commissions paintings (pictures), it supports museums (film libraries), and it is handed down across the generations (perhaps). It is also filled with strategic talk. Much later, the Sixth Earl, played by Ralph Richardson, will take his grandson to look at the estate wall and will explain the principles of studio rule: "I've seen other fellows sell off bits of theirs. . . . Never sell. Never, ever sell. Do anything to keep it whole. You understand me? Yourself whole." After the old earl dies, Tarzan replays this speech to himself.

This was rubbing Towne's (dog's) nose in it. Forced to give up his dream project, he could only watch as Warners endorsed his anxieties. Perhaps the studio understood writers after all. Despite all its talk of inheritance and baronial integrity, the film utterly forgets to sort out what happens to the title and the estate once Tarzan goes back into the jungle. Late in the floundering Act III, Tarzan's benevolent tutor and his imperial nemesis face off in a common room nature/nurture debate. The tutor (D'Arnot, "the humanist," Hudson calls him) declares that Tarzan is "what the jungle has made him." The nemesis (Sir Evelyn Blount, "the rationalist") responds that Tarzan must not only "be greater than the accident of his childhood" but "must be seen to be so." It is all so much pointless disputation, and we are meant to side with Jane, the American ward of the manor, who declares through her tears, "He must be allowed to decide for himself. . . . We want for him only what he wants for himself: to be whole." Yet there is no wholeness to be had—"Half of me is Greystoke; the other half is wild," Tarzan declares. Stay or go, he will always be divided. The ending will never make sense for him. It is Jane who exemplifies the Greystoke commitment to integrity and wholeness, Jane who lives the family motto: "Yielde to None." During production, there was some question about whether she would go with him in the end; she doesn't. And though her path to the inheritance is complicated by her gender and the distance of her relationship, she is the rightful heir. She is the enlightened studio exec. She is Lucy Fisher.

The screenwriter's story becomes the executive's story, but both are part of the studio's story. The movie is named for the house, not the man; *Greystoke*, not *John Clayton*. Towne's understanding of his role in the system becomes one part of the system as a whole, alongside Hugh Hudson's imperial dreamings and Lucy Fisher's affective inheritance. Hollywood movies are sites of conflict and collaboration, but they are just as readily sites of individual and collective self-reflection. In this era, those reflections are put to work across scales as studios strive to create and maintain both conglomerate corporate identities and the broader industrial framework—a context in which films might serve as mirrors of and figures for collective work. To have a reading of a film—even a partial reading such as this account of *Greystoke*—requires a detailed account of the business of which it is a part. But the converse is also true—the business would not exist in the same way without the stories it tells. This is the neoclassical balance between story and backstory.

. . .

The case of *Greystoke* suggests the following general form: allegory emerges where industrial pressures intersect and where creative actors are able to imagine symbolic solutions to real problems. As we trace the overarching question of the relationship between particular movies and the particular financial and labor relations underpinning their making and marketing, broader questions arise. There are questions of prevalence and significance, history and possibility, method and epistemology. How widespread are these allegories? And how important are they to the operation of the system? *How* and how *intensely* are movies about the business? On what occasions does that intensity wax and wane? Is there a history to the very possibility that a movie might be about the business? If movies are, "at some level" about the business, what are the contours of those levels? And if it is simple enough to say that movies are about the business, why don't we take that idea seriously? How could our culture continue to elude our attempts to understand it?

I assume there will be resistance to this sort of account, for several reasons. One is a general wariness about allegory, and it is worth treating first because it may be the most long-standing way of acknowledging and then denying the relationship between films and their production. If it is difficult enough for a Hollywood movie to tell one story properly, it seems greedy to expect it to tell at least two and foolish to expect those two stories to sync up sufficiently that they might be necessary for each other. What is worse, if we were to attempt to trace the allegory, the more the details of our reading began to pile up, the more those compelling bits and pieces would threaten to reduce the film to its allegories or to promise a secret key to a narrative that was compelling in its own right. Thus, when we do find the idea of allegory popping up in criticism, there we usually find a hasty denial of its importance. Implicit meanings are suggestive and fun to play around with but ultimately, for some reason, unbelievable.

You don't build a history of cinema out of inside jokes. Here, for example, is Peter Wollen backing away from his own reading of *Singin' in the Rain*:

> It is tempting to try to interpret *Singin' in the Rain* in terms of the political climate in which it was made: to note, for example, that the story hinges on the thwarting of a plot to blacklist Kathy Selden, launched by an informer and enforced by using the media to pressure a weak-willed studio, which ultimately puts profit before principle, until finally the situation is resolved and virtue triumphs in a wishful happy ending. Or perhaps the "Singin' in the Rain" dance sequence represents Kelly's determination to be optimistic in a miserable political climate, insisting that he may have behaved in an unorthodox, uninhibited way, but that basically he is joyous and generous and American whatever the law may think as it holds him in its disapproving gaze. Perhaps.[5]

The reading is tempting enough that Wollen cannot resist publishing it, but not so tempting that he can admit to believing it or, more important, that he can admit that MGM, or the Freed Unit, or Gene Kelly believed it. Even so, once we have begun moving down the path of temptation, we may also notice that the film is about "making stars talk," that it recognizes that this new force is not a passing fad, and that the sustained analog for this new situation is the decapitative violence of the French Revolution, from its tumbrils to its dummies to its display window filled with cloche-capped heads.[6] You can see why Wollen was tempted; you can also see why he applied the brakes.

One reason he is wary is specific to the era of the blacklist: the sort of subversive storytelling he sees in *Singin' in the Rain* is uncomfortably close to the subversive notions of Hollywood that the members of the House Un-American Activities Committee (HUAC) indulged in. And if one feels that the blacklist was a horrible squandering of American artistic talent and potential in the name of a paranoid delusion, as Wollen does, then it is hard to endorse the hermeneutic process that attended it. But the local reason for Wollen's self-doubt is only magnified when we wonder not simply whether a particular film has a hidden political meaning but whether movies in general depend on allegory in order to constitute themselves as a system. You may not *want* to believe that movies are up to something implicit, but you can certainly be tempted that way. You may not be *able* to believe that something as jury-rigged as an allegory could result in the consistencies we find in the Hollywood system—it seems impossible. That is, critics are wary of allegorical systems because they seem too intentional to account for systems that seem to exceed anyone's ability to master them. Even if we grant that the folks making these movies know what they are about, we don't credit the idea that this is one of the things that they know.

A second reason that industrial allegory has not been taken seriously as an underpinning for the Hollywood system is that there is too great a gap between the needs of the corporation and the power of the individual film. Individuals like Robert Towne might make a film mean what they want it to, but they can't do as much for Warner Bros. But if we are thinking this way, we are already endorsing the defenseless individual in the land of carnivores understanding of the industry, and that understanding is a *reading* of the industry, not a neutral description. We might change our premises by acknowledging that the overwhelming "real problem" of the contemporary entertainment conglomerate is the need for an ever-larger market. Paul Grainge runs directly into the gap between system and instance as he traces the ways in which the major conglomerates scour the globe to extend their brands, chasing down fugitive entertainment experiences in an effort to monetize them. As he puts it, that marketing effort—the "practice" of branding—necessarily entails image making and storytelling—the "poetics" of branding. Further, he argues that the logo is the essential trope of that corporate poem, the lever by which a dispersed audience is gathered together to be sold to. Logos "demonstrate industrial attempts to affect, or allegorize, the gestalt of total entertainment."[7] Grainge begins from the "postclassical" situation in which both the cinematic experience and the studio origin have become fragmented—hence the corporate anxieties, and hence the need for aggressive inclusion. Thomas Elsaesser concurs with Grainge's "focus on branding and the logo" as "a principle of homeostasis . . . a chief strategy for capturing and managing these volatile masses and markets."[8] But while Elsaesser can believe that logos are part of an essential strategy of brand extension, the notion that these efforts are worked out allegorically seems implausible to him. The elaboration of the poetics of branding into full-blown corporate allegorical readings results in interpretations that are, he says, "suggestive rather than persuasive, and perhaps too narrowly framed to lend themselves to generalization."[9] No matter how intense the corporate interest in its own brand of poetics, it cannot make the leap from the narrow frame to an account with systematic power.

If logos, which are everywhere, are a "chief strategy," but individual allegorical accounts of films like *Greystoke* are too narrowly framed, how might such readings achieve the sort of saturation that logos have? One way would be to look to genres, not individual films or studios, as the source of industrial allegory. Vivian Sobchack takes up the case of the grand historical epics of the fifties and sixties to do just that. Pursuing an account of audience experience in the last moments of the classical era, she argues that "the genre *formally repeats* the surge, splendor, and extravagance, the human labor and capital cost entailed by its narrative's *historical content* both in its *production process* and its *modes of representation.*" With the films standing as mirrors between the masses on-screen and the masses in the theater, "the genre *allegorically* and *carnally* inscribes on the model spectator" the sense of being a subject in and of History, but a history where she might recognize the excess on-screen as part of her experience of "a historically specific *consumer* culture."[10] That is, the historical epic says to its model audience that all this—all this money, all this blood, all this labor—has been expended for *you*, you as the inheritor of millennia of history, you as the audience for this monumental motion picture.

Compelling as Sobchack's account is, it remains partial. Genre is not the sole way in which industrial allegory comes to occupy the center of systemic self-reflection. Two other critics, John Thornton Caldwell and Jerome Christensen, have attempted to make clear how it is possible for corporate or industrial self-representation to result in something as durable as the system we have come to know. The emblem of this self-regard is indeed the logo, but the homeostatic operation of the logo, like the allegorical and carnal suture of the epic, is but one example. In *Production Culture*, his largely ethnographic account of the contemporary film-and-television system, Caldwell describes the postclassical system from the labor side outward rather than from the audience side in. For him, the ever-more-fragmented and -flexible industry of the last two decades requires ever-more-intense self-reflection. "Within the nomadic labor and serial employment system now in place, any area that wishes to remain vital—in the face of endless new technologies, increased competition, and changes in production—must constantly work, through symbolic means, to underscore the distinctiveness and importance of their artistic specialization." At most levels of the industry, these symbolic means are deep texts—demo reels, trade shows, producers' script notes. They are the "native theories" of practitioner groups at various levels of the hierarchy. The system is manic and anxious, and the results are self-reflexivity: "Film and television companies, in particular, acknowledge image making as their primary business, and they use reflexive images (images about images) to cultivate valuable forms of public awareness and employee recognition inside and outside of the organization."[11] Allegory thus wends its way through the industry, pushed along by everyone from below-the-line workers up through the executive ranks.

At the top of Caldwell's organizational hierarchy are "industrial identities" and "industrial auteurs," and they exist both as the accumulated sediments of thousands of individual participants and as independent categories. This is closer to the framework that would make something like my reading of *Greystoke* possible, but the industry here is always the integrated film-and-television industry, not "the movie business." And as a corollary to Caldwell's democratization of reflexivity, none of the symbolic means through which those industrial anxieties are processed holds pride of place. A digital effects bakeoff is as revelatory as, say, *Spider-Man* (Sam Raimi, Columbia, 2002). Motion pictures have no special place in this media ecosystem—they typically draw more labor and capital and have higher production values, but what makes the system a system is the generalized anxiety.

This is the point at which Christensen parts ways with Caldwell. In *America's Corporate Art*, Christensen makes the most sustained case yet that movies are about the business.[12] Early on, he notes that Caldwell is less interested in "the movies themselves" than the situation of workers in a "post-network industrial world" and proceeds to offer stunning accounts of individual films as a way of renormalizing film history around the idea that studios matter.[13] The distinction he draws has two aspects, though, and they ought to be separated. First, there is the apparent difference between someone interested in films-as-texts and someone interested in labor arrangements. Yet that difference seems to fall by the wayside when we realize that Caldwell and Christensen fundamentally agree that the texts are the locations in which corporate policies are worked through. The relationships between text/corporation/worker/union/and so on are ever shifting and certainly warrant investigation from each side, but Caldwell and Christensen share the sense that these relationships are of such intensity that they can generate industrial allegories. Which brings us to the second difference, between someone who conceives of the industry as fundamentally "the movies themselves" and someone who considers "cinema within the diverse contexts of electronic media," that is, between someone who appears to be an old-fashioned studio cinephile and someone for whom cinema no longer holds pride of place now that the labor situation has been flexibilized and the corporate situation has been conglomerated beyond recognition. Who is correct?

Either might be, and given that possibility, we ought to reformulate the question: Who is correct *now*? If we take the position that broad industrial continuities are at the same time subject to contingent rearrangements in the service of corporate strategies, we might see the opposition between Caldwell and Christensen as a historical question, and we might ask how someone could hold Christensen's position—that films are the privileged objects of interpretation—in Caldwell's world of diverse electronic media. Here is Sony America's chairman and CEO Howard Stringer, speaking in the summer of 2001, offering his explanation for why movies matter even when they are parts of conglomerates as far-flung as Sony:

> You could make the case that the movie is the most fundamentally symbolic piece of content that any media company develops. It drives all your content. It's the most

visible. It's the most conspicuous. It's the most dangerous. It's the most exciting. And as the world becomes ever more aware of content, movies will go wider and wider. When the digital world is really here, movies can be disseminated from satellite direct to homes and direct to small theaters in Mongolia and northern Russia and obscure places that the market for movies is going to grow and grow and grow. And it's really the flagship of your content. It's not the most profitable part at the moment. It can be profitable. But it drives everything else that you do and it lives forever.[14]

Stringer here is engaging in a bit of industrial reflection, as befits a CEO when asked to weigh in on the importance of a particular division. But he is in agreement with his contemporary CEOs across the industry—with Barry Diller and Michael Eisner and Steve Ross and Gerald Levin and others—that what is decisive about this period is the sense that movies remain the center of the conglomerate even within a post-network configuration of electronic media. If the practical project of this book is to justify the allegorical interpretation of individual films, and the theoretical project is to explain how those allegorical intentions add up to and drive the Hollywood motion picture industry, then the historical project is to show how that sort of self-representation was also self-enabling, how movies retained their hold on the center of the entertainment mediascape. How do motion pictures sustain their corporate prominence when the industry is no longer underwritten by the economic structures that supported the classical Hollywood studios? Why does Howard Stringer sound like Christensen in Caldwell's world?

When Christensen explains that movies embody corporate strategy, he is ever so close to Stringer explaining that movies "drive everything" (that's the strategy) and "live forever" (that's the corporate). And when Stringer unites critics, companies, and employees in a universal second person—"you could make the case," "drives all your content," and "drives everything else that you do"—he is close to Christensen's notion of movies as corporate speech. Christensen's version of corporate authorship goes like this: "There is no interpretation without meaning, no meaning without intention, no intention without an author, no author without a person, no person with greater right to or capacity for authorship than a corporate person, and finally, no corporate person who can act without an agent."[15] Since this book has such obvious similarities to Christensen's work, I want to pay particular attention to the difference between his fifth claim—"no person with greater right to or capacity for authorship than a corporate person"—and the other five. The other links in the chain are a set of absolute entailments, but this one is a qualitative judgment. That difference hides an awful lot of history. If studios become speaking subjects—become authors—because the legal regime recognizes them as such, then the crucial transformations in the nature of corporate subjectivity will be those moments that lie just outside the system as a whole. Movies will make sense of, say, the *Miracle* decision or *Citizens United* or the battle between QVC and Viacom for control of Paramount, but the history of corporate subjectivity will lie, importantly, outside the films themselves. This seems to mistake the precipitates of corporate behavior for its causes, and by taking the results in this way, we give up what our new modes of critical attention have found. Christensen looks at the studio system, and it shatters into its constituent parts, but by regrouping the studios, he risks underselling the particularity he has uncovered. The Hollywood system is a complex bundling of contingency and regularity, and the actions and actors that shape and are shaped by it are always being rearranged, reinterpreted, reorganized. The corporate allegory that emerges under such conditions is not merely a unified text but the result of the "jurisdictional conflict," as Rick Altman calls it, between the myriad forces that have come to bear on the production.[16]

Consider, for a moment, a "natural person" with at least some "right or capacity for authorship." Now enfold this person in an environment in which dozens if not hundreds of others seek to exercise similar rights and demonstrate such capacities. Who among them believes that the corporate person that employs them enjoys greater rights and capacities? Christensen's answer is that "corporate employees become effective executives insofar as they are able to discern a [strategic] pattern" to the corporation's actions and are able to "make a decision consistent with the operant intention of the whole." That is, the effective executive believes what Christensen posits and serves as the corporation's necessary agent. One difficulty with this account is that when someone steps forward to serve as the corporation's agent, that identification is one "that people may recognize, but not one to which anyone must consent."[17] The battle over the interpretation of corporate strategy continues.

In Christensen's theory, our interpretations need only the text in order to build the world of agents and intentions that make the allegory run. But in his practice, Christensen toggles back and forth between text and production history, providing readings that are contingent upon the differing economic arrangements and organizational imperatives at each studio. And it is, again, the practice that is worth following. The smoking guns of agents' intentions exist—not in every case, but in enough cases that we are able to coherently trace out the conflicts and cohesions between interests, programs, needs, and aims that underlie these collaborative creative works. We move back and forth between texts and actors not simply for hermeneutic reasons but because the texts that capture the interlocking agendas of their contributing authors are coherent and fractured, depending. A studio's self-reflections are essential—there is no denying that returning the studio to the category of necessary authors is an enormous leap forward in critical capacity—but within Hollywood, self-reflections are distributed across innumerable levels, from the lowliest term-contracted computer compositor to the studio production head to the conglomerate CEO; from Robert Towne to Hugh Hudson to Lucy Fisher; from union work-to-rule campaigns to Motion Picture Association of America (MPAA) lobbying efforts. In a context of potentially overwhelming anxiety the movie becomes the home of collective reflection, where competing visions of the current industrial configuration can play out.

The theoretical question of whether the meaningfulness of Hollywood movies depends on their being examples of corporate speech (Christensen's legal/ textual version) or the outcome of conflicts and cohesions among workers (Caldwell's labor/ethnographic version) can be similarly directed back into the historical project. How were the diverse interests of different laboring groups turned toward self-theorization? How were those theorizations harmonized so that they might serve even larger, transpersonal ends? How were those larger ends made to serve a particular corporate and industrial framework in which conglomerated entertainment companies could pin their identities onto particular texts that could nevertheless continue to provide possible avenues for workers' self-reflection? The opposition between corporate speech and labor struggle *is* the opposition between the movies themselves and the film/video industry. And the history of that opposition will be one in which studios compensated for the lack of balance in the work lives of their employees and the economic arrangements of their conglomerate owners by seeking balance in various ways on-screen.

* * *

In the chapter that follows, I lay out the interpretive protocols for the remainder of this book. Operating under the modern "package-unit" system of production—where each film is mounted by a new and one-off collection of talent rather than assembled from studio labor already under contract—studios face a great deal more uncertainty about their continuity as creative enterprises. Companies in creative industries, as economist Richard Caves argues, are uniquely dependent on their standing in the "creative community" for access to talent. As studios have become "mere" financiers and distributors, anxieties about identity and reputation have grown as well. In order to guarantee that their movies bear the corporate stamp, studios have allowed logos to bleed into the opening scenes of selected films: The WB becomes the Bat shield, the ice cap on the Universal globe melts to open *Waterworld*, and MGM, attempting to return to studio-level production after a decade of floundering, matches the lion's roar—the most famous studio logo of them all—to the StarGate itself, that portal to the good old days when MGM had "More Stars than there are in Heaven." Logorrhea is the most explicit and commonplace moment of branding within the cinematic experience.

In a time of remarkable mergers and a relentless drive for synergy, studios regularly sought the corporate control of the classical Hollywood era. "We're a new version of the old studio system," Jeffrey Katzenberg said of Disney (and then of DreamWorks).[18] But in an economic context radically different from the one that underpinned the classical studio system, the new classicism of the studios could never actually reconstitute a bygone era. Unable to restore the pillars of the past, studios aspired to that form of classicism they could achieve. It would be classicism at one remove, an idea of a studio, and it would be part of an economic strategy that would always be pre-aestheticized.

Once the framework is in place, the history proper can begin. The first section of the book investigates the paranoid narratives of the seventies. A generation of scholars regarded the paranoia of the New Hollywood directors as the cinematic realization of Watergate-era social unease. But a subsequent wave of writing has looked more closely at Hollywood's prolonged economic slump. For these critics, the financial successes of the movie brats somehow "saved" the old Hollywood—either by directing hits (as Biskind contends) or by replenishing the stock of genres and formal moves available to the system (as David Bordwell and Geoff King claim).

To be sure, in the late sixties and early seventies, studios turned to a variety of new directors in a rather desperate attempt to return to profitability. Still, no critic has yet suggested that in addition to providing a return on capital and a revivification of American film style, these self-conscious auteurs reinvented the studio as a powerful entity in its own right.[19] Yet every paranoid allegory of a large corporation crushing the "independent"—whether that was the independent crop duster in *Charley Varrick* (Don Siegel, Universal, 1973) or the independent surveillance man in *The Conversation* (Francis Ford Coppola, Paramount, 1974) or the independent truck drivers in *Sorcerer* (William Friedkin, Paramount/Universal, 1977)—added to the mythology of corporate power. And the major studios were only too glad to have someone fear them again. For directors of the New Hollywood, the readiest embodiments of the Watergate era were the studios themselves, and the auteurs' assertion of structural equivalence gave the studios the courage to be brands again.

To understand how that complex circulation of paranoia, allegory, production, and narrative might get under way, I begin with the most paradigmatic instance, Steven Spielberg and Universal's *Jaws* (1975). *Jaws* lies at the heart of most analyses of the New Hollywood for narrative reasons, but I show how the film's production and distribution gave rise to a particularly robust allegorical architecture that could serve the industry as a whole. If allegory is a method of reading that requires us to distinguish and then reconcile surface and depth, *Jaws* is a film positioned precisely where surface and depth meet. Its act breaks are confidently managed and insistently demarcated, a narrative assurance that carried over to its marketing. Universal and producers Richard Zanuck and David Brown were particularly attuned to the management of deep interpretations over its long run. That Universal drove the hardest bargain possible when negotiating with exhibitors is further evidence of that assurance.

The neoclassical era begins not with its full flowering in *Jaws* (or *Star Wars*) but piecemeal, spread across films and studios. I trace Paramount's version in part because in its deal to launch the Directors Company, it grappled more directly with the problem of institutionalized auteurism than its fellow studios did. Paramount was part of a typically seventies conglomerate, Gulf + Western; it had a charismatic CEO in Charlie Bluhdorn; and it clawed its way out of the industry slump by relying on the talents of key auteurs (Coppola, especially). Along the way, it installed design as the heart of the new system.

Paramount (and Warner Bros.) began the process of leading the studios out of the postclassical wilderness, but it was the rise and dominance of Creative Artists Agency (CAA) that set the terms for industrial success. Led by Mike Ovitz, the powerhouse agency achieved an unprecedented degree of authorial control over the projects its clients pursued. CAA represented more than simply a challenge to studio authority, though. Through Ovitz's particular fascinations—with Japan, with Armani, with pop art—the agency helped broker a certain Nipponization of the American economy.

In Part II, I survey several instances in which studios had to respond to radically changed contexts, some brought on by mergers, some by drastic shifts in the industry more generally. The inevitable gap between the development of a film and its reception, and the even longer gap between development and profitability, forced studios to imagine their films into a future they could not entirely control. Yet if they could not control the results of any particular film, the studios were living through an era of remarkable prosperity backstopped by cable, video, and eventually DVD revenues. Those bulwarks of profitability encouraged the studios to take on the task of projecting the futures of their corporate parents.

While the Directors Company was a financial fiasco, alongside it Paramount installed a new studio chief, Barry Diller. Diller and his fellow executives (Dawn Steel, Michael Eisner, Don Simpson, etc.) brought drastic change to the studio when they imported television-style discipline over both budgets and narratives. The "Killer Dillers" attempted to give the paranoid auteurs something worth fearing and agencies something to reckon with. At the same time, their vision of high-concept storytelling freed creative executives to concentrate on the allegorical relationships between the stories on film and the stories on the lot. The highest of the high-concept films showcased a hyperindustrial production design, usually at the expense of characterological depth. As Justin Wyatt has noted, these films and the stories they told emphasized style above all—the way one dresses, or takes pictures, or dances, or flies fighter jets, or fights crime, or practices medicine.[20] The ascendancy of production design capitalized on the paranoid gaze that the seventies auteurs had cultivated. And that combination not only opened the film to downstream markets that would reward repeated viewing; it also created space within the narrative for display, whether of stars or placed products mattered little. In other words, high-concept filmmaking was the formal antecedent to the emerging dominance of ancillary revenues.

Finding the correct balance between story and backstory required the efforts of artists and artisans, above and below the line. If they worked in contexts that undermined narrative coherence or encouraged design to run wild or pushed effects to extremes, the standards of their crafts pushed back. The formal bargain that was struck amounted to a cinema of controlled or motivated excess, and that bargain served as the baseline of the allegorical relationship between a studio and its conglomerate in the neoclassical era.

High-concept filmmaking invented the formal and narrative armature of neoclassicism, and studio resistance to agents spurred on the new ranks of creative executives in their efforts at control. The studios may have been merged into integrated conglomerates, but as publicly held companies, they were all answerable to their boards of directors and their shareholders. This and the culture of "suits" made studios notoriously risk averse. Some adopted risk-minimizing strategies on the financial side (Paramount and Disney most notably), while others believed that only enormous blockbusters might keep the studio profitable, however risky (Columbia and Warner Bros.). One genre to emerge from this endless quest to conquer risk I call the "chaos film." In these films, which stretched from *Groundhog Day* and *Jurassic Park* to *Pocahontas* and *The Butterfly Effect*, a popularized version of the sciences of nonlinear dynamics—chaos theory—served as a model and an alibi for Hollywood's negotiation with unpredictability and feedback. Studios later adopted certain nonlinear economic models as they attempted to predict their hits, but in this case as in others, the case for the economic strategy was made on-screen before it was made in the boardroom.

In Part III, I examine what may be the passing of the neoclassical era. In the wake of the AOL TimeWarner debacle and the implosion of Vivendi Universal, the case for the ever-more-integrated media company became harder to make. As these two companies learned their lesson the hard way, the films they created continued to serve as arenas in which they could imagine competing, yet plausible, accounts of their histories and their futures. That imagination has taken the form of rigorous questioning of expanse—of plans too great to attempt. At Universal (on its way from Matsushita to Vivendi Universal to GE to, now, Comcast), the expanse was the sea, the world of water. At Warners (on its way from TimeWarner to AOL TimeWarner and back), there were similar seaborne misadventures (*Poseidon*), but the studio was far more interested in personification: the Danny Ocean of *Ocean's 11* (and *12* and *13*). With Steven Soderbergh serving as its in-house auteur, Warner Bros. thought its way through, and beyond, the merger with AOL, ultimately finding itself in agreement with eventual CEO Jeff Bewkes, that synergy "is bullshit." However differently Universal and Warner Bros. reckoned with the megamerger gone bad, the studios' motion pictures continued to represent the studios to themselves, even as the conglomerates they thought for no longer believed in them.

In the recent cycle of empire films, the tight alliance between activist filmmaking and corporate critique that gave rise to neoclassical Hollywood in the seventies returned, inverted. The cycle took off following the success of *Gladiator* (Ridley Scott, DreamWorks/Universal, 2000), a neoclassical product par excellence. *Gladiator* hinged on the powers of entertainment, but with the attacks of 9/11 and the launch of the Iraq War, the imperial film took on new cultural and political relevance and provided certain filmmakers (Oliver Stone, Antoine Fuqua, and Ridley Scott again) with a chance to advertise their politics.

Yet where *Gladiator* did roughly equal business domestically and abroad, the next several imperial films were increasingly lopsided, taking in three or four times as much abroad as in the United States and Canada. For empire films, there appears to be a direct trade-off between the critique of American politics and success at the American box office. As such movies became more dependent on foreign box office, they became more dependent on the corporate distribution empires that could open a film around the globe. Filmmakers were forced to reconcile the critique of American military imperialism with their reliance on American cultural imperialism. As a result, the moment of retreat became central to the aesthetic and narrative aims of the empire films. The paranoid auteurs dreamed the studios back into power in the seventies; the imperial auteurs cleaved to them only long enough to dream them out of existence.

If 1970 serves as a rough beginning to a neoclassical era that had largely consolidated by 1975, 2010 is a similarly ragged end. Something different seems to have been at work in the industry since 2005—a move away from the confident assertions of economic, formal, and corporate integrity of the previous decade. It is always a risk to proclaim the end of a period, but if there has been an integrity to the system, such forecasts of its relative disintegration should seem less prognostications than answers to questions raised by the prior analysis: If the industrial configurations remain largely consistent, how might Hollywood filmmakers imagine their studios around the next corner? How, indeed, does any aesthetic formation so dependent on capital, so durable in its division of labor, so prevalent in a culture, pass away? If neoclassicism allowed the Hollywood studios to once again imagine themselves into the center of a mediascape they did not dominate, then this book might be taken as both a tribute to that imagination and a forecast of its ceremonies of abdication.

Logorrhea, or,
How to Watch a Hollywood Movie

Begin at the beginning of *The Core* (Jon Amiel, Paramount, 2003). The twenty-two stars rush into the screen in a twirling line before they form their graceful Paramontian arc. The logo freezes and holds for a moment. Then we push into the mountain and turn, suddenly, down into it, through the layers of rock into the warmer oranges and yellows of the mantle, until we reach the core, or, not really the core, but the textual stand-in for the core, the words *THE CORE*, with their own stand-in for the core's rotation, a rotating *O*. The journey from studio to title inaugurates the film as one that can be both *experienced*, as "a big ride," as director Jon Amiel puts it, and interpreted, or *read*: "It also kind of tells you the story, in a funny way."[1] For Hollywood films of the neoclassical era, this is the fundamental duality.

Through the *O* we move into a rather coloristic graphic spiral that shifts from yellow and orange to yellow and purple and, in the big reveal, turns out to be the spinning top of a temporary carnival ride erected for Green World Day. Taking up the title's invitation to read the ride, the graphic echoes Saul Bass's remarkable credits for Alfred Hitchcock's *Vertigo* (1958), which discovered celestial abstractions in the eye of the object of desire. Here, though, the abstraction is mere decor. With *Vertigo* in mind, we might tell this all-too-familiar story: Once upon a time there were authored, obsessional films, and now there are merely vertiginous rides given an arbitrary trade dress.

But the graphic reminder on the other side of the title is still part of the studio's story, not yet that of a more general history, since *Vertigo* was a Paramount film. That is, it *was*. As a result of some cagey dealings by Hitchcock and his agent, MCA's Lew Wasserman, the *Vertigo* negative reverted to the director. Hitchcock then moved to Wasserman's studio, Universal, where *Alfred Hitchcock Presents* was being filmed. When *Vertigo* was restored in 1996, it was Universal that restored and reissued it. And it is from Universal that you would buy it. So the opening of *The Core* is corporate cultural revanchism, an attempt to undo the mistake of letting *Vertigo* slip away, much as Scottie attempts

Figure 1.1. Journey to the center of the studio in *The Core* (Jon Amiel, Paramount, 2003)

to resurrect Madeleine, a resurrection that occurs, one might say, on another "green world day."

The Core then proceeds to represent and disavow its own aggressions by putting them in the mouth of a slick businessman, who thumpingly exhorts his team: "Let's hit 'em. Let's do it. Let's go make $30 million dollars." The line is both too craven and, strangely, not ambitious enough, because we know that if a movie like *The Core* were only to make $30 million, it would be considered a major disappointment.[2] The film, to Paramount's chagrin, *did* do about $30 million in US box office, and even throwing in international revenues, still did not make back its roughly $74 million budget.[3] Needless to say, the film kills off our money-obsessed pitchman right away, and as he dies, the carnival comes to a halt.

Not content to seize its "rightful" Hitchcockian patrimony, *The Core* goes on, in a subsequent sequence, to remake *The Birds* (1963), a Hitchcock film released by Universal. Taking back *The Birds* involves another substantial change. As Amiel explains, in the original the birds were "malevolent"; here they are simply "flying blind." The blind flying is caused by the earth's internal slowdown and—like the title image and the interrupted carnival—serves as an emblem of it. These birds no longer swirl around Piccadilly Circus as they are supposed to. Instead, they smash into and through things. Our inclination to believe the just-so story in which the waning of the Hollywood auteur and his murderous gaze makes a place for an unguided action cinema only strengthens.

But if we can again forestall the industrial diagnosis, we might better understand whose authorship is really threatened. In the opening logo bleed (which is what I mean by logorrhea), the journey to the earth's core is marked off as a journey to the corporate core. The rotating *O* of the title displays and blocks

Figure 1.2. The Paramontian gun. *The Core* (Amiel, Paramount, 2003)

our access to the corporate-planetary core that no longer rotates. The film is a lesson to be read by Paramount. It offers Viacom an urgent primer in how to restart one of its "core competencies" after a period of disastrous returns. The balance of the film, in which a ragtag group of terranauts must journey to the center of the earth and restart the core, drives this point home. The ship will be called *Virgil* (epic storyteller–cum–infernal navigator), and the Gatling gun–type laser that will clear the ship's path through the crust and mantle has twenty-two lenses—one for each star in the original logo.[4]

"Into the heart of the cosmos"

The logo bleed at the beginning of *The Core* is particularly elaborate, but not exceptional for its era. Even when the logo does not slide directly into the film, it is quite common for the leaders of the studios and production companies to be tinted or textured to mesh with the production design of the film. Warner Bros. has been the most assiduous in this—the WB shield is reflective, or cloudy, or stony at the beginning of *Harry Potter*s 2001–11), green at the beginning of *Matrix*es (The Wachowskis, 1999–2003), and an icon in a computer desktop in *You've Got Mail* (Nora Ephron, 1998). Finally, even when the logo does not bleed and the leaders are not colored, the snippet of studio sound track that backs the leader in its iconic form is frequently stripped away and replaced by an appropriate sonic lead-in. Warners, for instance, will drop the orchestrated version of "As Time Goes By" that became standard with its seventy-fifth anniversary for something else—a bleeping modem, a siren, heavy breathing, mood-setting silence. As the production process has been further and further divided, contracted out, and assembled piecemeal for singular efforts, sound and color have become corporate binding agents.

But the logo bleed remains the privileged sign of the intentional integration of studio and story. As a result, the frontier is fiercely guarded. "God forbid you should tamper with the logo," screenwriter Peter Rader said.[5] But in *Waterworld* (Kevin Reynolds, Universal, 1995), one of Rader's films, the logo bleed is both elaborate and narratively crucial. As the Universal globe turns, it zooms outward and tilts the polar ice cap toward us. The white region quickly vanishes into the neutral, near chromakey blue of the ocean. That impossibly monochrome ocean dissolves into a shot of a real ocean upon which we find Kevin Costner's trimaran. Decades of historical exposition are condensed into a single "shot" that quickly establishes the genre conventions—the narrative plausibility of hard, near-future, dystopian sci-fi on the one hand, and the cartoonish, or, rather, graphic reduction of motivation of most of the characters on the other. A film may open efficiently, as this one does, yet fail to find the necessary audience, as this one did. Or, more precisely, it failed to find the necessary *popular* audience that might have made it profitable. Yet given how quietly the logo bleed can pass by, how even when it tells us what we need to know about the *film*, we might still not take it as a sign of something we need to know about the *studio*, then the audience for the bleed may not need to be a popular one.

It would be more direct to say that the creation of a popular audience invested in the fate of the studio logo has been one of neoclassical Hollywood's fundamental projects.[6] To attach an audience to a corporation, to brand something as weakly branded as a contemporary studio, would be a major feat. The

Figure 1.3.
Taking the plunge.
Waterworld (Kevin
Reynolds, Universal,
1995)

neoclassical moviegoing experience smudges studio identity in as many ways as the classical Hollywood system reinforced it. Long gone are the days when one saw a Paramount newsreel, a Popeye cartoon, and a Paramount twin bill in a Paramount Publix theater. Today, one is more likely to catch Coke and Nike ads, a number of trailers (diverse in their studio pedigrees, united in their demographic aims) concluding with one from the same distributor as the feature, and finally a single Paramount feature, all in an AMC Loew's multiplex. Unless the film is one of the few strongly branded franchise films—a *Star Trek*, or an *Indiana Jones*, for example—the studio behind it is likely to be not simply unimportant to our viewing but irretrievably lost on us. The film's credits will be a hodgepodge of levels of attribution: Paramount Pictures presents a David Foster Cooper Layne Sean Bailey production of a Jon Amiel film (*The Core*, 2003), or Universal Pictures/Dreamworks LLC/Imagine Entertainment present a Brian Grazer production of a Bo Welch film (*The Cat in the Hat*, 2003). Inside the film, we may find far more effective Coke and Nike ads, extended paeans to the new Mini Cooper, or incongruous Louis Vuitton dropping.

The moment when we pivot from the multibranded exterior of the film to its multibranded interior ordinarily passes unremarked. The pivot is more visible on disc, where the ads are usually absent, and where the first thing one sees is the logo of the home video distribution arm of the studio. There are then the licensing stipulations, a disclaimer that the opinions expressed in the commentary track are not those of the corporation, and several trailers, all from the same studio this time. Still, even in this moment, the studio can slide by because the story, it seems, lies on the other side.

Yet the five or so minutes between the beginning of the final trailer in the theater and the end of the opening credits constitute the zone where every contingency of the film's production—from the labor that made it to the financing behind it, to the oversight that saved it (or wrecked it), to the distributor's best attempt to integrate it into that cultural kernel represented by the production slate as a whole—is rearticulated. For mass audiences, almost none of the crediting matters; for industrial audiences, everything from type size to duration carries intense significance.

If credits are the public inscription of the professionals' contracts, then the opening smudge is, for the vast world of what *Variety* quaintly calls the "nonpro," an allegory of our contract with the narrative. Writing about the openings of various films noirs, French critic Marc Vernet has argued that the "cinematic transaction" between the detective and his "dispatcher" is an emblem of the viewer's relationship to the investigative narrative.[7] In the neoclassical Hollywood cinema, the emblem is both more literal and ultimately less precise. The morphing of the contemporary animated logo is concrete to the point of being cartoonish, as in *Waterworld*, literal to the point of literation, as in *The Core*'s rolling *O*. Yet logos do not readily become protagonists that we might think alongside as they attempt to realize their goals in the face of increasing obstacles over the course of a balanced, multiact narrative. Instead, our identification is less with the logo as protagonist than with the emblematic nature of the logorrheal process as such. Will this bit of kitsch have consequences? Will the narrative be integrated with the conditions of its production? Will any of the concerns of the submissive, contracted, incorporated parties mirror our own concerns as the film unspools or the DVD spins?

Branding Utopia

To be sure, such abstract concerns are not typically what come before us as the theater finally darkens and the repeated promises of the feature slide into our experience of the presence of a film. Yet it is surely worth lingering over these openings since every studio has devoted itself to them. Paramount pushed into the mountain; Universal melted the ice cap; Warners morphed the shield into the Bat sign in *Batman Forever* (Joel Schumacher, 1995); Columbia flew into the lady's torch in *Big Fish* (Tim Burton, 2003); Disney turned the cerulean background to its white castle into the walls of Andy's room in *Toy Story*, a shot that quickly panned over to reveal Luxo, the Pixar desk lamp (John Lasseter, 1995).

Figure 1.4.
Corporate morphing.
Batman Forever (Joel
Schumacher, Warner
Bros., 1995)

Even MGM, the studio that has most struggled to find or maintain its identity throughout the period, played the Lion for all it was worth. The studio not

only morphed Leo into the screaming mouth of a boy-band fan in *Josie and the Pussycats* (Harry Elfont and Deborah Kaplan, 2001); it also attempted to launch an animated series based around him and his family, *Lionhearts* (1998). That series went nowhere, but at Warner Bros., Steven Spielberg's Amblin productions launched *Animaniacs*, which ran from 1993 to 1998 and told stories of Wakko, Yakko, and Dot Warner, three animated characters too "zany" to use in WB cartoons. They lived in the iconic water tower and made self-referential, faux-ironic mischief all over the studio lot.[8]

Perhaps the most important bit of logo play in the neoclassical era comes at the beginning of Paramount's *Raiders of the Lost Ark* (1981). Producer Frank Marshall explains that "Steven was always coming up with great ideas which were sometimes a challenge for the production. And we were setting up in Kauai and he called me over and he said, 'Look I need to find a mountain, I need you to go find a mountain that looks like the Paramount logo where we can shoot.' And I went, 'OK.' And because it was sort of a last minute request, and we didn't have CGI [computer-generated imagery] to fall back on, I had to drive around to the whole island until I found a location that would work for us, and for a few extra pineapples, we got it."[9] In this account, the opening is an improvised moment, a director having fun and bringing the film in line with some of the nostalgic techniques that shaped its narrative and its production design. The *idea* is Spielberg's; the property is Paramount's; the film is the consummation of the marriage between auteur and studio.

Yet, as has been the case throughout Spielberg's career, every solicitation of studio concern has been tempered, subverted, even completely undone by his assertion of a particularly broad claim of authorship. About the opening Spielberg says, "I just thought it would be fun to start with the Paramount mountain. I mean when I was a kid, my first company was called Play Mount Productions, and I had a mountain, which I painted myself. Now, Playmountain is my name in English from German. Spielberg means 'playmountain.'" However inspired he might have been by Paramount "as a kid," however "fun" it would be to start with the Paramount mountain, in the end, as he says, "I had a mountain, which I painted myself." Indeed, it is not the fact of the mountain that matters here but the fun, the play, with which it is deployed. The logo would have been there regardless. The affect behind the decision to bleed it into the film is Spielberg's patrimony. As a result of his bit of fun, Paramount may have been bound more tightly to the George Lucas–produced, Spielberg-directed film than it had any right to be, but that surplus identification of the studio with the film depended on a much larger identification of the director with the mode of production, the mode of autorepresentation, as a whole.[10]

Logorrhea is an imaginary solution to a constellation of problems that range from the economic and ideological to the narrative and back to the imaginary itself. And while logorrhea cannot dissolve these problems entirely, it can offer, at different times and in myriad ways, partial solutions. Yet what remains unsolved also remains available for further thought, for further repression, representation, systematization. If the opening of a neoclassical Hollywood film is a swamp of contingency reinscribed as the investigation of necessity, then the remainder of that contingency is available for further reinscription throughout the narrative. The bond between corporation and product can take the shape of an icon or a deus ex machina, of a protagonist or an emblem, of an element in a psychology or an ethics or in a discourse on economics. Yet in its most common form, the studio appears within the film as a place, a *locus classicus*, as it were. The mountainous landscape of Kauai is one way to bring Paramount into the picture; the Scottish highlands of *Braveheart* is another. As the property becomes more integral to the corporate imaginary, the logo reaches deeper into the film until the relationship between studio and story switches. Now, instead of slipping the logo into the film, the film takes place "inside" the logo, as in *The Core*, or *Waterworld*, or *The Matrix*.

The logo, in other words, turns into the utopia. In this era Columbia has its turfs; Fox has its mutant alien X worlds and its schools; Warner Bros., its Road Runner deserts; Paramount, its Final Frontiers and King's Dominions. The initial audience for studio logos was internal to the industry. But as films have become more elaborate parts of corporate efforts to unify the on-screen and the off-, studios have sought to extend their identification with particular stories. Much of this book maps and then navigates these corporate landscapes according to the protocols I am laying out here.

A glowing *X* at the beginning of Fox's *X-Men* (Bryan Singer, 2000) sets up a nifty reciprocity between franchise and studio. On the one hand the *X* is only part of *FOX*, necessary but appropriated; on the other, that *X* outlasts its studio, a slightly wistful nod to the reality of the audience's concern. The *X* will recur throughout the film—throughout the series—in the school logo, in the wheels of Professor X's wheelchair, the exposed supports of a host of modern buildings. The *X* is everywhere in X world, just as it was in Howard Hawks's *Scarface* (Caddo/United Artists, 1932), but where Hawks's *X* conveyed the entire range of authorial possibilities, *X-Men*'s *X* reverts always to the brand. It is a product placement for itself. Yet wherever we find the *X*, the mark of legibility, we also encounter a second source of meaning—the mutation, the sudden, inexplicable change. Professor X may rationally explain mutation in his prologue, but the twisted, writhing lines that represent mutating DNA are indecipherable.

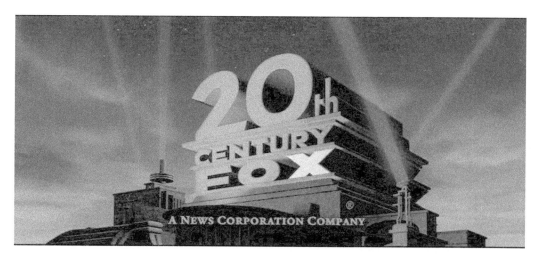

Figure 1.5. Franchise appropriation. *X-Men* (Bryan Singer, Fox, 2000)

The narrative competition between these two semiotic tempi structures the space of *X-Men*. The opening scene—Poland 1944—gives us Magneto's backstory, his moment of self-discovery. At the gate to a concentration camp, young Eric Lehnsherr is separated from his parents. He reaches desperately for them, attracted by and attracting the metal in the gate. The palette of the scene has been desaturated, leaving only rain-soaked grays and browns, with one exception: the yellow Stars of David with their Hebraized *Jüde* the Jews are forced to wear. "It's a very monochromatic scene except for the fact that yellow stars have been goosed up." The "goosed" yellow stars, like the glowing yellow *X* in the logo, certainly make the film more legible, but legibility is precisely the problem here. The bright stars and grim numerical tattoos are of a piece with the horrible order of the camp, an order exemplified by the *X* on its gate. And that horrible order is on the verge of realization in America where the Senate

Figure 1.6. The omnipresent X. *X-Men* (Singer, Fox, 2000)

is debating a new mutant registration law. In opposition to this rage for order, Magneto will build a mutation machine and use it on the senator leading the registration effort. The radiant force of the machine will graphically match the supercoiled DNA of the prologue and contrast with Professor X's clean-lined, mind-reading machine, Cerebro. The narrative opposition is spatialized.

But it is also nuanced. The opening sequence ended with a shot of the camp gate twisted into a large-scale version of the barbs on the wire and a tilt up an ominous smokestack. The shot suggests that disorder and illegibility are somehow consistent with and not opposed to hyperorder. In the world of the *X-Men* films, the alternative to the camp is not a place without order but a place with the right order, and the right reading, a place like Professor X's school in Westchester. Indeed, reciprocal logo reading seems to be only one element in a more general opposition between fundamental topoi. The concentration camp and the school are two analogues for the classic Fox logo, with its Albert Speer pedestal and vertical klieg lights. Dystopia, utopia, twinned and entwined, like Magneto and Professor X.

We might follow this intuition in two directions, one thematic, one corporate. What follows are the opening steps in each. Thematically, the notoriety of Fox's interest in mutants and aliens—from *X-Men* and *X-Files* to *Star Wars* and *Independence Day* has perhaps hidden the company's fascination with prison-schools. Dating back at least to the military school in *Taps* (Harold Becker, 1981), Fox has interrogated the limits of educational authority. *Taps* appeared with *Revenge of the Nerds* and *Porky's*. The nineties featured *The Simpsons'* Springfield Elementary and *PCU* (Hart Bochner, 1994; scripted by Zak Penn, who would also write for the *X-Men* series). Still later, there were *Boston Public*

Figure 1.7. The mangled wire. *X-Men* (Singer, Fox, 2000)

(which debuted the same year as *X-Men*), *Malcolm in the Middle*, *Swimfan*, and

Prison Break (with its tattooed instructions). Of course, high school movies from any studio will frequently turn on questions of authority, and the agenda for research would inquire into the differences between such total institutions *by studio*. How is Fox's Professor X's academy for the gifted different from Warners' Dumbledore's Hogwarts? Does the difference between studios apply at that level of generality, or is there a shared, and likely partial, industrial imaginary at work in which the boarding school may come to represent the happy studio lot, be it Fox or Warners?

The second direction would look to the *X-Men* films to track out the biography of their studio. Oddly enough, Marvel Enterprises, the "owner" of the *X-Men* franchise, does not get a leader at the opening of *X-Men*. By *X2*, three years later, it will. In the second film, the *FOX X* still glows, but it is quickly followed by Marvel's riffing comic images. The corporate leaders give way to the same Patrick Stewart–narrated prologue that takes us from the interstellar landscape deep into the neural architecture of an individual human. But once we come out of that, we are in a gallery of presidential portraits in the West Wing of the White House. These still images will come to life when Nightcrawler begins his assault on the Oval Office. His enlivening is an emblem of Marvel's own corporate career, beginning from a static origin in which the comprehensively tattooed mutant echoes JFK (Nightcrawler is a devout Catholic, making the pairing that much more logical; the X-Men also debuted in 1963). If *X2* quickly identifies Marvel with Magneto's gang through graphic matching, it does the same for the X-Men through montage. Jean Gray's telepathic abilities appear as a collection of voices that she sorts through much the same way that Marvel flips through its intellectual property, a sorting process that culminates in Jean's disruption of a collection of computer workstations and 2-D animated museum exhibits. (Indeed, the "frenetic" "whip-wipes" of the scene were a late substitution for what would have been a slow-motion version, according to Singer.)[11]

Avi Arad, the former CEO of Marvel and Marvel Studios, described the logo in his commentary for *X-Men: The Last Stand*: "Actually the history behind this logo is that when we started to make movies we tried to figure out how do we represent something typical for Marvel in front of a movie instead of just a logo? And the idea was just animate storyboards—comic books like the old fashioned cards and it became—actually it gets this mini-applause." By the third installment, the logo play had become old hat. "I really wanted to change this 20th Century Fox logo," director Brett Ratner says without elaborating. "But the X stays, watch it, oooh! Isn't that cool?" If the Fox logo stays the same, the Marvel logo has changed so that the flipping images are all X-Men frames "specific to the plot line of this movie," according to Zak Penn. Ratner goes on: "If you freeze frame each frame one-by-one, you'll see the entire story." Marvel, dispossessed in the opening film, has found a way to nest the franchise within itself again. The third installment, naturally enough, is based upon the X-Men story line called "Dark Phoenix."

Theories of Studio Equivalence I: Capital

This sort of intensive reading or overreading of corporate intentions runs headlong into broadly shared assumptions of contemporary Hollywood scholarship. For those who are willing to read films closely, the crucial imaginary location is Hollywood itself, not any of the studios or companies that compose it. It may be that certain important citizens—directors, stars, writers, producers—are able to leave their mark, yet that mark is inscribed on a slate that reads Hollywood. The assumption is that there is an ideal typical studio from which all actually existing studios necessarily but unfortunately differ. Instead of beginning with studios, analyses begin from Hollywood—the incarnations are only epiphenomenal.

Those who think that Hollywood studios are interchangeable think so for one of two reasons. Either studios are the same because they are all corporations and corporations are all the same, or they are the same because the people who work for them all live and breathe (or act and think in) the same culture. Both views draw some support from the revolving doors for executive and craft employees. If an exec can move from Fox to Paramount over the weekend, there cannot be much difference. If one Mel Gibson film can be Warners (*Lethal Weapon*), another Paramount (*Braveheart*), and another Columbia (*The Patriot*), the studio cannot be all that important to the film or to him. Indeed, his independent productions (*The Passion of the Christ*, *Apocalypto*) would make him the ideal contemporary auteur: willing to take financing from anyone but secretly dreaming of complete authority. It is either the system or the individual, and the mediating category is nothing but a convenient placeholder.

There is a long-standing debate over whether, when, and how studio fungibility has altered over time. One flank of the argument from corporate interchangeability updates a much older critique of the "culture industry." Writing during World War II, German exiles Max Horkheimer and Theodor Adorno argued that a uniform source of capital made corporate distinctions quaint. "Everything is so tightly clustered that the concentration of intellect reaches a level where it overflows the demarcations between company names and technical sectors." Just as "the difference between the models of Chrysler and General Motors is fundamentally illusory. . . . It is no different with the offerings of

Warner Brothers and Metro Goldwyn Mayer." "Enthusiasts" debate the subtlest distinctions "only to perpetuate the appearance of competition and choice."[12] After seventy years, it may be hard to gauge just how polemical Horkheimer and Adorno are being here. The difference between Warners and MGM was the biggest difference there was. MGM was all starry, production value–driven, Anglophilic conservatism; Warners was "gritty," realistic, genre-driven New Dealism: *Grand Hotel* vs. *G-Men*; Greer Garson vs. Bette Davis; gardening vs. smoking. MGM made *Mrs. Miniver* to convince Americans that World War II was worth fighting; Warner made *Casablanca* for the same reasons. Horkheimer and Adorno could see the differences between those two films and between those two studios; to say they didn't matter was to say a lot.

For them, the analogy between movies and cars, the homology between Hollywood movies and modern industrial society, goes deeper than their dependence on the same system of capital allocation. Films, they say, have perfected the use of "interchangeable parts" in their "interchangeable details": "The brief interval sequence has proved catchy in a hit song, the hero's temporary disgrace which he accepts as a 'good sport,' the wholesome slaps the heroine receives from the strong hand of the male star, his plain-speaking abruptness toward the pampered heiress, are, like all the details, ready-made clichés to be used here and there as desired." The details may overwhelm the story, Horkheimer and Adorno go on to say, but this is no Romantic triumph of expressive freedom—Stan Winston's monkeys and aliens are no rebellion against the idea of "totality." Instead, the triumph of the detail is the end of the "bourgeois" work of art with its integral idea. "Although operating only with effects, [the culture industry] subdues their unruliness and subordinates them to the formula which supplants the work. . . . The so-called leading idea is like a filing compartment which creates order, not connections." With no overweening authorial vision behind them, mass cultural doodads cannot offer a vision of transformed individuals or a reformed society; they can only hope to be advertisements for themselves. "Today every close-up of a film actress is an advert for her name, every hit song a plug for its tune. Advertising and the culture industry are merging technically no less than economically."[13]

This was a stern Marxist critique of the culture of the "free world," yet its very totalizing power seemed to produce exceptions to its rule. Those exceptions might take shape as culture heroes—Charlie Chaplin was certainly one—but they might also incarnate as the moguls whose studios could seem in the classical era to be both examples of the culture industry's general laws and extensions of their individual personalities. However true Horkheimer and Adorno's critique might have been, the reaction of the moguls who made that culture was never going to be "Oh, gosh, I hadn't realized that Donald Duck takes his punishment on screen so the audience will learn to take theirs. This shall stop at once." The only response the producers of the culture industry could make was to internalize or introject or co-opt the critique. If Hollywood cinema was part of the death knell of the Enlightenment, it was also, in the hands of what we might call, after André Bazin, the evil geniuses of the system, a necessary site for brand cultivation. "Look," they might say, "all our movies are made up of the same parts—yours, mine and Fox's. But they are spectacularly successful at selling things. Now that we have the parts figured out, I'm going to use my movies to sell my studio. Besides, I have to convince my contract players that there is something different about working here." If corporations are the same, they are the same in that they have to be different, even if they hire the same people.

There are places where Horkheimer and Adorno can see this possibility, where their critical Marxist position looks more like an insider's guide to the industry. When a movie needs to slot in its clichés, it turns to "the production team." The gags are written by "special experts." These experts, you can feel them saying, really know their business, the producers most of all. And to "feel" them saying this, one must read against the account of the audience's subjugation and toward a motivated account of production that Horkheimer and Adorno are loath to provide. "The familiar experience of the moviegoer, who perceives the street outside as a continuation of the film he has just left, because the film seeks strictly to reproduce the world of everyday perception, has become the guideline of production."[14] Part of the critical theorists' task in unmasking the culture industry, then, is to see the movie the way a producer would yet avoid being swept up into the system of advertising and promotion—distribution—themselves. "Sharp distinctions like those between A and B films . . . do not so much reflect real differences as assist in the classification, organization, and identification of consumers. Something is provided for all so that no one can escape."[15] Audiences see production values, they say, but the producers see demographics. They buy expensive audiences with A budgets; inexpensive ones with B's. These are the evil geniuses of the system at work. The genius appears most shimmeringly at the top of the studio org chart, but, as the remarks about the gag men imply, he or she can exist anywhere. Yet if one imagines the relationship between culture and audience to be homologous with and an instance of the relationship between capitalist and worker, then the mogul's intentions are of a fundamentally different order than his employees'. The expertise of the gag man—or any other potentially reflective member of the organization—is situationally, structurally, experientially an expertise shared horizontally across the craft and not vertically within the studio. Certainly the battles to establish and secure craft unions across the 1930s would have buttressed such a view.

Theories of Studio Equivalence II: Labor

To the extent that we see these craft interests as orthogonal to those of the studio bosses, we begin to construct an alternative but complementary theory of studio equivalence. The labor theory of studio interchangeability builds on the standardization of labor across the industry. This argument was first developed at the University of Wisconsin in the late seventies and achieved its grandest form in the publication of David Bordwell, Janet Staiger, and Kristin Thompson's *The Classical Hollywood Cinema: Film Style and Mode of Production to 1960.* No mode of argument was more productive for Hollywood-centered film studies than the (neo-)Marxist (neo-)formalism of *The Classical Hollywood Cinema.* It quickly established rules for historical rigor and archival depth that could be followed, and it served as a monitory response to histories based on legendary anecdotes. Yet since it was a stylistics, it required and rewarded (at least in principle) the fine attention to filmic instances that close reading had cultivated. At its core, it provided a much richer understanding of how a "group style" might emerge in a competitive, capitalist society. And it yoked the classical era of Hollywood to a classical aesthetic, one that would "rely on notions of decorum, proportion, formal harmony, respect for tradition, mimesis, self-effacing craftsmanship, and cool control of the perceiver's response."[16]

Naturally, *The Classical Hollywood Cinema* became a lightning rod for historical and theoretical debate. Partisans of close reading, though, largely had to content themselves with immanent justifications of the significance of their examples. The history of film style no longer seemed composed of "landmark movies." Instead, and as far as the industry was concerned, there were only deviations from the accepted norms. Industrial patterns might still be warped by a particular success or failure, genres or individual performances might reverberate throughout the culture, but the mode subsisted in the "ordinary film." Changes, when they came, accreted or came suddenly *to* the mode, not through it.

At the same time, the ordinary film was ruthlessly debranded. Cinematography established itself as an independent art bound by certain conventions within which Hollywood cinematographers, especially in the classical era, had to work. A qualified cinematographer might have a contract with Warner Bros., but when he wrote for *American Cinematographer*, he was writing to a skilled audience across studios, and that was what mattered. Hollywood films looked and felt consistent because they were made consistently by a consistent group of workers. A studio was just an "economic category."[17]

But standardized labor has never been an argument against brand identity. The United Automobile Workers (UAW) represents employees of the big three auto makers and their parts divisions, but no one doubts that the auto brands are carefully calculated to maintain real—perceived—differences. When Chrysler engineers sit down to design a new car, at least one of their major concerns is that it look like "a Chrysler," however that may be, and that it not look like a Ford. When Chrysler designed the PT Cruiser, it looked like nothing on the road. Yes, it had four wheels, airbags, antilock breaks, left-hand drive, and all those things were important, but the engineers knew (from focus groups, Jungian design consultants, and so on) that their audience was not interested in three-wheelers; they were interested in a wagon with aggressive retro-design on the outside and comfort on the inside.[18] In advanced capitalism, "connoisseurship" is a general phenomenon. (Horkheimer and Adorno were being polemical there, too.)

A Hollywood movie is not the same as a car model, precisely because it has a style that is executed throughout the production process. The assembly-line workers at a Chrysler plant have had their stylistic contribution engineered out of the product—their changes are called "defects"—whereas a sound editor can make a real difference in the film's style (she can make errors, too). And at least one of the categories that she could have in her head is "Paramount sound." From story construction to distribution, the phases of Hollywood production are brandable to the extent that they have a style at all. What remains to be seen is the extent to which style might have come to undergird its own industrial history.

Theories of Studio Equivalence III: History

A historically qualified version of the theory of labor interchangeability is more intuitively compelling. In this account, studios used to matter, back when everyone was on seven-year contracts and studios were run by the philistine, tyrannical, yet somehow "movie-loving" moguls who founded them. Once the studios were broken up, the dysfunctional family was gone and there was no longer any difference between them. What remained were industry-wide crafts no longer segmented by studio and liberated auteurs. The latter would take pitches from one studio to another and be glad to get the movie made at any of them; as for who supplied the money, the auteurs did not care. They would round up their usual suspects, or, if someone was busy, then the next-best person for the job, and get on with it.

Tom Schatz analyzes the industry studio by studio in *The Genius of the System*, producing a collection of remarkably careful histories. Capital flowed from

New York, but it was the strong production executives who gave the studios their house styles. "In the overall scheme of things, the West Coast management team was the key to studio operations, integrating the company's economic and creative resources, translating fiscal policy into filmmaking practice."[19] Without that delicately balanced integration, there was no system.

But this is where the evil genius idea creeps back in. If it does not matter who makes a film, then the a priori of studio filmmaking is reversed. Whereas a classical Hollywood film belonged unproblematically to its studio because it could not possibly escape such ownership, a neoclassical film belongs to its studio only through an act of monetary will. To see a contemporary film as a studio film is to realize *this* studio wanted to distribute *this* film badly enough that it passed on thousands of other possible stories and outcompeted its major rivals in order to put up the money for the project. The studio must have seen something it wanted to see when it agreed to make the film, and the task of its creative executives—aside from riding herd on the budget—must have been to keep that certain something alive. Labor and capital come together at this moment to perpetuate the studio after the studio.

Douglas Gomery's work has been the most important exception to the presumption of studio equivalence in the postclassical era. Where other historians see a series of changes in the mode of production, Gomery finds "a consistent pattern—with studios always selecting films for production and groups under studio control making them—rather than some fundamental set of transformations." As a result, his phrasing of the "key question"—"how did a collection of major studio corporations (Hollywood) come to dominate . . . and maintain its control?"—keeps the corporation at the center of the analysis.[20] He calls this a "minority view," and it is; yet his emphasis on the oligopoly encourages attention to both the limited number of central players and to their intercorporate efforts at self-regulation and defense. This shift in the null hypothesis inflects our understanding of what qualifies as a historical fracture; it locates our attention not in the inevitable continuities of style but in the efforts at continuity. It gives us backstories where others see only a single story, a system.

The most frequent attacks on *The Classical Hollywood Cinema* have come at its historical end point, where industrial fragmentation and independence would seem to have drastically changed the mode of production. And at this bleeding edge, Bordwell and Thompson have been vocal in their defense of the underlying historical framework. As the period after 1960 has lengthened until it exceeds the initial span of the classical, the defense of Hollywood as all-classical-all-the-time has become more complicated. Concessions may be made to the stylistic inroads made by television forms, or the "youthquake" of the late sixties, or a tightly delimited "high-concept" period in the early eighties, or the "intensified" continuity editing style more generally, but the narrative core has been redoubtable.[21]

In Kristin Thompson's *Storytelling in the New Hollywood*, she works through ten films that exemplify the resiliency of classical narrative techniques in the postclassical eighties and nineties. Many writers and directors have praised the book because it attends to "what Hollywood practitioners themselves have said they are doing," and that sanction is important.[22] As she constructs an inductive theory of screenwriting and directing, Thompson presumes that the organizing frame ought to reside "within" the narratives themselves. That is, she organizes the films according to the number of their protagonists, from the single to the dual to the group. Seen as a collection of practitioners' problems and solutions, the examples are a diverse lot. Yet reorganized by *studio*, something notable appears:

> *Tootsie*: Columbia, 1982
> *Groundhog Day*: Columbia, 1993
> *Alien*: Fox, 1979
> *Hunt for Red October*: Paramount, 1990
> *Back to the Future*: Universal, 1985
> *Parenthood*: Universal, 1989
> *Amadeus*: Orion, 1984
> *Desperately Seeking Susan*: Orion, 1985
> *Hannah and Her Sisters*: Orion, 1986
> *Silence of the Lambs*: Orion, 1990

Forty percent of the films that evidence classical narrative's enduring relevance are products of the smallest of studios, the only one that did not become the flagship of a gargantuan entertainment conglomerate, *the only one to go bankrupt in the period* (1992). Indeed, Orion was also the only one to be formed in that period. It began when the United Artists brain trust, Arthur Krim and Robert Benjamin, left the notoriously auteur-friendly studio after selling out to Transamerica. Their departure set the stage for the destruction of United Artists (UA) and the entire American New Wave in the *Heaven's Gate* debacle.

Of all the mini-majors formed in this era of tax code–driven incorporations (including Cannon, Carolco, New Century) Orion had the strongest connection to a classical studio, but the studio it was bound to had the peculiar pedigree of having been "built by the stars." UA benefited by not being a studio in the classical sense—it was not a signatory to the guild agreements, so it could finance nonunion films; and it maintained none of the expensive departments

that required other studios to slap a hefty overhead fee on the films they distributed. Instead, UA financed and distributed, and in order to entice producers, it offered substantial profit participations. Krim and Benjamin capitalized
on these strengths to build a real, operative brand:

> This was the most potent and enduring of lures and legacies Krim and Benjamin were
> to contribute to producers, United Artists, and, eventually, the industry: independent
> production in an atmosphere of autonomy and creative freedom. This laissez-faire
> approach to production—more than careful distribution, more than the absence of
> overhead charges, more even than the promise of profits—was the distinctive differ-
> ence that would make UA first unique, then the pacesetter for the industry.[23]

Krim and Benjamin carried that aura with them to Orion, and their films made
that evident. "The studio built by the stars" became the studio that put the stars
into logorrhific circulation. This history, this brand, indeed this studio focus
simply has to matter in the assessment of narrative coherence—it mattered to
everyone involved.[24]

Yet in Bordwell and Thompson's account, classicism persists no matter
what happens to it (almost). Having long outlived its inaugural industrial form,
it is now a zombie classicism that can be "intensified," made "mannerist," sped
up, chopped up, and riven with exceptions (or near exceptions—exceptions
that reinforce the rule-making apparatus, i.e., deviations). Still it marches on,
driven not by an insatiable lust for brains but by a preternatural fit with our
cognitive habits and a relatively stable labor regime.

One critic who has not welcomed the standard account of Hollywood
classicism is Richard Maltby. To his mind, the question of when or whether
Hollywood ceased to be classical is thoroughly wrongheaded since the industry
was never classical to begin with. It was, instead, built around an ideology of
entertainment. That is, Hollywood is "essentially opportunist in its economic
motivation. The argument that Hollywood movies are determined, in the first
instance, by their existence as commercial commodities sits uneasily with the
ideas of classicism and stylistic determination." How would one decide between
these views? Maltby's principal warrant is that the stylistic account necessarily
gives short shrift to audiences—"how viewers use movies," on the one hand,
and "how Hollywood movies are organized to deliver pleasure to their audiences," on the other.[25] Whereas Bordwell and Thompson evaluate screenplays
based on whether they are "coherent," Maltby's key determinant is whether they
efficiently "deliver."

This shift to a transactional aesthetic relieves Maltby of the need to write
the history of Hollywood as the history of an undead style. Instead, to "explain

how a 'classical' style can persist in a 'post-Classical' cinema," he tells "three sep-
arate but overlapping histories": of production, of reception, and of criticism.
Bordwell launched the classicist program by decrying the overemphasis on
textual criticism in film studies.[26] Maltby responds that Bordwell, Staiger, and
Thompson are themselves too reliant on integrated notions of the film as text.
However neo, it's still formalism.

As prominent as entertainment is in the ideology of Hollywood, other
quite readily available industrial discourses militate against it. The panoply of
awards—from the guilds to the Oscars themselves—reward not the most entertaining films but outstanding achievements. Indeed, if Hollywood guards its
aesthetic or political judgments closely, it is still able to judge individual contributions through the discourse of "achievement." Sometimes that achievement
dovetails neatly with popularity. But the long history of the "Oscar-bait" performance suggests that the discourse of "prestige" offers resistance to an ideology of
entertainment. What, indeed, were the indie divisions of studios but the attempt
to quantify those alternative discourses at the level of the production slate?

Considered from the perspective of the talented free agent or the packager
of talent (agent or producer), the ideology of entertainment is too limiting
a discourse. Creative workers find it essential to have access to some further
rationale for their massive labor commitments. Doubtless the collection of
reasons includes criteria of aesthetic success that are merely pragmatic: hits
command respect. But those criteria for aesthetic success also include industrial notions (channeled through guilds and other peer groups), individually
held beliefs that have been fed by institutions that cultivate taste and judgment,
and immanent frameworks that arise within the context of particular projects,
that is, standards that evolve in the close working conditions and relative independence of the one-off, package-unit mode of production.

Into this messy evaluative process comes a native level of reflection on the
relative balance between sets of criteria.[27] Following the legendary John Ford,
some stars and directors are able to adopt a "one-for-them, one-for-me" policy,
alternating between large, payday-driven projects and smaller, more personally meaningful films (John Malkovich, for instance, or Steven Soderbergh, or
perhaps Spielberg in the *Jurassic Park/Schindler's List* and *War of the Worlds/
Munich* and *Tintin/War Horse* pairings). This is an extreme version of self-
reflection, but something similar applies to any player in a creative industry
who confronts a sufficient range of choice. In these situations, when a career
reaches a stage we might call "managed," the individual must weigh a variety of
concrete options—different projects—against one another, including the possibility of doing nothing rather than something.

To the extent that studios and other developers find themselves across the table from individuals engaged in this sort of calculation, they also find themselves working through a parallel collection of considerations. How much money should be offered a major star for her "one-for-me" project? Where is the line between feeding the maw of distribution and maintaining respect in the creative community? What level of commitment to certain properties will be necessary to retain access to the best projects at early stages in the development process? The horizons of a decision expand and contract; its repercussions are bound more tightly to its conception or slip away. Individual executive careers are made and ruined based on the results of these decisions. But at the choke-point of responsibility, ordering and weighing these questions are a problem of matching the project to the source of capital: will *this movie* be right for *this studio*? "Rightness" and "fit" elude objective definition and might give rise to a system of accumulated contingencies. Yet when studios bleed their logos into their films, they are laboring their films into the corporation, effacing that systematic contingency. The logo bleed transmutes the individual decisions behind a film into the elements of a corporate career, a studio story.

Classicism and the Order of Composition:
Allegories Deniable and Otherwise

Since I will be reading the stories on the screen as the stories of Hollywood itself, I would like to be clearer about the broader bases of these allegorical readings, why it is that what I am calling neoclassical Hollywood requires such interpretations.[28] How does this historical framework interact with the history of style? Given that a collection of major studio corporations has maintained its control of financing, and given that intellectual property belongs to corporations and not the industry as a whole, how should we tell the story of the interactions of narrative and style? Although I hope the accounts of individual films will prove compelling, my understanding of the motivation for those allegories rests not on the readings themselves but rather on an account of classicism. I begin from what is, I think, a rather uncontroversial definition of the classical theory of the frame. As Jean-Claude Lebensztejn describes it, the theory is twofold. "First, a painting should be framed to avoid confusion between its objects and surrounding objects. . . . This separation is a landmark of classicism, which aims at the values of order, clarity, and distinction." By "landmark," it appears that Lebensztejn means that the classical frame both delimits classical space and serves as an emblem of the themes that will be dealt with in that space. The order the frame makes allows the painting to address "order." "The second point . . . is that the frame should be there, but not insistently there; it should not attract too much attention to itself." This balance should give the appearance of a "natural constraint."[29]

In the case of the cinema, there are obstacles to such a classicism. Cinematic space tends to risk colliding with what Lebensztejn calls "real space" because it can show very convincing pictures of real things over time and it shows them almost framelessly.[30] It is therefore biased toward the insistent thereness of trompe l'oeil. Beginning from the principle that films were necessarily pictures but they *should* tell stories, classical narrative introjected the self-divisions of its institutions to compensate for the relative weakness of its formal separations. But where the psychoanalytic valences of introjection suggest a process destined to produce legible symptoms when the defense mechanism encounters resistance, Hollywood's introjections may seem almost frictionless. Given that one principal aim of the system is to produce legible projections, what we read is not a *symptom* occasioned by the failed introjection but a *duplicate* of that occasion. Bordwell, Staiger, and Thompson famously call this "an excessively obvious" cinema. The overarching aesthetic is explicitly literalist.

Take, as an example, *The Big Clock* (John Farrow, Paramount, 1948). In Kenneth Fearing's jewel of a novel, the clock is a metaphor, no less obvious than "the big sleep" (the clock ticks for thee). Yet in the film, that metaphorical big clock appears as a *really big clock* that regulates all the little clocks throughout the mammoth Janoth Publications building. Indeed, the flashback that opens the film—which stars Ray Milland and Charles Laughton—is triggered inside the very workings of this enormous timekeeper. Classical Hollywood literalism solves the problem of trompe l'oeil duplication by suggesting an additional signification bobbing easily enough upon the surface tension of the narrative.

Historically, the crucial institution underwriting that equipoise was the Production Code Administration, which required meticulous precision about words and certain actions (one foot on the floor) but left unpoliced nearly the entire kingdom of nuance. "As Colonel Jason S. Joy, the Code's first administrator, explained, to entertain its undifferentiated audience, the movies needed a system of representational conventions 'from which conclusions might be drawn by the sophisticated mind, but which would mean nothing to the unsophisticated and inexperienced.'"[31] What emerges from such an internally divided system is a unique form of authorship, one pegged to what Ruth Vasey calls a "principle of deniability."[32] In Maltby's account, "entertainment" ideology is a way of consciously denying "authorial responsibility for whatever moral or political intent" might be imputed to a film.[33]

Deniability moves toward the center of an aesthetic when it buttresses an ideology of entertainment. One difficulty with depending upon that ideology as a critical anaclisis is its very conscious publicity. "That's entertainment" is *too* readily mounted by the industry in defense of its self-regulatory regimes. Indeed, part of its attraction (for Maltby) as a critical strategy is its surface availability. In place of a vast, unseen, fragmentarily elaborated style, entertainment offers the relief of a noninterpretation. This relief is entirely consistent with the pleasures of the literalist aesthetic it accounts for. Yet the notion of deniability suggests that interpretation—that depth—is inescapable. Before acceding to a zero degree of interpretation, we might ask, Does the inevitable recourse to the hidden or the implied stem from a critical imperative, an industrial one, or both? "Both" would seem to be the answer. Yet just as literalism and entertainment complement and extend one another, critical and industrial depth are yoked together precisely by industrial practices that attempt to admit sophisticated interpretations as far as possible—to admit them until they threaten deniability itself.

Having made a place for both its own and its critics' interpretations, this system interpellates viewers in a further, and perhaps more immersive, way. We project our desires into the illicit (and unstipulated or censored) contents of the narrative only to have the narrative dissolve that potentially guilt-inducing projection with its happy endings. "The movie's happy ending tells us that social sanctions to enforce good behavior are superfluous, since people are inherently good, and would behave impeccably if left to themselves."[34] Assertions of depth are deflected into surface phenomena by the discourse of entertainment only to return in a more abstract fashion in the film's openness to criticism. In the same way, nonnormative (buried) desire is projected into a narrative where it might be resolved outside the operation of formal rules (a world of authentic surfaces). If the happy ending is what I will call a disappearance-form of desire, its openness to interpretation reconstitutes an antecedent depth even if that openness disavows the desire that was cached there. Hollywood perpetuates these structures even as it effaces their content. Yet in both cases—the case of the deflected critic or the sublimated audience member—the converse possibility presents itself, particularly in the system's most compelling products. That is, our discomfort with the ideology of entertainment or our incredulity at the happy ending suggests to us or teaches us or inspires us to regard our interpretations or desires as antecedently deep. Hollywood produces these structures by denying the content that it (literally) projects. This replete, liberal subjectivity is perhaps the crowning effect of the classical Hollywood system.[35]

Intensive self-delimitation both made classical Hollywood classical and turned its technological-industrial constraints to its own advantage by naturalizing them. (Indeed, it did so and does so in large part by naturalizing *us*.) Classical Hollywood cinema overcame the structural weakness of the literal cinematic frame by substituting obvious divisions within what appears on-screen (between denotation and connotation) for the work of the frame. The bawdy implication should be there but not insistently there. The metaphor should be readily available yet unnecessary. What is stable or ordered about this system is not, then, the division between art space and real space but the division within art space between the "insistently there" and the "naturally constrained." Since the frame must encompass both the classically constrained and the unclassically insistent, the relatively simple emblematization of the frame's ordering as the picture's order appears at one remove. The emblem becomes the complicated allegory of the attempt to balance the insistent against the constrained.

With surprising frequency the classical Hollywood cinema makes this allegory appear effortless. The stories it spins on the classical themes—the justice of violence, state invasion of the private, the materialization of the perfect form, ambivalence in the face of passing youth, and so on—draw on the resources of genre to help right the anticlassical imbalances of their production (or their iteration of the generic narrative). *The Jazz Singer* is the story of the assimilation of European Jews *and* the story of the Warner brothers becoming Warner Bros.[36] *On the Waterfront* is the story of organized crime on the waterfront *and* the story of naming names before HUAC.[37] *Red River* is the story of the civilization of the West *and* the story of independent production and the perils of contract.[38] Each industrial crisis—the conversion to sound, the witch hunt, the breakup of the studios—becomes the occasion for yet another display of the power of the classical Hollywood framework.

Those displays seemed insistent for some and constrained for others, but the deniably allegorical narrative of Hollywood form and Hollywood industry is not simply a matter of aesthetic judgment. Instead, these ambiguities return us to the question of how we ought to tell the history of Hollywood. Maltby finds the principle of deniability at every level of classical Hollywood: It is insisted upon by the industry and its producers, inscribed in its great stories (*Casablanca* is one of his touchstones), and operating in the audience (or at least the imaginary audience). His initial suspicion that a formalist notion of classicism would be insufficient as the basis for an industrial history thus proved correct. But where he explicitly imagined that an ideology of entertainment might take its place, he has instead discovered that ideology to be the rhetoric of a system eerily ordered at every level of its function. "Hollywood's entertainment is self-explanatory, self-contained (in the safe space of the movie theater), self-justifying ('it's only entertainment'), and self-regulated. It is, then, hardly surprising that Hollywood represents itself so often in its movies."[39] Here, Maltby means movies such as *A Star Is Born* and *Singin' in the Rain*—movie movies—

but if we understand the principle of deniability as expansively as Maltby wants to or ought to, we might extend the category of the movie movie to include, potentially, any movie at all. Who is to say *this* movie is not self-reflexive?

Classicism and Neoclassicism:
History Consistent and Insistent

The integrity of the classical system does not depend on the system of production as such but rather on the representation of the conditions of production. Classical systems require that their principles of integrity be the subject of uninsistent public display. The obvious thematization of the limits of government—in *Red River*, what rights does a trail boss, even a mad one, have over his cowboys?—goes hand in hand with its tacit thematization by the governance of the image, its "classic look and feel." When such a system insistently publicizes the extrapictorial (the backstory, the behind the scenes, the scandalous), any actual distinction between cinematic space and real space becomes even more difficult to account for. The conditions of production are already on their way onto the screen.

Such a definition of the classical also repotentializes the individual film within the system. Classical Hollywood narrative is shadowed by its own meticulous negotiation with the problems of capital accumulation and artistic production to such a degree that its classicism lies in the balance it can strike between the conditions of its production and the demands of its literal narrative. For the authors of *The Classical Hollywood Cinema*, the system is so overwhelming that the actual instances that system produces can have no effect on its operation. There is no need to read the films of classical Hollywood for their self-understanding of that system because no such understanding is permissible. And any understanding one did find would simply be a deviation that enabled the system to maintain itself.

By returning representation—theme, style, allegory—to the center, it becomes easier to understand how a neoclassical iteration of a classical system might be launched or why TNT branded itself as The New Classics while AMC brought us its Classic Collection. For a system to take up the classicism of a predecessor, whatever was classical about that prior system had to be rethought as a feature that might be emulated. If one thing that made classical Hollywood classical was a stable of stars under long-term contract, then putting stars under long-term contracts in order to make a new classical system has aestheticized that apparently material feature even if that means giving the star a vanity production company and signing a lucrative first-look contract with the new producer-star.

Relative independence of production—even of studio-financed productions—has been dispositive for historians marking out the difference between the classical system and its contemporary successor.[40] The limit case of independence is the negative pickup, where the film is developed, financed, shot, and edited before the distributing studio commits to it. How could that distance be classicized, since it is the essence of what was *not* industrially classical? Here, again, I take my cue from Maltby, who sees the negative pickup as the return of the deniable: "The element of deniability that was built into the conventions of Classical Hollywood production has been transferred, like much else in the transition to post-Classical Hollywood, to the contractual relationship between distributor and independent producer."[41] Deniability—the deniable allegory—migrates further up the industrial ladder, reestablishing itself at the contractual level—the formal division reconstitutes itself at a second remove. Logorrhea, though, drives that allegory back down into the narrative. It is the crucial reassertion of identification in a truly Reaganite world of plausible deniability.[42]

Along that migration, of course, deniability passes through the very heart of the story, and we should expect something to have replaced the Production Code as the essential relay in the circulation of the discourse of deniability. Noël Carroll argues that beginning in the late sixties and into the seventies, in the wake of the code, in the new era of the ratings administration, filmmakers rely on "a two-tiered system of communication which sends an action/drama/fantasy-packed message to one segment of the audience, and an additional hermetic, camouflaged, and recondite one to another." Since that mid-seventies moment, such allusiveness has only proliferated and been, at every turn, further incorporated into the discourse of the industry. Recondite no longer, allusiveness and its explication are essential to the operation of the system. If we are looking for something to occupy the role of the frame in the neoclassical era, this would certainly carry sufficient weight: "the settling down of the industry in the mid-seventies through the increasing reliance on genres" encouraged film-literate directors to "[adjust] via the two-tiered system of allusion."[43] The frame, if this can be thought possible, is itself historicized and aestheticized.

Lurking in every classical cinema is the aestheticizability that makes neoclassicism possible. This is not a quasi-deconstructive aesthetic principle. Instead, it is a contingent phenomenon. The relationship between studio and story is not something always-and-everywhere the same. The contingency of the bond between the corporate and the industrial has meant that neoclassical Hollywood has lost the inevitability of its own allegorization. As a result, films that aspire to the classical must not only be allegories; they must insist on allegory, even at the expense of their literal narratives. To return to Lebensztejn's account of classicism, he notes that the painter Ad Reinhardt similarly insisted on the division between art space and real space when he wrote "Art is art-as-art and everything else is everything else." Lebensztejn says of Reinhardt that "he was a classicist with a vengeance, and excess of any sort is unclassical, especially an excess of classicism." In place of unclassical here, I would say neoclassical. Reinhardt's "pretense of making again and again 'the last painting which any-one can make'" gives his classicism the air of synthesized crisis that is endemic to, even defining for, contemporary Hollywood.[44] For neoclassical Hollywood, Reinhardt's dictum can be rewritten: "Movies are movie movies and everything else is everything else." What makes neoclassical Hollywood neo is the difficulty it confronts in containing its self-consciousness—something its participants clearly want to do—and not, as a Romantic account of neoclassicism might put it, the self-consciousness itself. The mismatch between the attention given to the allegorical and the attention given to the literal gives these films (and other artifacts of neoclassical systems) their whiff of pomposity (something that is true even of attempts to present neoclassicism neoclassically, for example, Peter Greenaway's *The Belly of an Architect* [Hemdale, 1987]). Neoclassical Holly-wood films are often overwhelmed by their allegories. Their stories frequently make no sense at all except as backstories.

The aspiration to the idea of a studio would be part of an economic strat-egy that would always be pre-aestheticized. They called that strategy synergy. Whereas a classical studio moved product through its distribution pipeline, a neoclassical studio moved "content" through a shifting collection of conglom-erate partners. When we regard classicism as the object of studio desire, we can assess its success in terms that are aesthetic and economic, artistic and strategic, elusive and measurable. Hollywood acquires a history as contingent and yet as immersive as the cultural totality it routinely figures.

Neoclassical Culture:
The Precession of Causality and the Implication of Criticism

Just as neoclassicism emerges as the dominant framework for the articulation of industry and artifact in Hollywood, so a belief in contingency comes to char-acterize the mechanisms of culture as a whole. When "raw facts"—economic or social or historical—appear only under the sign of the already aestheticized, our familiar accounts of cultural determination seem less apt. Is Hollywood best thought through notions of labor determination, or are corporations and other institutions decisive? In an industry built on the marketing of personal-ity and persona, one of the great worries is that individuals will come to exert decisive influence over the system as a whole. Yet at the same time, fickle audiences can shoulder the blame for particular misses or hits, as when a "foreign" audience is blamed for Hollywood's decision to produce simpleminded action films. All one can consistently say about a creative industry in this period of compounding flux is that the crucial cultural or economic determinant seems to move from one force to another. I will refer to this phenomenon as the precession of causality. The collective self-understanding of various creative actors within the system finds problems and locates solutions differently depending upon the current understanding of cultural determination. And that understanding of the system changes as other groups or individuals successfully assert control at different points in the process.

This conceptual horizon has evolved over decades. In their account of the conversion of Hollywood from a mass-production system to an era of "flexible specialization," economists Susan Christopherson and Michael Storper focus on the allocation and division of labor. They chart the emergence of a surplus labor pool necessary for the "flexibilization" of the industry, yet alongside these changes in the labor market there have also been marked shifts in skills. "In the contemporary motion picture industry, the skills of actors, writers, and directors have expanded to include collaborative and transaction skills, such as those needed to acquire a suitable film 'property' or solicit investors."[45] These "industry skills" include "conceiving, packaging, and financing productions," skills that sound remarkably like the development of the sorts of studio consciousness I have been describing. More and more, privileged individuals view their work as a "speculative enterprise" in which they are investing labor. "They have management as well as labor interests."[46] They are, in current industry parlance, hyphenates.

Within this new knowledge arrangement, though, there are micro-histories, waves of conventional wisdom that gather and break. Auteurs vie with studio executives for control; agents intervene, rebrokering the balance of power between talent and buyers; different models of how to secure talent for the long term are tried and emulated. Studios slough off risk by signing talent to multi-picture deals or to incentive-laden contracts; then everything changes and one studio veers toward negative pickups while another finds refuge in coproductions. New sources of capital decide to underwrite studio slates or fund new players. Stars following a one-for-them/one-for-me strategy compel studios to open their own indie labels. These are the stories that find ready allegorization on-screen. How closely should we pursue these micro-histories? How tightly should we bind our analysis to the vagaries and caprices of this industry and its players? When does criticism of the inside joke threaten to become too inside for its own good?

The phenomenon of logorrhea, even at its most expansive, seems nevertheless a small part of the story of contemporary Hollywood. Its importance for criticism derives from its position at the interface of art and industry, of show and business, an interface that continues to elude critics as it attracts them.[47] Within the collection of practices and techniques for interpretation, some will be more useful for excavating or analyzing particular strata than others. Deep readings will require different interpretive tools than less deep ones; there are different techniques for analyzing the social relays of a particular group of films than for seeking other sorts of meaning and function. If logorrhea locates the initial site of the interpretive contract, we will bind our reading to both its parties in turn.

The claim here is that the close-reading techniques that might seem best suited to the understanding of films as works or artworks should be extended to the processes of their creation and marketing for two reasons: because this methodological fusion captures the role of the particular film project in the elaboration of an ongoing corporate or collective identity; and because in the attempt to harmonize or at least simultaneously explore films and the labor that constitutes them, we find an equivalent for the attempt to harmonize the scales of attention and labor that the project requires. The elevation of harmony in the object-project and the analysis-interpretation is particularly characteristic of classical systems because the consistent aim—indeed, the definitive aim—of the classical is a reification, the extraction and naturalization of cultural processes as shareable cultural objects. Unsurprisingly, producers and I share a set of interpretive aims in the attempt to establish coherence among and within our objects-projects.

This suggests a necessary second step, the development of protocols that could indicate where the coherence of interpretive and productive aims should break off. The readiest division would seem to be the temporal split between the productive and the interpretive moments, but that is more apparent than real. Indeed, as I have claimed previously, Hollywood neoclassicism defines itself as an interpretive production oriented by its aspiration to an antecedent classicism. If we understand the question of industrial (systemic) or corporate (individual) primacy as a question of which aspect will win out, what accommodation each will strike with the other, then films are never simply applications of rules. Rather, they are at the same time investigations of rule making, and the rules in question are simultaneously social and aesthetic. That aspiration appears not only in the objects but significantly within the system as the ceaseless irruption of interpretation within production, a system of requisite checkpoints that gauge the likelihood of success of a given project in meeting its aims. Interpretation and forecasting collide, complicating any neat temporal division between production and analysis.[48] One might carry this further and note that fundamental economic differences between the classical system of vertical integration, long-term contracts, and general audiences and the neo-classicism of horizontal integration, option contracts, and segmented audiences are differences that multiply those checkpoints and outfit them with structured alternatives. The more fully neoclassical the system, the less purchase temporal sequence will have in distinguishing analysis from production.

Extending the immanence of interpretation to the production process compromises the independence of the interpretation. But where temporal division offers no reliable distinction between interpretation and production, the converse—simultaneity—suggests itself as a possible solution. The simultaneity of interpretive independence (auteurs) and productive implication (in studios) in classical Hollywood called for a reading protocol that could distinguish between them (the *politique des auteurs*). The neoclassical system aestheticized that analysis, converting it into part of the system itself, implicating it. The history of the system is crucially the history of the incorporation of a way of reading it. This in turn suggests that the exhaustion of that history of incorporation will appear as yet another reading, a reading of implication, and that the interpretation might well pause once it has traced the appearance of this latter reading. The advent of this new reading takes two forms: Corporations must choose whether to unwind their faltering synergistic conglomerates built around alliances of authorship; auteurs must avoid recognizing how incompatible their political position—their readerly position—has become with its critique of empire. Both must come to terms with the limits of extension—of the empire or the conglomerate. This new configuration restores the bifurcated interests of studios and authors, not in a raw economic sense but rather along a gradient of self-consciousness that might be swapped cleanly for a calculus of power. In the worst cases, studios cannot make sense of their conglomerates in the sense that they are unable to; auteurs cannot make sense of their politics in the sense that they must not. In addition to marking the end of a neoclassical period, this entente of impotences ejects the implicated interpretive position as well.

Part I

Last of the Independents
Paranoid Auteurs and the Invention of
Neoclassical Hollywood

At the end of *Charley Varrick* (1973), Don Siegel's underrated caper film, Charley throws his crop-dusting uniform into the trunk of a burning Imperial. As fire consumes the jumpsuit, we have sufficient time to appreciate Varrick's ingenuity and his narrow escape. We also have plenty of time to read the back of the uniform, which we have seen several times before: Charley Varrick: Last of the Independents. And once we are in the reading mode, Siegel is kind enough to superimpose "A Universal Picture" over the flames. We leave *Charley Varrick* knowing who to blame and recognizing that the sad condition of the independents is a general one.

As a brand, "Last of the Independents" combines the wistful and the cagey, a combination written everywhere on Walter Matthau's face. It is sentimental, to be sure, but it hides its sentimentality in supposedly clear-eyed revelations about crooks stealing from crooks and about the honor code among the

Figure PI.1. *Charley Varrick* (Don Siegel, Universal, 1973)

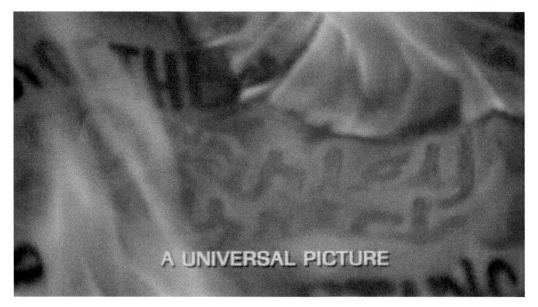

criminal class. Independence—tenuous and hard-won—was Siegel's auteurist political hallmark: from Kevin McCarthy's panicked run away from the pod people in *Invasion of the Body Snatchers* through Dirty Harry's laconic, anti-institutional vigilantism: "A man's got to know his limitations"; "You've got to ask yourself, 'Do I feel lucky?' Well, do ya, punk?" And at the end of *Charley Varrick*, that independence goes up in smoke.

What killed it? To begin with, the "independence" brand had always been a smokescreen. Varrick and his crew are only crop dusters by the way. Their proper job is robbing banks. And on one particularly fateful job, they happen to rob a bank far too full of cash. Charley knows at once that the bank must be a Mafia money drop. The big score means bigger trouble, Varrick explains to his gleeful partner. Unlike the FBI, the Mafia "never stops." It takes an elegant frame-up for Varrick to dispatch the inexorable Joe Don Baker and turn the mob-connected casino owner into the prime suspect. The frame-up turns on luck, or, rather, the implausibility of luck: no one is lucky enough to rob a drop bank on the day it is awash in Mafia money; that means someone, someone inside, is responsible. There is no luck, only knowledge.

This is the paranoid position, and *Charley Varrick* revels in it: Does Charley know enough to outsmart his ruthless Mafia pursuers? He does, and in the process, Charley sheds his dumb partner and his wife. In his disappearance he becomes the independent he had always claimed to be. This is the game that Jean-Paul Sartre called "loser wins." The three chapters that follow take a longer route through Hollywood's assimilation of auteurist paranoia. Still, we will end up more or less right here, with the last of the independents—or his uniform, at least—in flames, replaced by an Armani suit.

The Literal and the Littoral
Jaws

Here, at the edge of this history of the studios' great second age, we confront again a question of possibility. Where do the allegories come from? If we can locate them in individual and collective choices, what opened that field of choice in such a way that it might gather to it the principal vectors of corporate self-understanding? What delimited the field's contours so that it might be possible to incessantly promise a second, hidden meaning to some viewers while requiring it of none? *The Core* was a typical instance of logorrhea, if an atypically canny reimagining of an "action" movie as an "acting" movie. *Raiders of the Lost Ark* (Spielberg, Paramount/LucasFilm, 1981), two decades earlier, elevated auteurist play to the level of corporate identity. These allegories are insistent, yet their importance is always deniable, downgradable to an in-joke, reducible to a token of industrial privacy inessential to the appreciation of the surface of the plot. Where did that contemporary deniability come from?

It came from *Jaws*. Doubtless it might have come from some other source or been cobbled together from a collection of films of the early seventies. In the following chapter, I show how *The Godfather* (Coppola, Paramount, 1972) advanced crucial portions of the new industrial-aesthetic formation. But *Jaws'* particular combination of production history, distribution, narrative structure, editing, and shot composition twisted all the necessary strands of the emergent order into one of the sheets of neoclassicism.

To make the case for the film's fascination with denial, it would be simple enough to note that *Jaws* went into production beginning in the fall of 1973 and shot through the summer of 1974, coincident with the massive fallout of Watergate. The movie hit the screens just as the Church Committee had plunged into its investigations of CIA involvement in assassination plots. Domestic and international policy making had become hopelessly confounded and constitutionally contaminated. "What did the president know and when did he know it?" became the mantra of the Watergate hearings while the Senate Select Committee on Intelligence attempted to break through the wall of plausible denial to determine whether the CIA was behaving as a "rogue elephant" or whether presidents had known about the attempted assassinations. A long-standing term of art in the world of covert operations, "plausible denial" first reached the popular press in the document dump accompanying the *Pentagon Papers* in 1971. As the CIA was being repurposed as an all-purpose domestic spying agency, the conceptual apparatus of deniability was being ported into the White House's campaign of dirty tricks, where it sounded more sophisticated than the "rat fucking" it covered for. Senator William Proxmire had introduced intelligence oversight legislation in 1973, explaining that the root of the problem lay in deniability: "In domestic affairs . . . the use of 'plausible denial' becomes a frightening, antidemocratic device. The President must be accountable for his actions. He should not be able to hide behind the cloak of 'plausible denial.'"[1] Proxmire's bill died, but the first piece of successful legislation to emerge from the Watergate-era tumult was the Hughes-Ryan Amendment, which required a presidential "finding" approving any covert operation. Plausible denial was supposed to be a thing of the past.

This Nixonian aura was essential to *Jaws*, with its initial opposition between the "rogue" shark and what screenwriter Carl Gottlieb called "the smoothly corrupt but genuinely sincere" Mayor Larry Vaughn:

> Competent and gifted with an uncanny ability to portray weakness posing as strength, Murray [Hamilton] was a natural for the part. . . . [I]n *Jaws* he would be the foremost spokesman for the "rational" view, as well as the defender of the town's economy and architect of the cover-up. Quite coincidentally, he bears a passing resemblance to Richard Nixon, and would be a natural choice to play the Boy From Whittier, should that film ever be made.[2]

Midway through the film, Mayor Vaughn signs the contract allowing Sheriff Brody to hire Quint to hunt the shark. A mayoral "finding" of a sort, his signature is both his admission that the shark problem is real and his acceptance of responsibility for the consequences of deferred municipal action. Yet his carefully maintained denial—as much psychological ("sincere") as institutional ("architect of the cover-up")—slips away satisfyingly enough to make *Jaws* decidedly *post*-Watergate: the film *wants* the mayor to do the right thing. Vaughn's rank mercantilism and foolish attempts to manage the press do not hang over the seaborne sequences in the way that Nixon's malfeasance loomed over the mid-seventies.

Two aspects of this reading, though, are decidedly unsatisfying. First, as an account of the shark it is rudimentary at best—surely everyone from author

Peter Benchley and Gottlieb to producers Richard Zanuck and David Brown saw more in the beast than its role in the political allegory. Second, the resolution of the mayor's conversion narrative marks the midway point of the film, not its climax. Either our account of *Jaws'* narrative structure requires drastic revision or this aspect of the story must be somehow nested in the larger narrative.

We might better see *Jaws'* particular importance in the reconstitution of classical deniability by imagining a world where its temporary status as the most successful movie of all time still had the ring of novelty and not destiny. David Anthony Daly's dissertation, *A Comparison of Exhibition and Distribution Patterns in Three Recent Feature Motion Pictures* (submitted 1978, published 1980), is one of the first scholarly attempts to make sense of "sharkmania." He describes the lineaments of the first summer blockbuster this way: "Steven Spielberg, a twenty-seven year old Universal contract director who had made *The Sugarland Express* for Zanuck/Brown was chosen to direct." Think, for a moment, of how unfamiliar that sentence is: that Spielberg needs explaining; that an explanation would include *The Sugarland Express*, a film nearly forgotten today; that he was a contract director in an era when virtually no one was a contract director; and that his producers chose him and not the other way around.[3] By 1982 he had directed *Jaws, Close Encounters, Raiders*, and *E.T.*, along with the misstep *1941*. By the end of the eighties, he and George Lucas had eight of the top ten box-office hits of all time (unadjusted for inflation). Daly's dissertation marks the last time Spielberg would need contextualizing; it may also be the last moment when "Spielberg" would not be the self-justifying alibi for a film's performance, and when someone might hazard other causes for its market dominance.

Looking for sources of *Jaws'* success, Daly points to the film's saturation marketing campaign and Universal's brutal distribution policy. In the latter, the studio initially offered exhibitors the choice of nine weeks at a 90/10 split after the "house nut" was subtracted or 70 percent of the overall gross, along with substantial advances and high guarantees. Moreover, the contract was to be "blind bid"—that is, the exhibitors would be agreeing to Universal's terms without having seen the film first. After running afoul of the Justice Department, Universal backtracked from the blind bid by screening *Jaws* for exhibitors across the country. Yet the studio was now confident enough in the film that it *increased* the minimum playing time to twelve weeks. Moreover, for *Jaws*, the studio extended the "cooperative local media buy" in which theaters share the cost of advertisements in local papers and on radio to include charges for an unprecedented network television campaign. Exhibitors paid in advance, paid for three months, and paid more than they ever had.

Network advertising makes sense only when a film is saturation-released, and much has been made of Universal's decision to open *Jaws* in 464 theaters. More important, though, was Chairman Lew Wasserman's decision to *reduce* the initial release from more than 900 theaters in order to force exhibitors to accept more stringent terms. (By Christmas 1975, *Jaws* would still be playing in 2,460 theaters.)[4] If nothing else, *Jaws* would have a disciplining effect on the entire exhibition sector.

Not that the studio expected to wring its profits entirely at the exhibitors' expense. Zanuck/Brown and Universal were supreme promoters:

> The promotional tie-ins licensed by Universal were staggering. In eight weeks, over a half million *Jaws* t-shirts, two million plastic tumblers, and two hundred thousand soundtrack albums were sold. *The Jaws Log*, a quickly produced paperback about the making of the film, sold over one million copies the first month. Also available were beach towels, bike bags, blankets, costume jewelry, shark costumes, hosiery, hobby kits, inflatable sharks, iron-on transfers, games, two varieties of posters, shark's tooth gold charms, shark's tooth necklaces, sleepwear, children's sweaters, women's swimwear, ties for men, and a *Jaws* water squirter.[5]

Considering this tsunami of ancillary promotion, Daly and the generations of critics who have followed have found it hard to believe that the marketing was not responsible for the film's success. Clark Ramsay, then head of distribution at Universal, gave the classic response: "You can't hype your way to success in this business. The movie has to be good. What we did was create an opportunity for *Jaws* to take off. The advertising and promotion might have been responsible for the first three-day run, but it was word-of-mouth that carried it to the top."[6] Stanley Newman, the vice president of publishing at Universal, offered a more nuanced explanation. He would still disavow the notion that promotion *created* success, but that disavowal was less important than the chance to tout Universal's unified corporate effort. "*Jaws* was successful not because of some pre-meditated, well orchestrated advertising and media campaign, but because every part of the film was dealt with on a highly professional, top-flight level."[7] Daly finds this "perhaps somewhat less than completely believable," but without some enveloping account that would marl distribution to content, the selling to the story, Daly and others could only assert what the studio flacks denied, that marketing and distribution had independent causal power.

Yet wherever one turned in the cultural discourse, from the popular to the academic, the industrial to the aesthetic, that question resurfaced: *Why* were audiences flocking to *Jaws*? There were two categories of explanation, an audience-centered "anxieties" account and an industry-centered huckster's account.

Critics and editorial cartoonists immediately seized upon the shark image as an allegory of everything from Reagan challenging Ford in the 1976 primaries, to a Soviet sub build-up, inflation, oil profiteering, and even "undercover 'security' operations" (the rogue shark as rogue elephant). Unofficial national therapist Dr. Joyce Brothers contended that mid-seventies social and economic anxieties were readily figured by the shark: "The shark fantasy hits where we are the most tender—our fear of dismemberment, the invasion of our bodies." Fredric Jameson, whose "Reification and Utopia in Mass Culture" (1979) quickly followed Daly's dissertation, found the secret to the shark's appeal in its deployability. Reflecting on the myriad meanings of the shark for critics, Jameson contended that "the vocation of the symbol—the killer shark—lies less in any single message or meaning than in its very capacity to absorb and organize all of these quite distinct anxieties together." By "folding back" any number of Brothers's social anxieties into apparently natural ones, the shark performed a "profoundly ideological" function.[8]

One astute reader of the *Jaws* phenomenon was the Universal publicity department, which quickly "absorbed and organized" the editorial cartoonists' anxieties into a full-page ad headlined "Everybody's enJAWing it!" The studio regularly capitalized on and orchestrated the burgeoning behind-the-scenes coverage in the major magazines and daily newspapers. A massive article in the *New York Times Magazine* chronicled the crafting and marketing of Benchley's book, "Sharks: . . . and Then, and Then, and Then . . . The Making of a Best-Seller."[9] In September, the *Los Angeles Times* declared "*Jaws* Swims to Top in Ocean of Publicity."[10] As screenwriter Carl Gottlieb puts it in the wrap-up to *The* Jaws *Log*, "By April 1975, the rumors were out around Hollywood that the picture felt good, that it seemed to be playing well for audiences. This book was commissioned, researched, and written in a very short time."[11] A three-month turnaround on the book, a month on the cartoonists' advertisement: Universal is working very quickly indeed. For Jameson, the shark's polysemy exemplifies a popular culture intent on naturalizing and thereby disavowing social anxieties; but for Universal, as for the classical Hollywood studios, that openness speaks to the film's marketability, an ideological use of a different order, less "profound" by Jameson's standards but just as intent on universal incorporation: Everybody's enjawing it.

Yet if *Jaws* looks almost modern in the totality of its media exploitation, history was working very quickly as well to drastically alter the conceptual relationship between publicity and product. One can see a stark before and after, a divide between production and distribution. During the shooting of *Jaws* the production crew went to modest lengths to prevent outsiders from so much as seeing

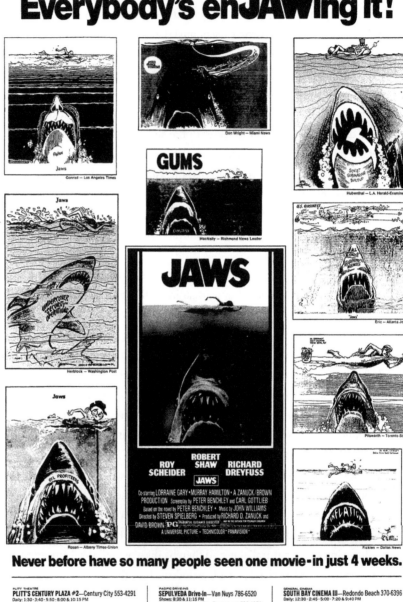

Figure 2.1. "Everybody's enJAWing it," especially distribution. Source: *Los Angeles Times*, July 19, 1975, F13. © 1975 Universal Pictures

the shark. "We all believed that an audience's enjoyment of the picture would be severely diminished if they had read for months in advance about how the shark was just a mechanical contraption." They particularly feared "wise guys" in the audience "thoroughly destroying the illusion for that happy majority that has willingly suspended its disbelief" by spouting off about the mechanical shark.[12] If Hollywood was about to turn over its prestige productions to genres that had been B-picture staples, if it was entering an era where it would regularly risk schlock in its drive for retro appeal, it was also making audience sophistication easier to come by. The classical hierarchy was returning: Two audiences—one sophisticated, one naïve (or believing)—only now one was potentially ruining it for the other. Detailing the travails of working with Bruce, the mechanical shark, Gottlieb explains, "The only reason this is being written now is because the book will be released a little after the movie, and many of you will have already seen what we're talking about so the mystery won't be destroyed for you if we tell you a little bit about how it was done." In a footnote for the twenty-fifth-anniversary edition, he recognizes that "[t]he efforts to protect the 'secret' of the shark seem a quaint anachronism today, when the special and virtual effects would be featured in hours of promotional material and 'Making of' pseudo-documentaries." "In 1975, nobody could have predicted the modern era of accessibility, where the details of every aspect of the entertainment industry are widely publicized."[13] *Jaws* pivots between these two audience-management regimes at the moment of its release; its production—technically proficient but generically nostalgic—was itself instantly nostalgized. On the one hand, the filmmakers profess a belief in secrecy and "movie magic"; on the other, they are swept up into an as-yet incompletely synergized drive to capitalize on any and all possible promotional avenues, including the behind the scenes. And bobbing in the "ocean of publicity" that surrounds the book, the film, and their reception,[14] Gottlieb's Jaws *Log* will tell the story of the limits of promotion, anchoring the film off the coast of the newly discovered world of accessibility.

Still, there was the lingering problem of the audience's belief in "movie magic." If secrecy was so important that disclosing the mechanical shark might have gotten Gottlieb fired in 1975 (the guard who let a reporter photograph the shark *was* fired), what competing value could have supplanted it? One answer would be to say that no value has supplanted studio secrecy, that "accessibility" is a sham, a carefully managed process of information dissemination, in which the studios and their conglomerate parents search for synergistic content that can be distributed across what Justin Wyatt has called the "enfotainment complex." That seems true enough, yet it does not speak to the central questions of an audience's experience; indeed, it seems to raise them more insistently.

Clark Ramsay is surely, in some way, right that promotion may be able to buy opening weekend success but that something more is required if the film is to have legs. Why are Hollywood films satisfying (when they are)? How does inside knowledge affect the willing suspension of disbelief? Does postmodern awareness spell the end of pleasure?

Let us take a step back. In the *Jaws* era there are three competing theories of the relationships between marketing, success, and quality, and each implies an answer to these questions about audiences. One, Ramsay's, assumes that marketing and success are fundamentally contingent but that success and quality are fundamentally connected. True, a weekend's worth of success might be bought, but "real" success depends on real quality. The difficulty with this view is that when confronted with a successful film, it must posit something "good" about it, lest it undermine its antecedent belief in the contingency of promotion and quality. The innocence of audiences must be preserved, lest they come to suspect that they are only tools in the promotional machine. The converse model, Daly's, assumes that marketing and success are strongly connected but that success and quality vary independently. If a weekend's success might be bought, so might a week's, a month's, and so on. That there are counter-examples—hugely, wondrously successfully promoted films that flop—is not particularly important. This view assumes that an audience in-the-know will react cynically; to know *how* the film works is to know that it is *working on you*, which is to be made aware, again, of the contingency of quality. This leaves a third view, Newman's, which takes no position on the necessary relationship between the three except to say that they are all signs of professionalism. For an audience full of these "wise guys," knowing how it is done is part of knowing that it was done *properly*. Newman's view makes room for an audience to know both *how* the film works and to judge *whether* it works, since both find shelter within a judgment of professionalism. The relentless drive to provide access to the backstory, then, functions to continuously reassure the audience, within the industry and otherwise, of the film's competence; at the same time, that drive reinforces a semiotic reading of the film. The willing suspension of disbelief passes over into a willing suspension of control: I know they know what they're doing. Here is the way Vincent Canby concluded his review in the *New York Times*: "Mr. Spielberg has so effectively spaced out the shocks that by the time we reach the spectacular final confrontation between the three men and the great white shark, we totally accept the makebelieve on its own foolishly entertaining terms."[15] Competence and immanence have supplanted criticism.

A substantial part of that competence is aesthetic. According to Gottlieb, "If anything had come out of the exhaustive analysis and rewritings of the basic story, it was that the film had a three-act structure, like a well-made play." The production would echo this narrative structure:

> The first two acts were played on land and with the exception of a couple of shark attacks in which the monster would only be hinted at and never fully revealed, there was nothing to cause any production man any concern. . . . But the crucial third act, in which the three men go to sea in the fishing boat and confront the great white— well, that hadn't been done before, not "live" on location with a fourteen-ton shark mechanism and a full crew.[16]

The pulse-pounding narrative climax would neatly coincide with the production's greatest challenge. Yet, from the beginning, there would also be a tension between the structure and the production precisely as a result of this coincidence. The identity of the ragtag band of misfit-experts might become too individualized, too authored, perhaps even undeniable. This would warp the underlying structure:

> Years ago, one of Broadway's great play doctors and original writers commented that the classical three-act structure of a well-made play could be summed up this way: In Act One, you get a guy up in a tree. In Act Two, you throw rocks at him. In Act Three, you get him down again. When I told this to Steven, he observed that making *Jaws* was a four-act structure: "In Act One, I get into a tree, and for the next three acts, people throw rocks at me." I think he was identifying a little closely with the picture.[17]

If Act III really were getting the men down from the tree, it seemed to go on far too long; it took almost half the film's running time. How could the structural competence of both the production and the plot be saved?

Kristin Thompson contends that the three-act model runs into difficulty because it elides a crucial midpoint shift in the second act. Instead of three parts, the well-made screenplay has four. At the very heart of the film, the protagonist's goals reset; the "complicating" action of the first half of Act II slips into the "developing" reaction of the second half. What is more, each part in the four-part model is roughly equal; the whole is, in her term, "balanced." In this framework, which seems incontrovertible in her analysis of *Jaws*, the move to the water is not the beginning of the third act but this midpoint pivot in the second. The third act begins when the shark attacks the boat while the men are belowdecks drinking and singing. Setting sail isolates the men; the convivial drinking brings the men *together*.

Thompson goes on to note that in *Jaws* each of the three turning points is highlighted for the viewer by being disarticulated from the overwhelming tension of the action sequences. Yet that disarticulation does not threaten the cohesiveness of the whole. Instead, clarity and causality amount to classicism; indeed, they amount to a warrant against an all-too-hasty declaration of Hollywood postclassicism: "The fact that the turning points of *Jaws* do not come at the moments of high action when the shark attacks is worth examining in light of claims that 'post-classical' films favor spectacle over causal logic."[18] Certainly *Jaws* turns on a collection of highly motivated moments, and in a system where, at the very least, screenwriters, actors, editors, and composers place a craft-derived premium on such motivations, we should expect nothing less.

But closer attention to the turning points reveals something more intriguing than simply their distance from the film's action pulses. The midpoint, as already noted, involves the signing of a contract. Act I concludes with Quint's offer to kill the shark for ten thousand dollars. That is, the *plot* of the terrestrial half of the film pivots around the poles of New Hollywood labor: independence and contracting. Even more particularly, it pivots around whether the contract will be "all in" or an option contract. Offered three thousand dollars to kill it, Quint negotiates up: "I value my neck a lot more than three thousand bucks, chief. I'll find him for three, but I'll catch him, and kill him, for ten. . . . For that you get the head, the tail, the whole damn thing." If the arc of a well-made play requires a constant escalation of the threat, *Jaws* conveys that escalation through the increasing bounty on the shark.

Does the third act commence with a similar moment of contract? Thompson's Act III begins when the men "break into song, confirming that Quint now accepts Hooper as a comrade."[19] The song certainly signifies *something*, but within the sequence belowdecks, comradeship becomes contract when Quint and Hooper compare shark-bite scars. The terrible scraping of Quint's nails against a chalkboard that initiated his economics lesson at the end of Act I becomes the competitive display of the squaline signatures that have already made blood brothers of the hunters. Unknowingly bound by their shared past, the men are incorporated through a scene of uncanny reading. When Hooper offers up his leg for Quint to examine, the shot alternatively suggests that the leg belongs to Quint or that it is entirely detached. "Here's to our legs!" they proclaim, recalling an earlier shot from the shark attack in the estuary. This final contract, then, is in blood, signed by the prey they are hunting.

To understand the film, one certainly need not have any sense of this drama of contract; or if one did have that sense, it would likely appear as a drama of male friendship in which the formalities of contract—however necessary—were always understood to be the tribute paid to civilization for the opportunity to temporarily escape that society in order to defend it. (This would also

Figure 2.2. The scars of contract. *Jaws* (Steven Spielberg, Universal, 1975)

explain Daly's omission of the first half when he summarizes the film: "The film focuses on three personalities. . . . It is the battle among these three and the shark that thoroughly engages our attention.")[20] As the men pack to set sail, Quint recites a bit of sexist doggerel—"Here lies the body of Mary Lee, / Died at the age of a hundred and three. / For fifteen years she kept her virginity; / Not a bad record for this vicinity." This drives away Ellen Brody, leaving the men alone. (The song they will break into belowdecks reratifies their newfound society: "Farewell and adieu, you fair Spanish ladies, / Farewell and adieu to you ladies of Spain.")

The ocean separates them from the world of women and children, but it also gives them the chance to recover from their gender's previous failures. The opening attack on Chrissie occurs when Tom Cassidy passes out on the beach, unable to follow her into the surf for a skinny dip. The film is naturally vague here about whether the shark attacks because Tom fails to defend her, whether the shark simply represents the fulfillment of his desires, or some of both. Tom is, rather simply, absolved, yet in this scene his guilt migrates to the aquaphobic Chief Brody, who will bear it until the film's epilogue. In the final scene, as he swims from the wreck of the *Orca* and the seaborne carnage, Brody quips to Hooper, his (male) swimming partner, "And to think I used to hate the water"—as though that were Tom's problem, as though the danger in the water were the water itself and not the sex it promised or threatened. The end of *Jaws* answers the beginning in all sorts of recognizably classical ways: an arena of failure becomes an arena of success, nonswimming becomes swimming, night becomes day, the female victim is avenged, and so on.

The initiating attack not only defined the parameters within which the film's classical narration would play out; it was crucial to both the movie's marketing and its style. The one-sheet, the image around which the entire campaign would revolve, yoked the attack *in* the film to the attack *of* the film. That image derived from the book jacket, where, stylized and out of scale, an enormous shark rose toward a lone female swimmer. Doubleday had tried several times to come up with the right cover. The hardcover jacket featured a blunt-snouted shark with a crescent mouth, "a penis with teeth" Doubleday editor Tom Congdon called it, although there were no visible teeth. Still, the penile profile was no accident; it had replaced an initial mockup that the sales force had rejected. That first cover had shown "a peaceful unsuspecting town through the bleached jaws of a shark." Yet when that version was shown to the Doubleday sales managers, "there was considerable resistance. . . . It made them think of Freud's classic dream of castration, the *vagina dentata*."[21] For the paperback, the penile hardcover was thoroughly revised: the lighting was brought up and color brought in, the swimmer came into sharper focus, the waterline was emphasized, the snout was sharpened, and the ragged jaws gaped; in short, the *dentata* returned.

The paperback cover was designed in coordination with the marketing for the film. Both centered on this image, yet no comparable long shot of shark and female victim appeared in the film itself. Instead, *Jaws* offered us repeated, lingering access to the shark's point of view. If the book-jacket image does not itself appear in the film, and certainly not in the attack on Chrissie, what does appear, particularly in Act III, are displaced renderings of its menace, a displacement that finally runs to ground when Brody shoots the (we might as well call it penile) air tank in the shark's mouth, causing both to explode: "Smile you son of a bitch." The film frames itself in versions of its own logo.

Inside that logo, we find ancillary self-promotion and something very like market analysis. Like the product autoplacements that will litter Hollywood neoclassicism, the video game for *Jaws* gets its close-up within the film (debranded, to be sure, but this is only a mark of the film's position at the gateway to the era). The market research included both Mayor Vaughn's claim to Brody that "it's all psychological. You yell barracuda, everybody says, 'Huh? What?' You yell shark, we've got a panic on our hands on the Fourth of July," and Quint's analysis of the choice facing the town council: "[Y]ou've gotta make up your minds. If you want to stay alive, then ante up. If you want to play it cheap, be on welfare the whole winter." While the production of *Jaws* dragged expensively into the Martha's Vineyard summer, the marketing of *Jaws* depended on being able to remake the summers to come as the high season for popcorn movies. These competing stories of production and distribution appeared as a stark choice within the film, but it would also be a choice between alternative ways of reckoning with the logo. Either option made the shark a symbol of itself.

Deep into the second act, Quint tells the story of the sinking of the USS *Indianapolis*. "So, eleven hundred men went in the water; 316 men come out and the sharks took the rest, June the 29th, 1945. Anyway, we delivered the bomb." Brody and Hooper listen with an awe they borrow from Spielberg himself, who will go on to spin a collection of less and more successful films on the same theme (*1941*, *Always*, *Saving Private Ryan*). Quint's tale does many things. It provides a backstory to the discourse of plausible denial and secret governance—the men weren't rescued because their mission to deliver the bomb was a secret that could not be acknowledged; it installs what we might anachronistically call the greatest generation gap; and it humanizes (the proper word, as we will see, is tenderizes) Quint before his death. But in its account of a fate worse than drowning, the story brings greater precision to the threat the shark-as-vagina-dentata poses. "On Thursday morning, Chief, I bumped into a friend of mine, Herbie Robinson from Cleveland. Baseball player. Boatswain's mate. I thought he was asleep. I reached over to wake him up. Bobbed up, down in the water just like a kinda top. Upended. Well, he'd been bitten in half below the waist." Hooper had said as much early in Act II when he noted into his tape recorder that Chrissie's "torso has been severed mid-thorax." And, indeed, this is how Quint will go: bitten in half at the waist, not, as he had promised at the end of Act I: "This shark, swallow you whole. No shakin', no tenderizin', down you go." "Here's to our legs" indeed.

Shark teeth halve men, just as the bleached jaws divide the film, echoing the original, discarded book-jacket design. That division is routinely coded as a castrative distillation of a feminine threat. And that division ramifies throughout all registers of the film, from production and narrative to character and editing. The biggest shock in the film—the sudden appearance of Ben Gardner's head—

Figure 2.3. At the waistline. *Jaws* (Spielberg, Universal, 1975)

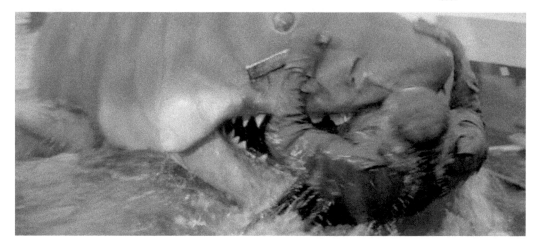

was the last piece to be filmed. It was shot, appropriately enough, in a swimming pool that belonged to editor Verna Fields. Fields, who spent the production on location, assembling footage on her then-state-of-the-art KEM table, would win an Academy Award for her work. Better than anyone had hoped, she hid the balky mechanical shark and matched the wildly varying sky conditions. Her nickname could not have been more appropriate: Mother Cutter.

Jameson is correct that the natural or psychological grounding of the shark's symbolic power is an alibi for its polysemy, but that polysemy was also a privileged site for the reconceptualization of an audience. *Jaws* worked not because audiences were all scared of the same thing but rather because audiences could reproject that underlying fear as they saw fit, reinforcing and constituting the logorrheic flow.

Ultimately, *Jaws* turns not on the particular *meaning* of its imagery but on its *control*. The first half of the film was positioned on the littoral, a dividing line that posed a particular cinematographic problem: How can one focus on both land and water simultaneously? Spielberg and cinematographer Bill Butler drew on a particularly seventies piece of technology, the diopter, a lens that offers two independent focal lengths and allows the viewer to focus on both an importuning resident in Wellesian close-up and the wading bathers in a long shot. But that technology was static—it did not zoom—and therefore did not convey the sudden profundity of depth. For that latter effect, Spielberg and Butler used a *Vertigo* zoom (tracking out while zooming in) on Brody as he sat on the beach. These allusive directorial quotes suggest an auteurist frame of reference for *Jaws* for those in the know, but they do not require any such reference since they not only refer but they *work*, particularly on the viewer's sensorium.

Figure 2.4. The jaws that divide the film as the *Orca* sets sail. *Jaws* (Spielberg, Universal, 1975)

In *Jaws*, the meeting of land and water at the littoral is not a vertical plane. There are projections (docks) and inlets (the estuary) that confound that border. Fundamentally, though, the encounter of sea and sand is a form of laminar superimposition; it is the lapping of water on the shore, of waves chasing up the beach and draining away. The opening attacks occur off these beaches, each time preceded by a low-angle shark's point-of-view shot and the ominous bass of the *Jaws* theme. The low angle on Chrissie is matched to a high angle on her—a displacement that only heightens the tension—before we are jerked back to the surface of the sea, neither below nor above her. This perspective is the heart of the film. As Spielberg explained,

> Bill Butler . . . reconfigured the water box so it was easy to get the focus, so that you could get your hand in there to pull focus. And still have the water lapping the lens. I really wanted this movie to be just at water level, the way we are when we're treading water. We don't see water three feet off the water; we see water like *this*. I wanted to get the camera down to where the human point of view is most accustomed to be when you're swimming, and that's why I shot at least 25% of the movie from that water box.[22]

The water box takes the layering of water on land and puts it on the lens, slicing our point of view just as the waterline divides the surface of the open sea from its depths. As Antonia Quirke phrases it, "This is *Jaws*' defining image—the shark's eye division of the world into above and below."[23]

Figure 2.5. Like *this*: the experience of the meniscus. *The Making of* Jaws (*Jaws* DVD supplement, 2005)

Figure 2.6. The shark's-eye view. *Jaws* (Spielberg, Universal, 1975)

Jaws goes further by twice staging our reaction to that self-division, to the terrible uncertainty over the relationship between what we see and what lies beneath. In the second attack, Alex Kintner dies far offshore, suddenly, in a fountain of blood. In place of a body bisected by the waterline, we are prepared for his death by lingering shots of the canary-yellow, ultraplastic raft holding him just out of the sea, perhaps just out of harm's way. When his lonely, deflated raft washes up on shore, the waterline has been sentimentalized. We miss the boy, but we see the plane.

In the third attack, a recreational sailor will die carrying Brody's son Sean to safety in the estuary. The paternal sacrifice implies that the threat has increased—the shark is now "within" the island—and personalized in a way that leaves Brody no choice but to act. The police chief, who had taken Tom's guilt upon himself, is now guilty of failing to protect his sons. The boys seem to have

Figure 2.7. The laminar littoral. *Jaws* (Spielberg, Universal, 1975)

done nothing wrong—they are swimming where they have been told to—yet we know them to be guilty of swimming around with a fake fin. That transgression nearly kills them when they emerge from the water at gunpoint—and nearly kills them again when the shark attacks. Yet their guilt also belongs to the filmmakers, boys playing with a fake fin in order to instill fear and panic. Spielberg, Gottlieb, Zanuck, and the rest were convinced that they could not reveal the shark without spoiling the effect, yet they could not resist this extravagant allegory of their own technical mastery, their own control over what is manifest and what is latent.

What do we know of the depths of the water from its surface? When we see a fin, does it belong to a shark or a boy? What meaning does it offer us? What meaning do we offer it back? *Jaws'* classicism lies in its ability to control the moments of allegorical obtrusion, to establish the balance between the literal and the allegorical and then to violate that balance, systematically, in the service of a further illustration of control. Something is present; something is intimated. That fin and hundreds of other instances form a collective allegory of Hollywood's capacity to move back and forth between the literal and the allegorical, an allegory waiting to be read as the industry's history of itself. Thus is the field of neoclassical deniability opened. The vehicle of this allegory of allegory, the meniscus, the slightest of betweens, is the movie screen; the tenor is the production process.

Paramount I

From the Directors Company to High Concept

On the Concept of High Concept

What is "high concept"? Most filmmakers and critics agree that it begins with simplified narrative. Ideas "you can hold in your hand," according to Spielberg—the kind of thing that fits on an index card (Jeffrey Katzenberg) or in the logline of a TV listing (Barry Diller). But the notion might be extended to other regular features of contemporary Hollywood production and distribution: genre-dependent plots built around likable characters, a preponderance of "pre-sold" elements, an emphasis on marketability and ancillary value.[1] Beyond a certain point, though, high concept becomes synonymous with Hollywood, and the concept ceases to exist. "Consider," Charles Sanders Peirce put it, "what effects, that might conceivably have practical bearings, we conceive the object of our conception to have. Then, our conception of these effects is the whole of our conception of the object."[2] That is the way it is with concepts: no effects, no concept.

This recourse to philosophy may seem unwarranted because it takes the "concept" in high concept quite literally and because producers are not philosophers (not usually). Yet as I have argued, literalism is one of Hollywood's systematic strengths. And it is worth testing the possible conceptual rigor of "high concept" if only because the notion has been such a point of contention in histories of Hollywood. David Bordwell, in his extended critique of Justin Wyatt's outline of high concept, points out that narrative simplicity and marketability are not novelties and that many films no one would call "high concept" can be handily summarized. Surely he is right. But if the elements of high concept are nothing new, why did it seem to be new? New to whom? Into what industrial configuration did high concept erupt, and what did it leave behind? These questions are methodologically decisive. By making high concept a matter of professional ideology and not, initially and essentially, a matter of style, we avoid battles over definitions. Instead, we operate at one remove: The thing we want to pay attention to exists at the level of the concept (what the studios and producers want) and not the level of style (how the film achieves that). As a consequence, what we are looking for when we look for evidence and attributes of high concept becomes evidence of professional attention.

At the heart of the critical debate over the meaning of high concept lies a particularly clarifying disagreement about what I have been calling industrial allegory, but which is more technically called homology. On the one side, there are critics who strongly believe that "production practices within the film industry are influenced by shifts in the industrial structure of Hollywood." In Wyatt's version, high concept "has been molded by several major structural and economic shifts."[3] But how "molded" is it? Phrased narrowly, and the suggestion of a homology is largely unobjectionable, but the tighter the link between industry and style, the more tenuous the claim seems. If the industry has fragmented, and if the forces of publicity and the proliferation of downstream uses for a film have changed the marketplace, that might imply a concomitant "collapse of narrative." In defense of the position they staked out in *The Classical Hollywood Cinema*, Kristin Thompson and David Bordwell have argued that the forces of integration are substantial. Thompson turned principally to screenwriting; Bordwell, to cinematography and editing conventions. But both saw little evidence of drastic change, of change that would qualify as epochal. Instead, what seemed to be happening was an "intensification" of classical practices; they were becoming "baroque" or "mannerist." Still, a decade into debates about high concept, Bordwell appeared willing to concede that Wyatt had (at least) highlighted a particular production cycle built around films with "bold music and slick visuals," a "fashion-layout gloss." Yet even this concession is begrudging. Such films were "rarities in a field dominated by films as stylistically unprepossessing as *9 to 5* (1980)."[4]

We might still say something about the frequency of those rarities. That is, we should extend Wyatt and Bordwell's sense that there is a history to high concept by asking—eventually—what its role was in the elaboration of the neoclassical studio. In particular we should ask, as Wyatt put it, why "Paramount's genre films are certainly not classical examples. More than other studios, Paramount utilizes the viewer's knowledge and understanding of mass/popular culture. The audience's recognition [of generic conventions] . . . gives the studio license to 'update' the films through the visual style and production design of the films."[5] Criticism has thus far focused on the contradiction between the narrative simplicity of the high-concept films and their (supposed) reliance on the viewer's knowledge of conventions. Before we turn to the economy of that complexity, though, we should be struck by the ease with which Wyatt notes what everyone in the industry noted at the time: Paramount was different.

Why was that studio able to parlay industry-wide trends into something like a brand? And how did Paramount shape those trends?

With this last question, style rejoins strategy as an object of critical importance. Not, again, because elements of the style are necessary or sufficient to high concept but because those elements are the "practical bearings" of the concept. One of the most illuminating descriptions of high-concept filmmaking, of its aesthetic ambitions and effects, appeared in Howard Kissel's *Women's Wear Daily* review of *The Hunger* (Tony Scott, MGM, 1983). "Tony Scott's *The Hunger* is supposed to be about such themes as death, immortality, violence and love, but it's really about art direction—the way blood looks splattered elegantly against a page of music, the way Catherine Deneuve's face looks lit from underneath by flames; the way a very fine lens can capture a tear moving slowly down her cheek; the way David Bowie and Susan Sarandon can be photographed to resemble each other; the way Sarandon can be reflected on the smooth surface of an immaculately polished pay phone."[6] One may be tempted to think that Kissel has put it incorrectly, that *The Hunger* is not "about" art direction but is an *example* of a certain kind of art direction and that only a critic aware of his fashion-magazine audience would so quickly read through an image to its professional origin. (Bordwell makes a corollary point in his dissection of high concept.) Yet Kissel knows what he is about here. Consider the list again. It may begin with the way blood and faces look, as though appearances were simply captured from reality, but it ends with intimations of authorship. The lens can capture a person, phones can reflect people, and one person can *be made* to look like another. There is a theory of spectatorship implicit in this sentence. The first time we encounter something on film, we are struck by its look (or its sound, or perhaps both); by the fifth time, we are attending to the particularities of its origin.

Our development of expertise or connoisseurship might follow several paths. In *The Hunger*, it follows the path where resistance is least: the lens is "very fine" and the pay phone surface is "immaculate." *There is no grit.* The ultra-high finish of *The Hunger* may today seem to be a hallmark of early Tony Scott, but in the eighties, it seemed to be a more general phenomenon, and its effects were profound. As Wyatt put it, "The self-consciousness of high concept suggests that some force ('the author'?) is constructing the style—the configuration of perfect images, stars, music, narrative, and genre—which has become coded across these films."[7] There are no perfect images without authors, and the more perfect the image, Kissel implies, the more quickly we begin to imagine its author.

Allegorical readings are naturally the products of experience. But it is a particular experience, the experience of design. Indeed, for all the discussion of high-concept narrative and stylistic allusion, what has been less remarked is the new prominence of production design within Hollywood's division of labor. Design establishes the contours of the continuous experience in which we develop our expertise. High concept is frequently blamed on philistines in the industry, on the dominance of studios by "suits," or on some change in the power of marketing within the studio to create movies it deemed salable. But in this chapter and Chapter 5, I want to show how the advent of high concept depended upon an essential leap of reading that confused image and author, how Paramount in particular made that leap of reading more widely available, and how that leap uniquely suited the studio in its efforts to brand itself into the eighties. What we want to know is how Paramount went from making films that looked like *The Conversation* to films that looked like *Top Gun*. That story ranges from the diffuse beginnings of the studio's reawakenings through a wide array of examples that included a host of neomusicals and the launching of Eddie Murphy's cinematic career.

Jaws renovated the elements of narrative in a way that could be consistent with Hollywood's long-standing commitment to deniable allegory. That discovery swept up its production-phase panics about secrecy into a distribution-phase confidence in polysemy. It was professional from top to bottom, or, as I said, from surface to depth. But it was Paramount that finally internalized the auteurist resistance to studio control. Told one way, as in Peter Biskind's *Easy Riders, Raging Bulls*, Paramount history captures the rise and

Figure 3.1.
The Paramount seventies... *The Conversation* (Francis Ford Coppola, Directors Company/ Paramount, 1974)

Figure 3.2. . . . and the Paramount eighties. *Top Gun* (Tony Scott, Paramount, 1986)

fall of the New Hollywood revolution, of rebellious authors undone by their own excesses and broad economic changes. Told another way, though, and Paramount becomes the site at which Hollywood's seemingly perpetual crisis of control found a moderately durable solution. Paramount began the seventies as the home of the auteurs; it ended the decade as something like an auteur itself. Something like, for Paramount was not, in 1980, an author in the way the classical studios were. It was a place where certain forms of authorship became possible. If *Jaws* was an allegory of allegory, high concept was the authorship of authorship.

Covens and Conglomerates: *Rosemary's Baby*

Paramount was consolidated into Gulf + Western in several steps between late 1966 and mid-1967. G+W was the creation of charismatic Austrian CEO Charlie Bluhdorn, and it would routinely run afoul of federal regulators. The initial impetus for Bluhdorn's purchase was the chance to monetize Paramount's post-1948 library by licensing it to television. That would result in a quick and easy profit. The studio, in contrast, was not making money, and G+W considered simply shuttering it. Instead, as Kevin Heffernan explains, the new owners attempted to create a "leisure core" out of Paramount, the Desilu television studio, and other components.[8] The centerpiece would not be film production but distribution and financing "expertise."

Committed, however marginally, to the continued existence of Paramount as a film studio, G+W overhauled the management. Out went veteran Howard Koch; in came novice Robert Evans and journalist-turned-executive Peter Bart.

Veteran schlock-horror producer-director William Castle signed on as a producer. At the same time, the studio signed a four-picture deal with Roman
Polanski. Castle acquired the rights to Ira Levin's *Rosemary's Baby* while still
in galleys and intended to direct it. Evans convinced Castle to step aside and
lured Polanski into the director's chair. The new guard had its first emblematic
production.

The film might have been simply an update of the old schlock. As Castle
put it, "Instead of a tingler under the seat . . . now I'm getting publicity by
bringing over Vidal Sassoon to cut Mia Farrow's hair."[9] High-class Sassoon may
have been, but Farrow's haircut was still gimmick-based marketing. What set
Rosemary's Baby on a different course, indeed what made it more than simply
a successful film, was its marketing. Instead of using its in-house staff, Paramount entrusted the entire campaign to Steve Frankfurt, then president of the
creative side of Young & Rubicam. Outsourcing the marketing of a major release—opening titles, the one-sheet, the tagline, the trailer, buttons, street-level
graffiti—constituted a dramatic break from Hollywood's past. It also broke
Evans's promise to Paramount's distribution executives. At their first meeting,
he went up to a chalkboard, "[T]urning my back, facing the blackboard, I made
a line straight down the middle. On one side I wrote in large letters, 'DON'T
TELL ME WHAT TO MAKE.' On the other side: '. . . AND I WON'T TELL YOU
HOW TO SELL.'"[10]

Rosemary's Baby set the pace for Hollywood marketing in the high-concept
era. Movie advertising campaigns build outward from a central image—the
one-sheet. In this case, we see the silhouette of an old-fashioned pram, tiny,
alone, on a rocky outcropping. Behind it, Mia Farrow in profile, suffused in
green. Below, the ominous tag, "Pray for Rosemary's Baby." The clean, modern
lines of the typeface and the stream-of-consciousness of the copy were typical
of the sixties revolution in advertising. So were the ellipses on the poster, which
were, in turn, picked up as the long silences in the trailer. (This is how a one-
sheet defines a campaign as a whole.) In the discourse of the time, such gaps created open space into which the viewer could project herself; this was the essence
of the soft sell.[11] But soft-selling a horror movie flew in the face of what Heffernan calls the hucksterish "three-SEEs!" approach.[12] In place of old-fashioned,
Castle-style sensation, Frankfurt offered "involvement." As he explained to the
New York Times in 1968, "I want to make great advertising. . . . People have got
to be involved. You've got to sell them one at a time. Get them involved, that's
the first step to persuasion."[13] More than that, though. As Frankfurt makes clear,
the soft sell raises the prestige of advertising as a whole. The "great advertising"
he makes is not great because it is the most efficient and effective but because

Pray
for
Rosemary's
Baby

Mia Farrow
In a William Castle Production
Rosemary's
Baby

John Cassavetes

Figure 3.3. The soft sell comes to horror. *Rosemary's Baby* (Roman Polanski, Paramount, 1968). Courtesy Paramount/Photofest

it is the most durable, the most involving, the most artistic. When Rosemary's actor husband, played by indie director John Cassavetes, is asked about his work in commercials—"That's where the money is, isn't it, commercials?"—he replies, "And the artistic thrills, too." Heard ironically, the line belongs naturally to Cassavetes, but if he is kidding on the square as he does throughout the first act of the film, then he is standing in for Frankfurt.

Frankfurt's later campaigns—for *Goodbye, Columbus*; *Superman*; *Forrest Gump*—would be legendary. Summing up his career, *Variety* called him the "one-sheet wonder." Thirty years on, he was still stressing "involvement," albeit in much more familiar, high-concept terms. As he explained to *Variety*, he always asked two questions: "'What is the essence of the story? And who will the picture appeal to? Every movie is like a new consumer product that has a brief window to pull it off.' The unconscious demand each consumer is making of an ad campaign, he says, is: 'Involve me.'"[14]

So, what is the essence of the story in *Rosemary's Baby*? Certainly it spoke to tremendous anxieties about female independence, maternal devotion, and faith—hence the tagline, and hence the rather bald-faced moment when Rosemary pulls out a copy of *Time* magazine at her obstetrician's office and the cover blares "Is God Dead?" (a real cover from April 8, 1966). But those anxieties are made volatile and paranoid by their setting. The reason the tagline is effective, even without the presence of any menacing force, is the pram's isolation. *This is no place to raise a baby.* Frankfurt was a master of parental emotions, from his truly startling opening titles for *To Kill a Mockingbird* (Robert Mulligan, Universal, 1962) to the lingering close-ups in his campaign for Johnson and Johnson's baby powder, "looking at the baby as the mother would."[15] *Rosemary's Baby* made cultural anxieties parental; the next year, Frankfurt's campaign for *Goodbye, Columbus* (Larry Peerce, Paramount, 1969) would make parental anxieties a joke: "Every father's daughter is a virgin."

Taking our cue from the poster that *Rosemary's Baby* generates anxiety through setting, and looking ahead to Kissel's intuition that these films are really about art direction, we find the film stretched around two worlds of design. On the one hand, there is the history-encrusted Bramford (actually the Dakota), home to the coven and to the Woodhouses. Richard Sylbert, the production designer, chose the Dakota even before the screenplay was written. (Levin likely had it in mind.) It is the past, Castle's castle. If Sylbert cast the Dakota as a character, Polanski chose the character actors as historical decor: "I thought of all those secondary roles in the book in a certain way. And I thought that I would like to use old Hollywood actors for these parts. In order to explain what I really wanted to the casting director of the studio at that time, I drew all the characters. And I said that the physical aspect of each of those characters was more important to me than some kind of acting abilities."[16] Their pasts are inescapable, like the Bram's, like the Castevets'. Right away Rosemary notices that they have taken down their pictures because there are discolored "empty spaces" on the walls. The past might be repressed, but it leaves traces even so.

The other design domain is younger and more modern. Rosemary remakes her apartment as a world of yellow and white: dishes, sheets, towels, dresses, shoes, wallpaper, and paint. (There is no montage sequence accompanied by a pop song during the makeover in 1967.) Yellow is a color-capsule for her. For the cemetery scene, Polanski ordered a yellow cab to replace the red one the prop department had ordered. As Evans remembers it, "'This crazy Polack doesn't like the color of the cab' became Charlie [Bluhdorn]'s favorite line whenever Roman's name came up. Roman wasn't crazy. He was right in insisting on an authentic yellow banner."[17] Yet authenticity is not the right criterion. There were numerous red-and-yellow and even green cabs in New York at the time—they can be seen in the background of many shots. What mattered to Polanski was not *authenticity* but *design*.

When Rosemary ventures out of the apartment to meet an old friend (who intends to present her with a book detailing the witches' history), she goes to the Time-Life Building, where Gulf + Western was headquartered. This is a telling change; in the novel, the meeting is supposed to occur at the Seagram Building. The October that *Rosemary's Baby* was shooting in New York, G+W announced plans to build a new tower on Columbus Circle, a dozen blocks south of the Dakota. Paramount would leave its famous Times Square building and move Uptown. When the existing building on Columbus Circle was demolished to make way for the new headquarters, "it was revealed that it contained a mysterious Gothic room, reputedly built as a chapel for [William Randolph] Hearst's longtime companion, the actress Marion Davies."[18] Everywhere, there were ghosts of the old Hollywood.

Rosemary's Baby turns on just such hidden gothic significances. Late in the film Rosemary shuffles Scrabble tiles in an attempt to work out the anagram that will reveal her situation. Roman Castevet, the elderly man with the missing pictures, is anagrammatically revealed to be Steven Marcato, warlock. There is something irresistible, though, about the link between Roman Castevet and the two directors in the film, Roman Polanski and John Cassavetes. With such revelations, a second, more ominous significance attaches to the film's one-sheet. Whereas the image initially played on general anxieties on behalf of the powerless infant, by the end of the film, we know that the horror and the power lie within the old-fashioned pram.

In late 1969, Gulf + Western was again considering shuttering Paramount. Occasional successes like *Rosemary's Baby* had not transformed the studio's ongoing operations into a reliable profit center, and much as Bluhdorn enjoyed owning a studio, the board of directors had had enough. Evans convinced Mike Nichols to direct a short film touting Paramount's upcoming releases in order to sway the board. The case was simple: times were hard in the movie business; studios had made mistakes; some had learned from them; some hadn't. Paramount, Evans claimed, had. In this uncertain climate, studio president Stanley Jaffe proposed a novel form of product differentiation: "'Every half-assed guy in the business is making films about where it's at,' said Stanley. 'Let's take a different road, Bob . . . give the audiences something they haven't had for a while—stories about how it feels.' Paramount's strategy of telling stories about how it feels was the secret flag we were going to carry in the years to come."[19] *Love Story*, with its old-fashioned doomed-romance plot, would be the beacon of that strategy. But on top of its affective commitment, Paramount would commit itself to developing its stories in-house. Evans explained to the board:

> We didn't sit back in our plush chairs and write a check for a million or a million and a half dollars for the books, which happens so often in our industry. We developed both of these books. If it weren't for Paramount, the book *Love Story* would never have been written. If it weren't for Paramount, *The Godfather* would never have been written. Because we were in there in the beginning, spurring the writers on, working closely with them to make these books the best-sellers they are and what we think will be the great movies that they're going to be.
>
> We at Paramount don't look at ourselves as passive backers of film, we look at ourselves as a creative force unto ourself. And that is why Paramount is going to be paramount in the industry in the seventies. I promise you that.[20]

At first glance, Evans's strategy may seem to be merely an intensification of industry-wide trends. Studio competition pushed producers to acquire properties earlier and earlier in the process. True, Evans had made a name for himself as an independent producer by jumping on the rights to books still in the galley stage. Indeed, it was Peter Bart's glowing profile of Evans doing just that— "I like it. I want it. Let's sew it up"—that had brought Evans to the attention of Bluhdorn and Bart to Evans.[21] But as the case of *Rosemary's Baby* makes clear, galley options were hardly unique in the late 1960s.

By taking the process a step further, Paramount turned the competitive race to acquire a pre-sold property turned into something like its opposite, a race to produce a property that might be sold at the same time as the film. The author-screenwriter's name would appear on the book, but the books would be more simultaneous novelizations than acquisitions. Evans is selling G+W the idea that Paramount can make authors. In some cases, this would be literal (as it would be for Mario Puzo and *The Godfather*). In some cases, the authors would be directors; in others, they would be producers. And by extension, Paramount would be "a creative force."

This was a very expansive idea of the studio. Evans might have emphasized Paramount's modern aspects, such as its cutting-edge marketing and ruthless distribution, but he chose to look backward, beyond the package-unit system, beyond the producer-unit system, to the supervising producer mode best exemplified by Irving Thalberg at MGM. Indeed, if Evans modeled himself on anyone, it was Thalberg, and for good reason. Evans had abandoned his floundering acting career to be an executive at his brother's fashion house, Evan-Picone, but was "rediscovered," poolside, by Thalberg's widow, Norma Shearer. She wanted him to play her husband in the Lon Chaney biopic *Man of a Thousand Faces* and, eventually, in *The Last Tycoon*. He was already acting the part. Through Evans's identification with Thalberg, Paramount began rebuilding itself as an epigone of the thirties, and that transformation turned the design-and-marketing complex that the studio had wielded on individual films into something approaching a studio style.

The Paramount Thirties and the Idea of Italy

At the grandest scale, the career of high concept serves as both skin and support for the emerging culture of postmodernism. For Fredric Jameson, one cornerstone of the postmodern loss of historical possibility is nostalgia for a time when the political left was possible. In the 1970s, that was nostalgia for the 1930s, emblematized for him by *The Conformist* (Bernardo Bertolucci, 1970) and *Chinatown* (Polanski, 1974). Jameson does not, though, note that both films were distributed by Paramount. Indeed, while there was plenty of thirties nostalgia to go around, Paramount made a specialty of it, producing or picking up a dozen such films. *The Conformist* and *Chinatown* were tremendous successes, but there were also *Paper Moon, Murder on the Orient Express, The Postman Always Rings Twice, Day of the Locust* (1975), *The Last Tycoon* (1976), *Bugsy Malone*, and, eventually, *Raiders of the Lost Ark*. Throw in a trilogy of African American–themed films set in the period—*Sounder, Lady Sings the Blues*, and *Leadbelly*—some of the twenties with *The Great Gatsby*, and the studious avoidance of the thirties in the *Godfather* films, and Paramount is the most nostalgic of studios. Or, if nostalgia is not exactly the right word, then the studio most concerned with achieving renovation by retelling its own history.

However determined Evans, Jaffe, Frank Yablans, Bluhdorn, and others might have been to restore Paramount to some previous greatness, they could not specify which newfangled take on the old studio would offer the most success. Rather than commit themselves to one particular reincarnation of the classic era, they tried on several versions, each of which emphasized a particular aspect of the contemporary industrial configuration. To put it another way, the industry's deep recession at the end of the sixties threw Hollywood into chaos and reopened the question of systemic causality. Where did power lie? With the studios? Directors? Producers? Somewhere else? Who could make the most effective argument that they were "in charge"? Paramount chose to answer those questions through experiment, and they cast those experiments into the imaginary 1930s. To be sure, those thirties were an era of historical possibility, as Jameson put it, but that possibility overlay a surprisingly durable industrial configuration—one that, at Paramount, was presided over by a commitment to style. So when Jameson laments the reduction of Depression-era social unrest to art deco stylization, he is, in part, missing the attraction of the period for the studios. Paramount loved the thirties because the system endured, stylishly, despite the wrenching changes in the industry. Come 1970, as the studio confronted another shatterbelt in the precession of causality, it imagined the emerging order along three lines. One extended the emphasis on external style and design that it had pioneered with the marketing of *Rosemary's Baby*. The second attempted to institutionalize auteurism through the creation and support of the Directors Company. The last turned to explicit meditations on the nature of the classical studio (or, in the case of *Chinatown*, Los Angeles), particularly to analogs of the supervising producer that Evans imagined himself to be. In the end, neither the supervising producer nor the director would become the model for Paramount's creativity going forward. Instead, the studio would remake itself around the designer as such.

Paramount proved its commitment to the auteur with *The Conformist* and *The Italian Job* (Peter Collinson, 1969), and each of them contributed to the studio's particular notion of the thirties. *The Conformist* was a Franco-Italian coproduction, helped along by some German funds, but that complicated financing was less important to the movie than its distributor, Paramount. Bertolucci first heard the outline of the plot from his wife, who was reading Alberto Moravia's novel. Without reading it himself (he was occupied with the editing of *The Spider's Stratagem*—a Borgesian investigation of identity; like *The Conformist*, set in a fascist Italy), he rushed to Luigi Luraschi, head of Paramount Rome. Luraschi had been the head of censorship at Paramount in the United States from the thirties through the fifties and was the CIA's man in Hollywood.[22] In 1960 he went to work for Dino De Laurentiis and eventually came back to Paramount.[23] Thus, Luraschi had strong connections to the studio in America. And after Brando's comeback in *The Godfather*, it was Luraschi who managed to secure his performance in *Last Tango in Paris*. He was the crucial mediator in Paramount's crucial foreign location. Bertolucci knew where to take the pitch.

The eventual reviews of *The Conformist* stressed its differences from the director's more challenging earlier work. Stephen Farber thought that what set it apart was its portability: It "travels better than the others; visually and dramatically, it is one of the most exciting Italian movies in years, but its political ideas seem bewildering or facile."[24] A portable, heightened style and narration crowding out politics: Farber's account may not be entirely accurate, but this would be the characteristic trade-off of the new cinema. And it depended crucially on below-the-line talent. Editor Franco Arcalli introduced the multiple flashbacks to the narration; cinematographer Vittorio Storaro constructed a visual language of smoke and light, of languid tracking shots and handheld jitteriness; and production designer Ferdinando Scarfiotti found parodic and monumental locations against which individual stories might play out. Later, Storaro shot *Apocalypse Now* (Coppola, UA, 1980), and Scarfiotti designed *American Gigolo* (Paul Schrader, Paramount, 1980). Arcalli never worked in America, but his imbricated flashbacks would decisively influence the structure of *The Godfather Part II*. In short, Paramount's take on the American New Wave came by way of Bertolucci and company.

The Italian Job had little in common with *The Conformist*, but the heist picture rebalanced the relationship between auteur, studio, and mise-en-scène in a way that nearly foresaw the product-integrated design concepts of the eighties. At its core *The Italian Job* was a very odd sort of product placement for Fiat. If high concept is assembled out of a particular configuration of auteur, studio, design, and marketing, one of its essential elements is a broad recognition of the essential marketability of elements within the film narrative. Early on, Fiat understood that the film could be a "huge opportunity to promote the product," as producer Michael Deeley put it. If the production had simply been willing to trade the Minis for Fiat 500s, the Italian company would have provided them with "all the cars you want to destroy," fifty thousand dollars, and the "top of the line Ferrari." Deeley refused, not because British Motors offered more—they "were completely disinterested in helping . . . in any way," according to Matthew Field—but because the politics of the film required it. "The whole point of the movie, which I had grasped by that time, was us against them. It was the first Euroskeptic movie. It was us showing the Italians a thing or two,"

Deeley said. Yet the film still revolves around Fiat: The target is the Fiat payroll; the Mini jumps from building to building were filmed at the plant; the Mafia guys drive Fiat Dinos; and the giant traffic jam that bottles up Turin came courtesy of Fiat head Gianni Agnelli. "All it took was one call from David Harlick to Agnelli and Agnelli passed the word down to the police and others that we were to be helped, and they gave us amazing—they gave us lots of vehicles of course, and drivers and things like that, but they gave us Turin," Deeley explained.[25] In exchange, the production planted Fiats wherever they could.

Deeley's insistence that the film is Euroskeptic is accurate, but it wears its politics as a kind of knowing British pride. The job itself is bankrolled by Noël Coward from behind bars. Coward's Bridger may be a criminal mastermind, but he is unswervingly nationalist (and Royalist). His prison cell resembles a perverse gentlemen's den with its deep leather club chair and walls papered with photos of the queen. When it comes to robbery, the Bank of England is off limits (for nationalist reasons or because Coward has seen *The Lavender Hill Mob*?). Michael Caine initially attempts to interest him by explaining that the robbery in Turin will be good for the country's balance of payments. Bridger refuses. Caine, who has gone to the trouble of breaking back into prison to make the offer, then addresses the camera directly: "I could always take it to the Americans—they're people who . . . recognize young talent, give it a chance, they are." And the Americans are the ones backing *The Italian Job*, making Caine's remark, like the alpine backdrops of the Italian scenes, a product placement for the studio in the era of the auteur.

Figure 3.4. An advertisement for the alpine studio itself. *The Italian Job* (Peter Collinson, Paramount, 1969)

Indeed, the Paramount roots of *The Italian Job* run deeper than such simple nudges. Just as *Rosemary's Baby* cast character actors as decor in the service of its overarching design, so the casting of Coward carried with it a wave of

Paramount history. *The Italian Job* was Coward's last film role; his first, thirty-four years earlier, had been in another Paramount film, *The Scoundrel*. For that project, several major players were trying on new roles. Coward moved from writing to acting while Ben Hecht and Charles MacArthur moved from writing to directing. Most notably, it was made during the brief tenure of director Ernst Lubitsch as head of production at the studio. As part of Paramount's emergence from Depression-induced receivership, Lubitsch was given the key production job. The studio's strongest brand was the "Lubitsch Touch," and its board sought to make that identity more explicit and intense. Lubitsch quickly signed King Vidor, Lewis Milestone, and Frank Borzage, a move that cemented Paramount's reputation as the most director-friendly of the majors. Lubitsch declared, "Directing at Paramount will be entirely a matter of personal taste and ability," and that declaration seems to have been borne out.[26] Ethan Mordden, surveying the Lubitsch era concludes, "What is most essential to the Paramount style, however, is not the slyness of its sex comedy alone but the studio's reliance on directorial initiative."[27]

In the late sixties, the studio did not need a change of leadership—Deeley considered Evans "a very, very good studio head."[28] What it needed was a way of cultivating "directorial initiative." *The Italian Job* marked one successful culmination of Paramount's cultivation process. Bluhdorn wanted Peter Collinson for the project, but Deeley felt that Collinson did not have the requisite experience (he preferred Peter Yates, fresh off the chases in *Robbery* and *Bullitt*). So Deeley arranged for Collinson to direct *The Long Day's Dying*. This was classical studio thinking—the company would manage the career of a contract employee, laddering him up from one assignment to the next; it was, in the late sixties, utterly exceptional. But what made it more than simply an instance of a studio looking beyond its immediate need for a director for a particular package to the longer-term need for loyal talent was Collinson's backstory. Collinson had been raised in the Actors' Orphanage, and Coward had been his godfather. Through that relationship, Collinson was able to convince Coward to play Bridger, the on-screen godfather—the on-screen producer—of the "young talent." The solution to one studio problem, then, generated further proof of Paramount's intensive self-reflection. All that remained was an open declaration of principles, a manifesto of the studio's desires, a literalization of the mutual exploitation of story and backstory. What Paramount wanted out of *The Italian Job* was the openness to young talent associated with the Americans, the total control of Agnelli, and the loyalty of the Brits. But what it wanted most of all were the foresight and the ruthlessness of the Mafia ("It's a matter of prestige," as Bridger explains). It got all of those on *The Godfather*.

The Godfather has been the subject of more good criticism than perhaps any other film from its era, in part because Coppola was as voluble about the project as he was. He told anyone who would listen that the film was really about capitalism, about business, about family—about the great American themes. And writers were willing to listen to him because he was the auteur. Paramount had settled on him not simply because it trusted his relatively young talent (Peter Bart did; Evans did not) but because he gave them cover as the expected backlash against the portrayal of mob life built. Stanley Jaffe was blunt: "He fits the party line, you'll smell the spaghetti."[29] And as the squabble for credit between Coppola and Evans dragged on, a great deal of the production backstory has been available, either through interviews or Coppola's generous release of working documents. Finally, perhaps more than its blockbuster contemporaries *Love Story*, *The Exorcist*, and *Jaws*, *The Godfather* saga yields to the traditional pressures of academic film study. A movie that begins with someone saying, "I believe in America," and that manages to pull off such histrionics, is ideally suited to the sorts of interpretation that were waiting for it. Coppola imagined that movies were directors' creations; critics imagined the same; and in this case, the film itself could bear the attention.

None of which is meant to belittle the remarkable work that has been done on *The Godfather*, only to suggest that the meanings that have been read out of it seem to have been fully anticipated. Why does that matter? Because the essence of leadership in *The Godfather* is the ability to turn recognition into anticipation. That may seem implausible: Surely the film's emphasis on the proximity of family, business, politics, and crime is more important. "Business," of course, is the film's key word: the "family business," the "dirty business" of drugs, this "Solazzo business" that has sent Michael to Sicily, and on and on. The opposite of business (it sometimes seems) is the personal. Tom and Sonny fight over the line between the two spheres: "They shoot my father and it's business, my ass!" "Even shooting your father was business, not personal, Sonny!" And Michael insists that something as extreme as killing a cop could be justified. "It's not personal, Sonny. It's strictly business." Even when the opposition between the two turns out to be hollow, it would seem that critics are right to focus on the film's avowed concerns. It does not particularly matter whether all the male boasting about what is personal and what is business is antisentimental posturing (which suggests only the real depths of their feelings) or sociopathic denial (as Kay finally suspects) because both versions only suggest the dangers of the proximity between them—"Don't ask me about my business."[30] Psychology has given way to what we might call configuration. What looks like a theme turns out to be a map of American society.

As a result of this melding, the morality of *The Godfather* continually runs the risk of getting lost in the Long Island marshes. All the discourse about the domestic and the criminal ("Leave the gun, take the cannoli") emerges from the configuration of zones of action within the film, and those zones come preprogrammed with motivations (family, business, revenge, etc.). We feel, at times, that the revelation of *The Godfather* lies precisely in the display of the arrangements of underworld life—hence the availability of these mobsters for hero worship; hence the endless arguability of the righteousness of particular actions. Yet the problems of configuration are far less explanatory of the film's operation than is the scene-setting force of anticipation. More important than any thematic is the structuring principle of Mafia action: this has been foreseen. The Mafia in *The Italian Job* were waiting for Rossano Brazzi as he crossed the Alps; later, they were waiting for Michael Caine and his gang as they did the same. In *The Godfather*, that preternatural sense of anticipation is what Don Vito and Michael Corleone share. Consider, as a first instance, the scene at the hospital, where Michael recognizes the impending hit. When he whispers, "I'm with you now" to his father, we hear that as a kind of enlistment in the family business— we *know* that it means more than simply that he is present. But the film takes our knowledge and immediately compounds it. Don Vito is pained to realize that his attempts to insulate Michael from the family business have failed even as he is relieved that Michael is there protecting him. Yet the thrill of the scene comes not from Michael's new allegiance but rather from his unexpected competence as he stage-manages a response. "I'm with you" turns out to be a declaration that he is on the same page as his father—that, like the Don, he knows what is coming.

The second, similarly thrilling moment passes between Don Vito and Tom Hagen as they rehash the pseudo-board meeting of the Five Families. As Jon Lewis describes it,

> Tom asks: "When I meet with the Tattaglia people, should I insist that his drug middlemen all have clean records?" Vito replies, "Mention it, but don't insist. Barzini is a man who'll know without being told." Tom catches what he assumes is a mistake, a sign that the aging Don is slipping: "You mean Tattaglia." But Vito has read the previous scene better and more closely than his attorney. "Tattaglia's a pimp," Vito snarls, "He never could have outfought Santino. I didn't know it till this day that it was Barzini all along."[31]

What makes this moment work is that even here, when the Don is admitting his failing, he is still a step ahead of us all.

The climax of the cult of the piety of anticipation comes in the succession discussion between Don Vito and Michael. It was a scene insisted upon by Brando, doctored by Robert Towne, and shot exceptionally patiently by Coppola. As the Don's powers are fading, now visibly, he struggles to sort out the various threads of the discussion: the threats to the family, his dreams for his son, and the intersection of the two. What remains clear for him is the pattern of the game: "Whoever comes to you with this Barzini meeting, he's the traitor. Don't forget that." He simply *knows*, and Michael, who has been told this, already knows that it will be Tessio. This last claim may seem even more implausible than my insistence that anticipation shapes the film, especially given the staging of the Don's funeral. There, Michael appears to be searching the crowd for the man who will suggest the meeting with Barzini. Yet if that were the case, then Michael's subsequent exchange with Tom ("I always thought it would be Clemenza, not Tessio." "No, it's the smart move. Tessio was always smarter.") would be Michael disguising his own post hoc rationalization. But we don't take it as that: His scene with Tom is the parallel to Don Vito's Barzini-all-along conversation. Michael is nearing his peak here, which implies that he is simply looking for Tessio at the funeral, that he has anticipated the entire sequence of events. In the earlier draft of the scene, Tom was the more knowledgeable partner ("I guess you've figured it all out," Michael says to him), just as he had known that Vito and Michael were up to something when they pushed him aside as consigliere. But in the film as shot, Tom is less canny, and he needs to be told, first by Vito and then by Michael, what is what. As confirmation of Michael's foreknowledge, we look to the end

Figure 3.5.
The burden of anticipation . . .
The Godfather
(Coppola,
Paramount, 1972)

Figure 3.6.
. . . registered in
Michael's body. *The
Godfather* (Coppola,
Paramount, 1972)

of his conversation with his father, when he slouches back into his chair. The move echoes the end of the scene in the Don's office when Tessio and Clemenza ask to be turned loose to fight for their territories. They are put off—"There are things being negotiated now that will solve all your problems and answer all your questions. That's all I can tell you now"—as though the family were meekly winding up its affairs before heading to Nevada in "six months." Yet the setup of the Corleones' Vegas enemies has already been put in motion—Tom is being moved out of his role as consigliere (as far as he knows), and a third regime is being built up within the family. As Michael sits in his father's chair for the first time, Tessio and Clemenza take their leave—Clemenza, diffidently, still clearly chafing at being put off; Tessio more formally, more apparently at ease with Michael's new role running the family business. He extends his hand, and Michael takes it. Then, when he has thrown Tom out, Michael drops back in the chair. He has measured the two capi, and in the later scene, he is playing out the betrayal still to come.

Tessio's fate is more than another picket in the film's jury-rigged fence between what is business and what is personal. "Tell him it was just business. I always liked him," he says before futilely asking for a personal favor: "Can you get me off the hook, Tom? For old time's sake?" His death completes the handoff from Vito to Michael, and it is the apocalypse of anticipation: "It messes up all my plans." The irony is thick as the film reaches its climax in the grand, symphonic montage in which Michael forswears "Satan and all his works" while his enemies are being liquidated. Yet as we have known since the opening scene, the relationship between the godfather and the Don is not ironic but enabling—it is, in the terms I have been using, allegorical.

That enabling relationship extends to the production itself, from the studio's early involvement with Puzo's treatment to its awkward attempts to appease the Italian-American Civil Rights League by excising any explicit mention of the Mafia. In the wake of its very public agreement with the league, Paramount faced press criticism. The studio was accused, rightly, of playing along with the league's founder, notorious mob boss Joseph Colombo. But while critics called that acquiescence "ironic," it was, again, essential to the production's success since Colombo was the key to the city's unions. By ostensibly playing down the film's references to the Mafia, Paramount was able to shoot the movie it wanted. Just as Agnelli "gave them" Turin, Colombo "opened up the city."[32]

But for Colombo to play the Agnelli role, he had to be both appeased *and* sacrificed. Fiat got its product placements, but the company became the patsy of British Motors. Agnelli's behind-the-scenes control was partitioned out on-screen between the lads (who seized control of Turin) and the Mafia (who ultimately controlled the Italian scene more generally). No on-screen thank you could bridge the gap between the production and its reading. Colombo, in turn, was appeased long enough to get *The Godfather* shot. On June 28, 1971, he was gunned down in pseudeponymous Columbus Circle, outside the Gulf + Western building, as he prepared to lead an Italian-American Civil Rights League rally. He lingered in a coma for years. The button man was executed on the scene (his assassin was never apprehended). The man who ordered the hit, Crazy Joe Gallo, hoped to supplant Colombo, going so far as to set up his own mob-washing organization, Americans of Italian Descent. Gallo was killed the following April at Umberto's Clam House in Little Italy in a scene that nearly duplicated Michael's hit on Solazzo.[33] For *The Godfather*, which had opened only the month before, the gang war was good for business.

The claim here is not that Paramount staged Gallo or Colombo's death (it didn't) but that their deaths required only the same sort of recognition-as-anticipation to which the studio had been aspiring. Critics have registered the distinction between the first sort of action ("agency") and the second ("fit") as irony, only to find that the studio's relationships with the mob continually outstrip the trope. Just when one imagines that there is (only) a coincidence between the fictional world of the studio's stories and the nonfictional machinations of the studio's story, yet another "ironic" detail appears. So in 1971, Paramount negotiated in public with Colombo to guarantee that filming in New York would go smoothly, only to partially disavow its willingness to play along with the mob. Yet Evans had rehearsed that negotiation in his struggle to extricate Al Pacino from his commitment to star in MGM's *The Gang That Couldn't Shoot Straight*. When Coppola wanted Pacino for *The Godfather*, Evans turned to his friend and notorious Hollywood fixer Sidney Korshak to pressure MGM's Kirk Kerkorian into letting the actor go. "I asked him if he wanted to finish building his hotel."[34] It was a power play on the same order as the offer Tom Hagen makes to Hollywood producer Woltz in order to secure a role for Johnny Fontaine: "You're going to have some union problems. My client could make them disappear." Was the Pacino story apocryphal? Had Evans simply rewritten the novel as corporate backstory so that it could be "ironically" displayed in the film? The answer is less important than the commitment to the instant repurposing of stories across the organization's various levels.

The line between irony and allegory—between image and author—is as fraught as the line between what's business and what's personal. But where *The Godfather* reveals that the latter is ultimately a hollow opposition, the former is essential to the emergence of the neoclassical era. When does the contingent seem necessary? The passage from a world of coincidences to a world of causes is, for corporations and audiences alike, the experience of design. When does that experience become compelling: with the Kerkorian deal, the Colombo agreement, the Gallo hit, *The Italian Job*, or the development of Puzo's novel? Is it merely a matter of accumulation of instances? Or is there a foundational moment that locks these events into a pattern inescapably? In October 1969, still pondering the sale of the studio as a whole, G+W put the Paramount lot on the market, spinning it into a new subsidiary (Marathon Holdings). The next June, Bluhdorn announced that half the lot had been sold to Società Generale Immobiliare (SGI), an enormous Italian real estate company, one backed by the Vatican. In exchange, G+W purchased fifteen million shares of SGI from an undisclosed "major corporate stockholder." That shareholder turned out to be Michele Sindona, a banker with close ties to the Vatican and the subject of persistent rumors surrounding his ties to the Mafia—rumors that seemed confirmed when he was tried and convicted of murder and various financial crimes. In the most lurid detail, fellow banker and sometime partner Roberto Calvi was found hanging under London's Blackfriars bridge on June 18, 1982. Calvi's death, Sindona's conviction, and the unspooling conspiracy theories regarding the death of Pope John Paul I were enough to entice Coppola back to Paramount to make *The Godfather Part III*, a film that was all but explicit about its narrative and financial debts to the studio's underworld ties.[35] The year 1970 found Korshak and Colombo running interference for the studio between Los Angeles, Las Vegas, and New York; Luraschi and Sindona brokering deals in Rome; and Jaffe and Evans relying on all of them while simultaneously bringing along Puzo and Coppola. Given how tightly the studio was being wound around its organized criminal core, it would be willful to persist in calling Paramount's corporate arrangements "ironic." But criticism persists because the alternative requires us to believe that the studio is in the business of foreseeing such events, that its identity and aspirations consist of a projective reading of its own possibilities, one that leaves little room for criticism beyond certification.[36] To say that the new Paramount would forgo stories about "where it's at" for stories about "how it feels" amounted to saying it would be built around the conversion of image into authorship.

The Directors Company:
"Something Like" the Paramount Thirties II

In the wake of *The Godfather*, Paramount attempted to institutionalize an auteurist mode of production. Despite the arguments between Coppola and Evans, it was obvious that the studio would strive to keep the Oscar-winning director on board for *The Godfather Part II*. To accomplish that, in 1973 Paramount signed a deal with Coppola, William Friedkin, and Peter Bogdanovich creating the Directors Company. The terms were legendarily generous. The studio would stake them to $31.5 million in development and production funds in exchange for twelve movies over the next six years. The agreement was non-exclusive, meaning that directors were free to make pictures at other studios. Evans was cut out of the process; control rested with the three directors. At a time when the studio was reducing its average budgets to $2.5 million, the directors would be able to green-light their own films if the budgets were under $3 million; over that, and the board of the new company (half of whom were from Paramount) would have to approve the project.[37] Despite the terms, the Directors Company would yield only three films before it dissolved: *Paper Moon* (Bogdanovich, 1973), *The Conversation* (Coppola, 1974), and *Daisy Miller* (Bogdanovich, 1974).

Coppola was the most assiduous brander of the new company. After soliciting logo designs, he wrote to Friedkin (and, presumably, Bogdanovich): "I hope for something like the old logos—Rank, MGM—something like the *30's*."[38] Bogdanovich, preparing to shoot Depression-set *Paper Moon*, would certainly have agreed. At the same time, through his other studio project, American Zoetrope, Coppola pitched his partners a behind-the-scenes television special about the Directors Company itself. The documentary would capture each of the directors at a different point in the moviemaking process—pre-production,

production, and post-production—and was to be a model of the future of enfotainment marketing:

> The special would be designed to appeal most directly to the audience with the fol-
> lowing demographic characteristics:
>
> Age: 18–35 years
>
> Income: $10,000 plus
>
> Education: Some college exposure
>
> Life Style: Contemporary, well-informed, media-oriented

What would set the show apart from the routine behind-the-scenes coverage
would be its studio focus. It would not tell the story of *The Exorcist*, *Paper Moon*,
or *The Conversation*, but the story of this unique corporation. "At some point,
during the final third of the picture, Mr. Bludhorn [*sic*] or another appropriate
Gulf & Western or Paramount executive would be fitted in to briefly reveal the
involvement of the management and how The Directors' Company arrangement differs from the classic director/producer relationship."[39] Whether this
last statement was designed to appeal to Coppola within Zoetrope, to the other
directors, to Paramount, or to the audience is less important than the sense it
gives that the corporate structure could be, and should be, part of what would
set the Directors Company apart for its audience.

Coppola needed the Directors Company because Zoetrope, his previous
attempt at institutionalization, had been cast adrift by Warners. In 1968, he was
driving around the country shooting *The Rain People*. "It was like independent filmmaking under the auspices of the studios, kind of, but it was nice
because we were isolated and on our own," according to star Robert Duvall.[40]
The romance of the production of *The Rain People* spilled over in all directions.
George Lucas was traveling with the company, ostensibly shooting a making-of
documentary, but more intently developing the feature version of the script for
THX-1138. Coppola was conjuring an independent studio, financed and distributed by a major but controlled by him.

Lucas, typically mythologizing his own origins, offered this account of Zoetrope's beginnings: "The day that John Calley and Ted Ashley and all those guys
showed up for work, their first day of work at this new Warner Brothers Seven
Arts, Francis sent them a note which said, you know, we have a picture in production here and we're here waiting for your go-ahead, and you better shape up
or ship out. And that's really where American Zoetrope started." Calley, naturally, had a much savvier and more rational explanation for the arrangement.
"We bought the notion that we would help subsidize Zoetrope, that they would
work out of San Francisco, that the paradigm would be one of modestly bud-

geted films done in a hands-off manner. Francis would be the parental figure, at least as he presented it, and that we would say yes and wait."[41] Zoetrope offered seven films in its initial package: *THX*, *The Conversation*, *Apocalypse Now*, Willard Huyck's *The Naked Gypsies*, John Korty's *Have We Seen the Elephant*, Carroll Ballard's *Vesuvia*, *Santa Rita*, and a film about People's Park. *THX* would be the first to shoot, the inaugural American Zoetrope production.

The film began as George Lucas's student film at the University of Southern California. Lucas amplified it into a feature script, and in the summer of 1969 he and Walter Murch collaborated on the screenplay. Their institutional situation was nearly total independence with access to substantial capital. Sheltered under Coppola's wing, and the beneficiary of his remarkable deal-making skills, Lucas fashioned a perfect illustration of the cognitive structure of paranoid auteurism. No allegory of its own production, *THX* was, if this can be believed, nostalgic for an era when the studio could plausibly be a figure of total knowledge and endless malefaction. Only against such complete oppression would it be possible to imagine an individualism as radical as the one Lucas envisioned.

It was only fitting that Zoetrope was located in San Francisco. By the late sixties, the Bay Area had become a hotbed of paranoid political thinking. And fears of that paranoia gave rise to complementary counter-paranoias. Joan Didion, writing about the possible political underside of the Summer of Love, was drawn to the gnomic mimeographed dispatches from "The Communication Company," whose "missives are regarded with some apprehension in the [Haight-Ashbury] District and with considerable interest by outsiders, who study them, like China watchers, for subtle shifts in obscure ideologies."[42] *THX* was plugged into the San Francisco paranoid scene in a very particular way. When the production needed hundreds of bald extras, it turned to a bountiful local source, Synanon. The drug-treatment center was famous for its confrontational, acephalic group-therapy sessions, called "The Synanon Game." The place had enjoyed remarkably good press throughout the sixties. But by the end of the seventies it, like much of the human potential movement, would lie in ruins. As Scientology would, it incorporated as a church in order to avoid taxes.

Fredric Jameson, writing about the paranoid seventies in *The Geopolitical Aesthetic*, draws particular attention to a sequence in *Three Days of the Condor* (Sidney Pollack, Paramount, 1975) in which Robert Redford hacks a telephone-switching station. For Jameson, it is the station itself and not the individual hijacking of it that is most emblematic.[43] Like the panorama of San Narciso in Thomas Pynchon's *The Crying of Lot 49*, the switching network holds out the promise of meaningfulness, of analogon, in the midst of a society that seems to lack a central author. Four years earlier, the creators of *THX* had also staged a chase scene through a telephone exchange, and for very Jamesonian reasons. As Murch put it, "The most particular and peculiar thing about this world is that there is nobody in charge. In that sense it's like the precursor to the internet which is a web, a social, electronic web, which is so large and diffuse that there doesn't have to be a central brain that controls it. It's self-controlling in a way by virtue of all of the people who participate in it." This net-before-the-net frisson implies that the film, as a bit of near-future, hard science fiction, is forward looking. But Lucas understood it to be simply descriptive, not predictive: "The world is becoming this way, but it seemed to me at the time that it already *was* this way."[44]

Yet if *THX* offered both a look into a dystopian future and a cloaked representation of a dystopian present, it did so precisely through a design concept that emphasized nostalgic recognizability. True, it did not offer up the recent past as *American Graffiti* would, nor did it resemble thirties serials as *Star Wars* and the *Indiana Jones* films would. But like those other Lucas films, it stressed the combined and uneven progress of history. Murch, describing the sequence in the telephone-switching room, put it this way: "It's one of a number of wonderful incongruities in the film where you're looking at an obviously advanced society but some of the hardware and the devices that people use are charmingly anachronistic—telephones with wires coming out of them, ordinary handsets and this room which is a telephone switching room. . . . [A]ll of this equipment was rapidly becoming obsolete."[45] Whatever privilege those mechanical switches had in representing the social would shortly disappear as relays were replaced by the electronics of touch-tone switching. In this sense, *THX* not only represents a future through the present; it presents itself as nostalgia for that possibility.[46]

Lucas and Murch were able to realize their involuted time signatures through cohesive design. In order to clear the political pathway through that complex temporality, they relied on the sorts of limited narrative that would be Lucas's hallmark. As he described it, the film's three acts were "the same story three times": first told conventionally (the domestic drama), then abstractly (the debate about how to escape), then through action (the chase picture). Moreover, the arc of the story would be lifted from or, rather, harmonized with Joseph Campbell's *Hero with a Thousand Faces*. Lucas had read the book in his sophomore year in an anthropology class. Now he was putting it to use not as an analytic but as a recipe. "You know in mythology there's always the magical character along the side of the road that they always pick up on the way? This is sort of my first use of that magical character [a magic Negro, it turns out] who isn't real but isn't not real, but is smarter than everybody else, and doesn't live in this world so he doesn't quite know how to open the door but is very wise."[47]

The paranoid backdrop to *THX* appears on-screen as design coherence and excessively redundant narrative. As a result, the film suggests a degree of planning that would seem to be consistent with the sort of repressive, totalitarian society it laments. That was the risk of making the movie: that you would end up replicating the system you wanted to destroy. One way of tempering that risk was to cast it backward, literally, via historicism, or tonally, via nostalgia. But the only way of utterly liquidating the risk of replication was through magical thinking.[48] The flip side of late-sixties paranoia is a belief in telepathy, a kind of frictionless society or signless communication. At its most ordinary, this is a belief in intuition, and however implausible it might seem, it nevertheless seems absolutely necessary for social action. This implausible-but-necessary combination holds true even for highly cephalic forms, like, for instance, a motion picture unit. Here is Murch:

> Why are films basically on time and on budget? I think it has to do with the amount that people follow their own intuition and are somehow intuitively tied in to the intuition of others. The fact is that if you had to articulate all the decisions that get made on a film, if everything had to be written out, let's do this, and then you do this, and then you do this, every acting decision, every decision in cinematography, every decision of production design, every editorial decision—if all of those had to be overtly articulated, the film would never get done. At the very heart of the filmmaking process is a reliance by everyone involved, particularly the heads of departments, on a gut feeling about what might be right. And it's delegated to the director to supervise and choreograph all these decisions, some of which the director is making but many of which are being presented to the director so the director in that sense is kind of like the immune system of the film.[49]

This is a remarkable vision of collective creation, of relatively homeostatic independence. Yet Lucas, however much he might have needed his collaborators, and however independent his productions, could not manage to dwell within this utopia of presence for long.

> And I realized very much that the unique situation I found myself in being at American Zoetrope, being away from the studios, having them approve the film, the studios being confused about what kind of movies work and what kind of movies don't work, I said this is my one chance to make you know a really avant-garde movie in the mainstream. I may never get this chance again. This may be a little open window that's gonna close right up again because it's a completely unique opportunity. And so I took it.[50]

THX told the same story three times; Lucas's account of its backstory constitutes the fourth version. His "avant-garde movie" was less a tale pulled from the reaches of his individuality than it was the story of his narrow escape through the little window afforded by the floundering studios. The allegory becomes increasingly clear across the film. Act I tells the story of narcotized entertainment consumers and seems to be a broad social critique. Act II recasts that story as an existential-political fable in which stand-ins for classical philosophers argue with a character who "does nothing but quote Richard Nixon speeches." Act III, the action iteration, is not a pure chase, for the pursuit is continuously monitored for its adherence to an initial budget, and once the budget is blown, THX is allowed to escape. Lucas made the allegory explicit: "One of the final statements of the movie is that you're dealing with a social system where everything is on budget, money kind of rules everything. I guess it was a bit of a statement of my feelings about the studios at the time."[51]

And those feelings were, naturally, confirmed. *THX* was not yet a model the studio could recognize. At the studio screening, Calley was baffled. "There was nobody in the room, I must confess, that thought they knew what to do with *THX 1138.* . . . It was as though George was making this movie that Francis was managing and producing, and it was clear that he wasn't." The Zoetroopers ran off with the print as soon as it had been screened to prevent Warners from attempting to recut it. Lucas's paranoia was dovetailing with reality: "There was no point for them to do that other than to exercise some power. 'We can screw around with your movie so we're going to.'" Lucas's heroic stab at independence "almost brought American Zoetrope down at the end and almost destroyed my career, but it was definitely worth the attempt at the time."[52] The Zoetrope deal with Warners came apart; the indie was now saddled with tremendous overhead and precious little income. The solution to their problems would come via Paramount.

The success of *The Godfather* allowed Coppola to pay Zoetrope's debts and secure his independence through the Directors Company. In mid-1972, Coppola cashed in another of his chits with the studio when he walked into a San Francisco car dealer with Lucas, ordered the Mercedes-Benz 600 Pullman—"the big stretch limo," "the one with the six doors"—and had the bill sent to Paramount.[53] The limousine was quickly put to use on-screen in *The Conversation*, where the car belongs to Robert Duvall. Since Duvall's character is known only as "The Director," we might say the director's limo becomes the Director's limo when the Directors Company needs a limo. As the materialization of the pun, the car is both personal and corporate, a perfect emblem of Coppola's thematic obsessions. Indeed, the film seems of a piece with *The Godfather* in its insistence that business is ineradicably personal. The Mercedes may be a company car but bears the brand of personality in its custom license plate: C1. (Coppola was able to secure the plate in part because California had only begun issuing vanity plates in August 1970.)[54]

The car seems to belong to the Director, but it appears on-screen only after he has been killed by his wife and her lover, just as she is about to assume control of the company. In the ensuing press scrum one reporter shouts, "What about your corporate control? Will your stock now give you controlling interest?" while another drives home the irony by asking, "Do you feel now that there's an enemy within the company?" Reading Coppola's take on his film's corporate succession is difficult. On the one hand, he clearly relished the idea of toppling the old guard at the studios and installing himself. On the other hand, he has loaded that regime change with all the pathos of a mock suicide: his car, his initial, his job title. The film's solution to this dilemma is to search for a moral actor who can embody Coppola's ambivalence yet at the same time offer a clearer resolution. This is the function of surveillance expert Harry Caul (Gene Hackman). Caul is a shrouded wiretapper, obsessed with his own privacy and consumed by guilt. He is legible from his plastic raincoat to his jingly ring of keys. His links to the betrayed Director become obvious during the murder scene. The killers attack Duvall, wrapping his body in plastic sheeting. Still, in the struggle, he escapes long enough to slap his bloody hand against a wall of obscure glass for Harry to see. And see he must. At that moment, the barrier between the professional and the personal becomes lurid and translucent. Indeed, whenever Harry appeals to the distinction between his work and his life, whenever he insists that there be a wall between his work and what his clients do with it, we know he is repressing. "What they do with the tapes is their own business," he says, unconvincingly and unconvinced. We may not be able to sort through Coppola's ambivalence in the face of corporate succession; we know he thinks it's personal.

One way of taking *The Conversation*, then, is to understand it as a loser-wins parable in which Harry overcomes his repressions only to have his most paranoid fears come true: he is not only culpable, but he has been found out. Just over halfway through the movie, he lets his guard down and confesses his romantic troubles to his rival's "demo girl." It turns out that he has been recorded. "The bugger got bugged." (The film makes the link between bugging and buggering clearer when Harry tells a joke about a "fag wiretapper" who "could only bug a princess phone.") This midpoint turning of the tables is played for awkward laughs, but the peripateia plays it deadpan as Harry methodically rips apart his apartment looking for a bug he never finds.

Harry's problem is not simply that he keeps things bottled up but that he is stuck in a rhythm of repression and confession. In the film, he confesses three times: to a priest, to the demo girl, and to Ann, the Director's wife, in a dream. Harry appeals to dream-Ann for understanding, having taken real-Ann's easy empathy with a bum on a park bench for a character trait rather than recognize it as the displaced acknowledgment of her own culpability. But the fog that shrouds the dream foreshadows the clouds of exhaust from the Mercedes that envelop Harry when he finally sees her in person. The car convinces him that she had everything to gain from the recording, that her confession has been staged.

Harry is stuck in this rhythm because he feels inexpiable guilt over a previous job. His rival, William P. Moran, talks everyone through the scenario: A Teamster boss has set up a sham "welfare fund" and has taken every precaution to keep his discussions with his accountant secret—they talk about it only while out on a lake, fishing, and they clam up whenever a boat so much as appears on the horizon. Harry, working for the district attorney, has successfully recorded their conversation. The union boss, convinced the accountant has turned informer, has the accountant, his wife, and child murdered. "Their heads were found in different places." Moran is uninterested in Harry's guilt ("ancient history"); he only wants to understand his technique. "C'mon, Harry, show and tell." In the script, Harry explains that he has prebugged the tackle box, but in the film, he is spared that moment when his assistant Stan starts to play back Harry's most recent technical triumph, the recording of the eponymous conversation. This is his loaded backstory, the thing he cannot confess, and the thing that his latest project might give him the chance to undo.

For both the Teamster accountant and the Director, Harry's recording becomes a crucial piece of evidence, and what makes it central to their fates is its openness to misunderstanding. In the earlier case, the impossibility of the recording dictates the Teamster president's response: If a conversation is unrecordable *and* unique details of that conversation have been made public, then one of the participants must have leaked them. Here, the Teamster president is tracking the pathway of information. In the latter case, though, the content of the recording dictates the Director's response: If a conversation is secret *and* it has been recorded, then the unique details of that conversation must be true. Here, the Director is tracking the veracity of the information. The Teamster president was wrong when he assumed his conversation was unrecordable—a mistake born of arrogance. The Director's mistake is more interesting, since he is wrong when he assumes that the conversation's unrecordability testifies to its privacy and its truth. His is a mistake born of a faith in the ordinary course of things—he simply isn't paranoid enough to believe that his wife, her lover, and his secretary have set him up, that the world is a clandestine performance for his benefit.

Only after Harry comes to understand the plot does he become a target of the conspirators, and only after he realizes that he is a target does he deconstruct his apartment looking for a bug he will never find. Literalist viewers often believe that the bug is hidden in his saxophone strap (the one thing he doesn't break down; it also looks like a lavaliere microphone). More transcendental types believe the bug is the (unlocatable) cinematic apparatus itself. Coppola tends that way when he denies the bug is in the strap and explains his camerawork in similar terms. "I also had an idea in making the movie that the camera would be an eavesdropper; unlike most modern movies if you watch the lower corner or the upper corner of any movie you'll see that it's constantly adjusting, the cameraman is constantly trying to make a good picture and follow the conversation. I wanted the camera just to be dead."[55] But the most logical explanation is that the bug is not findable because it is not in the room.

Early on, Harry and Stan are discussing the upcoming surveillance convention at the St. Francis Hotel. "Among those pre-eminent in the field expected are Hal Lipset and Harry Caul from San Francisco." Stan is impressed that Harry is mentioned in the publicity blurb as being in attendance—he does not yet know about Harry's past or his stature. He continues: "Also attending will be William P. Moran of Detroit, Michigan." Harry snipes, "Since when is William P. Moran of Detroit, Michigan pre-eminent in the field?" That is the film's not-so-hidden story arc: the rise of Moran. Harry thinks Moran's equipment is "junk," and we know much of it is copied from competitors (Moran specializes in industrial espionage). But Moran does have a particularly nifty product, the Moran S-15 Harmonica Tap. As he demonstrates, it allows anyone, anywhere to turn a phone into a room microphone. A version of this seems to be working in Harry's apartment. He is playing saxophone along with a record. His phone rings, no one is there, and he hangs up. He receives a second call, and the voice on the line (the Director's secretary) explains that they are listening to him and plays back Harry's sax playing. That Harry cannot find the bug when he takes apart the phone only means that he wasn't paying attention at the convention. He has been slipping. In contrast, Moran has been on a roll. First he steals Harry's assistant, then he bugs Harry at the party, then his demo girl steals the tape of the conversation, and then he bugs Harry again. He is "pre-eminent in the field" since now.[56]

How is this change possible? The simplest way to put it would be to say Harry *bugs* people but Moran bugs *people*. Harry doesn't know, and all but refuses to learn, that "the field" comprises all of its observers as participants. He believes in a professional/operational distinction that does not exist. At one level, there is the world of "surveillance and security technicians" in which he is preeminent. At another level, there is the arena in which he carries out his recordings. Yet those two locations are the same: just outside Union Square. The wiretappers convene at the St. Francis Hotel, the same hotel in which Harry placed one of his microphone recordists in the opening scene. From the hotel one can see (and with the right technology, hear) the goings-on in the square. As the script put it: "The man working under the neon Eiffel Tower scans the field through his telescopic sight, searching for his subjects."[57] Even the opposition between hotel and square (edge and field) breaks down when we see the scale model of Union Square in the hotel. The model room will be the site of Harry's assertive auteurism—"I'm telling you I'm not giving those tapes to anybody but The Director."[58] Just as he believes in the distinction between professional and operational life, so Harry retains his belief in the solitary power of the Director.

The film knows better and Harry should too. When he is actually at work in his studio, he seems to recognize the contingent arrangement of the elements of the field. The opening sequence announced its artifice in the electronic burbles that erupted on the sound track. In his meticulous editing, Harry will work to remove those bleeps and phase shifts just as diligently as Murch worked to generate them. Echoing his screenplay, Murch called that editing work "shifting the various fields" and contrasted the process of remixing with photographic enlargement: "And as you go deeper and deeper into the film *Blowup*, you find that hidden piece of evidence through a series of enlargements of the photograph. Well, in sound, we are doing this same kind of enlargement, if you will, although it's rather a shifting of the various fields of sound to reveal a field formerly hidden or obscured by the foreground music."[59] What Harry knows about sound fields he fails to understand about professional fields. When he sees the outline of Union Square on his chalkboard, he thinks it is a diagram, a representation. It is, rather, an extension of the field into the studio, the vehicle and the emblem of the union between individual and institution. The repeated occurrences of Union Square in *The Conversation* amount to logorrhea without a logo.

The Conversation, like the *Godfather* movies and, as we will see, *Chinatown*, insists on its fascination with the line between what's personal and what's business in order to maintain the fiction that the contest for preeminence is fundamentally one between individuals and institutions, and in order to relish those moments when the line is blurred beyond recognition. Harry's story has a happy ending from this point of view: he knows his (individual) performance has an audience; he has guaranteed himself that someone in the world cares about him again; he can stop confessing. Coppola's ambivalence over creative control drove him toward paranoid solutions, toward Harry's solution, toward fantasies of a dead Director and a dead camera. But the film, as Murch put it together, continually insists on the unceasing contestation for control of the field as a whole. Furthermore, in *The Conversation*, the contest itself establishes the parameters or, better, the design, of the field. This looks like a matter of professional autonomy, and it is, but because the players determine the design, the professional demarcation of the field can be replaced—often suddenly—by something else that successfully claims the authority to determine preeminence. These changes are what I have been calling the precession of causality, and *The Conversation* is its crucial thought experiment. Appearing at the high-water mark of the auteur in the New Hollywood, *The Conversation* turns the opposition between the individual and the corporation, between what's personal and what's business, into history. That history will be the product of its players and their actions across different scales at particular moments' time, which is to say that this history will be designed, linear, and one-directional, which is, finally, to say that it will unspool like Harry's master tape.

The Paramount Thirties III: *Chinatown*

One side effect of Evans's reliance on Korshak was the bizarre deal he struck when his contract was up for renewal. Evans wanted a percentage of the gross of every film the studio made—something like what Jeffrey Katzenberg would later claim at Disney. Bluhdorn said no, and Korshak, who was negotiating on Evans's behalf, instead suggested that Evans have the right to independently produce one film a year that the studio would distribute. Instead of a percentage of everything, he would get all of one thing. The difficulties were baked into the arrangement. As Evans described it: "*Chinatown* was my first film as a bonus, because no person ever ran a studio and could make their own films. . . . And it worked against me not for me. If the picture were not a success, it wouldn't have mattered, but the picture being the hit that it was, all the other filmmakers around Paramount said, 'It's not right, he's working on *Chinatown*, why isn't he spending time with us on our film?' So it reverberated negatively towards me."[60] The organizational mess of his production deal lasted only a short while—Evans was, indeed, flaming out, and he would move aside for Sylbert. Yet while it lasted, Evans's deal resulted in another decisive film in the progress of Paramount's achievement of high concept.

The Godfather is a film that appears to be about the antinomies of business, family, and crime but is instead driven by the anguish of executive function. *The Conversation* appears to be about the ineradicably personal aspects of "the field" but is more intent on redefining the field as a zone where the potential for secret knowledge is inexhaustible. *Chinatown* appears to be a film in which the eradication of the line between the governmental and the personal (the public and the private) has horrific consequences, consequences that make the discovery of that erasure more traumatic than it is worth. In its final repressive imperative—"Forget it, Jake. It's Chinatown"—*Chinatown* joins Paramount's host of loser-wins dramas of 1974. It is another perfect complement to *The Godfather Part II*. *The Godfather* insisted on the frisson of "family business" in its climactic montage; *Part II* staged its climactic execution within earshot, as anticlimax, as the already repressed (as the backstory of *The Conversation*). *The Godfather* kept its politicians and judges off-screen, hidden in Don Vito's pockets; *Part II* put them on display. As another successor project to *The Godfather*, *Chinatown* also took up the dialectic of the personal and the institutional. For Robert Evans, as for Michael Corleone, it was all personal and it was all institutional at the same time.

In *Chinatown*, the discussion of what is business and what is personal occurs at the end of Act I, when Jake Gittes explains to Evelyn Mulwray that he intends to go on with his investigation. "The point is, is I'm not in business to be loved, but I am in business, and believe me, Mrs. Mulwray, whoever set your husband up set me up." What follows is a massive disavowal of the sort Sonny expressed in his half-wise state: "It's nothing personal, Mrs. Mulwray—" She gives Michael's answer: "It's very personal, it couldn't be more personal." Of course her answer is burdened with the film's incest subplot, but here again the discussion is less about what is personal and what is business (even though that's what they appear to be disagreeing about) than the *degrees* of personality and business-ness: "*nothing* personal" "couldn't be *more* personal."

If we take Evelyn as speaking an unspoken truth, the most personal thing would be incest since it marks the degeneration of the social institutions of reproduction into the core family unit. It is both maximally personal and maximally private. What would be the opposite? One opposite would be Jake's assumption that what appears to be personal is really business. In his world reputation is decisive, and the worst that could happen would be to be made "a local joke." A second opposite would be something maximally private but maximally institutional as well. The film figures this possibility in the sealed-off landscapes of the Oak Pass Reservoir ("Sorry, this is closed to the public, sir." "It's all right. Russ Yelburton, Deputy Chief in the Department," Gittes responds) and the orange groves with their "No Trespassing" signs, which turn out to be filled with "dumb okies." (The oak pun here is something of a "locale joke.") Finally, the most rigorously opposite force in the film would be the public institution, here figured as the hearing in which Hollis Mulwray will publicly declare, "I won't build it. It's that simple. I am not making that kind of mistake twice." His announcement is followed by something like a "regional joke," when a farmer lets his sheep loose in the council room.

The film cycles neatly through these possibilities, balancing public against private, personal against institutional. This is its classical narrative harmony. At the intersection of these two axes lies a publicly enforceable private agreement in which an individual (Evelyn) seeks institutional answers (who killed Hollis?); that is, at the center of these axes lies the contract, a contract signed fifty-nine minutes into the film, at roughly Thompson's Act II midpoint. (The exact midpoint comes during Gittes's lunch with Noah Cross, when the patriarch will propose a more lucrative contract. We never see the papers drawn up, but Gittes will refer to the "figures" in that contract late in Act III.) His contract with Evelyn will be sealed by love twenty-four minutes later. Gittes will immediately suspect her of killing Hollis, and twenty-four minutes after that he will beat the real explanation out of her. The last twenty minutes begin with a renegotiation of the terms of his contract with Curly, pass from there to the faux conclusion of his faux contract with Noah, and on to the concluding sequence in Chinatown.

Chinatown, then, works very much like *Jaws*, and for very similar reasons. What both of them want to master is the evanescent balance between the obtrusive and the implicit, to assert a control beyond mere control by controlling both pace and allegiance. *The Conversation* is still in thrall to the telepathic, acephalic, ultraparanoid San Franciscan social utopia, while *The Godfather Part II* slumps into its sociopathic legacy clearing out both wife and brother in Michael's failed attempt to remove the evidence of his own rapacity. *Chinatown*, in contrast, as "neo-noir," appears to fit neatly into Jameson's postmodernity. In his BFI monograph on the film, Michael Eaton has taken up Jameson's argument and disagrees with his conclusions for very particular reasons. Those reasons are worth noting, because in them we see an emergent configuration of larger concepts, the postmodern and the classical:

> Though this film can evidently be seen as very definitely a product of its time, its predominant concerns cannot be simply reduced to those of a phoney reflection of the past. Only think of how it avoids all the pitfalls of a retrospective soundtrack. If there is an argument to be had with *Chinatown* it will not be because of its knowing evocation of the past, but rather with its romantic anxiety about the present. The ultimate problem of this film for me lies not in the complicit wink of the post-modern but the unblinking stare of the classical.[61]

Eaton, I think, underestimates the automaticity of Jamesonian nostalgia when he calls it "phoney" and "knowing." He has taken the agency from Carroll's account of seventies allusionism and extended it until it can be subjected to a kind of moralizing against the retro. (One alternative would be to channel that agency into the sorts of avowed politics or industrial expressivity that I have been tracing.) More productive, though, is his conflation of a certain "romantic anxiety" with "the unblinking stare of the classical." How would that pair function together?

Let us take this problem and compound it in the hope that our conceptual difficulty will find at least the vector of its practical bearings. When we wonder who might be the unblinking yet anxious subject behind this film, Eaton gives us an answer that seems to have taken the film's repressive imperative to heart. "Only the obsessive drive of an individual . . . can get a picture off the launch pad. In the case of *Chinatown* it seems evident that the individual who quite simply made this film happen, even if he cannot be credited with weaving its complex web of meanings, was the producer."[62] Evans, then, is responsible for the film but not its meaning. Yet he is the obsessively driven individual who would seem to be able to synthesize both romantic anxiety and the unblinking stare. He is, in this regard, like Gittes: "Is this a business or an obsession with you?" Evelyn asks.

Tiny emblems of the film's "unblinking stare" are spread throughout *Chinatown*, from the discovery of Hollis Mulwray's glasses, to Jake's trick with the watch, to the gunshot wound through Evelyn's head. As this list makes clear, the unblinking stare is the stare of death. Interruptions in the stare are necessary if we are to register life or history (hence Jake's *coitus interruptus* joke). The blink is the space of possibility, of cinema, and the way the film registers the slow progress of history in Jake's wound. Against the emblems of the deathly stare, *Chinatown* offers the tiniest flickers of life. The film opens with a scene of "romantic

Figure 3.7. The flicker of possibility in the recognition of changes in ownership. *Chinatown* (Polanski, Paramount, 1974)

anxiety" as Curly flips through photos of his wife. Jake discovers the film's central real estate scheme at the county clerk's office by noticing the narrow strips that register changes in ownership and flicking one back and forth. Even the way Jake flips his cigarette epitomizes the film's coolly arid style. *Chinatown* bares its device ever so slightly, across the registers of narrative and character, plot and prop. These are the consistencies of design and the center of the film's energy. The blink is more essential than the winking retrospection of the film's sepia opening but less fatal than the unblinking stare. And with every blink, every hesitation, every "reverberation," as Evans put it, the film retains its tenuous ability to separate the public and the private.

The Paramount Thirties IV: On the Lot

In the wake of the classical studio system, two forces have vied for dominance. We ordinarily refer to them as the studios and the independents, but one might more generally think of them as system and instance. Dialectics quickly emerge in which studios cultivate individuals that, as systems, they can exploit, or in which individuals seek institutional forms that might insulate their independence from the demands of the studios. Corporation and auteur oscillate uncomfortably.

Yet there are decisive vectors to this fluctuation. The deep studio depression in the early seventies set the stage for auteurist successes and "The New Hollywood"; the overreaching auteurs of the late seventies all but guaranteed the return of consolidated studio power. How was this pivot accomplished? What mechanisms swung the dialectic in the studios' favor? Peter Biskind contends that a combination of auteurist burnout and the rise of retro-auteurists such as Spielberg and Lucas were decisive. Yet each studio had to ground its reassertion of control in an ideology that would simultaneously appeal to industry-wide conditions and justify the studio's unique ability to capitalize on those conditions. Moreover, that rhetoric needed spokespeople. Beyond the logic of the argument, there would be the force and energy of the execs who made it.

Each director's success was not only an advertisement for his own authorship; it hinted at a model that might reoccupy the space once held by the classical studio. But what would constitute that generalization? *THX* was utterly ungeneralizable, even if its story centered on the workings of studio control. *The Godfather* required attention as a result of its success, but the generalization it suggested was fraught. A studio modeled on *The Godfather* required a similar hollowing out of the difference between personal conviction and organizational rationale. Turned into narrative, though, and the collapse of the personal becomes a particular vision of tragedy—one we glimpse at the end of *Part I*, one at the center of *The Conversation* and *Chinatown*. Ultimately, the solution to the problem of systematization depended on how one accounted for a film's success in the first place. If success were the logical outcome of the production system, then the essential condition for the success of the New Hollywood would be the autonomy accorded directors. Understood that way, the generalization of the model should take the form of a broadening of the auteurist mode of production. But if the mode of production were less important than the particular narratives that might emerge from it, the generalization of auteurist success would require nearly the opposite approach, the assertion of narrative control. The collapse of the Directors Company, like the collapse of the Zoetrope–Warner Bros. deal, encouraged Paramount to seek fresh routes to that control. In *Jaws*, narrative control might have resided in the script, but it was figured as control over pacing, point of view, and audience reaction. At Paramount, the studio tradition had always meant a particular look, and in the swing from the authored seventies to the conceived eighties, the control of the look would be decisive.

I have been using the term "control" because it suggests the social and organizational aspect of the process, but for Paramount, the crucial term would be "design." The "Paramount look" in the thirties had rested on deep continuities in the art department headed by Hans Dreier and massive investments in art deco sets and costumes. Rick Altman's notion of the "jurisdictional struggle" proves useful here.[63] The Lubitsch/Dreier era was a negotiated settlement to such a conflict (here, between market demands and style), now ramified through the corporate hierarchy. The mid-seventies replayed that standoff in its own terms: in the wake of the Directors Company no one believed in the radical auteurist experiment, but there was no obvious way to systematize studio and auteur. Directors still had a great deal of power; studios still had no way of disciplining that independence. The peculiarly balled-up dialectic that would allow Paramount to become its own auteur and the home of high concept had not yet found traction among the necessary players, had not yet crested the horizon of plausibility. The standstill encouraged an interim solution. The year 1975 uncannily echoed 1935, but where classical Paramount put its faith in a director, emerging neoclassical Paramount put its faith in a designer: Richard Sylbert. Like Lubitsch, he lasted about a year.

But in that year, he green-lit half a dozen films that would carry the studio from its neo-Thalberg era to the Killer Dillers. Two of those were high-toned adaptations of Hollywood novels. Neither *The Day of the Locust* (John Schlesinger, 1975) nor *The Last Tycoon* (Elia Kazan, 1976) was financially successful, but both fit neatly within the studio's continuing project of using the thirties to rethink the seventies. Nostalgia gave the studio purchase on its present troubles, and in these cases it did so by exploring two possible modes of studio control. *Locust* asks what it means for the studio to be under the control of the art department (the designers), while *Tycoon* explores a very particular vision of a supervising producer. However animated each film was by its tight fit with Paramount's changes in governance, each marked a step along the way from a studio in the hands of the auteurs to the studio as its own auteur.

Film criticism has seen *Locust* as out-Adornoing Adorno. As Richard Keller Simon puts it, "In his cynical and mocking parody of popular movies, and especially in his trashing of Capra, West crafted a story that demonstrates much of what Benjamin and Adorno asserted in theoretical prose."[64] Robert van Dassanowsky is surely right when he says that *Day of the Locust* does not yet belong to the "neoclassic Hollywood phase," he dates from *Star Wars* two years later. *Chinatown* "managed to make a success of the 1930s but it avoids both Hollywood and the Depression." In contrast *Locust* seemed to be fighting against "the air-tight cinematic fantasies that deny intellectual response" at every turn by "insisting on its artificiality," eventually burning away the film stock itself in a bit of modernist distanciation.[65]

Locust collapses semiotic artificiality into urban artificiality. Its endless shots of sprinklers insist on "Hollywood's facade-like nature as a city built on a desert."[66] *Chinatown*, by focusing on the actual "desert beneath our feet," leaves the semiotic contrivance relatively intact. Polanski's film provides a deniable allegory of the cinematic facade before our faces. Everywhere one turns in *Locust*, though, one finds thuddingly obvious politics and thuddingly obvious ironies—from the montage of adding machine and prayer service to the culminating riot in which a newspaper headlined "Roosevelt Pledges Nation to Continue Fight for Tolerance" burns.

All of this would seem to make the film a misstep in the progress of neoclassicism. And to the extent that neoclassical Hollywood required, depended on, abetted, and perhaps culturally codified the reemergence of conservative politics after the interruptions of Watergate, the oil shock, and the fall of Saigon, the film's relative failure at the box office confirms its own misfit cultural status. Yet if the film ruthlessly indicts the classical Hollywood virtue of spectacular transcendence, it also sets up Paramount in particular as the embodiment of that transcendent power. If *Locust* advanced the neoclassical agenda, it did so under the radar of criticism. *Everyone* knew it was an indictment of Hollywood; no one recognized it as an homage to Paramount as Hollywood's privileged metonym.

Whenever the novel slams "Hollywood," the film finds a way to direct that energy at the studio. Textual Tod works at "National Films"; cinematic Tod, at

Paramount. The textual transvestite nightclub singer croons the sentimental
"Little Man You've Had a Busy Day" (a song that regularly appeared in Warner Bros.' Porky Pig cartoons); the cinematic transvestite rips through Marlene
Dietrich's "Hot Voodoo" (from Josef von Sternberg/Paramount's *Blonde Venus*,
1932). Adore Loomis, the sexually disconcerting child, propositions Tod with
Mae West's come-up-and-see-me line from *She Done Him Wrong* (Lowell Sher-
man, Paramount, 1933). Early on, we see the famous arched Bronson gate. Late
in the film the climactic riot occurs outside the premiere of Cecil B. DeMille's
The Buccaneer, a Paramount film from 1938. As the Paramount newsreel cameras
roll, the on-screen announcer hypes the madness: "If you don't believe me, go to
your favorite theater next week"—his mic cuts out, but his next words are "Paramount News." Around the corner, where Donald Sutherland's Homer Simpson
is stomping Adore to death, a billboard above him advertises three films: *College
Swing*, *Texas Trail*, and *Spawn of the North*—all Paramount. When another studio should appear, it goes unmentioned. Faye Greener, Tod's muse, asks him
where he's going. When he says Paramount, she says they can't even share a cab,
without saying where she's headed. When she and Tod leave a screening of a film
she appears in, Fox's *Ali Baba Goes to Town*, we don't see the closing Fox logo but
instead jump right into Paramount News coverage of the Anschluss. Even the
San Bernardino Arms, Tod's apartment, has been given a Paramount makeover.
In West's novel, it is a three-story apartment block; in the film, it is a garden
apartment with a Paramontian entrance and arched doorways everywhere.

Figure 3.8. The
Paramount arc
supplants the
Fox searchlight.
Day of the Locust
(John Schlesinger,
Paramount, 1975)

Figure 3.9. The arc as architecture. *Day of the Locust* (Schlesinger, Paramount, 1975)

Perhaps none of these studio references is surprising. But this last, more speculative instance draws our attention away from the verifiable intonations of Paramount-Paramount-Paramount and toward the more suffusive concerns of production design or art direction. It may be too much to see 1930s "Paramount white" in the white telephone at the "sporting house" where Tod goes to watch pornographic films, but the import of design in *Locust* does not lie in reference but in articulation. Simply put, in *Locust*, the studio *is* design. There are no writers or stars, no orchestras or editors, no flacks or producers. (There is a director—played by William Castle—and an assistant, but they are at the mercy of the set Tod has designed. In the novel, as in the film, the set collapses, but in the novel Tod is not the designer.) Production and hiring at the studio seem to be overseen by Claude Estee, a supervising art director in the mold of Dreier or, more aptly, Sylbert.

West's novel leaves Tod's design career by the wayside as it skips about through his abortive affair with Faye. The film, though, gives him both a career arc and a professional context. At first, he lounges about with a number of other underutilized young would-be art directors, boosting the overhead. "But if there isn't anything for us to do, then why do we come?" one asks. "You're getting paid. . . . Relax, it's better than relief." Tod quickly plays up his Yale background to Estee—"Boola-boola and all that"—and gets assigned to *Waterloo*. He pulls from Goya and Daumier, and Estee approves of his initial sketches: "I like your work. You're probably a little too facile for your own good. Can be an advantage out here." Tod's work reaches another level when he creates a battle-field for the charge up Mt. Jena. It resembles nothing so much as the opening direction of *Godot*: "A country road. A tree. Evening." After it collapses, Tod will be part of the postmortem cover-up orchestrated by Estee, and his Hollywood education will near completion.

In the novel, Estee is an experienced screenwriter who trades barbs with Tod, taking stories to their ultimate conclusions and determining whether they will "play." In the film, he wields tremendous power at the studio, combining his profession with his corporate responsibilities. An aging aesthete forever in search of new stimulations, Estee relishes pornography and cockfighting. Yet his eye for the main chance has given him access to the great works of mod-ernism that Tod hopes to produce himself. Estee lives in Frank Lloyd Wright's Ennis House, one of the "textile block" homes Wright built around LA. "I fell in love with the house, and Alice came with it." Alice may not understand art—she's insisted that there be a statue of a dead horse in the pool—but Estee does, and dwelling within it is worth whatever compromises that might entail.

The scene at the Ennis House constitutes an addition to West's novel, and the context establishes crucial distinctions between the two designers. Estee can no longer make fine art—his oils are unopened and his canvas is blank. This seems to be a consequence of his lack of moral compunction. Asked whether it would have made any difference if someone had died in the collapsing set, Estee says no. If Tod is marked as somehow (for now) more morally inclined

Figure 3.10. The designer at home in Frank Lloyd Wright's Ennis House. *Day of the Locust* (Schlesinger, Paramount, 1975)

that Claude, every part of the production design comes together to make it clear that Tod nevertheless belongs here, in Estee's world. His glorious brown suit blends perfectly with the rich, brown living room, and when he is left by himself, his pinstripes pick up the angles of one of Wright's leaded windows. He will still be wearing that suit when his leg is crushed in the riot.

The film presents us with an articulated hierarchy of design. Estee sits at the pinnacle of the design mountain in the studio. Tod is scaling its heights, drawing from both the people and places he knows and more historical sources as he develops the look of *Waterloo* for the studio and assembles the faces for *The Burning of Los Angeles* in his apartment. (He shares this aspiration with Faye, who produces a montage of star images on her own bedroom door.) Beneath Tod, in what we might call the role of "domestic designer," we find Homer Simpson. As part of his "business arrangement" with Faye, he goes to great pains to faithfully replicate an image of strawberries and Corn Flakes from a magazine in real food to serve her for breakfast. The film emphasizes the connection between Estee and Tod and Homer: As Estee leads Tod away toward the *Waterloo* set, the camera will push in on Tod's scale model of Mt. Jena; from there we dissolve to Homer's hands at work on breakfast. Homer rules the breakfast plate; Tod, the model; Claude, the studio.

In the end, *Day of the Locust* conjured memories of Paramount's lost greatness but hitched them to a continuing tradition of design, a tradition of *privileging* design as integration. *The Last Tycoon* may have been the studio's send-off for Evans, but *Locust* was its tribute to its new head of production. The studio that began the decade with a former actor as the head of production and with a notorious deal with a group of directors pivoted through one of the most remarkable episodes in Hollywood history when a production designer took on that role. If Sylbert was followed by the Killer Dillers, it was not entirely because the financial imperatives of the conglomerate had trumped the studio's historic reliance on style. Indeed, the preeminence of production design would mark off the high-concept era, but it would do so in a way fundamentally continuous with the studio's historic elevation of design as such.

The adaptation never got the green light, but a decade later, Evans had become the producer he might have played. And a decade after that, having exhausted his welcome at Paramount, the studio did manage to mount *The Last Tycoon*. The film is equal parts stunt-nostalgia, with Robert Mitchum, Ray Milland, Tony Curtis, and Jeanne Moreau in supporting roles; and test-track for future stars, with Theresa Russell, Anjelica Huston, and Ingrid Boulting joining Robert De Niro as Monroe Stahr. Harold Pinter wrote the screenplay and Elia Kazan directed; it was Kazan's last film.

In its landmark scene, the legendary producer becomes an actor. Stahr is explaining movies to George Boxley, a novelist who feels he is slumming by writing pictures. Stahr's point is that movies are not really about their ludicrous scenarios or their dialogue. To prove this, the producer spins a yarn about a young woman who sneaks into the office on a mission: "She takes off her gloves, she opens her purse, she dumps it out on a table. You watch her. This is you. . . . Now, she has two dimes, a matchbox and a nickel. She leaves the nickel on the table; she puts the two dimes back into her purse; she takes the gloves—black—puts them into the stove." Eventually, Stahr breaks off. "Go on," said Boxley smiling. "What happens?" "I don't know. I was just making pictures." Boxley is hooked.

Fitzgerald's version of this scene reads too earnestly, as though the failed screenwriter were trying to prove to his former bosses that he understood how to create tension through action and not dialogue. He is playing both Stahr (who understands movies) and Boxley (Fitzgerald's tyro self and, eventually, his drunken self). On-screen, this veiled narcissism vanishes, in part because Stahr is acting it out while he narrates it and in part because the lesson is slightly altered. The novel's Boxley asks what the nickel is for, and Stahr says, "'I don't know.' . . . Suddenly he laughed. 'Oh yes—the nickel was for the movies.'" It is an allegorical frisson in which the surplus element almost literally pays tribute to the desire to go to the movies. The film gets the same zing but makes it clear that this is a *professional* lesson. When Boxley asks about the nickel, Stahr turns to one of the "hacks" Boxley has been disparaging and prompts, "Jane, what was the nickel for?" "The nickel was for the movies." Caught out, Boxley can only say, "What do you pay me for? I don't understand the damn stuff." The novel emphasizes Boxley's education—"But you will"—while the movie points out that Boxley already understands, he simply needs to understand what he understands. "Yes, you do, or you wouldn't have asked about the nickel." Stahr caps his point about the nickel by pretending to toss it to Boxley, who reflexively moves to catch it. Cause : effect :: shot : reverse shot. The job of the novelist, at least in the film, is not to jam his dialogue into pictures but to turn his reflexive reliance on cause and effect and his intuitive understanding of story construction into a professional expertise. De Niro's Stahr knows movies, Boxley is going to school, and the lesson is not simply about narrative causality but about collective intelligence.

The scene is so good the film repeats it at its conclusion, but in a new key. Now, Stahr breaks the fourth wall and addresses the audience directly. (We are the reverse shot that will never come.) Intercut with his speech are shots of Kathleen, his lost love, burning a letter he has sent her. (She has read it; we haven't.) In the first version, Stahr's narration made us pay attention to things that were not there—the color of the imaginary gloves—while in this one the slight mismatches between the narrated story (burning gloves) and displayed story (burning letter) draw our attention to the possibilities of narrative. If the first version of Stahr's performance was classical Hollywood deniably bearing the device, this second version is more modernist, *Tycoon*'s version of *Locust*'s burning film stock. Kathleen kisses her new husband, breaks it off, and stares into the camera. Her look falls halfway between a direct address to us and an eyeline match with Stahr. He returns the gaze and declares, to her and to us equally, "I don't want to lose you." A few shots later, Stahr's distant, echoey voice slowly repeats this line as he walks down an empty studio street. He is now addressing the studio itself while standing in for Kazan. And Evans. And ideally for us. "This is you," he has explained to us, twice.

The ending was more or less improvised. Fitzgerald's notes and drafts suggested all sorts of possibilities, but this apostrophe was not one of them. It is too precious by half. Yet *The Last Tycoon*, for all its aloofness and imbalance manages something extraordinary: it rediscovers the studio as the actor-producer's natural or, better, rightful beloved. The second version of the glove-burning scene turned classical Hollywood technique into an occasion for more explicit, modernist display. It made the thirties into the seventies. But the ending of the film turns modernist display back into classical restraint. The film's allegorical impulse may have been a widely shared nostalgia for an era of studio greatness (under Thalberg or Evans), but its final lesson for us is that the cinema will no longer address us as directly as it might. The nickel is for the movies; the love is for the studio.

Pressing Hard for the White Suit

Richard Sylbert's decision to hire Don Simpson as head of production (the role Peter Bart had under Robert Evans) was a way of complementing his own visual strength by bringing in someone with a deep commitment to narrative clarity. Yet with TV-veteran Diller as CEO and story-memo-crazy Simpson in charge of production, Sylbert appeared to be sandwiched between them, a placeholder until Michael Eisner took his job. *The Day of the Locust* and *The Last Tycoon* hardly seemed like a way forward; the Killer Dillers (the group that would include Katzenberg, Dawn Steel, Ricardo Mestres, and others) were just around the corner. How should we think about such corporate successions when even the apparently central participant (Sylbert) was aware that his time at the top was limited?

For Bernard Dick, it seemed a foregone conclusion that a cadre of executives with television experience would remake Paramount in that image.

> What Diller and Eisner achieved was not so much "high concept" as "high transfer." Their world was television, viewed as a concentric universe within which lay smaller circles such as news, sitcoms, talk shows, and film. "Film" then was a microcosm within a universe called television. Diller and Eisner reconfigured that universe so that the small world—and therefore the small screen—became the big world and the big screen. It was simply a matter of converting a microcosm into a macrocosm.
>
> "Barry and I began to run Paramount like a real business," Eisner boasted. But the business was television.[67]

The Leibnizian tone of Diller and Eisner's reconfiguration of the universe aside, the movies were accommodating themselves to the small screen in new ways. Most basically, the arrival of video-assist technology allowed directors and directors of photography to watch the scene play out on a screen and not through the eyepiece. Stephen Prince, Geoff King, and others have noted that this video-first approach could distort lighting and shot-scaling choices. Second, and at least as important, the emergence of the home video-rental industry encouraged directors to "shoot for the box"—to frame the action for the 4:3 ratio of the television rather than the widescreen of theatrical exhibition.[68] The more apposite consequences of the shifts in scale in the late seventies, then, were not narrative but pictorial—little seems to have changed in the screenwriting process.

What would it mean, in any case, to convert a microcosm into a macrocosm? And how could such sublime transfer be simple? Paramount did not ratchet up production to televisual levels; they did not scale back budgets of films to match TV movies; and the company's finances had not swung drastically toward TV. Or, rather, not more drastically than they had in the 1960s when Bluhdorn bought the studio principally to monetize the library by licensing it to TV. For Dick, I think, the conversion is ideological; simply changing the center of aesthetic gravity from film to television would count as changing the universe. Put another way, however influenced the studio had been by TV forms and funds, Yablans and Evans's belief that they were movie people kept television at bay.

Dick's sense that television had fatally compromised the glorious Paramount of the early 1970s despite any evidence that television had changed the studio's mode of production ironically echoes Norma Desmond's remark in Paramount's *Sunset Blvd.* that she is still big: "It's the pictures that got small."

This notion of small pictures is the sort of concrete aesthetic belief that is most fully worked out on-screen. There, micro and macro might appear as social scales (town and city, for example), or they might appear as children and adults. Can we make such a scalar reading work? If the 1970s were defined by *grit*, as detailed by Carlo Rotella, and nostalgia, particularly for the 1930s, as Jameson contends, Paramount found itself pulled between the two.[69] Even when Sylbert reached out for children's fare, the same conceptual pair reappeared: The foul-mouthed, off-brand *Bad News Bears* are the avatars of grit, and the preternaturally odd kiddie gangsters of *Bugsy Malone* are the children of the 1930s. The latter film is a gangster musical where everyone is pubescent, and the guns drench the victims in creamy white "splurge." In *Bears* Tatum O'Neal plays a contemporary Addie Pray (her character in the thirties comedy *Paper Moon*); in *Bugsy*, Jodie Foster plays a throwback Iris (her character in the ultra-gritty *Taxi Driver* from Columbia). After *Bugsy* flopped, the two films were often run as a double feature. If the children of *Bears* are effectively ungoverned and ungovernable, the children of *Bugsy Malone* are strangely possessed: When they talk, their voices are their own; but when they sing, they sing with the voices of adults. The pint-sized Dooley Wilson character, for instance, has composer Paul Williams's voice—truly bizarre.

Bugsy Malone matters not because it stages the micro-macro inversion at the heart of the Diller regime but because Australian-born Robert Stigwood was one of its producers. A legendary music producer (the Beatles, Clapton, the BeeGees) he had moved from popular music to legitimate theater to film, acquiring the rights to several successful stage musicals and converting *Jesus Christ Superstar* and The Who's *Tommy* into movies. His first movie with Paramount was a dubbed version of a Mexican film about the crash of the Uruguayan rugby team in the Andes. He and American Allan Carr had partnered to bring the low-budget, true-life cannibalism story to the United States. They next planned to go into production on a much more significant property they owned together, the hit musical *Grease*. On the strength of *Welcome Back, Kotter*, in late 1976 Stigwood signed John Travolta to a three-picture deal worth $1 million. The centerpiece of the deal was to be *Grease*, but the producers' option prohibited them from releasing a film before Easter 1978 so it would not compete with the Broadway production. Stigwood needed a project to tide over Travolta and, ideally, prepare the way for the musical.

They found it in Nik Cohn's article "Tribal Rights of the New Saturday Night."[70] Ostensibly nonfiction, Cohn's article had displaced very particular class fantasies of his upbringing in the United Kingdom onto some Brooklynites he never really got to know. Fiction or not, the social dynamic seemed utterly recognizable and authentic to Allen and Stigwood. More important, the project would allow Stigwood to include several songs by the BeeGees, who were then at a crossroads. A hugely successful group, their sales had begun to tail off; Barry shifted to falsetto, and the band bolstered its rhythm section after working with Ahmet Ertegun at Atlantic Records. *Saturday Night Fever* would take RSO's musical expertise and use that to leverage both the BeeGees and John Travolta. If Paramount was temporarily weakened by the executive changes at the studio, RSO took the opportunity to move from music to film.

Weakened or not, Paramount retained its commitment to design. On the one hand, visual design would migrate down the hierarchy and would, in essence, overtake narrative. At the same time, the studio would be playing catchup with its new structure. If the film business was to be run as part of a much more integrated entertainment conglomeration, then it made sense to partner with individuals and organizations that might model this emergent synergy. As the new Paramount sought to leverage television into cinema (as with Travolta and *Star Trek*), RSO would be the tutor. From costume to corporation, Paramount would be dedicated to design. As with *Jaws*, that dedication yoked the micro to the macro allegorically, and the beneficiary of that allegory was the studio itself.

Certainly *Fever* was not a director's film. John Avildsen, who directed *Rocky*, was hired and quickly fired when he ordered extensive rewrites of Norman Wexler's script and derided the songs the BeeGees cut for the film as "passé."[71] John Badham replaced him much as he would replace Martin Brest on *WarGames*. Charles Bailey was the production designer and one of the central figures behind the gritty New York movies of the New Hollywood. He had worked as an assistant on *The Exorcist* and had designed *Serpico*, *Dog Day Afternoon*, and *The Front*. (Tony has a *Serpico* poster on his wall; he quotes *Dog Day Afternoon* to his grandma.) In 1977, Bailey's curbside perspective on urban social decay still counted as realist. But the broken concrete and landtime-forgot storefronts are so conventional—and cinematographer Ralf Bode shoots with such limited depth of field—that the actors hold more of our attention. If, as Carlo Rotella has rather brilliantly argued, *The French Connection* insists on its urban specificity, merging character and locale, by 1977 the New-York-fiscal-crisis-as-usual production design makes a place for performance and costume.[72]

But of the below-the-line talent on *Fever*, the most important was clearly costume designer Patrizia von Brandenstein. Trained as a set designer, von Brandenstein was in something like an apprentice period, yet unlike most aspiring production designers, she did not work as an assistant art director but in costume. After *Fever*, she would quickly become a major production designer in her own right, winning an Oscar for *Amadeus* and creating the signature looks for films as different as *Beat Street* and *The Untouchables*.

How did she understand her role in the design continuum of the film? Taking her cue from the faux-ethnographic Cohn article that served as the basis for the film, she adopted just such an approach. "Grooming was intensely important for the guys. I virtually do not recall seeing face hair at all, but I saw lots of hair, lots of hair." What they lacked monetarily, they compensated for through ritual and narcissistic labor. "The fashion ideas in the film were based on kids who didn't have a lot of money but who lived to dance on Saturday night." But where Cohn's ethnography was ersatz, displaced from a British situation he knew better, von Brandenstein took up the ethnographic imperative in the form of a productive constraint. She would buy rather than make the clothes. To be sure, the clothes were "geared toward movement and light," but the characters were "not fashionable people. We wanted them to not look custom and we wanted them to look not expensive."[73]

The white suit first appears three-quarters of the way into the film, when Tony and the gang visit Gus in his hospital room. It is the twelfth or thirteenth outfit Tony has worn—not including those times when he appears in his tank undershirts or his briefs or when he tries on his brother's priestly collar—and it will be the last. He wears the suit through the long night of the dance competition, his attempted rape of Stephanie, his friend Bobby C.'s suicide and its aftermath, his subway ride to the Village, and his reconciliation with Stephanie there. It first appears almost casually—a sleeve, a medium close-up, and then bathed in the red light outside 2001. We don't see it in its full glory until Tony and the boys approach Stephanie at the club entrance. Joey tells her, "Hey, jeez, look at this, you're beautiful," but while he is saying it, we aren't looking at Stephanie but at Tony, and his suit, as they emerge in a pool of clean, white light.

During the dance sequence, the suit does nothing particularly striking—nothing as dramatic as we see in the centerfold of the *Saturday Night Fever* sound track double album, where Travolta jumps and poses in multiple shots, and nothing as dramatic as the original one-sheet with its iconic raised arm and skyward index finger. That move appears in the first visit to 2001, when he is wearing a rose and gray Nik Nik shirt and rose pants.[74] We might believe that what makes the suit iconic is its cultivation as an icon in the film's paratexts. Badham seems to have thought so. Stigwood hired legendary dance photographer Martha Swope to take the publicity photos, and "[t]hey finally picked a shot that had a little sparkle coming off John's finger from a star filter Swope

Figure 3.11. "Look at this, you're beautiful." *Saturday Night Fever* (John Badham, RSO/ Paramount, 1977)

had used. In retrospect, it would have been nice to have choreographed that into the movie."[75]

The iconic shot may have been created outside the narrative, but it synthesizes the Act I dance move and the Act III costume. Its self-conscious posture is a perfect emanation from the imagined character of Tony; that is, although the shot exists outside the narrative, it exists inside Tony's iconic self-understanding. Ethnography and marketing have converged. This convergence, or collapse, is central to the establishment of a new, design-centric, commercial cinema in the way it remains decisively conceptually anchored in the immersed realisms of the earlier part of the decade and puts that commitment in the service of an emerging reprioritization of that realism. And while all the key players in the making of *Fever* have some sense of this articulation, ethnography becomes marketing most emblematically when von Brandenstein imagines that the characters in the diegesis believe that their clothes possess symbolic significance and that symbolism is in turn taken up by Stigwood, Swope, and unnamed marketing executives who will then sell it back to a mass audience. "I pressed hard for the white suit because I think in this world that these guys lived in I think heroes wore white."[76]

This nativization of convention conforms to Derek Nystrom's sense that "if Tony seems to lack any critical awareness of his concern for his appearance, the film is at pains to establish *its* critical distance."[77] Yet Tony's unselfconsciousness

Figure 3.12. The star, and the star filter. Courtesy Paramount/Photofest

is not quite as total as it appears. Over coffee with Stephanie, she tells him, "You're a cliché, you're nowhere, and you're going no place." The BeeGees had made that clear at the beginning, although in their version, the singer is aware ("I'm goin' nowhere. Somebody help me, somebody help me there"). Stephanie's own painful class anxieties are themselves cliché, and the outcome of this scene is to deepen our sense that while the makers or the audience might attempt to distance themselves from Tony, his candor will undercut any such move. Nystrom's point is that Tony does not recognize the proximity between his intensely groomed, disco-going lifestyle and New York's gay culture of the time. And while producer Stigwood and CEO Diller certainly did recognize that proximity—they were frequently accused of being charter members of the Lavender Mafia in the entertainment industry—it might still seem that Tony becomes increasingly self-conscious about his social position but never reaches any such insight into his own narcissism. We might, then, look closely to see if that is the case.

At 2001, Tony's clothes don't *perform*, they are *performed*. In his first and only solo (to "You Should Be Dancing"), he is wearing the shiny blue shirt he put on layaway in the film's opening sequence. Twice he draws attention to his multiple-button cuffs, before checking his waist. At the end of "More Than a Woman," as he and Stephanie dance off the floor, Tony does a similar, but more restrained, move with his cuffs. (The camera angles match almost perfectly.) He pulls his lapels, fluffs his collar, draws down his vest, and pulls his lapels again; she follows along obediently, one hand on his shoulder. She kissed *him*; she follows *the suit*.

It is a very particular outfit. The jacket has large, peaked lapels, but by no means the largest in the film—Bobby sports those, on a powder blue jacket that, like all his clothes, is clownishly overstated. The lapels have pronounced pic-stitching, and the gorges are high. The suit has patch pockets, which mark it as inexpensive. The buttons are white, and plastic; the vest has five, the jacket has two, and there are four at each cuff—it may be inexpensive, but it is a suit with aspirations. The pants, like all the pants Tony wears, are flat-front and uncuffed, and they pull tight across his crotch. They are flared. The shirt is black, with a double pinstripe, pearlized plastic buttons, and standard cuffs. He wears it without a tie and with multiple gold chains. The shoes, which appear clearly only on his subway trip into Manhattan, are two-tone black-and-gray wingtips with Tony's usual platform heel. He has them square-laced.

In the last scene, at Stephanie's apartment in the Village, the suit is broken down. But its indomitable whiteness, paired with Stephanie's white robe, mark these characters as decidedly, definitively, aesthetic. The Village is the land of aesthetic people, at least as far as Tony is concerned; jazz wafts through the streets and the apartments have classical piano sound tracks. The production design agrees with him. The emblem of the apartment is a copy of Matisse's *Icarus*, from his book *Jazz*, and the furniture picks up the primary colors of the background. The scene is quite legible: Tony goes up the steps to Stephanie's (what he called "a fuckin' stairway to the stars" when they had coffee), and, unlike Icarus, there is no risk that he will fly too high.

But where Icarus is black, Tony and Stephanie are obtrusively white. And in a fairly conventional way, the explicit whiteness of the clothing vouches for the newfound contingency of their own racial identity. What matters is not race, or ethnicity, or faith, but ability. Tony's discovery, the one that has made his continued existence in Bay Ridge intolerable, is that he wants to be in a place where the meritocracy is purer: "Good is good." Racism has blocked honest judgments of talent, and while Tony was a willing participant in its crudest forms—early on, he jokes, "Would you put your dick in a spic? Does it get bigger in a nigger?"—by the end of the dance contest he has reached a kind of epiphany. Of course, just because he has seen through ethnic pride does not mean that he won't attempt to rape Stephanie in order, the film implies, to certify his manhood in the face of the overwhelming crisis of social categories he has precipitated.

Fever narrates as a moment of social and especially aesthetic recognition what was more broadly a transformation of class and race. The class changes of the seventies could put outer-borough women in pink-collar occupations in better position to take advantage of the new world of knowledge-work. (See Mike Nichols's *Working Girl* [Fox, 1988, also designed by von Brandenstein].) As Nystrom points out, "The U.S. working class was beginning to look less like the hard hats of *Joe* or *Five Easy Pieces* and more like the low-skill service workers of *Saturday Night Fever*, which is to say, they were starting, in some ways, to be less easily distinguished from the high-skill, high-value service workers of the P[rofessional] M[idle] C[lass]," and this was true first for women.[78] Tony's one encounter with a bona fide member of a higher class, Jay Langhart, is legible on every level. Langhart wears jeans (Tony never does) and a blue workshirt (but ironed); where Stephanie introduces Tony as "a friend," Jay announces that he has "unspecified status."

When Tony confronts Stephanie about her relationship, she explains that they had an affair that has ended amicably. When Tony pushes, she lashes out:

> He helped me, man, you don't know what it's like at that place. It's crazy, you don't know shit, you know? I didn't know how to do stuff so I would go to him and I would ask him, and he would tell me how to do things, and then I'd go back to work

and everything would be alright. . . . What do you expect me to do? What the hell do you expect me to do? He helped me.

The world of work is hopelessly vague here. She is supposed to "do things" but doesn't know how; he tells her "how to do things," and in exchange they sleep together: "what do you expect me to do?" But if the work that she does is vague, the venue is particular—particular in the way that Hollywood has always particularized class advancement: Stephanie works at a talent agency (it seems to be William Morris; it goes unnamed), and from this strategic perch, she will be able to rub elbows with celebrities (Laurence Olivier, David Bowie, Joe Namath). Langhart is, she says, "an arranger, record producer, wants to do films"—someone like Allan Carr or Robert Stigwood, for example.

At the end of the film, Tony has either forgotten or repressed or, we might say, aestheticized the sexual exchange at the heart of Stephanie's qualified success. He announces he will move to Manhattan, and the conversation remains nebulous.

S: What are you gonna do?

T: What do you do? You come in, you get a job, you know, do what *you* do. Get a nice apartment.

S: Oh yeah, what kind a job?

T: I don't know, what did you do? You couldn't do nothin', right?

S: I could type when I came in.

T: No big deal, I'm an able person. I can do these things.

The film has no idea how Tony might follow her up the class ladder—or, rather, it has no idea how he might follow her without learning to type and sleeping with his boss. Lost in the supposedly meritocratic metropolis where everything has "unspecified status" ("Everything is beautiful there," Stephanie says, "even the lunch hours"), Tony can only declare, "I'm an able person."

Recalibration

Saturday Night Fever was always intended as a prelude to the much bigger *Grease*, and one might see the passage from the gritty disco to the kitchy "Shakin' Shack" as sufficient evidence of the cultural turn I am describing. Yet as nostalgic as *Grease* obviously was, even it had been, in its stage version, grittier. "The authors were a little mad at me because it was my vision to suburbanize it for a wider audience. I didn't want the characters grabbing their crotch and using vulgar language," said Stigwood's partner Carr, who wrote the screenplay. Choreographer Patricia Birch was one of those angry authors. "The play was about these gritty kids from the raw side of Chicago. Though Tom Moore was from Yale and I was from the Martha Graham company and there wasn't a greaser in the cast, we had played it documentary-real."[79] The same tensions were present in Travolta's next film, *Urban Cowboy*. Already shunted off to the side since it was being produced by Robert Evans, the production became a rearguard battleground where grit, authenticity, and just plain sordidness were fought over by producer and studio. The usual arguments were between Evans and everyone else, but the alliances were fluid. Still, as he put it, "Grit was the issue. Travolta, Bridges, and company wanted *Grease* in chaps. I wanted *Saturday Night Fever*, raunchy ranch style."[80] Yet the *Saturday Night Fever* he wanted was disappearing even as he appealed to it.

It is unclear exactly when Paramount decided to put *Saturday Night Fever* back into theaters in a recut, PG-rated version, but that event marks the decisive reassertion of studio control over the film and, through the film, the design and management of American entertainment. Stigwood had fought for the linguistic grit of the film—had even changed directors rather than drastically alter Wexler's script—"Everyone was nervous about the film," he said. "Paramount about the language, particularly. I wouldn't budge on that because Norman's dialogue was perfect, it's how the kids spoke."[81] A moderately cleaned-up version, six and a half minutes shorter, with hundreds of lexical and other changes, had been playing on airplanes through much of 1978 and was submitted to the ratings administration on December 4. By then, *Fever* had returned over $100 million in rentals to Paramount, the most ever for an R-rated film. Or that is what Aljean Harmetz of the *Times* and Gene Siskel of the *Chicago Tribune* believed. In 2002, though, Paramount told Box Office Mojo, that the film had *grossed* only $85 million domestically, making the earlier rental figures impossible—even a revised figure of $74 million in rentals was utterly implausible.[82] In any event, in January 1979, Paramount announced that *Fever* would be pulled from release so that it could reappear in a recut, PG-rated version in March; the MPAA ratings administration required a sixty-day hiatus between versions of a film.

The re-release of *Fever* was a way of getting a jump on the television audience; indeed, much of the new footage had been shot for the eventual television release. Instead of thinking of the movie's revenue cycle as an extended theatrical run as an R-rated film followed by a general-audience release on television, Diller & Co. used the re-edited, airline version of the film to poach the teen (or non-R-attending) audience. Paramount was able to monetize the general audience a second time, and more directly. Under late-seventies arrangements, networks paid a lump sum for television rights (not a sliding scale based on box-office revenues), and while Travolta's *Kotter*-derived star power boosted the studio's quote, the second-run theatrical haul would be marginal income—the TV deal had already been made. The PG *Fever* was, in this regard, the moral equivalent of pay per view in an era of network dominance. (It was also a canny risk to take: by relying on the airline version, Paramount incurred minimal additional costs in assembling the PG cut.) Whether there would be sufficient audience for that tamer version was a question; Paramount hedged its bets by repeating the platform model of expansion with the new version. Reviewers all thought the PG version was a way of "cooling down" the film, stripping away its authenticity and grit, but that sanitization was happening anyway.[83]

Moreover, the rerelease of *Fever* provided Barry Diller with an opportunity to frame the critical understanding of the studio's process in public. In the early seventies, the most interesting accounts of individual films at Paramount came from their directors, writers, and actors. But in its Diller-led incarnation, the most compelling accounts of films and filmmaking came from Paramount's executive ranks. Central to this successful arrogation of interpretive authority were Diller's own apparently limitless candor and his willingness to make cinematic quality only one of a set of institutional variables, variables over which Paramount had control. It is worth quoting at length:

> "Why?" asked Barry Diller, chairman of Paramount, rhetorically. "Because we felt a lot of people who would enjoy the film were excluded from seeing it. Why shouldn't we let them see it and make ourselves some money? Young people knew and responded to the music. We would not be doing this without the immense appeal of the BeeGees' music."
>
> Mr. Diller is candid enough to question whether the revised "Saturday Night Fever" will be the artistic equivalent of the original movie. "I don't know. It is not the same film because it doesn't have the impact of that raw reality. Is it as good a film? I doubt it, but, at the same time, I don't think people who go to see the PG version will be cheated. They'll see the same story, hear the same music, see John Travolta—although he'll be more like the Travolta they've seen in 'Grease.'"[84]

As he considered whether to take the role in *Fever*, Travolta worried that it was too close to his TV character, Vinnie Barbarino. Reviewers were kind and noted the spread between the two Italian Brooklynites, but Diller was even sharper: however televisual the PG *Fever* might be, the frame of reference for its audience would be cinematic. A star's passage from TV to film is, for Diller, one-directional. Just as Carr stripped the "documentary" aspects out of *Grease*, turning it into a nostalgic parody of the fifties, so Paramount stripped the explicitness from *Fever*, turning it into, well, *Grease*, or, more pointedly, a nostalgic version of itself. This level of immanence defines the studio's self-imaginary in Hollywood's emerging neoclassical era, when cadres of Armani-clad agents and risk-averse executives would be accused of killing off the New Hollywood. What would be true of the industry was true of the PG *Saturday Night Fever*. The film was different—not as good, by Diller's own admission; the suit remained the same.

Our Man in Armani

The Ovitz Interregnum

The suit does not cover the body, but instead puts it in evidence.

Giorgio Armani[1]

Japan, Inc.

In *Maid to Order* (Amy Holden Jones, New Century, 1987), Ally Sheedy is a spoiled rich girl forced to become a maid when her father cuts her off. She goes to work for Stan and Georgette Starkey, a couple of decidedly tacky Hollywood agents. Early on, she presses her boss's suit, and he is peeved: "You're not supposed to press it. It's a wrinkled suit. I bought it wrinkled. It's a Giorgio Armano [*sic*] wrinkled suit. Wrinkles are *in*. It's the eighties, kiddo; wake up!"

The joke is more about him than her. Anyone still saying "It's the eighties" in 1987 is desperately trying to remain young and hip, and Stan has the hair plugs to prove it. His client list consists of Rat Pack hangers-on like Steve Lawrence and Eydie Gormé. This, too, is something of an inside joke since Stan is talking to one of the founding members of the Brat Pack at the zenith of their domination of middling Hollywood fare. *The Lost Boys* (Kiefer Sutherland, Jason Patric, and Jami Gertz) was released the same weekend; *Stakeout* (Emilio Estevez) was released the next week; *La Bamba* (Lou Diamond Phillips) the week before.

Stan's belatedness extends to the edge of his fashion sense. He assumes that agents wear Armani and wants to make sure that his competition knows he knows that. The film's satire of this politics of perception works only if the Armani-clad agent is a familiar enough figure to be satirized but not yet a conventional or hackneyed target. In all likelihood the film is wrong about the joke's currency but right that there is something significant at work in the culture when it becomes possible to assume an audience might care how Hollywood agents dress.

The fish-out-of-water comedy forms one strand in the high-concept cordon that segregates eighties Hollywood historically. As I argued in the previous chapter, self-consciously high-concept filmmaking served the interests of aggressive studios as they sought to exert a greater degree of control over the creative process than the auteurist model of the seventies offered. In Hollywood's corporate comedy, high concept was the terza rima that led from the infernos of *Heaven's Gate* and *Sorcerer* to the synergistic heaven of *Batman*.

Yet studios were not the only players struggling for control in the wake of the auteurist seventies. As the studios campaigned against the stars under the banner of a return to discipline, chastened auteurs needed greater protection from the distributors' oligopoly, particularly if they harbored dreams of making risky movies. In the battle between the studios and the stars, talent agencies sided with the stars. And none was more strategic about that alliance than the newcomer, Creative Artists Agency (CAA).

In 1974, there were three major agencies in Hollywood—William Morris, by far the largest; Ashley Famous; and International Creative Artists (ICA). At the end of that year, Ashley Famous and ICA announced their merger. Meanwhile, five ambitious agents at William Morris had grown frustrated by the firm's layers of supervision; they broke away to found CAA. Such events compose the typical rhythms of a mature oligopoly. What made CAA different from the usual boutique agency was its growth. By the end of 1976, it had merged with Martin Baum's literary agency and had 90 clients; by 1989, it had 675 clients.[2]

Driving this growth was Michael Ovitz. Although the original five agents were equal partners, Ovitz quickly emerged as the head of CAA, and, in time, he would be regarded as the most powerful man in Hollywood. Much has been made of his relentless push to make the agency succeed, and of his style and the style of the agency, but almost nothing of the relationship between CAA's success and the projects it packaged. Part of that silence stems from the general anonymity of intermediaries in creative industries: Agents are generally unseen, their work is complicated, and their internal successes are not necessarily visible on-screen. Worse, successful agenting is at best a necessary condition of aesthetic success; it is never sufficient. In such a situation, agents can shoulder blame for the assembly of talent but can never take credit for the success of the project since the proximate cause of the film's success lies in the work of the writers, directors, actors, editors, and so on. Since aesthetic credit is unavailable to agencies, they have an incentive to define success as control over the antecedent and largely economic elements of a film, not the consequent, more aesthetic result. What set CAA apart was its assertion of control over the early phases of a film production in so complete a fashion that the ultimate economic and artistic success of the project could not be alienated from the agency. Thus was power defined, and thus did CAA become a target.

CAA found its niche in the Hollywood ecosystem first by devoting its energies to television packaging. In the seventies, this was the sector of the industry most open to new players. One might initially suppose that agencies would have had a harder time breaking into TV because the three broadcast networks controlled the ultimate scarce quantity via their franchise rights to a state-regulated frequency. But in recognition of that scarcity, the government had installed a strong antitrust regime of financial interest and syndication rules (fin-syn). These prevented networks from owning most of their own shows. Beginning in 1970, and reaffirmed by consent decrees issued in 1980, networks could not maintain a financial interest in their shows when the series entered syndication, nor could they set up domestic syndication arms. The major broadcast networks were compelled to be buyers and could do very little to strengthen their negotiating position.[3]

Agencies and movie studios thus emerged as strong players in the packaging of programs, particularly those shown outside prime time. For agencies, TV packaging was a remarkable economic system. Representing individuals, an agency might earn 10 percent from two or three clients on a particular show. But if the agency packaged the show, it could earn a percentage of the entire production budget—at William Morris, it was 5 percent up front, 5 percent deferred, and 10 percent of the eventual syndication fees.[4] On top of that, clients no longer had to pay agents out of their negotiated salaries. The agency made out, the client made out, and their interests were more closely harmonized. The networks paid.

But in CAA's case, the networks paid less. As part of its jump into independence, the agency cut the packaging fee from 5-5-10 to 3-3-6.[5] It was a strategy that CAA pursued in other areas; rumors abounded throughout the eighties that part of the way CAA was able to win over major stars was by cutting the agency's 10 percent to 5 percent. Yet the realities of a particular deal mattered less to CAA and Mike Ovitz than the perception of those realities. And if that perception was murky, it only heightened the exclusivity of the CAA mode of operation.

CAA's first major television package was for the miniseries of James Clavell's *Shōgun*. The novel was a blockbuster in 1975, but the development of a feature film from the one thousand–page book stalled. When Baum's agency merged with CAA, Ovitz rallied to the project. According to Robert Slater, it was Ovitz's idea to recast *Shōgun* as a miniseries and to pump up the authenticity values of the production. NBC bought it; CAA received $1 million in commissions, "four times as much as its largest fee prior to then."[6] The miniseries aired on NBC in September 1980 to tremendous ratings: 32.1 and a 51 share.[7] Still, it received only grudgingly positive reviews. Nearly every critic questioned the decision to include large chunks of untranslated, unsubtitled Japanese. "Long stretches of dialogue are either translated directly—and tediously—for Blackthorne by someone in the story or they are left untranslated on the theory that their 'emotional content' will be evident." "It's not much comfort but somewhat empathetic when Chamberlain shouts, twice, in the (literally) eleventh hour, 'What the hell is going on?'" and "[t]he question . . . is: Should I stay with it for the whole week? The answer at this point is as inscrutable as Orientals are portrayed on the screen in 'Shōgun.' And, perhaps, as inscrutable as the plot of the series itself."[8] If *Shōgun* was only a qualified success as entertainment, it was an unqualified hit.

Shōgun achieved on-screen what it had not quite managed in print: exemplary authority over the intersection of convergent cultural waves. It was, and remains, the crucial artifact of the American fascination with Japan at the beginning of the eighties. Among American business leaders, a crisis of confidence attending the recession of the late seventies spawned a search for ways out of the stagflationary bind. The principal model of high-tech success was Japan. Ezra Vogel's *Japan as Number One* (1979) set records for an American nonfiction title in Japan.[9] Vogel centrally claimed that Japanese industrial success was not simply the product of macroeconomic policy or investment in plant or training but crucially of Japanese cultural factors. For the next several years, American commentators would attempt to work out just how culturally exceptional Japan's economic success was and whether it might be copied.

In June 1980, three months before it aired *Shōgun*, NBC aired *If Japan Can . . . Why Can't We?*, a highly regarded white paper on Japanese industry. The show spawned numerous requests for video copies—a novelty at that time. It also made "total quality management" (TQM) more palatable by introducing W. Edwards Deming to a mass American audience. Deming had "brought" quality management to Japanese manufacturing during the postwar occupation; now the guru was bringing the ideology of continuous improvement "home." At the same time, the statistical techniques that were at the heart of quality control could carry the whiff of the exotic—the control chart as *japonaiserie*. The sense that Japan succeeded because it aestheticized capitalism pervaded Richard Pascale and Anthony Athos's *The Art of Japanese Management: Applications for American Executives* (1981). Deming's own book followed in 1982. The American TQM revolution was at hand.[10]

That revolution solidified the belief that what ailed American corporations was something called "culture." Peter Drucker had likely been the first (he is cited by others as the first) to redescribe the practice and principles of business management as a "culture" in 1973: "Management is a social function, embedded in a tradition of values, customs, and beliefs, and in governmental and political systems. Management is—and should be—culture-conditioned; in turn, management and managers shape culture and society. Thus, although management is an organized body of knowledge and as such applicable everywhere, it is also a 'culture.' It is not 'value free' science."[11] Athos and Pascale put it this way: "This subculture (of U.S. management) lies within the nation's larger culture. Both cultures contain the root causes of our recent managerial decline. . . . The 'enemy' isn't the Japanese or the Germans; it is the limitations of our managerial 'culture.'"[12] Within three years, the scare quotes would come off, and corporate culture would be an ordinary topic of discussion.

The pervasive sense that Japan could be a model, or what Athos and Pascale call a "special mirror," for America shaped the re-reception of Clavell's novel on the way to the small screen. As part of the run-up to the miniseries, Henry Smith, then a professor of Japanese history at University of California, Santa Barbara, edited a volume entitled *Learning from* Shōgun. He thought that Clavell's novel differed from earlier versions of the Will Adams myth in "its instructional quality. . . . [It is] a virtual encyclopedia of Japanese history and culture: somewhere among those half-million words, one can find a brief description of virtually everything one wanted to know about Japan."[13] But when Smith and his fellow contributors were able to view the miniseries, they were disappointed. Gone was the "cross-cultural learner" and back was the "stubborn ethnocentrist"; "virtually all of the political intrigue" was eliminated.[14] Only the romance remained. The disappointment here is the product of a reformist academic frame of reference: *Shōgun should* have been a cultural model; it was merely a diversion.

But if we keep our frame of reference steadily on the business, *Shōgun* seems far more successful. Not only did it put CAA on the map financially; it also suggested that the agency was an unseen power—unseen but not unheard. Here, the "haughty" decision to leave the Japanese untranslated finds an explanation: It demonstrates the agency's control. *Shōgun* the novel had led its readers through the complicated web of Japanese language, culture, and politics. When *Shōgun* the miniseries concentrated its instructional energies on Blackthorne's language lessons, a second, shadow lesson was intimated: the audience did not understand the power structure of Japan, but someone else certainly did. When he tried to determine why the miniseries failed to live up to the book, Tom Shales, then the most powerful TV critic in the country, concluded that the "likely botcher" was Clavell, "who as executive producer . . . probably had too much control. . . . Eric Bercovici wrote the script, but Clavell's name is omnipresent—'James Clavell's Shōgun,' it says at each commercial break and in all promotional material. Clavell may have a great agent, but he could use a bit more self-restraint."[15]

Shōgun is not exactly the story of an agent. But in its stripped-down, romance-centered, miniseries form, it dwells on the pathos of the intermediary.

If we cast aside the obvious stranger-in-a-strange-land identification with Blackthorne and ask where the miniseries' heart lies, it is with Mariko, his translator. She is both Buddhist and Christian, and when she prepares to commit seppuku, she does so with a crucifix around her neck. At the last minute, she is spared the choice between honor and damnation. Yet this relief from responsibility has its price: "Lord Toranaga reminds me that my opinions have no value and that interpreters should only interpret." Always an intermediary, Mariko can achieve some measure of autonomy only through suffering. She will not "give herself freely" to her husband, so he beats her. When Blackthorne asks why, she explains, "Because that is my revenge. To repay him for leaving me alive." This is what it means to be in a service industry. "We are taught from childhood to disappear within ourselves. To grow impenetrable walls behind which we live."

Her relationship with Blackthorne will allow her to escape the role of "inscrutable" go-between and become his spiritual guide. She dispenses the crucial piece of sagacity: "Life and death are the same. There is only this moment." When Blackthorne grows wistful—"Sad, isn't it, not being able to trust anyone?"—she draws on her corporate-zen resolve: "It is not sad, Anjin-san. It is just one of life's most important rules. No more, no less." Once he learns these rules for the subordination of affect, he will be made a samurai by Lord Toranaga. Late in the series, Toranaga will again reward Blackthorne for his valor by presenting him

Figure 4.1. The interpreter as agent of mediation. *Shōgun* (Jerry London, NBC/Asahi, 1980)

with a maid's "contract." He, in turn, will pass it on to her beloved, earning their gratitude and demonstrating his mastery of the agent's code.

This intermediary status suffuses *Shōgun* formally as well as narratively. For the US market, it was to be a miniseries, but abroad it would be edited and shown as a feature film. The conventions of the two media conflicted, especially in the cinematography. Shooting both for television, with its smaller screen and lower contrast ratio, and for cinema, where scale would be bigger and brightness would be greater, director Jerry London had to choose: "I had to think to myself 'I know that this scene will be in both the feature and the television show. What size do I pick? Do I go for the closeup closeup or do I go for the feature closeup?' . . . I always had that feature version/TV version thing on my mind, and how to bridge it."[16]

If in some ways, *Shōgun* sacrificed certain feature values because it was destined for TV, in other ways *Shōgun* was bigger than an ordinary movie. Director London called *Shōgun* "the greatest team effort that has ever been made in [the] motion picture industry." The mixed crew—Japanese and American; the mixed cast—Japanese, English, and Richard Chamberlain; and the mixed financing— with NBC airing it in the United States and Paramount Television and Toho splitting the production costs; make London's claim plausible. By making TV bigger than film, *Shōgun* proved that the "TV guys" at CAA could move beyond feature production. Even as the agency became the dominant movie packager, it held fast to this idea that it was somehow more than that.

Service Professions

Ovitz was not the only person in Hollywood fascinated by the interplay of Japanese art and industry. Writer-director Paul Schrader had written a book on Yasujiro Ozu in 1972. He and his brother had co-written the screenplay for *The Yakuza* in 1975. In 1984, they wrote and Paul directed *Mishima: A Life in Four Chapters*. In the intervening decade, the Schraders turned to more domestic concerns with media-induced anesthesia and purgative violence in *Taxi Driver*, *Hard Core*, and *Blue Collar*. By the time Paul reached *American Gigolo* (Paramount, 1980), he imagined that his films had turned a corner. He had "exchanged 'violence for design.'"[17] The exchange was not yet complete. When the film's hero, Julian Kaye, meets his lover for lunch at a Japanese restaurant, Schrader shoots their conversation frontally, an homage to Ozu. Yet this almost effortless interlude contrasts with the rest of Julian's life, a complicated balancing of style against commerce. The plot, in which Julian attempts to extricate himself from responsibility for the death of a trick while the onrush of notoriety destroys his carefully won independence, demonstrates how susceptible any commercialized aesthetic is to impositions of political power and vengeance. When sexual desire has been stripped of its moral sanction and reduced to money, power throws off its limits as well, and violence becomes an ever-present threat. As it works through the possibilities of desire—framed and unframed, bought and freely given—*American Gigolo* becomes something of a think piece on economic culture.

American Gigolo was also the first Hollywood film to feature Armani's clothing prominently. It came just five years after Armani's first solo collection for his own house, yet the designer already had a substantial presence in America by 1978, when *Time* magazine could refer to him as "the greatest evangelist of male unkempt" in a piece about "the rumpled, crumpled, wrinkled, crinkled look."[18] And while there are no wrinkled suits in the film, there are wrinkled separates. Early on, Richard Gere mixes and matches his lissome Armani sport coats and ties while singing along to Smokey Robinson and the Miracles' "The Love I Saw in You Was Just a Mirage." It is, perhaps, the happiest we see him.[19]

But the crumpled look was not the only fashion novelty of the seventies. The prêt-à-porter revolution, in which couturiers like Saint Laurent launched lines that could be sold in department stores, began in 1975 as well. Armani was among the early converts. He parlayed that broad distribution into a "look." Where distribution and style intersect, we find a figure Germano Celant has called the "mass dandy," and the embodiment of that dandy is Gere's Julian Kaye. He is a "behavioral model, conveyed by a system of mass communica-

Figure 4.2. Paul Schrader's homage to Ozu's frontality. *American Gigolo* (Paramount, 1980)

tion, invit[ing] individuals—the spectators—to forge their own self-image, and therefore their own destinies" through prêt-à-porter fashion.[20]

This dandy's trick is to walk the fine line between individuality and generality, to convey the magnetic availability of a good-looking body that is not eccentrically styled. "The gigolo is neither original, nor unique, nor rare, nor disturbing, nor different. Rather, he repeats gestures and behaviors he assumes will please others and lead to triumphs." It might seem that this endless masquerade would threaten his identity—he is, Celant says, "a multiple being"— yet that multiplicity is a way of reconceiving the gigolo as an expert in "the everyday management of one's appearance."[21] A sexed-up version of David Riesman's other-directed individual, the mass-dandy-as-appearance-manager puts Hollywood's new MBA and agenting class on-screen. As Pauline Kael described the New Hollywood executives that same year, "Their talent is being able to anticipate their superiors' opinions; in meetings, they show a sixth sense for guessing what the most powerful person in the room wants to hear. . . . They could be selling neckties just as well as movies, except that they are drawn to glamour and power."[22] *American Gigolo* proves that one need not choose between movies and neckties in the search for glamour and power.

Julian Kaye manages more than his appearance. In his defense of his career he is a master negotiator. He takes 50 or 60 percent of each trick from his madam; he's "already cut [her] out of the repeaters." When he freelances for his former pimp—the trick that will embroil him in murder—he works on a 90/10 split. Julie is, in short, a professional. When asked why he dates older women, he explains that no else cares about them enough to get them to come. In his description of a three-hour trick, prostitution becomes more than work: "When it was over, I felt like I'd done something—something worthwhile." It is, like agenting, a service profession. Still, though he may be available, and committed to his craft, "They get possessive. And I can't be possessed."

The murder, though, highlights his vulnerability—"If those bitches ever turned on you, you're through," his pimp tells him. His private space is first compromised by his lover, Lauren Hutton—"How did you find me? . . . This is my apartment; women don't come here." As she awkwardly confesses to her overwhelming desire, he studies one of the many unhung paintings that lean against the wall. He is less blissful but just as intent, as when he contemplates his wardrobe choices. His apartment maintains a studied incompleteness, the interior-decorating equivalent of the Armani casual look. It seems always to await its master's decision to finally have someone hang the paintings, to finally have someone iron the jacket. Whether from indecision or demurral, the commanded labor does not come; instead, it is always promised. To enter, the guest must only accede to this fantasy of control in abeyance, a fantasy of management.

"Women don't come here." There are several reasons, and several readings, for this line. Among them is a version that takes this as an implied address to the audience, as though Julian were his own Chorus, singing monitory songs of the moral law. Once the rules of entry are broken, the violations only get worse. The police work Julian's apartment over and leave it a mess in their search for evidence that might tie him to the murder. (The mess highlights just how studied the casual disarray of its ordinary state is.) At this point, he must rouse himself to have the apartment cleaned. He is passing beyond studied indifference to a chaotic state where he veers wildly between paranoia and a thorough lack of concern with appearances. Eventually, he himself will tear the place apart looking for incriminating evidence that might have been planted there. Throughout the second half of the film, he recognizes, dimly, that it is his aesthetic status that endangers him—"I'm in a frame." "Who's framing you?" "I don't know. All I can see is the frame." In the end, he flips over the painting on the wall in the hope of finding something, anything, behind it. One of "those bitches" has "turned on him," and he responds by turning on himself.[23]

There are two important allusions here. His line about seeing only the frame comes from *Out of the Past* (Jacques Tourneur, RKO, 1947); the high-angle shot as he searches his own apartment echoes the final scenes in *The Conversation*. Each of these precursors tells the story of a threatened independent investigator (the private eye, the surveillance expert), who has become himself the target of machinations of which he has only imperfect awareness. To put Julian in this context does more than bolster his investigative credentials and the film's claim to membership in a genre; it anchors him in an aesthetic allegory that has only just flashed into possibility in 1980. When Robert Mitchum delivered the line about the frame, he was, as usual, completely at peace with the idea that someone was out to get him. When Gene Hackman ripped up the floorboards of his apartment looking for a hidden microphone, he had become a victim of the paranoia he was used to visiting upon others. Mitchum was vulnerable to the setup because he broke the rules and ran off with the boss's girl; Hackman was vulnerable because he was paranoid by profession and sentimental by nature. Mitchum was possessed by a late-modern insouciance about baring the device—"I'm in a frame"—Hackman, by a postmodern fear that found its allegory in something unframed and uncontained—that is, sound. In Julian's case, the frame has been his ally, a buffer, the aesthetic equivalent of his apartment, a technology for insulating him from his actions. What he discovers, though, is that the frame is not of his own making, however independently he operates inside it. He deals, and dresses, in an arena carved out by much larger forces; this is what it means to be the mass dandy.

Julian's dedication to his independence and the paranoia that comes with it look back to the auteurist seventies, while the ruthless artistry of his deal making anticipates the era when the twin oligopolies—agencies and studios—would face off. (It may do more than that: when Julian replaces his usual 50/50 split with a 90/10 "favor" to a rival pimp, Paramount would have seen an echo of its great innovation in the distribution of *The Godfather*.)[24] The intersection of these two concerns—the cultivation of individuality and the pricing

Figure 4.3. High angles on the hero's apartment, with diagonals: (*top*) before Julian can rip his place apart; (*bottom*) after Harry has. *American Gigolo* (Schrader, Paramount 1980); *The Conversation* (Coppola, Directors Company/ Paramount, 1974)

of individuality in the market—occupies much of Julian's discussion of his percentage, his shopping, and his sexuality. The Armani-wearing gigolo is not yet identical to the agent because the battle for control is still amorphous. In *American Gigolo* authorship is diffuse, as the signatures in the credits attest. Yet however close Julian Kaye and Mike Ovitz are, there are no agents and there are no studios in the film. There are procurers, and there are independent contractors, and there are politicians.

Restraint of Trade

Exercising power, testing the limits of self-restraint, and aestheticizing commerce are the building blocks of the story of *American Gigolo*, the careers of Mike Ovitz and Giorgio Armani, and, ultimately, the reaction of American business to the challenge of "Japan, Inc." For Ovitz, power, restraint, and aesthetics first came together in *Shōgun*. Fresh off his work in *American Gigolo*, Armani would find inspiration in Akira Kurosawa's *Kagemusha* (Toho, 1980) for his fall/winter 1981 collection. "When I wanted to express the sensation of the greatest wealth of the decade, instinctively I turned to the images of a vague East, that of the Japanese samurai, of Imperial China, of the herdsmen of Mongolia, or of the maharajas of India, who have always fascinated me because of their dignity, composure, luxury, character."[25] Yet Armani quickly pulled back, eventually regarding the collection as a mistake: "In the early 1980s I did a collection inspired by Japan that was too theatrical. The colors were not mine."[26]

It seemed that the attraction to things Japanese piggybacked on a preoccupation with discipline. On the one hand, the way of the samurai was balanced, artistic, and restrained. On the other hand, modern businessmen who imagined they were following the way of the samurai were vulnerable to a dangerous overconfidence, the product of the sense that they had mastered an esoteric knowledge. The totem of this overconfidence might be Julian's array of Armani neckware in *American Gigolo*, but in the corporate high ground of America's corner offices, it would be a copy of Sun Tzu's *The Art of War*.

Mike Ovitz had come to know *The Art of War* in college. However versed in Sun Tzu he had been then, by 1981 he would have had enough time to reabsorb the slender classic, since that year a new edition, introduced by James Clavell, was published in both the United Kingdom and the United States. Clavell confesses that he had never heard of the book until 1977. "I was totally shocked that, in all of my reading about Asia, about Japan and China particularly, I had not come across this book before. Since that time, it has been a constant companion for me, so much so that during the course of the writing of *Noble House* many of the characters in it refer to Sun Tzu in all his glory."[27] The irony is thick.

When he writes his military history of Japan, Clavell knows nothing of Sun Tzu. Only when he settles down to tell the story of one of the British trading houses in Hong Kong does the manual of strategy become essential. In its first popular American appearance, the applications of Sun Tzu are already allegorical: the art of business as the art of war. In the person of Clavell we have the yoke that joins an ancient Chinese text to the martial history of Tokugawa Japan to the spectacle of contemporary Asian economic success. And through Clavell, we can see the precise moment when problems of the American economy disappeared into problems of culture. After *Shōgun*, *Noble House*, and *The Art of War*, the Japanified businessman is dressed to sell.

As central as *Shōgun* was to the ultimate high-concept project of making economics into cultural studies, it also allowed CAA to bridge from TV to film. That had been the plan all along. In June 1975, Ovitz told his partners, "You guys should really stick to TV. That's where you're selling shows. But I'm going to start to get myself known in the motion picture business."[28] There were good reasons to branch out from television. It would be hard to convince clients that the agency could fulfill their dreams unless CAA could offer the chance for motion picture success. There was also the very real question of prestige; when then-superagent Sue Mengers called them "TV boys," it was a slur, and one that could taint the projects they were pitching.[29] Economically, though, the move into film was less certain, as Ovitz acknowledged. Here, then, was a place where confidence, even overconfidence, was essential for the strategy to work. Indeed, taking a cue from *The Art of War*'s emphasis on perceptual victories, we might say that the strategy was a projective overconfidence backed by a ruthless pragmatism.

There were two phases to the CAA plan, which in this martial context we might call the attractive encampment and the fortification. To make an attractive encampment, the agency pursued film personnel with the same focus it had brought to television. In addition to signing a critical mass of above-the-line talent, CAA sought to distinguish its talent pool within the agency oligopoly: It would particularly target directors and writers. In that way, CAA would be able to offer potential stars a vehicle that already came with a vision. After the writers and directors were on board, the agency would hunt out the biggest stars, those whose work seemed allergic to the crapshoot complacency of the movie business. The agency would seek to demonize risk, arguing that certain stars, once committed to a project, would inoculate the studio against financial losses. Still, there was little new in this strategy; it simply amounted to doing what the other agencies did but doing it better.

To fortify its gains, CAA was able to use its success in TV as a model for feature production. Unlike TV, the film industry had no firewall between producers and distributors—quite the opposite. The unity of production and distribution had been the studio creed since the twenties; from a belief in that form of organization all power flowed. Without something like fin-syn rules, the agencies had no government body giving them a leg up in the negotiations. Yet CAA could carry the *knowledge* it gained from its history of packaging for television into a different economic context. If the Federal Communications Commission (FCC) kept the networks weak, in the film industry CAA could look for weak studios, studios that could not afford to say no to a package. Thus did the emergence of a new agency amount to the emergence of a new mode of control. It was, in other words, yet another case of an instance with structural effects.

At one level, the mode of production was all but determined. The package-unit mode in which each film was developed, produced, and distributed on its own was the nearly inevitable result of the disintegration of the classical Hollywood studios and the extremely high marginal tax rates of the fifties and sixties—beginning in 1954, the marginal tax rate on income over two hundred thousand dollars was 91 percent; it stayed there until 1964, when it was lowered to 70 percent. Newly liberated talent no longer needed constant work; indeed, the marginal film did not yield much income unless the star had found a way to amortize it. Yet taxes are only part of the story. As part of the Reagan Revolution, the marginal rate on the highest bracket was cut again to 50 percent in 1981. The Tax Reform Act of 1986 slashed that rate to 28 percent and equalized the tax rate on income and capital gains. Both of these might have encouraged stars to work more (and invest less). At the same time, though, the 1986 act eliminated many tax shelters that had channeled production funds to Hollywood studios. In particular, it repealed the investment tax credit. Studios that had previously secured access to capital by offering tax shelters now enlisted investors in limited partnerships such as Disney's Silver Screen Partners. The partnerships in effect provided interest-free financing in exchange for a share of the film's revenues.[30]

But if the antitrust regime and the tax code all but dictated that films would be made as one-off productions, that mode did not dictate who would *control* the content. If distribution were scarce, then distributors would dominate; but if talent were scarce, stars would. The tremendous expansion of ancillary markets in television and video led to a proliferation of well-heeled independent producers and distributors—like *Maid to Order*'s New Century, but including Carolco, Cannon, Embassy, Vestron, and DeLaurentiis Entertainment Group. And those indies chipped away at the studios' distribution oligopoly. Where there was effective competition—and there would be more competition in less expensive genres, like fish-out-of-water comedies—the scarcity of bankable talent intensified. And that scarcity, in turn, made it possible for agencies to bid up star salaries.

But simple inflation was not the only impact. A small portion of Hollywood's above-the-line talent is offered more work than it can take. For them, agents and managers guide their clients through the tricky process of selection and career cultivation. (When the tension between income maximization and career management is strong enough, an actor or writer will have an agent look out for the first of these and a manager look out for the second.)[31] To the extent that an agency could convince important Hollywood players that it did a better job of managing the artist's career—that it was not simply interested in maximizing its own income—that agency could emerge from the oligopoly. CAA did just this.

William Goldman's law, that in Hollywood "nobody knows anything," can be taken two ways. In one, it provides a great deal of comfort, recasting the business as an endless source of surprise and liberating individuals from their obligation to follow the herd. Such a utopian reading is nearly impossible to follow in practice. Taken the other way and the movie business is a bottomless pit of risk. For someone who "tests high" on paranoia, as Goldman put it, Hollywood is a place of routine, even numbing peril. That is how he first formulates his law, and he first applies it to studio executives. "Studio executives are intelligent, brutally overworked men and women who share one thing in common with baseball managers: they wake up every morning with the knowledge that sooner or later they are going to get fired." Gone, though, are the days when "a studio head might have said 'Let's make the goddam movie and hope the business guys know how to sell it.'"[32] Goldman's law, like the theme of risk paralysis, emerged in the early eighties, along with the consolidation of agency control.

This was no accident. As agencies initiated more projects, they sought, like CAA, to collect stars and protect them when necessary from worry that the films they wanted to be part of were not likely to succeed. At the same time that CAA was providing shelter to stars, it could also provide reassurance to studios. In this two-sided game, the specter of disaster was the agents' ever-present ally. Nestled within the discourse of risk CAA could alter the calculus; it could be an institution that predigested uncertainty in its ability to bring such an array of talented performers together. The agency promised to turn the unknowable into the ownable. CAA, in turn, could be embodied in the figure of its leader, Mike Ovitz, who could then be reembedded in the broader network of institutional and cultural relations that made him possible in the first place. The agency's challenge to studio control could become the basis for a much broader cultural reckoning because it cycled such a wide range of causes.

Here we reencounter the precession of causality from the economy through institutions, personalities, and cultural artifacts. One thing that separates creative industries from many similarly scaled capitalist enterprises is the way they make self-consciousness about this precession available across their component parts. As competing individuals and institutions attempt to sort through the myriad determinants of an industry's present state and its likely evolution, they seek competitive advantages. But as they compete, it is not enough for them to find a particular point of control. Instead, they must compete for control over which causes will be seen as controlling; they compete for the ground of generality and the suitability of a particular model to serve as the model of choice. "Perception is reality," as Sun Tzu put it.

The Agent Fairy

CAA's early recognition that filmmaking could be forced into the television mold paralleled Paramount's move to high concept. Both built on lessons from network television. Those lessons encouraged energized executives to seek drastic simplifications in certain aspects of feature film production in the hope that the yield would be a greater measure of control over an unpredictable process. And in both cases, the new narrative economy had a secondary yield: it opened or reopened a new channel for corporate self-definition. Changes in the industrial economy could be emblematized in particular projects, and a history of institutions would find ways of writing itself across the screen. Thus, by a second route, neoclassicism became possible.

The difference between strong studio and weak studio was the difference between Paramount and Columbia. By 1980 CAA had signed several *Saturday Night Live* stars (John Belushi, Dan Aykroyd, Bill Murray) as well as young director Ivan Reitman. Despite having representation, Reitman had an ex parte conversation with Eisner at Paramount about his idea for *Stripes*. He left believing he had come away with an enormous deal: three pictures to direct and five to produce. Overnight, though, Eisner reneged. In retaliation, Ovitz suggested taking *Stripes* to Frank Price at Columbia, where it became a hit.

The situation at Columbia was dire. Chief David Begelman had been forced to resign over an embezzlement scandal, and Price had been brought in to turn the studio around. After the success of *Stripes*, CAA found him a willing customer for its first major package, *Tootsie* (1982). The director (Sydney Pollack) and the stars (Dustin Hoffman, Murray, Teri Garr) were all clients. *American Gigolo*'s pimp and prostitute become *Tootsie*'s agent and client. Like all foundational moments in neoclassical Hollywood, the film becomes an allegory of its own authorship.

When Hoffman comes to call on his agent (played by director Pollack), the CAA offices he visits are not simply a set. They are the Columbia offices in drag as the New York office CAA did not yet have. Pollack doesn't wear Armani, and his office has none of the faux feng shui that the agency would cultivate. Nor is Pollack particularly dedicated to his client, explaining that his job is to "field offers." Michael retorts, "Who told you that, the agent fairy?" The joke here has at least two faces. To a broad audience, Hoffman seems to be entirely right in his demand for more attention from his agent. But to an internal, industrial audience, the real joke is in the idea that CAA agents would simply sit around fielding offers.

The proof of CAA's determination was on the screen, in its logo. *Tootsie* was an object lesson to the agency's clients that it would do right by them. And it signaled other studios and agencies that CAA was a force to be reckoned with. At the premiere, "an audible murmur swept through the audience" when the red CAA appeared.[33] When Laurie Perlman applied to be an agent trainee in 1976, "CAA was so poor they couldn't even afford a cover with the official CAA logo" when they sent out a script.[34] Now they had logos where they didn't even have offices. Indeed, like the infamous CAA license plates that adorned the Jaguars of the original five partners, the CAA plaque on Columbia's wall captured the agency at a time when notoriety served its interests.

Beyond this bit of logorrhea, the film showed that the attempt to port the packaging strategy from TV to film was working. At the most literal level, *Tootsie* was evidence that CAA could get its clients work. But Hollywood films don't live solely at the literal level. And when they tell stories of other kinds of performance—legitimate theater or television—Hollywood films usually proclaim the superiority of cinema to any possible alternative. In *A Face in the*

Figure 4.4.
Columbia's New York headquarters in drag as a CAA office. *Tootsie* (Sydney Pollack, Columbia, 1982)

Crowd (Kazan, Warners, 1957), a prototypical example, Hollywood's classical assuredness became the contention that only cinema could reveal the truth of television—could show us how venal the producer or the star might be when the cameras aren't supposed to be on (as in *Broadcast News* or *Scrooged* or *Death to Smoochy*). But in order to get the TV audience to see what the film audience already knows, there must be a rupture in the smooth flow of televisual lies. True to this history, in *Tootsie* Michael can break out of his Dorothy Michaels character only when the soap opera is forced to broadcast live, and only when he breaks out of television can he go on to the legitimate theater. Theater, here, stands as the truth of acting, just as live television is the truth of television. But both these truths are things film has known (and shown us) all along. And just as Michael needed to earn money and learn lessons from television in order to discover the truth of acting, so CAA learned its trade from television only to discover the truth of cinematic superiority. *Tootsie* and CAA pay lip service to the cult of cinema and the myth of television as mere apprenticeship to help justify the agency's increasing focus on film.

1987 Part I: Like Origami

By 1987, CAA constituted an industry-wide force, and the monopoly power it aspired to was nearly real. Because it controlled a substantial portion of the supply of talent, the agency could drive up its cost. At the same time, junk bonds and other new modes of studio finance joined the influx of independents to boost the demand. The exploding market for films on cable television and video supported this inflationary spiral on the way to a new equilibrium. While inflation had been conquered in the economy as a whole, it now congealed in the motion picture industry.

Still, each studio faced different and particular challenges, and each met them in its own way. What united the studios was not their shared economic context; that was too relentlessly particularized to define them. Instead, they shared a particular *view* of their position vis-à-vis the economy. They were all operating after the cultural divide. The Reagan era began by redescribing the problems of the American economy as problems of American culture. Once those enantiomorphic zones of concern had been folded upon one another, attention to "corporate culture" could stand in for, or even constitute, attention to culture or the economy as such. Every film might be read as a film about the film business, and as long as the situation held, that business would not need to be particularly disguised. The auteurs of the New Hollywood may have refired the personalities of the studios, but they had collectively failed to institutionalize their individual efforts. Now, as the studios individually reckoned with

CAA, their responses would be more than mere instances of inside baseball. The grandest efforts would contest for cultural authority and control, because that is what the stakes had become.

In this transition 1987 was the year of equipoise. Each part of the CAA assemblage—Armani, Japan, and packaging—had become notorious enough that it might be parodied, yet there was sufficient force behind each element that respectful homage remained possible. In 1982, CAA needed publicity. In 1987, it was no longer certain it did. On the one hand, *Maid to Order* could take potshots at the CAA fashion sense. On the other, *The Untouchables* (Brian De Palma, Paramount, 1987), with its Armani wardrobe, successfully reimagined Depression-era Chicago as a prêt-à-porter collection, with the Windy City's grand staircases substituting for the catwalk.

Into this balance strode the newly invigorated Disney, still looking for its first blockbuster. It already had a notoriously pecunious corporate culture. Eisner and Katzenberg had become infamous for casting outside the back door of the Betty Ford Clinic—that is, for seeking out stars whose bargaining power was no longer in line with their potential draw for audiences.[35] Disney's public desire to contain costs pitted it directly against CAA's inflationary plans. Out of that struggle emerged *Three Men and a Baby* (Leonard Nimoy, Disney, 1987), the *Citizen Kane* of anti-agency allegory. The most successful film of 1987, *Three Men* dominated the box office from Thanksgiving to New Year's. Yet alongside that financial dominance we find a near-total defense of the emergent neoclassical studio system.

Roger Ebert, reviewing the French predecessor, *Trois hommes et un couffin* (Coline Serreau, AAA, 1985), was disgusted: "I hated every second of this movie because it was so blind to psychology and reality, and so willing to settle for

Figure 4.5. Stairs are catwalks. *The Untouchables* (Brian De Palma, Paramount, 1987)

every relentless cliché. . . . Now comes the really bad news": Disney had bought it and was eager to remake it.[36] Chairman Michael Eisner offered a simple explanation: It was a huge hit in France. It also seemed exportable. While negotiating to build Euro-Disney, Eisner saw the film in Paris. (He was working on his French.) "I understood perhaps a third of what I heard, but responded to all the visual humor."[37]

But more than a possible hit, *Three Men* might be the first blockbuster of the Eisner regime at Disney—a "threshold" film he felt might be "the equivalent of *Stripes* or *Tootsie*." Eisner names those two films almost at random as successful comedies. But they were, as we have seen, crucial films for CAA. The first had been negotiated *away* from Eisner at Paramount; the second boldly displayed the agency's power over the studios it negotiated with. That agonistic background explains some of Eisner's determination to hold the line on costs. "We seriously considered stars for the two main roles, and even negotiated with Mike Ovitz for two of his biggest CAA clients, Dustin Hoffman and Bill Murray. Either one would have literally doubled the price of a film we were convinced was going to work on its own merits."[38] So what were the merits? A triumvirate of unrepentant bachelors are just getting used to their newly redesigned penthouse when they are presented with a baby to raise. The three men function as a self-contained studio with an actor (Ted Danson), an architect/editor/video librarian (Tom Selleck), and an artist/videographer (Steve Guttenberg).

The credits montage—with Gloria Estefan and the Miami Sound Machine singing "Bad Boys"—establishes them in the penthouse of the Prasada, an art deco apartment building on Central Park. Selleck sees his face reflected in the brass plaque that lets every visitor know that he redesigned the apartment. Comics artist Guttenberg is busy painting the elevator lobby with imagined scenes of them stepping out in white ties and tails against a Busby Berkeley backdrop. And Danson welcomes his agent—a buttoned-up professional woman in a red suit and big glasses—into the apartment, only to usher her out moments later, untucked, mussed, deglassed.

When the baby arrives, Selleck directs Guttenberg to "entertain it" while he is out buying food. Guttenberg asks, "How do you entertain a baby?" First, he tries a prismatic crystal ashtray, but the attractions of the colors and the expense are lost on the infant. Then he flaps his hands like wings. "Oh, look, it's almost like, look, Japanese origami, almost, with a hand." No good either, and another shot at Ovitz's Japanophilia. What entertains the baby is the three men singing together (the classics—fifties and sixties doo-wop); that is what entertains us, too, and that is what Disney knows and Ovitz does not.

Figure 4.6. The Armani-clad dealer arrives to collect his "package." *Three Men and a Baby* (Leonard Nimoy, Touchstone, 1987)

Set against our mini-studio is a drug dealer in the requisite unconstructed Armani jacket who arrives to claim his "package." Through a misunderstanding, the guys assume the dealer wants the baby. Selleck, for one, is disgusted: "I love how everyone keeps calling it 'the package.'" Eventually, they realize their mistake and fight to get the kid back. The dealer just wants the drugs. The opposition is implicit: studios nurture films like babies; agents sell packages like drugs.

Disney was willing to overpay for the rights to make *Three Men* and to fight to exclude Ovitz's stable of actors in order to show that in the studio's hands, the story of the "package" that could turn yuppie scum into adoring fathers could be the story of the right package at the right time, a movie that could turn TV actors like Ted Danson and Tom Selleck into movie stars. And in doing so, the film could confirm Disney's corporate emphasis on in-house development of stories and talent and increased control of the distribution process. Even Ebert loved it, down to the diaper-changing clichés. Of course, in between his pan of *Trois hommes* and his rave for *Three Men*, he and Siskel had signed a lucrative contract with Disney's newly launched Buena Vista Television.[39]

Katzenberg nearly took the allegory public. *Three Men* was the cost-conscious studio's revenge against CAA. In a *New York Times* profile that helped publicize the Katzenberg legend, Aljean Harmetz channeled him: "For two decades, studios have served as little more than traffic managers, buying expensive packages of stars and directors from ever-more-powerful agents. At Disney, the studio is once again in control."[40] Or, as he put himself, "We're a new version of the old studio system."

1987 Part II: The Art of the Art of the Deal

That winter of 1987, while Touchstone's *Three Men and a Baby* dominated the box office, Oliver Stone's *Wall Street* (Fox) blustered its way to the center of the cultural imaginary. Gordon Gekko's "greed is good" speech seemed to be the retroactive manifesto of the trading classes when it appeared two months after Black Monday, October 19. (The Dow lost more than a fifth of its value on that day.) That December, Donald Trump's *Trump: The Art of the Deal* appeared, and it opened with an almost modernist appreciation: "I don't do it for the money. I've got enough, much more than I'll ever need. I do it to do it. Deals are my art form."[41] In a sense, *Wall Street* encultured nearly every element of the CAA model: Sun Tzuian business strategy, a conflation of art with the art of the deal, and fine attention to the fashion system. Ovitz's victory was complete (Stone and Michael Douglas were both clients). Yet by the same token, the dispatching of these networked elements into the culture at large freed them from their origins. These signs and strategies were no longer the exclusive purview of agents and their adversaries; they could be put to other uses. In Stone's case, his ambivalence about financial legerdemain and the abuse of economic power turned inward, toward the necessities of studio decision making. Surely agents were important to the assembling of *Wall Street*, but the film does not seek to justify the ways of agents to men. Rather, it sidesteps them as it sorts through the studio biography. *Wall Street* was a memo and a mash note to Rupert Murdoch.

Gekko does not wear Armani; his bespoke suits do have an Italian designer, but they are as tightly structured as his deals. His formality is partly that of the Street, partly New York, and partly a defensive reaction to his class ascendancy ("Not bad for a City College boy"). He does, though, take Sun Tzu as his bible: "I don't throw darts at a board. I bet on sure things. Read Sun Tzu *The Art of War*: 'Every battle is won before it is ever fought.' Think about it." Here the ancient strategist is enlisted to justify insider trading. When America's business press first turned to "Japan, Inc.," the lure of Japanese business methods lay in labor-management partnerships, quality control, and state-backed industrial policy. By 1987, Sun Tzu made the Mephistophelean seductions of success at any price seem "strategic."

The object of Gekko's charms is Charlie Sheen, playing the studionymous Bud Fox. Bud managed to attract Gekko's attention through the CAA technique of deeply researching his personal life and giving him some Cuban cigars on his birthday. But he convinced Gekko to take his advice by slipping him inside information about his father's company, Bluestar Airlines. As Bud is drawn further into Gekko's circle, he becomes an expert in corporate espionage, eventually running an office cleaning company that specializes in stealing secrets. In the film's terms, Bud now wears his father's working-class uniform, but it is only a disguise.

Bud's initial assignment is Larry Wildman, a British raider modeled on Sir James Goldsmith and one of Gekko's principal competitors. Early in the film, Wildman seems to have tired of his greenmailing past. "This time I'm in for the long term. This is not a liquidation, Gordon. I'm going to turn it around. You're getting a free ride on my tail, mate, and with the dollars you're costing me to buy back the stock, I could modernize the plant. I'm not the only one who pays here, Gordon. We're talking about lives and jobs; three and four generations of steel workers." This solidarity has no attraction for Gekko, who responds by citing the numbers of workers Wildman has fired in the past. Nor does it appeal to Bud, who is still extricating himself from his own working-class background. Once Wildman leaves, Bud says to Gekko, "'All warfare is based on deception.' Sun Tzu says, 'If your enemy is superior, evade him; if angry, irritate him; if equally matched, fight . . . if not, split and reevaluate.'" In the third act, when Bud is forced to pit his loyalty to his father's airline against his loyalty to Gekko, Wildman will reappear as the white knight, a powerful, surrogate father Bud can turn to.[42] The battle is cleanly drawn. Despite a plan to turn Bluestar around, Gekko intends to wreck it. "Because it's wreckable, alright?!" If Wildman is Goldsmith, Gekko here would be Carl Icahn, who took apart TWA. Bud will swing the deal to Wildman and save his father's job.

A month before *Wall Street* premiered, *Time* described Sir James Goldsmith's strategy as "simple." "His targets were almost invariably old companies that had strayed from their original purpose through diversification, acquired too many senior managers, and were selling at a good deal below their breakup value. He would break them up, sell off the odds and ends, streamline the core and move on to the next project."[43] Goldsmith, the Shiva of the business world, was the avatar of "core competency" and the unraveller of conglomerates. Wildman is the same, but with a crucial difference: Because he has been angling for control of an airline, he has had to revoke his British citizenship and become an American.

The story may be about airlines, but the allusions are to battles for media control. From 1982 to 1984, Murdoch had, more or less hostilely, moved in on Warners. In response, CEO Steve Ross executed a complicated stock swap with Chris-Craft that gave WCI control over a large number of television stations.

And television stations, like airlines, are some of the very few companies re-stricted to American owners. Ownership restrictions cost Murdoch Warners, but he did manage to cash out. Yet his new status as a greenmailer seemed to bother him; Wildmanian pangs of conscience were breaking out: "I'm about building a company. I'm not about making money in the stock market. I thought I was getting quite the wrong reputation."[44] Murdoch began "repair-ing" that reputation by agreeing to buy 50 percent of Fox from Marvin Davis in March 1985 and then by buying Metromedia later that spring. In a two-month period, Murdoch had managed to buy half a major studio and a chain of televi-sion stations that would eventually form the backbone of the Fox network. The fictional Wildman became an American citizen on February 15, 1985; the actual Murdoch did so on September 4.[45]

If in the media allegory, Wildman is Murdoch, then Gekko is Kirk Ker-korian. In his directorial commentary, Stone redescribes the scene in which Bud discovers Gekko's real plan for the airline. It is no longer about Icahn and TWA; this is a Hollywood story:

> They're gonna cannibalize that airline. . . . Strip it, and sell the parts. Just like Kirk
> Kerkorian destroyed MGM and UA. When the United States allowed Kerkorian to
> buy both companies, studios and destroy both of them it was like the end of the
> movie business as we used to know it. UA and MGM were two great companies.
> Suddenly they were one lousy company. And Kerkorian did it for the same reasons
> that Gekko [did]; he did it for money. He didn't care one *iota* for making a good
> film. Never. That was never his intention. It was only to sell things. He's the guy who
> sold titles, he sold the name, he sold the naming rights, he sold the lion. He sold
> pieces. He cannibalized. That's what Gekko is doing.[46]

At the end of the film, when Martin Sheen tells his son that jail might be good for him so he will learn to "create instead of living off the buying and selling of others," it may sound like an old-style populist critique of finance capital-ism. But in the late 1980s, populism had been almost completely co-opted by right-wing ideologues like Murdoch. When the naturalized American visited Reagan's FCC to seek their blessing of his studio/TV station purchase, govern-ment approval was a foregone conclusion. As James H. Quello, a Nixon ap-pointee still serving on the FCC at the time, put it, "There was a good feeling at the commission about having an Australian turn American and becoming a big player in the communications industry."[47] They were confident that Murdoch was not going to "bust up" Metromedia but rather use it to "create" a competi-tor to the big three networks. Which is just what he did.

1987 Part III: Making Connections

If *Three Men and a Baby* defended the new classical studio against the predations of the arriviste agent-dealers, *Wall Street* displaced that battle onto a struggle between potential studio bosses. The battles of the studios against the agencies were particularized and internalized in preparation for the takeover mania that would seize the industry for the next decade. In those transactions, agents might be important—indeed, Ovitz would play a crucial role in the Matsushita purchase of Universal—but they no longer occupied the crucial spot in the value chain where assemblage might morph into creativity. Before the precession of causality overtook them, CAA offered a grand apologia for the agent's life.

Rain Man is the story of a dealer who finds his soul. It was also a package that, by all accounts, Ovitz held together and restarted several times, first when director Martin Brest left the production, then when Steven Spielberg had to leave to direct *Indiana Jones and the Last Crusade.* The project had been set up at UA with Peter Guber and Jon Peters producing, but had stalled as the studio imploded (again) under Kerkorian's machinations. The film was a hit, but UA had already shuttered its studio and could not gain any momentum from it. For CAA, though, it confirmed the packaging strategy by winning Best Picture, Director, Actor, and Screenplay. This was the confluence of talent that Ovitz and his partners had sought, and now they were being recognized for the aesthetic results of their economic model.

Rain Man opens with the arrival of four Lamborghinis and Tom Cruise's attempts to get them sold. The cars have not been approved by the Environmental Protection Agency (EPA), his swing loans are coming due, and the buyers are getting cold feet, so he bluffs his way through several phone calls. Along the way, he tells his banker the check is in the mail, he suggests bribing the EPA inspector, and he knocks five thousand dollars off the price of two of the cars to keep the buyers happy. Fires doused, he asks his girlfriend, "Ready for Palm Springs?" When she is incredulous that he would leave before the deals are actually settled, he is ultraconfident: "We're seconds away from closing this deal and clearing seventy-five grand. Not bad for a couple of phone calls, huh?"

If actors can have stock scenes, then this is Tom Cruise's. His trademark set piece consists of him rolling calls, often in a headset. Narratively, it is a dialogue, but experientially, it is a monologue. Such scenes allow him to use his body against his voice. Because he is an acousmatic figure for the person on the other end of the phone, he can tip us to moments when he is lying or secretly overjoyed or hiding his true feelings. The phone, like the suit, puts the body in evidence.

Figure 4.7. Tom Cruise on the phone: in the 1980s, closing a deal in *Rain Man*; in the 1990s, demanding someone show him the money in *Jerry Maguire*; and in the 2000s, promising to "rain down an ungodly fucking firestorm" on the terrorists in *Tropic Thunder*. *Rain Man* (Barry Levinson, UA, 1988); *Jerry Maguire* (Cameron Crowe, TriStar, 1996); *Tropic Thunder* (Ben Stiller, DreamWorks, 2008)

Cruise's Italian clothes (like his Italian cars and his Italian girlfriend) fit him especially well. He wears his shirt buttoned to the top without a tie—"we just thought it was an unusual look for the time," Levinson said. And when he enlists his autistic brother, Raymond, in a card-counting scheme at Caesar's Palace, there will be the de rigueur eighties makeover scene, this time shot largely from Raymond's perspective, "[o]nly sort of showing things that Raymond would react to: lines, shadows, forms, the tassel."[48] They emerge dressed for success.

It is too simple, perhaps, to see the mathematical savant Raymond as the logical extreme of the deal-juggling agent. And it is certainly too simple to see the film as a sympathy plea on behalf of agents everywhere. Still, when Hoffman says of the autistic adults he studied in preparation for the role, "Each of us felt that if we gave these people enough love, if we conversed with them—because we liked them—if we hugged them, if we kissed them, that somehow it would be like a magic wand and they would be released from it," or when Cruise says, "And really Charlie is kind of an emotional autistic is kind of the way we looked at him," such parallels are hard to overlook.[49]

In the film's pivotal scene, Charlie discovers that Raymond is the "Rain Man," the mysterious voice who sang to him and comforted him when he was a baby. They share a chorus of the Beatles' "I Saw Her Standing There." But that wistful revelation is swiftly doubled when Charlie figures out that Raymond was sent away to an institution after accidentally scalding him in the bathtub. Raymond's present horror at "[h]ot water burn baby" is out of place, but it literalizes the

Figure 4.8. The Brothers Babbitt, sporting the buttoned-up-yet-tieless look that Sean Connery wore in *The Untouchables*. *Rain Man* (Levinson, UA, 1988)

ongoing moral violation that has kept the brothers apart or the viewer's sense of that violation, or both. Raymond has been held in guilty abeyance for decades. Not that he could apologize, but had the brothers been kept together, he would have been able to demonstrate his good will. Yet as producer Mark Johnson put it, "The movie's about Charlie. It's not about Raymond. Because Charlie's the one who changes and quite frankly that's why we go to the movies."[50] Charlie recognizes not merely that he has been deprived of his brother but also that he has been somehow responsible for his brother's institutionalization, and that had he known as much, he might have been able to demonstrate his own good will, at least to Raymond. "I'm not burned. It's okay."

This is a complicated and sentimental moment for Charlie, but it is a more complicated and sentimental moment for the agent who might see himself caught up in a system that allocates responsibility unjustly, and without recourse. If it vouches for the Babbitts' humanity, it vouches for Ovitz's as well. The film withdraws from this anagnorisis when it turns to the broad humor of the card-counting scenes in Las Vegas and the brutal black humor of the hearing on Raymond's confinement. In this penultimate scene, Hoffman and Cruise (CAA clients) sit at the table with two doctors, played by Jerry Molen, the film's producer, and Barry Levinson, the director (and another agency client). Charlie, back in his soulful-agent mode, speaks of "making a connection" with Raymond, and the viewer knows that connection is what matters. Cruise-as-Babbitt may be the avatar of CAA, but when Cruise and Hoffman put their heads together, they are the agency's emblem. The logo in *Tootsie* announced CAA's presence where it did not have one; by 1988, such puffery was no longer necessary.

Looking back, the pinnacle of Ovitz's power was likely early 1989. In a cover story for the *New York Times Magazine*, L. J. Davis noted, "Four films released late [in 1988] with deep CAA involvement—*Rain Man, Twins, Scrooged,* and *Mississippi Burning*"—had grossed $380 million by July.[51] The agency moved into its landmark I. M. Pei building on Wilshire that summer. Producer Mark Johnson, director Barry Levinson, and Dustin Hoffman all thanked Ovitz from the stage at the Academy Awards. Yet by the end of that year, Ovitz would be—after Gordon Gekko—the most prominent example of a man whose infatuation with Sun Tzu and Japanese discipline had led to his (partial) undoing. When screenwriter Joe Eszterhas wanted to leave the agency to return to his former agent, Ovitz, apparently, told him, "My foot soldiers who go up and down Wilshire Boulevard each day will blow your brains out."[52] The system that Ovitz claimed to manage whipsawed between extremes of adulation and notoriety. Now that CAA no longer needed press, it was impossible to avoid. For the cover story in the *New York Times Magazine*, he could say, "We represent a lot of gifted people, and I've felt consistently that those are the ones the press should be talking about, not those of us who work behind the scenes,"[53] but this gnomic posture only fed the momentum.

CAA did not vanish because Disney or Fox was able to work around it in a particular instance. Accumulations of power in institutions often outlive their sustaining logics. Still, in 1987, even *Maid to Order* knew the score. Late in the film, there is a charity event designed to showcase Stan Starkey's latest "discovery," a singer named "Dude." In the audience are the imaginary Harvey Bessman, head of Universal; George Sterling, head of Capitol Records; and Alicia Nolin, of CAA. "These three could make or break Dude and I overnight," Stan says. He may not know much about fashion (or grammar), but he knows power when he sees it.

Part II

The Projections
Neoclassicism in Action

How should we attend to the surface of the world? If that is too grand a question, it might be brought back to instances: How should we attend to what we see on-screen? What does it hide? What does it cover? What does it inevitably reveal? And what might we mean by the depths of that surface?

A confident, self-conscious play of surfaces characterizes neoclassical Hollywood. The classical demand for legibility and the pressures of the system recast striking images as corporate or industrial emblems. One-sheets, trailers, production stills to accompany reviews, catchphrases and mottoes that appeal to critics and audiences, occasions for word of mouth, fodder for annual reports and compilation reels—such destinies color the emblems themselves. All the phases of Hollywood production may find their allegories in such moments. Yet this surplus meaning, slipped in between the compressed planes of the surface, might always go uncomprehended. Emergent or dissolving, immanent or pro-

Figure PII.1.
Groundhog Day
(Harold Ramis, Columbia, 1993)

Figure PII.2. *Jurassic Park* (Spielberg, Universal, 1993)

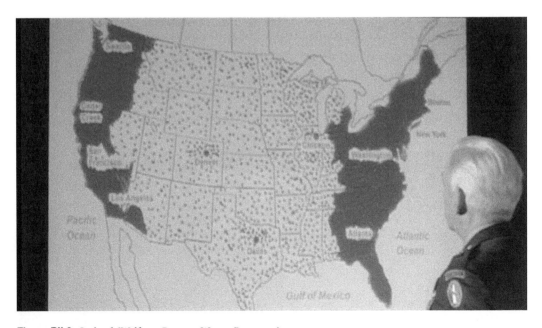

Figure PII.3. *Outbreak* (Wolfgang Petersen, Warner Bros., 1995)

Figure PII.4. *Speed* (Jan De Bont, Fox, 1994)

jective, these stratigraphic meanings retain their deniability, and in deniability neoclassicism reins in its insistence on complete legibility. "Read me!" the image says. "Oh. But not *that* way."

The stills pictured are postcards from the stages of the moviemaking process. In the first, from *Groundhog Day* (Harold Ramis, Columbia, 1993), a producer's body vanishes into the map, into the nation; only her head, hands, and buttons linger. She is about to embark on a location shoot while simultaneously developing the script with "the talent." Production design anticipates special effects in *Jurassic Park* (Steven Spielberg, Universal, 1993) when a dinosaur's head becomes the screen on which we read her genetic code. She may be animatronic, but the code upon her face stands in for the computer code that generates the film's digital dinosaurs.[1] In *Outbreak* (Wolfgang Petersen, Warner Bros., 1995), another map appears behind a general going over "the projections" for the president. How will a horrible disease spread throughout the United States? His answer constitutes a guess at the riddle of distribution. *Speed* (Jan De Bont, Fox, 1994) rescues the passengers of a doomed city bus so that they might watch it plow into an airplane and explode. We see the explosion twice before the reflection of the fireball ripples across the windows in front of the former passengers and they are blown back. That audience is us, more or less. Under the sway of such powerful images, we all become passengers on Plato's public transit system.

These images join dozens and perhaps hundreds of others that solicit but do not require such reading and identification. That gap between possibility and necessity is the arena in which identity may be tried on and the future (or the past) imagined. Sealed into this thinnest of envelopes may be a letter for a studio, a producer, a star-turned-auteur. In the chapters that follow, we will match the decryption of such letters with the circumstances and motives behind their composition. Yet no matter how metonymic or discursive those moments and contexts may be, what matters most is their projective capacity, their power to suggest an ideal order of composition.

Paramount II
The Residue of Design

The Mountain's on Fire

In the classical era, formulas provided filmmakers with an alibi of stability and control. To Adorno, though, that control evacuated the aesthetic potential of the work, leaving a desert of self-advertisement. "The so-called leading idea is like a filing compartment which creates order, not connections."[1] But in the emergent neoclassical era, the "leading idea" was rechristened high concept, and the point of high concept was not that it might make the risky business of film controllable, although certainly many of its great practitioners at times believed as much. Rather, the point of high concept was that it would make the assertion of control explicit, and this explicit assertion could then serve as the basis for a systematic approach to the movie business. At its most intense, the flurry of self-reference might manage to fashion a web of ersatz connections thick enough to revivify the studio. At Paramount this assertion was ramified throughout the studio and its products. At the conceptual level it appeared as the confident claim that the studio could control (craft, calibrate, design) the level of aesthetic achievement of its films; at the practical level it appeared in the form of design as such.

In the wake of Sylbert's replacement by Eisner, Paramount's commitment to design migrated down the studio hierarchy. And while production designers would continue to benefit from their new status—on William Friedkin's *Sorcerer*, for example, designer John Box is credited before screenwriter Walon Green—the more enduring continuity appeared as the studio's preference for art school–trained directors such as Adrian Lyne (*Flashdance*), Michael Mann (*The Keep*), and Tony Scott (*Top Gun*) or for directors who were themselves willing to accommodate themselves to the new order, to trade "violence for design," as Schrader put it.[2]

How does one make that trade? Conceptually it is not a radical exchange, for the violence of the mid-seventies was a paranoid violence, and paranoia entails implicit design. The radical suspicion necessary to understand the system—whether that system was the US government or a Hollywood studio—required a belief in the coherence of the system's effects, and that coherence irresistibly suggests authorship. Paramount was the likeliest place for that attribution of authorship to take root. The paranoid narrative at the center of the New Hollywood of the seventies was more pervasive there than at other studios, whether in its films (*The Parallax View*, *Chinatown*, *Nashville*) or its own auteur-institution (the Directors Company). Directors, writers, stars, and others could (and did) see studios as both instances and analogues of the system they opposed. Accused of the worst sorts of manipulation, studios might react in various ways, but they had to react. They could be appeasing, as the executive corps at United Artists continued to be up through the *Heaven's Gate* debacle; they could up the ante, as Warners did; or they could be oddly appreciative, as Paramount was. This last reaction redirects rebellious energy in ways that prove useful to the organization. So it is not surprising that when Schrader moved from Universal (*Blue Collar*, 1978) and Columbia (*Hardcore*, 1978) to Paramount and Bruckheimer (*American Gigolo*), he felt that something had changed. At the mountain, every warrant for studio authorship was also a warrant for design (that is, concept) over violence (that is, practical bearings). Or, to put it in both more Adornian and more practical terms, with high concept, Paramount turned paranoia into advertising.

That process took more than a decade to run its course. First, the last of the New Hollywood projects had to be liquidated. In their wake, the studio pieced together an identity out of nostalgic pieces of intellectual property (*Star Trek: The Motion Picture* and its sequel, *The Wrath of Khan*), its defining agon with CAA, its quasi-properties (Eddie Murphy, the "popsical" genre), and, ultimately, what Bordwell will call a "stylish style."[3] Indeed, at each step, Paramount will test its ownership claims—its identity—by asking whether its style is more important than its material assets. That dialectic reached one of its crises with Friedkin's *Sorcerer*.

Friedkin did not entirely leave Paramount when he left the Directors Company without directing a feature for it. His long-gestating remake of Henri Clouzot's *Wages of Fear* (Cinédis, 1953) was set up by Paramount and Universal and eventually financed through Cinema International Corporation (CIC)—their joint venture for European distribution.[4] Studios were allowed to coproduce on a case-by-case basis, but they could not codistribute in the United States. In Europe, where the antitrust regime was weaker, Paramount enticed Universal to set up a joint distribution arm in 1970 (MGM would join three years later). In rare cases, such as *Sorcerer*, that entity would bankroll particular films. There were three reasons to go through the shell game. First, and most significantly, by setting up the company abroad (Paramount chose the

Netherlands), they could avoid paying taxes on the money until it was repatriated to the United States. And as a pioneering multinational, Paramount could defer the day of repatriation indefinitely. "[T]he end result, for both companies, was the same," Diller explained; "the money was mainly not to be repatriated, the taxes not paid. It was a brilliant tax dodge." Arthur Barron, executive vice president of Paramount, estimated that between $100 million and $200 million was deferred each year.[5] Second, films could be funded with money—"captive profits"—that was held abroad. (MGM had used its London studio in precisely this way in the postwar period.) In ideal cases, such films could even benefit from European production subsidies.

Finally, one could pursue such economic convolutions for reasons that were almost aesthetic. Gulf + Western under Charlie Bluhdorn conducted virtually all of its business this way and on a grand, even imperial scale. Thanks to G+W, the economy of the Dominican Republic was being run along the CIC model. The Balaguer government had imposed capital constraints that limited the amount of money G+W could repatriate annually to a percentage based on the overall value of the company's investment in the country. But whenever, at the end of the calendar year, the Dominican central bank found itself short of foreign exchange reserves, G+W "prepaid" its first-quarter taxes, amounting to tens of millions of dollars. In exchange, the government would raise the value it placed on the company's investment, thus increasing the amount of money G+W could extract. The scheme was both dangerous and illegal. Dangerous because Balaguer's government faced leftist opposition that wanted to nationalize the country's sugar industry, and cutting a sweetheart deal with the foreign multinational was precisely the wrong sort of publicity. Illegal because these machinations were never disclosed to G+W shareholders. Piqued by reports of misdeeds in the Dominican Republic, the complex Paramount-related tax schemes, and the use of corporate assets and relationships with banks to enrich key executives, the Securities and Exchange Commission (SEC) had launched a multiyear investigation into the company in 1975. A series of articles written by Seymour Hersh detailing the allegations ran in the *New York Times* over the course of three days in July 1977, only a month after *Sorcerer* opened. Eighteen months later, when negotiations between G+W and the SEC broke down, the government filed charges. Finally, a settlement that required virtually nothing from the company was struck in 1981.[6]

Sorcerer's narrative mimicked, even, we might say, plumbed the multinationality of its underwriters. The production shot in Tel Aviv, Paris, New Jersey, Mexico, New Mexico, and, its longest and most frustrating location, the Dominican Republic. Gone were the days when a range of French locations would have to stand in for the rugged terrain of the Ruritanian Latin American country in *Wages of Fear*. Now, running from unions and into the open arms of waiting tax havens, it often became cheaper to mount a Bond-style travelogue than to search for ersatz locations closer to L.A. Still, within this peregrine mode of production, the Dominican Republic stood out. However onerous the conditions and however difficult it was to undertake a major production in a country without a substantial film industry, for Friedkin, it was a zone of moral clarity. It was Gulf + Western's industrial backlot, a place where the complexities of contemporary cinematic contracts and the opacities of authorship could perhaps be pushed to the side in favor of strongly delineated hierarchies of exploitation. At the top there were absent capitalists in a tense but mutually enabling partnership with the militarized state. At the bottom, there were hordes of casual laborers in a society of unrelenting squalor. Between them one found only the thinnest sliver of a managerial class. Whatever his class position in Los Angeles, on location, Friedkin could find himself on the side of the angels, at worst a comprador and at best one of the laboring many. He carried that class masquerade back to Los Angeles. Taking after his protagonist, Friedkin wore mechanic's coveralls to a grand, drunken, post-production clash with Diller and Universal's Sid Sheinberg in the Universal cafeteria.[7]

In its characters and its society, *Sorcerer* was a drastic simplification of Clouzot's film. To begin with, in *Wages of Fear*, there are far more managers in country. The corporation, SOC, is clean, efficient, and American. Its plant is modern; its employees uniformed; its trucks new and well maintained. Despite the neocolonialists' best efforts, a gas pocket has blown up one of their oil wells. Worse, the locals are fed up with the company's poor safety record, and they talk of organizing against it. When O'Brien, the Coca-Cola-drinking boss, goes looking for desperate men to drive trucks full of nitro to the site, he does it because "those bums don't have any union." The bums do have a fairly robust emotional life, masking their traumatic backstories with world-weary humor. Meanwhile, the folks around them wallow in sentimental piety and a relatively noble poverty. In *Sorcerer*, this familiar social world goes by the wayside. The rig explosion is the result of anti-imperial terrorism (the terrorists never appear; they will go unpunished); the locals rise up in a blind rage; and the idea of a union is ludicrous. *Wages of Fear* rests its political allegory on a bedrock of existential actuality, and the plot of the film is, in part, the excavation of that universal ground. *Sorcerer*, in contrast, rigs the game from the start. Politics and society are a veneer, barely covering the animalistic violence of this backward hellhole. Reviewing the film for the *New York Times*, Vincent Canby thought the film was "pretty tame"; "the poverty of

Latin America and the ruthlessness of the oil company . . . are of less political than atmospheric importance."[8]

What are the formal consequences of the political or philosophical shift from *Wages'* existentialism to *Sorcerer's* ironies? When nuance gives way to a relentless (and that is the word critics pro and con have always used for the film) actuality, any attempt to reopen the fictive world to interpretation is bound to seem arbitrary. That is, for a rounded character like O'Brien, his every action constitutes and reinforces his Americanness. But in the semiotically impoverished world of *Sorcerer*, what signs we do have are charged—they are vehicles of irony or allegory. And in the Dominican Republic, the privileged referent of that allegory was Gulf + Western. As Biskind recounts, "When Friedkin needed a photo for the office wall of the board of directors of the rapacious oil company that has a death grip on the fictional Latin American country where the action is set, he tore a photo out of Gulf + Western's annual report and used it. 'To me, they looked like a bunch of thugs,' says Friedkin. According to [screenwriter Walon] Green, 'When Bluhdorn saw his picture, he had a shit hemorrhage.'"[9]

Or so Green and Friedkin might have wished. There is a problem with this last, irresistible anecdote. The picture, from the company's 1975 annual report, does not include Bluhdorn, who actually appears on the next page, where he does not look like a thug at all. Moreover, the remaining executives (who do, it is true, look like thugs) would have been all but anonymous, and that anonymity allowed the studio to leave the scene untouched. (It is hard to imagine a

Figure 5.1. The Corepet board of directors, a "bunch of thugs," from the Gulf + Western annual report. *Sorcerer* (William Friedkin, Paramount/ Universal, 1977)

CEO having "a shit hemorrhage" and allowing the offending image to remain if he thought it would be recognized.) Friedkin, then, had happened upon a deniable, allegorical assertion of corporate responsibility. It was a sharper accusation against Gulf + Western than Mel Brooks's shot at "Engulf and Devour" in *Silent Movie* (Fox, 1976), but it was also safely *inside*. The gag in *Sorcerer* is as solipsistic and perverse as the rest of the film.

Given the rank egotism of its production, one might expect *Sorcerer* to be a strident assertion of directorial authorship. Yet as explicit as its allegory could be, and as private as its symbology might seem, *Sorcerer* is an oddly tacit film. While the title seems a fitting sequel to *The Exorcist*, and there are flashes of that film's demon Pazuzu—it looms darkly behind the title credit and later shows up on a rock face and a truck—these glimpses would be missed by any but the most obsessive fans. Moreover, the eponymous sorcerer is not a person but rather one of the trucks loaded with nitro that the men will drive through the jungle. More perversely still, it is not the truck that Roy Scheider manages to get within a couple kilometers of the raging oil well—that truck is *Lázaro*—but rather the truck that will explode far from the finish line when (thuddingly ironically) a tire blows out just after the French driver grows sentimental about his engraved watch and his abandoned wife. To know even this much about the trucks, though, one would have to be paying very careful attention. (Canby called the title "meaningless," suspected it had something to do with *The Exorcist*, and left it at that.) There is simply no discourse about *Sorcerer* the truck in *Sorcerer* the film.

And it is a scene without discourse that lies at the heart of the film. An hour in, the men have been chosen, and they will soon set off. Before they do so, they must prepare their trucks. In *The Wages of Fear*, competent mechanics assure the trucks are road-ready and a gang of uniformed laborers load them with cans of nitro while the men drink shots of company liquor to steady their nerves. In Friedkin's version, our teams of drivers must scavenge barely functional parts from the wrecking yard in order to fashion their Frankenstein's monster trucks. As a montage, it is canny and efficient. It falls into four parts: choosing the trucks, working on the engines, working on the exteriors, and loading the cargo. The last is handled as a separate sequence in long takes of nearly half a minute each in order to keep the tension high. The first three parts are punctuated by shots of an assassin planning his next move and of the raging well fire. Backing the whole is a Tangerine Dream cue ("Creation") that only rarely syncs up with the action on-screen. The assembly process culminates with a shot of the patched-together *Sorcerer*, now decked out in a motley assemblage of lights. (We know it is the culmination because the score plinks as each bank of lights is switched on.) In keeping with the film's infernal imagination, the montage makes clear that with the lighting array, the men have borrowed some of the oil fire's power and some of the assassin's malice. But where the fire is chaotic and the assassin is dark and murky, the truck is overwhelmingly backlit, and the surrounding fog only etches its silhouette more sharply. There is no other shot in the film like it. Were this a makeover sequence from half a decade hence, this would be the big reveal.

That is how Universal's marketing arm understood it.[10] When it came time to market the film—that is, to find its metadiscourse—the trailer took its cue from this sequence, beginning with the score. We hear "Creation" while a voice-over plays up Friedkin's authorship—touting, understandably, *The French Connection* and *The Exorcist* before introducing *Sorcerer*. Pazuzu's face fades up from the blackness and the title is laid over it, tightening the connection between the Friedkin the audience knows and the Friedkin they will get. More than half the trailer then passes without any voice-over or, even more strikingly, any diegetic sound. And in that ninety seconds, the backstories of the four men are told, telescopically. The voice-over returns to tell us the men will "risk the only thing they have left to lose" (this is when we see the backlit truck), only to fall silent again. A montage collapses the entire cross-country drive into less than a minute before the voice returns: "Roy Scheider, in a new film by William Friedkin, *Sorcerer*." Only credits, the corporate title ("A Paramount-Universal Release"), and the rating information remain. Like the one-sheet, the trailer is tacit—we never hear what the sorcerer is—and depersonalized—no character

Figure 5.2.
The automotive makeover. *Sorcerer* (Friedkin, Paramount/ Universal, 1977)

is named. What humans we see appear as unreliable appendages of the systems they have created. In the climactic shot, Amidou hangs off the side of the truck in silhouette; similarly, he (or his stuntman) is the lone visible person in the one-sheet as well, but he is crawling on all fours and looking downward while the gate-mouthed face of the demonomorphic truck dominates the image.[11]

With *Sorcerer*, Friedkin wanted to strip away the niceties of first-world corporate life to reveal the brutal processes that made that life possible. The men who have sought refuge in Porvenir are looking for an escape from their responsibilities—three are on the run from the law (Rabal, the assassin; Amidou, the terrorist; and Cremer, the bankster); one, from the mob (Scheider). They discover that life outside the system is no life at all. This discovery can seem existential, as it does in *Wages of Fear*, or it can seem ironic, as it does when Cremer and Scheider meet their ends. The men have all realized this, so they are willing to submit to the whims of Corepet, the American oil company—anything to get back inside the system.

Seen one way, Friedkin's paranoia, like Lucas's, was the cost of doing business with an auteur. An executive might harbor doubts about the marketability of the project, but in his very person, the successful auteur answered them. Seen another way, that paranoia was not an obvious and unfortunate cost but an implicit benefit. Friedkin (and Lucas, and Coppola) had a deeper belief in the omnipotence of the studio than most studio executives and owners did, and if those owners could come to understand precisely how it was that a company could exercise power through its freelancers, they might be able to reconstruct something like a studio system, one appropriate to the modes of labor and contract that now underpinned the industry. Indeed, by locating the *Sorcerer* project at CIC, Friedkin found himself stretched between the newest New Hollywood economics and some of the oldest. The deal, the financing, the labor force, and the production process were all unquestionably modern. Yet the same undeveloped antitrust regime that made CIC possible encouraged the three member studios to set it up as an epigone of the classical era: it handled some production, a great deal of distribution, and, through its own theater chain, exhibition. Thirty years after the Paramount case consent decrees had ended the classical system, Friedkin found himself working for the remake. In *Sorcerer*, he reminded the studio of that fact.

Dance Yourself Clean

If high concept at Paramount originated as both a reaction to and a counterreading of the auteurist revolt, it quickly found its principal target: CAA. The studio and the agency battled for control over individual projects, and each struggle was legible as a metonym for the system as a whole. As CAA attempted to monopolize talent, Paramount responded both economically and aesthetically. The economic response, widely adopted in the industry, was the multipicture deal. In these arrangements (which, of course, varied in every case), the studio guaranteed a star's salary in exchange for his or her services on a defined number of films. To the extent that the star was interested in control, the studio might set her up in a first-look production deal that would front a certain amount of overhead in exchange for the first option to finance any projects her company developed for a delimited period. While these deals created enduring ties between studio and star that might serve as a counterweight to the star's allegiance to her talent agency, such arrangements contributed to the morass of opening credits on particular films. Thus, such deals complicated studio planning even as they routinized it, and studios, particularly Paramount, could find themselves ever more dependent on deal making while simultaneously forced into their classic roles as cultivators of star personae. The interplay between money, stardom, and credit may have been contractually secured off-screen, but the continuing value of those settlements, as ever, depended on their on-screen success. At Paramount, the crucial figure in this new system, the figure that promised to convert an arrangement into a system, was Eddie Murphy.

We will return to Murphy's career, but it is sufficient to say that at Paramount he performs the role that Japan did for CAA: It is through him that the disposition of productive forces can be reimagined as the exercise of a particular aesthetic knack; it was through Japan that, for Hollywood and America, economics became culture. In the case of Paramount, I have been arguing, the aesthetic antedates the new economics, whether that aesthetic is simply the relative prominence of design or the apparently disposable bits of allegory, be they photos on a wall (*Sorcerer*) or logo bleeds out of the credits (*Raiders*). The material adjustments of the eighties complicated the production process, but they were ultimately consistent with the industry's overarching drive to find the appropriate degree of contingency—to balance risk and certainty. And while these new arrangements required justification, they did not require a *particular* rationale. CAA's discourse of risk mitigation was one readily available theory of how the system should work. In contrast, Paramount's response to CAA's promise of risk mitigation was to trumpet the importance of *choice*. On that account, a collection of cofinancing arrangements and back-end deals could contain risk, when risk needed to be contained. (Diller explained it this way: "Movies are risks. . . . You can never believe you've got it figured out. Well, I happen to believe in sharing risk. I don't mind giving up some of the upside— and believe me, we always get more than we give in these deals—to protect the downside.")[12] And with the financial risk managed, the decision to make or not make a particular film with particular players could be reinterpreted not as a willingness to take on a certain level of risk—even if it remained just that—but rather as the exercise of studio prerogative. This is the ground tone of every reflection by the Killer Dillers on their Paramount days. "The one thing you cannot be bad at in this business is choosing material. . . . This is a business based on ten to twelve decisions a year. They are very important. Nothing else is close," Eisner asserted in 1984.[13] We have already seen how he later converted anti-CAA animus into an allegory of Disney's newfound commitment to live action. Dawn Steel, who would move up the Paramount executive ladder before leaving to head production at Columbia, considered "break[ing] the agents' hold on Hollywood" Diller's overarching strategy:

> He refused to sit around waiting for agents to sell him packages that already came with a script, an actor and a director. By and large, movies were much more expensive that way, to say nothing of the fact that you didn't get to choose the combination of talent you wanted to work with. Under Diller, Paramount developed its own movies, created its own packages. It was our responsibility to get our own ideas and develop them.[14]

Steel accuses "the agents" in general, but Don Simpson was more direct: "[CAA] would say, Look, we got this project, so-and-so is the writer, we want to connect so-and-so to it. . . . We would get into big fights. I would say I'm not interested in so-and-so. I'm interested in the idea and the writer. We will make the choices as to who will produce it, and who will direct it."[15]

What exactly did the Killer Dillers bring to the fight? They had confidence and commitment to be sure, but also the assurance of a deep-pocketed corporate parent; the resources of genre, particularly the new musicals and fish-out-of-water comedies; and, finally, a certain degree of luck. But luck, Dodgers manager Branch Rickey often said, is the residue of design.[16] And the institutional and aesthetic elevation of choice required a particular facility with the permutations of Hollywood. At the highest level, it meant choosing "the combination of talent you wanted" as Steel put it, "who will produce it, and who will direct it," as Simpson said. But this belief in choice-as-combination imposed far-reaching requirements. It entailed a theory of narrative, of stardom, of editing, of cinematography, and of promotion. The greatest threat to choice was, unsurprisingly, grit: "'There are rare times when the material you read in a script plays better on the screen,' says Diller, 'but in general it gets worse. If you keep the selection process clean—in the mainstream of your interest—you've got a prayer of success.'"[17]

Whether it was called the "dance musical" or the neomusical or the popsical, it was at home at Paramount. In the genre's decade-long heyday, only *Fame* (Alan Parker, MGM, 1980) and *Dirty Dancing* (Emile Ardolino, Vestron, 1987) would be hits for other studios, while Paramount had *Saturday Night Fever, Grease, Urban Cowboy, Flashdance, Staying Alive,* and *Footloose.* For *Fever* and *Grease,* the studio initially found itself in the position of student. But it became clear within months that the fundamental requirement of the new musical was that it match its audience with its image. So Paramount watched as *Grease* was cleansed and immediately applied that lesson, remaking *Fever* in the new *Grease*'s image, remaking Travolta as his televisual self. If high concept depended on the "pre-sold property" for its success, Paramount seemed determined to pump up that dependence until it evacuated any novelty at all. Yet these lessons in risk aversion did not exhaust the possibilities of the popsical, and Paramount would find its next successes by ratcheting up its commitment to its own control.

To understand just how particular the Paramount version of the new musical was, we might contrast it with *Fame,* the most significant entry in the genre between the reissued *Saturday Night Fever* and *Flashdance. Fame* turned on the inveterate questions of talent: Where does it come from? How is it recognized? How is it developed? What are its proper institutions? What is its audience? At MGM, a studio that had been destroyed and would spend an astounding thirty years (and counting) promising to rebuild itself, these questions of talent were native. *Fame*'s answer to the last was, ultimately, small scale: The audience consists of the profession itself; the rest of us are simply eavesdroppers and voyeurs. There are fragments of other audiences—an adoring father and an overbearing stage mother; a brutal comedy club crowd and the ocean of New York passersby—but the film's proper tensions are *between* the arts: What do the dancers make of the musicians? What do they make of the actors? This film, then, is as modernist as they come. Its great montage takes us through the introductions to each of the school's divisions and the array of requirements and the difficulties the students will face. Each has its basis—the body of the dancer, the self of the actor, the mind of the musician—but each can consider itself its own paragon: "Dance is the hardest department in the school." [CUT] "Acting is the hardest profession in the world." [CUT] "Music is the hardest profession of them all." Yet these diverse particularities make one society, a society of *Ars Gratia Artis.* Thus, the scene that immediately follows the whirlwind introductions takes Doris, the most naïve of the students and the least obviously talented, into the cafeteria, a rathskeller beanery, where she will be assaulted visually and sonically—and forced, almost, to confront her own sexual doubts. The hubbub, though, will quickly harmonize itself as a total work of improvisatory art rises from the mass of students. This turn will prove even more baffling to Doris. She has just been told that art comes from the school's own disciplinary program, yet here it seems to well up of its own accord, across those barriers. *Fame* has it both ways: art is planned magic, and the role of the institution oscillates between that of a place where hermetic knowledge can be inculcated in the elect and that of a zone where native talent and appetite find sufficient concentration that they might reveal themselves.

Fame refuses to pin down the origins of art, but it is convinced that art is rare. Scarcity makes art desirable. The film is also, then, of a piece with MGM's desperation. At Paramount, where there was no doubt that talent could be recognized and developed or that art could be crafted and calibrated, *Fame* would have been utterly out of place. In its stead, we find more populist stories in which only institutions can stand in the way of art, and in which individuals mature not through some occult process of self-development but through participation in far more demotic rituals.

Paramount picked up *Flashdance* in turnaround from Universal, which was going to produce it for PolyGram (the Philips-Siemens conglomerate that owned RSO, producers of *Fever* and *Grease*). The acquisition might have been motivated by simple familiarity or a conviction that Paramount could now make dance musicals without the help of its record company partner, but in this case it was driven by Dawn Steel's desire to prove herself to Simpson (and Diller and Eisner) and the neat fit between her own desires and those she read in the film. Here, in utterly simple sentences, is the way identification becomes allegory:

> I loved this script. It was the story of young girl who works as a welder. She does sexy dancing at night in a club but doesn't feel entitled to anything better.
>
> She was me. I totally identified. Not with the sexy dancing, but I had always seen myself as the underdog. Rocky was an underdog and the way I saw *Flashdance* was *Rocky* with a female underdog.[18]

The production seems to have been particularly fraught, with Paramount's executives taking a great deal of credit while Peter Guber and Jon Peters, the original producers on the project, attempted to get their share. Simpson, characteristically, dictated dozens of pages of script notes; Steel ordered changes to the sets ("Get that cum-stained couch out of here!"); and Eisner asked for reshoots to make the climactic dance tryout more exciting. Even before shooting began, Tom Hedley's original script was extensively reworked, first by Joe Eszterhas and then (uncredited) by Katherine Reback. The original choreographer was fired and replaced by Jeffrey Hornaday, who was then seeing Jon Peters's ex-wife. Adrian Lyne and his D. P., Don Peterman, new to the genre, shot enormous amounts of footage for the dance sequence, using multiple cameras. The editing fell to Walt Mulconery and Bud Smith (who had cut *Sorcerer*). Taking twelve-hour shifts, "We worked seventy-two days and nights without stopping," Smith said. Whatever the pressures, the craftwork enjoyed remarkable support from within the industry. Smith and Mulconery won the Eddie (American Society of Editors) and BAFTA awards for best editing and were nominated for the Oscar; Peterman was nominated for an Oscar; and the film picked up numerous awards for its music, including Best Song. "Flashdance . . . What a Feeling!" was sung (and co-written) by Irene Cara, who had sung *Fame*'s Oscar-winning title song three years earlier. In *Flashdance*, Paramount had picked what it wanted from *Fame* and moved on.

Where *Fame* hinged on a display of social synthesis—of "Mr. Martelli" playing his bank of synthesizers while Cara sang and the whole school danced along—*Flashdance* channeled its synthesis through a single character, Alex, played by Jennifer Beals. She welds by day and flashdances by night. Her style draws on the street, taking cues from a highly performative traffic cop and a b-boy crew; her body is sculpted through marathon, "maniacal" sessions in her loft and rhythmic workouts in the gym; and her aspirations are channeled through WQED and trips to the Pittsburgh Repertory with her friend, former Ziegfeld girl Hanna Long (Lilia Scala). As in the film, so in its making. Choreographer Hornaday told Simpson and Bruckheimer, "We've gotta get a double. We've gotta get somebody who's a professional dancer to do this. She's not a trained dancer. I can make it work perfect and seamless with Jennifer as long as I get a double."[19] They hired Marine Jahan to double nearly all of the dancing, but even that was insufficient, so when Eisner asked them to punch up the climax, they brought in a gymnast to execute Alex's leap and one of the Rock Steady Crew to do the downrock spin moves. Lyne was struck by the result. "So in that last sequence there are literally four people: there's Jennifer's face, there's Marine Jahan's dancing, plus the breakdancer, plus the gymnast flying through the air."[20] If *Fame* imagined the school as *Gesamtkunstwerk*, *Flashdance* imagined the character as composite: Alex is a welder.

To elide the differences between these bodies on film, *Flashdance* relied on backlighting, makeup, and montage. In the "Maniac" sequence, montage united Jahan's feet, torso, and full-body profile with six strategic inserts of Beals's face; in the climactic "Flashdance," Beals does not appear after she asks to start over. Indeed, in that dance, Jahan will face the camera directly, pointing at each of the judges in turn. The film prepares for this audacious move in "Imagination," the last dance Alex performs before her tryout. Through three costume changes and several medium close-ups, Beals never appears at all, her absence hidden by Alex's faux-kabuki whiteface. Given how readily critics initially accepted the fiction that Alex was the result of a single performance, these two strategies would have been sufficient for the climactic scene to go over. Moreover, montage and makeup performed crucial cultural and narrative work as well. Editing united Beals's face and others' bodies in a way that was entirely consistent with the film's alternate assertion of Alex's integrity and her auto-affection. On the one hand, "I never see them [the audience]" she says; "I am rhythm now," the song avers. On the other, "It's like I'm someone else." At the same time, the disarticulation of Alex's body into feet, face, torso, and profile undercut that phallic power, making her available for a slobbering audience, human or canine. Similarly, the whiteface makeup that allows Alex to play at being Japanese implies her own whiteness, or, if one takes the performance more seriously, it vouches for her ability to pass. Alex's racial status draws on Beals's own. Without ever being explicitly marked, she will mediate, first between her fellow dancers, the hung-up Tina (who is white) and the forthright Heels ("I'm glad I ain't no honky"), and then between Heels and white bar owner Mawby, who come together through an appreciation of Alex's performance in "Imagination." Montage and makeup serve gender and race even as they make character, yet neither rises to the level of aesthetic principle. In *Flashdance*, the decisive technique is backlighting.

The film opens with Alex riding her bike, backlit, to her work site. On the job, welders and others will appear swathed in fog, strongly backlit and singled out by dim red bulbs. One wall is covered in an endless sheet of dripping water. The detritus of this "world made of stone, made of steel" surrounds the erstwhile androgyne as she makes sparks with her arc-welding torch. (She lifts her welding helmet to shake out her hair and smile—an irresistible image that appeared in the trailer, most commercials, and the music videos for the film's singles "Flashdance . . . What a Feeling" and "Maniac.") The whole credit sequence is cut rhythmically and shot with almost no regard for verisimilitude. Surely the water would have been shut off; surely the lights would be brighter; surely no one would be welding in one pipe while someone else was welding in the pipe beneath him. The next sequence puts us at Mawby's Bar, where Alex will dance to "He's a Dream." Nearly all the elements of the "steeltown girl's" day job recur: dominant backlighting tinged by red lighting for effect (neon this time), industrial nostalgia (the pull chain to release the WC), the wet look, and the hair shake. Lyne, who had asked that the water be kept on in the opening scene, extended the motif: "I knew I wanted the dance to involve water, because obviously water looks good on skin, and it's kind of erotic and it flies around, you know what I'm saying, when it's backlit. And I'd never seen a wet dance." The climax comes when Alex douses herself, and in order to capture the water as dramatically as possible—to make it look like sparks—Lyne, Peterman, and Hornaday jumped across the axis to shoot out at the audience. It would be the film's iconic moment:

> We had designed the sequence for the opening number with the water shot. And the first day, the set was shot from the front looking towards a backlit milked plexiglass. And consequently when the water fell it didn't have this dynamic impact that we thought it was going to. . . . We went back the next day to shoot out the sequence, and I remember standing next to [Adrian] as we were watching rehearsal, and we were upstage watching the dancer from behind, and there was a super-trooper spotlight out in front, illuminating her, and Adrian saw her silhouette against that backlight and went, "That's it!" you know, "That's what we gotta do for the water shot."[21]

When Justin Wyatt was enumerating the stylistic hallmarks of high concept, he settled on "extreme backlighting, a minimal (almost black-and-white) color scheme, a predominance of reflected images, and a tendency toward settings of high technology and industrial design."[22] He might very well have been describing this scene. Here, backlighting is *more* than stylistic, *more* than a strategy for occluding Jahan's performance. It outlines style and strategy even as it outlines bodies. As Hornaday put it, "The story is obviously very thin, and it pretty much has cartoon characters." Backlighting made that weakness a virtue.

Figure 5.3. The backlit water dance. *Flashdance* (Adrian Lyne, Paramount, 1983)

By reducing characters to two-dimensional composites and outlining them, high concept re-created the frame as a space that could be filled with hyper-legible signs. Backlighting drastically simplified the visual field in which the chaotic performances occurred. Similarly, no matter how dynamic or extreme the shooting and editing of the dances may be, their chaos is contained by rigorously balanced establishing shots of the performance venues—Mawby's, Iceland, the Pittsburgh Rep., the Zanzibar strip club, even the gym. A line is drawn—around the frame, within the frame, through the space, around the characters, through the narrative. High concept is an aesthetic of *disegno*, not *colore*, of composition, not application, and that emphasis extends all the way through the organization. Diller prayed for a clean selection process at the studio as a whole; Lyne and the others answered that prayer within *Flashdance*: "I've always thought my job should be called 'selector' rather than 'director.'" Within this aesthetic, filmmaking became, again, an advertisement for itself.

Despite the best efforts of the crew and the studio executives' insistence on secrecy surrounding the dance doubling, the secret did not survive very long. *Flashdance* opened domestically April 15 and finished the weekend a close second behind *Lone Wolf McQuade* with $4 million; on April 20 the *Los Angeles Times* published an extensive article explaining Jahan's work. The *Times* published a long follow-up two days later, and a wire service story went national that same day. Jahan's performance had been elided, and she had been given no credit. Various executives named and unnamed explained that she had been left out of the brief end credits for space reasons and that many others had been left out as well. One explained that Jahan had asked for credit among the performers, something Screen Actors Guild (SAG) rules would not allow. "Being a dancing double isn't a character. . . . There are times when a studio does rotten things, but this wasn't one of them. It was a very unfortunate oversight."[23]

The "oversight" proved to be the leading edge of the wedge for the *Times* to report on the extensive battle for credit as *Flashdance* became a hit. Nonprofessional readers could understand what it meant to fail to credit the principal dancer in a film or for the third screenwriter (Reback) to do an uncredited polish. From those basics, Dale Pollock built an account of the other controversial credits on the film—the credits for producers Guber and Peters, the absent credits for executives Eisner and Steel, the question of what the director, choreographer, or producer's credits might mean. As Pollock framed it, and, doubtless, as the Paramount executives thought of it, the elision of Jahan served as the analog for the studio's characteristic arrogation of authorship. "Such a discussion question[s] the entire theory of the director as *auteur*, or single author of a movie," he wrote.[24] Lyne gave way to line. As with any narrative of revelation, though, there was a complication to the moral. At the end of "Flashfight" Pollock recounts a story told by Reback. "The box boy at her local market" had seen the movie "six or seven times" and had bought "the album and the cassette and the poster." Synergy, in its 1983 version, was working. But "when news stories began to appear discussing the question of just who did the dancing or who really produced the movie or who was responsible for the music, the box boy became upset." Reback offers the following theory: "He didn't want to know. . . . That's not why people go to the movies. He went because *in spite* of all these people and hands, the magic was on the screen."[25] Lyne agreed with Reback at the time, telling the *Times*, "Raising the issue destroys the fantasy and magic of the film. Now everyone will go just to dissect the dancing."[26]

The idea that behind-the-scenes coverage "spoils it" for naïve enthusiasts is comforting and may even seem plausible when what is behind the scenes undercuts particular emotional investments in the reality of a shark attack or a dancer's leap. Then again, if one thought that naïve enthusiasm *needed* spoiling, one could look to the behind-the-scenes for disenchanting material. *Washington Post* TV critic Tom Shales did just that, decrying the film as little more than "an inflated version of MTV." Part music video, part commercial, *Flashdance* was, nevertheless, something new. Where "the typical commercial of the '80s . . . deploys sensory stimuli organized so as to induce a certain 'feeling' in the viewer, one that presumably will trigger a conditioned response when the viewer gets to the supermarket, *Flashdance* has even less content than a commercial because it's not really trying to get people to do anything." Here, he is manifestly wrong, since at the very least the film is trying to get people to buy the sound track to the film and to come back "six or seven times." Still, Shales contends that the "feeling" the movie inspires is but a sham that the viewer misrecognizes. And while he willingly admits that "television itself is sometimes something that makes you want to bury your head under the covers, just to escape the sheer clattering banality of it," a new threat comes from "television blown up to motion-picture size."[27] Like Bernard Dick, Shales worries that the specialness of movies is threatened by a particularly machinic (televisual) understanding of them.

Where Reback worried that the naïve audience's faith would be rocked by the exposure of the film's mechanics, Shales felt the need to puncture that faith by exposing those mechanics. *Flashdance*, though, stages its own very different understanding of the importance of media critique in two scenes in which Alex watches TV. In the first, Alex sits down on the couch in her cut-just-so sweatshirt. She is drinking a Diet Pepsi. She changes the channel away from the banal redundancies of the local news (channel 22, WPTT, hosted by Kevin Evans; there has been a fire in a lumberyard) and the motormouth deal making in a Federal Express commercial ("I'mputtingyoudownforadeal withDallas,Don. Isitadeal? Dowehaveadeal? It'sadeal. Igottago. Igotacallcoming in.") before she settles. The cue is sonic, not visual, since we do not see the screen. Instead, we are relieved that all the talking has been replaced by orchestral strings (Albinoni's "Adagio in G major"). But if the audience is relieved, Alex is not. She sits up straighter and focuses on the television set as the panning camera finally centers her in the shot, between the antennae. Only following a cut do we see that she is watching a filmed performance of a classical ballet. Eyes on the dancers, she stands in order to duplicate one of their spins. At this moment, the shot comes together: the grid of the windows, the well-tended plants, the ideographic calligraphy on her sweatshirt, and the image of Mount Fuji on the wall behind her. As she turns, she slops soda onto her sweatshirt, swears, and absentmindedly sops it up. After her long day at work, she may have been planning to skip her workout. Now, she has resolved to practice; the next scene will be "Maniac." The second crucial scene of media consumption is the "Imagination" dance. That number begins with Alex in her kabuki makeup, blown away by her television, à la the famous Maxell ad. As the song proceeds, her involvement with the television intensifies, and she has an appropriately Shalesian freakout, apparently at the prospect of losing her soul to a televised, Japanified modernity. While we might be tempted to read that as Reagan-era anti-Japanese sentiment or as prescient anti-CAA sentiment, the dance matters more as a performance of and alibi for her earlier anxiety at the prospect of trying out for the Pittsburgh Rep. What *Flashdance* suggests here is that critics who decry the effects of television on the audience are taking neither television nor audiences as seriously as this film does. And taking these things seriously, at Paramount, means calibrating them precisely. Just as Diller could explain what was at stake in the bowdlerization of *Saturday Night Fever*, so Simpson could explain his aspirations for *Flashdance*: "I thought there was a chance for popular art, not high art, in the concept. . . . [T]he casting, the concept, and the look and sound of the movie all come together."[28]

By 2007, Lyne had changed his mind about the audience's interest in the film's backstory: "[I]t's curious how the press found out that [Jahan] had done most of Jennifer's dancing, and they felt that it was a kind of a cheat or something, I guess. And there was a huge amount of press about it, which I think worked for the film, funny enough. You know I think people were kind of fascinated by the fact that it was a kind of a composite if you like."[29] On *Flashdance*,

Figure 5.4. Alex, between the horns of the antenna. *Flashdance* (Lyne, Paramount, 1983)

or just after, Paramount learned this same lesson, the lesson Universal had learned on *Jaws*: that there was no trade-off between "magic" and "dissection." As in the case of *Jaws*, the backstory could be, and was, turned to the picture's advantage. At the most immediate and practical level, widespread knowledge that the dancing in the film was "a kind of composite" could only elevate the status of its editors and cinematographer (which it did). And to the extent that the film itself was, on an even higher and more contentious level, "a kind of composite," press coverage had the effect of elevating the status of its creative executives. Indeed, the happy results suggest that what these new musicals offered to executives and audiences alike was feeling and formula at the same time. "Take your passion, and make it happen," as both the Oscar-winning song and the film's one-sheet had it. It was a reflection of Paramount's own internal guidance. Dawn Steel explained that Diller's "attitude was that the process of making a movie—starting with an idea and surviving through development, through production, and through release—could take years. And if you weren't completely passionate at the very beginning of the process, you weren't going to give a damn at the end of the process. A bored executive was going to make boring movies."[30] Or, as Diller put it in his legendary description of Paramount from 1984, "Our process is advocacy and yelling."[31]

Paramount released two dance musicals in the wake of *Flashdance* and its credit fiasco. They represented two possible lessons the studio might draw from the "flashfight." In *Staying Alive*, which opened July 15, there are no dance doubles, only dancers. In *Footloose*, which opened February 17, 1984, Kevin Bacon is doubled, but the studio decided to get out in front of the potential bad publicity in order to make it serve the film. These films are the cinematic equivalent of "mopping up" actions following a decisive battle.

Staying Alive was the sequel to *Saturday Night Fever*, and it polished away whatever grit survived the PG-ification of the original. As Tony explains at one point, he has stopped drinking, smoking, and swearing. He has also stopped having friends or a family (only his mother remains); there are no competing pulls on his attention, and there is no good music to dance to. Writer-director Sylvester Stallone has forced the BeeGees to take a back seat to his brother Frank. Meanwhile, the dancers in *Staying Alive* do their own dancing. Cynthia Rhodes, who played Tina Tech, was the one "real" dancer in *Flashdance*. Offstage, she could fret about getting up the courage to call her boyfriend on the phone, while onstage she would flip, crawl, and sidle her way through a "Manhunt." It was a patently obvious opposition, of a piece with Alex's fear of television, but it was still more nuanced than her role in *Staying Alive*, where she tags after Tony, or doesn't, depending. Travolta, of course, does all his own dancing, but instead of dressing to fit the part of the hero he imagines himself to be, he now shows off his shaved, baby-oiled body and, in the climax, wears only soft boots, a loincloth, and a gold headband—Rambo on Broadway. Stallone has reinvented the dance movie as an action movie. Yet the result feels hemmed in by its own residual commitment to authenticity: dancer-stars, writer-directors, musician Frank Stallone playing the musician who threatens to steal Tony's girl. After Travolta's Broadway triumph, he leaves his girlfriend, his lover/costar, and his other cast mates backstage because he wants to hit the streets, alone, and, as he puts it, "strut." The end of *Staying Alive* thus finds Tony where he was at the opening of *Fever*, only now he has earned the right to strut through Times Square, not down Bay Ridge Avenue.

Whatever its obvious failings, the film is, in its way, of a piece with the new Paramount. The director of the dance spectaculars sounds like a studio mouthpiece, yelling about concepts and feelings: "What we're having here is a conceptual interpretation problem," and "Don't waste my time going through the motions of emotion. You've got to feel what the hell you're doing *here* [gestures]." Even more than the characters, the lighting and production design anchor the film at Paramount. The star filter that Swope used for *Fever*'s one-sheet is now everywhere. Crucial introductions and conversations happen in smoky backlight. Even Robert Boyle's production design has been all but drained of color. The film climaxes with a performance of *Satan's Alley* at the Broadway Theatre. During the run-up to the premiere, the dancers' rehearsals and the construction of the industrial set overlap, giving us the same dancing/welding overlay that *Flashdance* pioneered. The production itself, about a man's journey to hell and back, is an extended clash between the hoariest tropes of the backstage musical—Travolta improvises a solo and becomes a star; the director fumes; a girlfriend is lost and won—and the film's utterly over-the-top design. The chorus take their positions on a set that is more scaffolding than Pandemonium, with the exception of a multistory chrome skull. While the cornpone plot unwinds backstage, succubi in costumes daubed with bloody smears across their breasts and genitals attempt to pull Tony into the lake of rock-star fog onstage; after intermission a demon horde in Bob Mackie–designed S&M wear will whip him without mercy until he fights them off like Bruce Lee taking on a troupe of ninja assassins. Finally Tony's character wins the heart of Satan's chief minion as they dance in a crowd-scanning laser à la Michael Jackson in "Rock with You."

The dancing in *Staying Alive* is authentic but awful. The dancing in *Footloose* is a mix of intentionally awkward rehearsals, bits of authentic feature dancing, low-stress group dancing, and one major set piece. The last, to the song "Never," is the most *Flashdance*-y. Shot in an empty rail shed with angular slashes of light and strong backlighting throughout, it drew heavily on director Harold Ross's immersion in MTV. "MTV became a textbook for him," said screenwriter-songwriter Dean Pitchford. Ross "turned on MTV in his living room and left it on 18 hours a day."[32] Again the backlighting was necessary to obscure the work of other dancers—two gymnastic doubles, a stunt double

Figure 5.5. Satan's minions vanquished by the power of backlighting. *Staying Alive* (Sylvester Stallone, Paramount, 1983)

who did a huge swing on a pulley, and a dance double who did the most complicated moves. Bacon tells the story this way:

> It's funny when the movie came out it was right on the heels of *Flashdance*, and Jennifer Beals had gotten a lot of shit for—the studio had asked her to say that she wasn't doubled in the movie at all, and I just said, look, you know, I'm not gonna do it, because it came out that she was, and everybody sort of blamed her when it was really the studio saying look, this is the way we have to market this movie.[33]

As *Flashdance* became a hit, the publicity was managed entirely differently. First, dance double Peter Tramm was credited. Second, since there was no "news" to break, reporting could take the form of what Wyatt calls "enfotainment" coverage. In this case, *People* magazine ran a cover story in April featuring a heartthrobby image of Bacon surrounded by tiny action shots of Tramm: "America Goes *Footloose*: A double does the fancy footwork but KEVIN BACON kicks up a *Flashdance* frenzy." And while the cover article described Bacon's unlikely stardom, a sidebar concentrated on dance doubles, explaining how both Jahan and her ex-husband Tramm parlayed their dance roles into credited acting gigs. "Hoofers hidden in the shadows dream of the limelight" the headline promised; the two-page spread delivered, showing Jahan and Tramm in iconic silhouettes on the left and casually working out on the right. The article rehearsed Jahan's story but gave the studio equal time: "A new breed of young directors . . . take a bionic approach to filmmaking. 'Young directors are very specific about their needs, and very departmentalized,' Hornaday says. 'If they can't get great acting and brilliant dancing in one person, they'll invent ways to have it.'"[34]

He might have added singing to the list. For the striking thing about the Paramount dance musicals is that, with the exception of *Grease*, the major characters do not sing.[35] Yet as in an integrated musical, the songs were intended to be continuous with the story, and that continuity reached its height with *Footloose*. Dean Pitchford, the Oscar-winning songwriter of *Fame* who wrote the script and co-wrote the songs for *Footloose*, detailed the process. "We went about casting it as if we were casting voices for a Disney animated movie. The voices of the singers were the subconscious voices of the actors. So Kenny Loggins was Kevin Bacon."[36] The result was a modular musicality in which songs that were tightly integrated in the story could nevertheless be detached and turned into "scout singles." As composer Tom Snow explained, "The whole innovative idea with this film was that you could write songs that alluded to the action onscreen but none of the characters were actually singing them. And then those same songs could easily be lifted from the musical and then put on the radio and become hits. And that was what the tremendous success of *Footloose* was.

No film had ever done it quite like that before." With Pitchford overseeing both music and dialogue, the result was "an organic musical film," as producer Craig Zadan put it. "It didn't feel like somebody had written the screenplay and then all of a sudden you're *sticking* a song in, and you're stopping everything to do a number. It felt like it flowed from song to song to song." At the same time, by "casting" the songs, the sound track retained one of the singular advantages of the compilation score: It mitigated the risk that a given single would fail to hit. According to Jeff Smith, "This stress on spreading risk helps to explain the specific form of the compilation score. By using a number of songs and recording artists, film producers and record executives hedged their bets."[37]

Part of the payoff of that organic connection was that it allowed Paramount to release a video for the eponymous single composed principally of the shots from the big "Never" number. (While the sound track ruled the charts in the spring of 1984, spawning half a dozen singles, "Never" failed to make the *Billboard* top 100.) True, the cinematic version was punctuated by diegetic sounds—a crashing beer bottle, the squeak of a hand as it slides down a railing—that let you know the performance was occurring in ostensibly the same space as the music, while the video used only the music. Still, the theory of the scout single was largely untouched by the video revolution. Bacon explained how it worked:

> Songs had been used in films before, but generally they were pop or rock songs of an earlier era, either from the fifties or from the sixties—a lot of Motown is still constantly used in movies in order to push an audience to some sort of an emotional point. And the reason that that's so effective is because you know the song, you've heard it a million times, it comes on, you already have an emotional attachment to the song, you just add to that whatever's going on with the characters and it heightens the whole experience. It's hard to have much of an emotional attachment to a record you haven't heard a few times. . . . So, these guys were so smart because they put out the sound track . . . and the songs were really taking off. And when the audience sat down, you didn't have to play an old Chuck Berry song or Motown or something. You could play "Footloose"; you could play "Let's Hear It for the Boy" because you already were into that song, and the track comes on and you're already grooving along with it. It was very smart of them.[38]

Another way to think of this process is to read "emotional attachment" as instant nostalgia. If we understand the cultivation of such feelings as central to the success of the popsical, then we better understand both the theory of synergy they embodied and the formal pressure to reprise the titular songs at the climaxes of both *Footloose* and *Flashdance*. For those few in the audience who did not know the songs, the performances over the opening credits set the emotional trap that will spring at the climax. At the same time, since the songs were original to the movie, they avoided any troubling associations. According to Smith, "Well-known music of any kind was thought to carry associational baggage for the spectator, and . . . these associations might . . . clash with those established by the narrative."[39] By the late eighties, that presumption had been vanquished. The nostalgia wave gave rise to a cycle of films titled after old songs. "It creates a certain resonance, calling individual audience members back to a certain time," said David Kirkpatrick, then president of Paramount Motion Picture Group.[40] The eighties dance musical existed at a crucial turning point, when associations could cut both ways. The trick, then, was to create music that was well known for being in the movie it would be in.

Without an urban setting to motivate an astringent production design, *Footloose* cultivated another version of classical rigor, one determined by formal durability and untimeliness. Its landscape is both natural and worked; its fashions are both timeless and practical. After an opening montage of myriad dancing feet, *Footloose* plunges into a rural landscape backed by dramatic Paramontian peaks. As Pitchford recalled, while he had imagined the movie as taking place in "vast rolling flatlands like Oklahoma," Ross wanted to shoot in Utah. "The great thing about Utah is that you've got those long flat valleys and then those majestic mountains rising in the distance. Please trust me that it will make a much more interesting frame." The town is Bomont, and the mountains are indeed beautiful. With its landscape corporatized, *Footloose* "became a parable" unanchored in a particular town or year. The decision to find a sort of cultural Shangri-La governed the overall design. Pitchford continued,

> One of the things about *Footloose* that continues to keep it in people's consciousness is that it floats above the era in which it was created on so many levels, not simply because the story is a fable but also because there are not too many design elements that mire it in the eighties. Not only does the score partake of real classic form[s] like rock'n'roll and ballad and in some cases show writing but also the look of the picture in terms of costumes. . . . [T]he uniform for these is blue jeans, boots, cowboy hats, flannel shirts, and it was twenty years before the movie was made, and it is today.[41]

Boots replace the bewildering array of footwear that opens the film, and cultural untimeliness both conveys and supports formal classicism. Kevin Bacon's character, Ren, may be a fish out of water in Bomont, but what he brings with him is not (except musically and tonsorially) the shock of the new. Instead, his look is vintage, classic: the maroon, shawl-collar dinner jacket he wears to the prom; the seventies VW bug; the Chuck Taylors he wears to his tractor chicken run. What he wants most of all is for the town to have an old-fashioned senior dance.

The film's emblem for its mix of teenage confidence and inexorability is the train. Ren's long, fictional story of a passionate sexual encounter describes it as "goin' like a fucking freight train." Thus, it is no surprise that the opening shot of Bomont pairs the church cross with a railroad crossing. These crossings will be the places where teenage sexuality ("boundary testing") will play out. When Ariel plays chicken with a Peterbilt truck, it is at a railroad crossing and she, herself, forms the debarring X. Ren will duplicate her pose when he dances in the train shed. When Ariel faces down an actual train, she raises only one hand, not two, and, as if in compensation, Ren will have to save her at the last minute. In the train shed, an abandoned locomotive is now called "the yearbook" because its walls are covered with quotations from banned books. Breaking the rules—going over the line—is universal, or, as *Footloose* puts it: classic. Early in the film, Ren voices his approval for *Slaughterhouse-Five*, a book the town busybodies want to ban, by saying, "It's a classic." "Maybe in another town it's a classic," one snipes. "In any town," Ren responds.

After Ren's bid to gain permission to have the dance in Bomont fails, his boss wants to wise him up: "You know you were railroaded, doncha?" It would be easy to ignore the phrase if the railroad weren't central to the plan to hold the dance in the town of Basin. "Basin's what, thirty miles away?" Ren asks. "Not where it runs up to these tracks, it ain't. Now, I figure if the Bomont firetrucks can't cross these

Figure 5.6. The debarring *Xes. Footloose* (Herbert Ross, Paramount, 1984)

tracks, well, neither can the long arm of the law." The film lays out a very precise geography: There is Bomont, a zone of righteousness, repression, and law; and there is Basin, a zone of license, leisure, and labor. Between them lies a line along which the virtuous of Bomont can watch the vicious of Basin. When the dance finally comes to pass, thanks to the begrudging approval of the Reverend Shaw Moore (John Lithgow), the pastor and his wife (Dianne Wiest) stand on the Bomont side and look on, approvingly, at the flower of Bomont youth dancing in the dark, Satanic mill of Basin. This borderline configuration monopolizes the discourse. Ren's boss tells Shaw, "You done a good thing here." When the minister demurs, "Well, I'm still not sure it was the right thing," the miller is pragmatic and proxemic: "Comes close." Or, as Wiest puts it: "Shaw, we're almost dancing."

Neoclassical Synergy

It was "Almost Paradise" at Paramount. "We're getting closer, closer everyday" as the "Love Theme from *Footloose*" put it. And paradise, in the Paramount dance musicals, is a place where dance venues and industrial locales merge. There is a progression. In April 1983, there is a robust narrative and stylistic continuity between Alex's day job and her night work. She may aspire to being a full-time classical dancer, but for now, the halves of her life are, more or less, complementary and interchangeable. Welding pays the bills; dancing keeps her sane. In July 1983, Tony has almost no life outside dance spaces, but all his studio work culminates in a setting that blends intense industrial design with sexual display. The convergence may seem just another of the film's false steps, or it may seem desperately à la mode, but in its striving *Staying Alive* indicates the depths of its anxiety, its yearning to fit in. (It is, in this way, pure Stallone.) In *Footloose*, the climactic dance is not the fusion of work and sex but the replacement of labor by entertainment. The Bomont high school students (however temporarily) take over the Lehi Roller Mills. In the span of less than a year, Paramount moves from imagining dance as complementary to industry to imagining complementarity is contingent to imagining a trade-off between them.

Over nearly the same span, Gulf + Western went from a monstrous, diversified conglomerate with interests in everything "from automotive parts to zinc" to a "highly focused" media conglomerate. Charismatic chairman Bluhdorn died in February 1983 and was quickly succeeded by Martin Davis. Believing that the diversity of corporate interests depressed the company's stock price, Davis took it as his mission to unwind G+W. The 1985 annual report boasted that the project was complete: "Over a 30-month period, Gulf + Western has received more than $2.6 billion in funds as a result of divestitures and securities sales and has reinvested more than $1 billion in target growth areas, primarily publishing."[42] Gone were natural resources, consumer and industrial products, and agriculture; what remained were financial services, publishing, and entertainment. In 1982, the movie studio accounted for 7 percent of the company's revenues; film and television, for 13 percent of the company's income. "Leisure Time" as a whole was more significant, about a quarter of the conglomerate's revenues and income. By the time Davis had undone his predecessor's empire building, Paramount was the center of the company: film and television accounted for 60 percent of Gulf + Western's operating income. Overall revenue was less than half of what it had been in 1982, and operating income was only a quarter. Or, to put it in narrative terms: In 1982, G+W's business segments are complementary and largely interchangeable. By 1985, industry has been replaced by entertainment and financial services. The next year, Davis would rename the company Paramount Communications.

Does this parallelism between the drastic changes at the company and the changes within its dance musicals seem strained, a post hoc reading, and merely surplus when considered alongside the manifold drivers behind the progression of the three films? It may. We might trace that doubt (or resistance) to three lacunae in our thought. The first is disciplinary and historical: We are not prepared to read the films of the modern studio system as particularly systematically related. Criticism and industrial self-description have converged in this regard. A guiding assumption of both has been that the package-unit system of production has made the management of studio identities across projects, producers, and years less consequential, less possible. Brand management, when it exists, seems to be restricted to franchises—at Paramount, *Star Trek*—and even those might be controlled elsewhere—at Paramount, *Indiana Jones*. These exceptions indicate another possible source of our resistance. Parallels may seem tenuous when the resources of narration, form, promotion, and so on have not yet rendered the surface of the screen sufficiently legible—have not yet yielded a hyperlegible cinema. In contrast, franchises seem to solicit allegorical readings to such a degree that resistances to their allegories fall by the wayside only to be replaced by a conviction that however intentional, those allegories are nevertheless powerless. Whatever lies "inside" these stories, or on their surfaces, could never apply sufficient pressure to move the bolus of actuality, contingency, and economic reality that underlies the industry's operations. That is, when we do find ourselves convinced by story and style, we turn against that formalism toward an apparently hardheaded materialism. Allegories are impossible, illegible, and inconsequential as need be.

As I have been arguing, though, the structural weaknesses in the system create as many opportunities for elective affinity as they obscure. Or, to be more precise, the changes in the mechanisms that cultivate studio identity do not determine the number and intensity of the bonds between individual films and the studio that might oversee them. In the case of Paramount, a constellation of diverse factors alters even that null hypothesis. Most important, the studio's industrial reputation was built on its unique ability to find points of control and then apply decisive force to them. The underlying assumption was that Paramount movies were Paramount movies first and foremost, and that whenever that seemed not to be the case (*Raiders of the Lost Ark*, *Reds*, even *Terms of Endearment*), those were the exceptions that required explanation. At one focal length, the studio oversaw the hyperstylization of its own product and a drastic reduction in narrative complexity *in order to* bring its films more firmly under executive control, a control that it then could deploy in future instances, a control that was called "high concept." Thus, while *Staying Alive* was clearly a Paramount film from its inception, both *Flashdance* and *Footloose* were picked up in turnaround (from Universal and Fox, respectively). With their ambiguous corporate parentage these movies might have seemed unauthored products of the genre, but in fact they did not. They became Paramount films because, and only because, of the work done to them by creative executives, crucial technical personnel, casts, directors, and marketers.

But to say that they are all products of and evidence for a particular systematic assertion of studio control is one thing; to argue that their narrative shifts also speak to an underlying transformation in the studio's relationship to its corporate parent is something else. The first requires only a reading of the origins and deployments of narrative, style, and backstory; these are all strongly marked as Paramount films. A second focal length requires a reading of the *content* of the narratives at a level that seems hard to sustain, even if the default assumption of the producers of these films (producers understood as widely as possible) was that their existence as films was owed to the very particular circumstances of their being mounted at Paramount. How do we test that reading? How do we justify that interpretive move?

The second question has primacy. We are not testing the adequacy of a particular allegorical reading so much as locating a time and place in which the material and formal possibilities of such a reading become insistent and systematic. The organizational cleanliness behind the dance musicals made them a natural fit for the studio. They were its embodiment and its ideal: The advocacy and yelling process made passion happen. But those same films seemed only tangentially related to the rest of the conglomerate's business, perhaps even more tangentially than the insistent films by directors such as Coppola and Friedkin. What our reading protocols require, then, is a claim something like this: The elaboration of a collection of organizational and formal strategies in the service of Paramount's relative autonomy in the motion picture industry had the effect of binding those strategies to the aims of the corporation as a whole. In light of Paramount's success, those strategies—again, what I am calling high concept—became the basis for the bond between studio and conglomerate. If the popsicals seem an unlikely place to make that claim, if they seem unable to sustain it compellingly, we might attribute that insufficiency to an economy operating *within* the studio that allocated to those films the achievement of a suitable and stable formal basis for the sorts of corporate elaboration that would be more readily carried out elsewhere.

That elsewhere might have been in the Indiana Jones and Star Trek franchises, and those films certainly performed important work in the emergence of the neoclassical system. In the 1983 Gulf + Western annual report, the introduction to the work of the Entertainment and Communications Group makes the case for "the natural synergism" between film, television, and publishing. Naturally, *Star Trek* is the privileged example: "[T]he legendary television series . . . led to two highly successful feature films from Paramount with a third currently in production. It has also inspired a video arcade game that has been converted for home use and the publishing of a *Star Trek* series of books by Simon & Schuster. In the meantime, the original television series continues to generate revenue as one of the most successful shows in syndication." As the company sought "synergy" "in virtually every communications medium," one might have expected the studio to take a back seat to a more central administration of intellectual property. Yet Diller (it seems clear from the rhetoric that each group head oversaw his section of the annual report) puts the movies at the center of this new economy: "The possibilities for this concept are limitless and the catalyst is Paramount's Motion Pictures Division."[43] The franchises, as sites of synergy, are realizations of this limitless concept—this highest of high concepts.

Synergy, with its cognate forms, has a twisted history. According to the Oxford English Dictionary, the word featured prominently in fifth-century debates over the role of will in salvation but did not come to mean "surplus action" until the eighteenth century. This surplus became more or less mathematical when the word appeared in scientific settings, more or less figurative everywhere else. But whatever its roots, by the mid-twentieth century, synergy had become a social and cognitive concept, part of evolving systems theory. It was this last version that was most easily ported into management theory, partially on the back of the reputation of R. Buckminster Fuller, but primarily through the work of J. Fred Weston (*The Case for the Multinational Corpora-*

tion, Large Corporations in a Changing Society, Industrial Concentration: The New Learning) and H. Igor Ansoff's classic *Corporate Strategy*.[44] Ansoff's tools were abstract, but they were abstract in precisely the ways that evolving and diversifying conglomerates would be attracted to. His central mission was the evaluation of new business moves by a firm—whether through acquisition or start-up, whether in a new market or a new product. At a given moment, a business could be mapped into various "competence grids" and "competitive profiles." That static evaluation could then be dynamized via a set of "decision rules and guidelines," that is, as a "*strategy*" or what he calls "*the concept of the firm's business*." Finally, that concept relies on an evaluation of the "common thread" uniting the firm's actions, an ever-changing "product-market scope," its "growth vector," and its "competitive advantages." All of these "describe the firm's product-market path in the *external environment*." What is left is the firm's understanding of its own competence: "[S]ynergy is a measure of the firm's ability to make good on a new product-market entry."[45] Only the most flexible firms will be able to remake themselves continually, to allow "structure to follow synergy." It was the agenda for the era. But while synergy was a "rage word" in 1969 and one of "the basic buzzwords of the '60s," by the eighties it had already lost its sheen.[46] In 1978, a profile of GE could say that its "strategic planning system . . . made the word 'synergy' a corporate cliché." Chairman Reginald H. Jones was apologetic, even as the company doubled down: "We felt we were not getting the synergy—I hate to use the word—that we should. . . . This revised system moves G.E. from strategic planning as a process to strategic management as a system for all levels."[47]

As diversified conglomerates became media conglomerates, synergy returned. Behemoths with media components such as Gulf + Western, Kinney National Service, or TransAmerica, and those without, such as LTV, Litton, and Textron, had been highly dependent on financial jugglery to make their acquisitions pay off. Two plus two equaled five only if accounting could make the quarterly and annual numbers come out right and only if acquisitions could drive up the companies' price-to-earnings ratios. As the big conglomerates struggled in the seventies, "synergism," as it was usually called, seemed to be a myth wrapped in cliché. But by the eighties, synergy had become the executive's version of Chesterton's Christianity: it hadn't been found wanting because it had never been tried. The new model conglomerate would be pared down, and strategy, not finance, would lie at its center. Davis's chairman's letter in the 1985 annual report captured the change: "Gulf + Western's transformation in terms of the composition of its core operations is being accompanied by changes in its corporate culture. Annual business planning was formalized at Gulf + Western in the 1960s. It was financially oriented and concentrated on the near term. Strategic planning—though an integral part of the process—did not receive as much emphasis."[48]

Thus, when Diller refers to the synergies of the entertainment group, or when Pollock says that "*Flashdance* has achieved that rare synergy between a movie and its music" in 1983, these are revivifications and purifications of the discourse of the diversified conglomerate.[49] And if we have grown accustomed to thinking of this sort of talk as native to the new era of media consolidation, that is only because we have lost sight of the impetus for such discourse in the first place: The studios never really fit with the corporations that had swallowed them. Their talk of synergy is strangely aspirational; it is the self-representation of a unit that wants to find its place in the larger organization. After Bluhdorn's death, Davis set to work remaking G+W. The Entertainment unit would be a laboratory of the new: "The synergies in the companies were never really utilized when we acquired them," according to Davis. "Now we hope to have better controls, and to put all the creative forces in the company at work together."[50] No longer was the motion picture studio "the catalyst"—it was, Davis said, a "weakness" in the strategic plan. "Now we're free to make all the pieces come together."[51] *Flashdance*, which seemed a model of the new ancillary-driven Hollywood, was, by Davis's lights, a failure. Paramount did not distribute the record (they had no record division at the time); the apparel division did not design the clothing line; Simon & Schuster did not publish a novel. In the final step of Davis's reorganization, Diller had to be replaced by Arthur Barron. The shake-up was necessary to, as Barron awkwardly put it, "get the synergies that exist in this company working together."[52]

With the right concept, all the facets of a particular movie could come together, resulting in what Simpson called "popular art." When Paramount turned its sights on Gulf + Western, though, the right concept was called synergy, and despite the management turmoil following Bluhdorn's death, that concept took hold of the conglomerate and reshaped it in the studio's image. Form and organization drew closer to one another, overcoming the distance between instance and system, bridging the gap not through Romantic will but through mutually reinforcing connecting threads. As the new form congealed, it suggested that we might judge the success of this corporate redesign and reconception through its practical effects. And within this new paradigm of judgment, we find a way of periodizing Hollywood history: When the allegorical implications of the studio's films no longer seem tendentious, then, we might say, has neoclassicism arrived.

Diller dismissed the management of financial risk in favor of a rhetoric of control. But given that the studio's ultimate project was the reshaping of its conglomerate parent in its own image, and given that that reshaping depended on both formal and material changes, we might wonder about the neglected side of Paramount's management efforts. How, exactly, did it grapple with the agencies' attempts to exert inflationary pressure on the price of talent? How, exactly, did it maintain creative continuity? What did those efforts cost? And how did high concept fit with this seemingly more material agenda? If the popsicals were a small but central part of what had already begun to be thought of as high concept, they were joined by souped-up B movies and buddy cop or fish-out-of-water comedies. Paramount sought to control these dominant modes of eighties Hollywood cinema and bring them within the stylistic and allegorical ambit of its other work. In both cases, the studio ultimately chose between story and style, with wildly varying success.

Designed to Be Effective

High concept at Paramount demanded a reduction in narrative complexity in favor of an assertion of stylistic control. The increasing legibility of both the action within the frame and the action of the frame itself pushed audiences toward a different sort of audio-viewing, viewing as reading, hearing as feeling (or, to use the relevant terms, toward process and passion). This transformation happened remarkably quickly—over the span of a decade, with crucial pivots taking less than eighteen months. It might seem that such a swift reorientation of American cinematic storytelling would necessarily be efficient, but even in such a compressed time frame it was possible for Paramount to produce films that did not advance the overall agenda. In the context of a broad production slate, most of these are "ordinary" films, relics of a prior system still working through its possibilities—Bordwell calls these films, such as Fox's *9 to 5* (Colin Higgins, 1980) "stylistically unprepossessing." In contrast, there are also films that however stylistically prepossessing point only to a potential settlement of the competing claims of the system. At Paramount in the early eighties, the most important false prophecy was *The Keep*.

Michael Mann's *The Keep*, like its genre mate *The Hunger*, tested the limits of stylishness. It has shots of perfectly calibrated beauty, as when a tramp steamer sails off into a sunrise; and monumental sublimity, particularly of the keep itself. In many ways, the terms of that test were exactly those of *Sorcerer*—as with Friedkin's film, *The Keep* was designed by John Box and the score was provided by Tangerine Dream. But if *Sorcerer* was an auteur's self-destructive envoi that helped convince Paramount of its power, *The Keep* was a volley in the continuing battle to retain that power. In this case, it was power vis-à-vis two of the only auteurs that remained standing, auteurs animated by their own deep investments in the studio system as an object of adulation, emulation, and danger; auteurs who paid for their autonomy by aiming for, or catering to, or sometimes even pandering to the heart of popular expectations, which is to say, George Lucas and Steven Spielberg. Where *Sorcerer* was a remake of a minor French classic, *The Keep* functioned as the negation of *Raiders of the Lost Ark*.

The Keep is *Raiders* stripped of its fun, its intense plotting, and its linear progress. Its negation of the *Indiana Jones* films appears at virtually all levels of analysis. Both pit the Nazis against a supernatural power, but where the *Jones* films have nothing to say about Jews, *The Keep*'s most compelling story line involves the Nazis' decision to enlist a Jewish scholar and his daughter in their attempts to understand what force occupies the keep. "The idea of making this film within the genre of horror films appealed to me not at all. It also did not appeal to Paramount."[53] Mann said he wanted the film to resemble a dream—it does not, not in any good way. Its central battle, between the increasingly in-carnate demon Molasar and his eternal adversary Glaeken Trismegistus makes no sense on-screen. In a brief scene in some versions, Glaeken's reflection does not appear in a mirror. Does this imply he is a vampire? Nothing else does—he does not need to be invited into spaces; he has no fear of the daylight; he does not feed on blood.

Surely Paramount did not anticipate the indirection of the film. The source novel declares everything, even its ironies—"Kaempffer knew that Hossbach's good wishes were as hollow as the promises of resettlement he made to the Polish Jews."[54] And Mann's previous film had been *Thief*, like *American Gigolo* a "last of the independents" story for the eighties—both were produced by Bruckheimer, both dressed their heroes in Armani, and both turn on the allocation of various percentages. In *Thief*, James Caan's Frank refuses to cut the police in for their standard 10 percent; crime boss Joe (Robert Prosky) gives Frank only 10 percent of his cut in cash (he invests the other 90 percent in shopping centers). Frank objects, "You are making big profits from my work, my risk, my sweat, but that is okay, because I elected to make that deal. But now, the deal is over. I want my end and I am out." Mann says, "What you're hearing here is Marx's labor theory of value applied to his life." Frank "is now a wage slave, that's what he's reduced to."[55] Still, *Thief* shapes itself to Mann's abiding aestheticism. Frank aims to realize a vision of the good life he has pieced together in prison and that he now carries with him in collage form. As Frank bullies the world until it accords with his designs, the film plays along. Early rain-slicked streets and backlit fire escapes give way to a period of color-ful shirts, pink trees, and sunny San Diego. But the tropicalia is short lived, and the third act features "more and more metallic colors and sounds, glare and reflections off metal," as Mann described it.⁵⁶ In the end Frank is alone again, bruised, and iconic: a man with a gun, a black leather jacket, ripped T-shirt, and jeans. Classic.

It would not have taken much for Mann to have made *The Keep* a film to fit with *Jaws, Star Wars, Raiders,* and the rest of the emerging neoclassical canon. The centerpiece of the new aesthetic was, as I have said, a two-track appeal. *Raiders* seemed to tell a thirties story in a thirties package, but while it was able to conjure the idea of the thirties serial in the minds of those in its audience who could remember such a thing, it pushed that idea without either making it necessary to the appreciation of the film or (and this deserves more emphasis than it has received) actually duplicating serial forms. *Raiders* posited that its thirties narrative and thirties form would seem mutually attractive, and this nostalgia for the apt container was wildly successful with audiences.⁵⁷ None of this would be true of *The Keep*. With a key exception, Mann's film was shot and sound-recorded in a style that wanted nothing to do with its origins (the very early forties).

The exception to this rule against period form is its lighting. Mann tells of using "arc lamps that date from the Twenties and Thirties to get a certain kind of hard blue shaft of light coming through all the openings of the keep. And it usually comes from behind people and makes shafts across them, creating a kind of Albert Speer–Mussolini monumental quality."⁵⁸ In the wake of *Flashdance* and *Staying Alive*, this is no surprise. Backlighting is *the* aesthetic of the 1980s, the way that deep chiaroscuro is the light of the forties and "available" light and near darkness make up the light of the seventies (*The Godfather, Days of Heaven*). Backlighting carves out figures, simplifies their surfaces, but it also makes substitutions possible by disguising crucial features. It squeezes out lens flare. It makes cartoons. And in *The Keep* the arc lights weld story and style. The thirties technology turns eighties moviemaking into an epigone of thirties political aesthetics.

Speerian monumentality came naturally to Mann, who wanted "to sweep [the] audience away—be very big, to have them transport themselves into this dream-reality so that they're in those landscapes, there with the characters. You can't sweep people away in 1.85 and mono." As a consequence, Mann refused to "shoot for the box." When asked, "Are you pushing your compositions toward the middle of the screen?," Mann was adamant: No. Whatever happens to it when [*The Keep*] goes out on television or video, that's the breaks. I can't do anything about that. But I can do everything about the cinema experience which, for me, is obviously primary. So the shots are composed for the big screen and the film is designed to be effective for theater audiences." For Mann,

Figure 5.7. Speerian backlighting. *The Keep* (Michael Mann, Paramount, 1983)

control, and control achieved through stylistic rigor, took priority over multiplatform success. "Commercial reasons aside, I'm interested in the theatrical experience, not in the small-screen experience." The "aggressive seduction" achieved through period lighting and contemporary widescreen constitutes a warrant for going to the cinema. Movies must offer "a different order of experience. Otherwise stay home and watch the idiot box."[59]

Mann's modernist commitment to cinematic specificity at the expense of downstream revenues—and *The Keep* has had at best a fitful afterlife on video—might seem out of place at synergy-hungry Paramount. But his attempt to "get at the way you think and feel in the way dreams work" was, for the studio, some compensation. For if *The Keep* is a dream, it is *Paramount's* dream of a *Raiders* under studio control. Paramount may have been happy with the amount of money *Raiders* made ($363 million in rentals), but they were also annoyed that they had been handed the deal terms. (Fox felt the same way about *Star Wars*.) The deal for *Raiders* was ridiculous. Lucas and Spielberg initially demanded high salaries ($4 million and $1.5 million, respectively), full financing, and profit participation from the moment the negative cost had been recouped, with no overhead or distribution fee. Paramount won some concessions, but Lucasfilm retained ownership of the film, and thus the franchise.[60] When Lucas and Spielberg came back with *Temple of Doom*, *Last Crusade*, and, eventually, *Kingdom of the Crystal Skull*, Paramount had to negotiate all over. So *The Keep* was an experiment, an attempt to see whether one might build a studio around Mann's hyperstylized, "more experimental" films.[61] It premiered in December 1983 and fared poorly with critics and at the box office. By July 1984, when Tony Schwartz's love letter to the Killer Dillers appeared in *New York*, *The Keep* had become the grit in Paramount's process: "Put simply, Paramount has figured out, better than any other studio, how to make the right movies. This scarcely means flawless judgment, just that successes like *48 Hrs.* are big enough to overshadow failures like *The Keep.*"[62]

Strategic Stardom

Eddie Murphy came to Paramount through an inspired suggestion by Hildy Gottlieb, an agent at ICM. *48 Hrs.* was an ICM package—they represented director Walter Hill, Nick Nolte, and writer Roger Spottiswoode in addition to *Saturday Night Live* star Murphy.[63] By 1982, all three major agencies—ICM, CAA, and William Morris—were intently packaging, and Paramount was usually resisting. *48 Hrs.* was the exception. But if Murphy was a late addition to the package and a replacement for another, more expensive actor (Gregory Hines and Richard Pryor have been named), he quickly became the best argument for making the film. And by getting out in front of Murphy's career, the studio was able to buy the sort of labor continuity studios benefited from in the classical era: From his debut in 1982 to *Boomerang* (1992), every movie Eddie Murphy starred in was distributed by Paramount. Over that remarkable decade, the studio succeeded in keeping him working, for them, in vehicles that were generally highly profitable and that grossed more than $1.5 billion. The legal and material bases for that relationship were not the traditional seven-year contract but a multipicture deal and a vanity production shingle. While neither was unique in 1982, the speed and thoroughness with which Paramount assimilated its new star were striking. Before his first film had even been released, the studio had offered Murphy a $1 million signing bonus, $1 million a picture, and $250,000 to underwrite Eddie Murphy Productions. With each new success, Paramount would renegotiate the deal, upward. The downside of such a headlong rush was inflation, but the upside was control.[64] Where Paramount had to woo and win Lucas and Spielberg anew with each fresh installment of the *Indiana Jones* saga, they would have the rights to Murphy's services and the first look at anything he wanted to develop. At the same time, given its sizable "investment" in Murphy's career, the studio would seek to shape his screen persona in such a way that it would be reliable and iterable. *The Keep* was an experiment in control through *style*, of control *as* style; Murphy's career would be a *story* of control, of control *as* story. *48 Hrs., Trading Places, Best Defense,* and *Beverly Hills Cop* made him a star, but they also solidified the importance of studio management in the eighties.

Shot in the 1982 summer hiatus of *Saturday Night Live, 48 Hrs.* was released that November. The plot is simple enough: Murphy is sprung from jail to help catch a cop killer. He has two days. If he is successful, he will get to keep $500,000 in stolen money. That simplicity helps open the channel between story and backstory: The narrative deadline mimics and draws some of its force from the production deadline. Such communication is traditional. When a star migrates from one medium to another—from TV or music or the stage to film the debut project ordinarily figures that move. Such easy allegories are part of the star-making process, as essential as the close-up, the catchphrase, the characteristic gesture (in Murphy's case, the laugh), or the big post-makeover reveal. Microscopic pieces of the performance will be extracted for use in marketing—whether on the one-sheet or in trailers and TV spots—while the film's story is shaped to the audience's experience of the star, in a kind of narrative repoussage.

The strongly generic story that made Murphy a plausible substitute for Gregory Hines also made the film reliable. If we imagine that producers have a certain level of risk they are willing to allocate to a given project, then to the extent that genre mitigates narrative risk, it "frees up" a quantum of uncertainty that might be allocated to a novice director or actor.[65] At the same time, genres provide a narrative and tonal contour onto which an actor can map a performance. Buddy cop films, or, in the case of *48 Hrs.*, cop-and-con films, have tightly wound logic engines at their core. Virtually every narrative element moves in concert with the others, and in an effective instance, the film's narrative tensions are framed by a style that puts just enough distance between the ostensibly contingent byplay of the central pair and the underlying case they are busy talking over. The emblematic scene in *48 Hrs.* comes halfway through, just after Nolte (Cates) and Murphy (Hammond) have reached a dead end. In their pursuit of the bad guys, Gans and Billy Bear, they have been tracking "known haunts" and "known associates," that is, looking at externals. Cates is giving up on this strategy and wants to understand what drove Gans to break out of jail in the first place. This is the dialogue that sets up the action:

> Cates: This sucks. Maniac gets ahold of my gun and runs all over the streets killing people with it. So instead of being where I oughtta be, home in bed with my gal giving her the high hard one, I'm here doin' this shit, roamin' around the streets with an overdressed, charcoal-colored loser like you.
>
> Hammond: Look, man if you don't like it, why don't you just leave? I can take care of Gans by myself, alright?
>
> Cates: Don't make me laugh. You can't take care of shit. You've been dicking me around since we started this turd hunt. The only thing you're good for is games. So far what I got out of you is nothin'.
>
> Hammond: Yeah, well, I'm real impressed with you, too, man. It took a real skilled cop to kick in the bedroom door of a couple a dykes.

> Cates: Luther knows more than he told me, and so do you. I want to know what the
> fuck this is all about. I gave you 48 hours to come up with somethin', and the
> clock's runnin'.
>
> Hammond: Yeah, well, maybe I don't like the way you asked me, alright?
>
> Cates: Who gives a goddamn what you like? You're just a crook on a weekend pass.
> You're not even a goddamn name any more. You're just a spearchucker with a
> number stenciled on the back of his prison fatigues. Alright. I'm through fuckin'
> around. You tell me the truth or you're gonna get the livin' shit beat out of you.

This scene constitutes the midpoint pivot of the film. But it also serves as a
handy digest of the animating features of the interracial buddy flick. First, the
central relationship demands the contained display of social anxieties. It is, in
the way that it cultivates racial tensions, a melodramatic structure, although
unlike most melodramas, it ultimately blocks rather than reveals the social consequences of racial difference. Nick Nolte and Eddie Murphy can slug it out, call
each other horrible names, and still put their differences aside.

Second, as is also typically the case, the buddy flick requires that those differences be put aside at the expense of the women in the film—what two men
as different as a white cop and a black con share is trouble managing women;
whether by preference or fate, they find themselves together. At the same time,
this partnership has to manage the implicit sexual tensions of working together.
Cates is with Hammond instead of his girlfriend; meanwhile, Hammond has
been "dicking" him around on "this turd hunt," a nasty bit of implicit homophobia. Whatever the tensions between the men, though, they can be projected
onto the "couple a dykes." On the one hand, the lesbians' lack of interest in
them is the alibi for the guys' heterosexuality; on the other, the women are
themselves unforthcoming about their own sexuality. Though they claim not to
be attracted to men, they will take in Gans and Billy Bear. All told, the film gives
us a pair of heroes, a pair of villains, the villains' girlfriends, the villains' prosti-
tutes, Cates's girlfriend, and the woman Hammond will have sex with in the epilogue. Thus, *48 Hrs.* has reinvented the homosocial triangle as a parallelepiped.

The combinatorics of *48 Hrs.* are solid from top to bottom, from character
to production design. The villains pair off with the heroes racially and narratively as well as sexually. Cates and Hammond are white and black; Gans
and Billy Bear are white and Indian. Hammond is sprung from jail on parole
by the white cop; Gans is sprung from jail by Billy Bear (the guards are dis-
tracted when the two come to blows over a series of racial taunts—Gans calls
Bear "Tonto"; it is the prologue's version of the midpoint fight). In Act III, the
motormouth Hammond will kill the stereotypically silent, laughing Indian

motorman; monomaniacal Cates will kill simply maniacal Gans. "I got hit! I don't believe it. *I* got *shot!*" The film opens in dusty, heat-shimmering *Cool Hand Luke* territory before heading into San Francisco, a city of Paramontian neon and steamy backlighting. The country returns in the city at Torchy's, a bar Billy Bear used to frequent, a bar where Murphy will proclaim, "There's a new sheriff in town." And just as Murphy is the fish out of water at Torchy's, Nolte will be at Vroman's.

One of the ways we might judge the rigor of a particular member of the buddy genre would be to search for moments in which the logical merry-go-round produces formally consistent but socially implausible scenes. Late in *48 Hrs.*, Nolte gets into it with his boss. The African American lieutenant screams that Murphy is "a lousy nigger convict. That's right, I called him a nigger," while Nolte defends him as having "more brains that you'll ever know, got more guts than any partner I ever had." "Just cause you say it with conviction, it don't mean shit to me." By this point, if the film has worked, the shock of the lieutenant's slur fades behind the more important opposition between something said "with conviction" and being a convict. Good for more than games, more than Gans, Murphy is a legitimate partner.

That partnership, though, had its own story. By the time *48 Hrs.* was in previews, Murphy was already cast in *Trading Places*, a film that would shoot in *SNL*'s winter hiatus and be released in the summer of 1983. Three weeks before *48 Hrs.* was released, Paramount moved to sign Murphy to the multi-picture deal. And just as the film allegorized Murphy's temporary liberation from television as his forty-eight-hour parole, so the million-dollar bonus Murphy would receive for signing with Paramount was figured by the five hundred thousand dollars his character was allowed to keep at the end of the film. Nolte's cop called it "the merit system," which seems as good a name as any. When the negotiating team descended on Murphy backstage at *SNL*, he made them wait outside his dressing room while the TV show he was watching ran its course. Yet what seems at first glance to be mere petulance, an omen of Murphy's on-set antics to come, is better thought of as due diligence. The show he was watching was *Star Trek*. If Paramount was going to "own his ass," Murphy wanted to know what it was like to be a proprietary franchise.

Trading Places and *Beverly Hills Cop* extend the star-making allegory of *48 Hrs.* In *Trading Places* Murphy, first seen as a low-rent con man, becomes the subject of an experiment carried out by a matched set of fusty brothers, Mortimer and Randolph Duke, who own a commodities brokerage: Which is more important, they wonder, breeding or opportunity? After they successfully install Murphy (Billy Ray Valentine) in the brokerage house and just as successfully debase Dan Aykroyd's snobby broker, the Dukes become, in turn, the victims of a switcheroo, bankrupted on the trading floor. Though *48 Hrs.* gave Murphy a "weekend pass" and the chance to earn several hundred thousand dollars, at the end of the film he went back to prison to serve out his time. *Trading Places* gave him the chance to escape poverty (television) forever. *Beverly Hills Cop* completed the star-making process by reversing it. In his first two roles, Murphy's character needs to prove his worth—to become a partner—and someone else is responsible for his rise. But in *Beverly Hills Cop*, Murphy brings his urban sensibility (his Detroit street smarts, his authenticity, that is, his blackness) to Beverly Hills in order to solve a case and liberate the Beverly Hills Police Department from the strictures of its adherence to the rules.

These films trace the arc of a career that is being managed nearly perfectly—by Paramount, by ICM, by Robert Wachs, and, not least, by Murphy himself. Between November 1982, when *48 Hrs.* premiered and Murphy-the-*SNL*-cast-member was quickly elevated to Murphy-the-host, and December 1984, when *Beverly Hills Cop* debuted and he hosted *SNL* again, he made only one serious misstep. Tucked in the middle of 1984 was Murphy's star turn in *Best Defense*. Over the years, a legend has grown that his part was added after the film previewed terribly, but the earliest trade announcements, from October 1983, have Dudley Moore and Murphy starring together.[66] (Murphy shot his scenes, again, in the winter break from *SNL*.) In his many apologies for the film, Murphy never implied that he stepped in to do Paramount a favor but rather that he did it for the money.[67] He was certainly a star, but his role was little more than an inflated cameo—a sex scene intercut with one between Moore and Kate Capshaw; a brief scene on a base in Kuwait; scenes of him field-testing a tank. Murphy felt guilty in part because the movie was unfunny and in part because Paramount had given him nearly equal prominence in the marketing. Marketing, in other words, had made the studio's failure his failure.

The only hint that Murphy's role was as small as it was came in his billing: "Strategic Guest Star." Given that the film was ostensibly a comedy about shoddy defense contracting, this credit was doubtless a play on President Reagan's Strategic Defense Initiative, the "Star Wars" program of advanced weaponry first floated in public on March 23, 1983.[68] What the movies had given to Reagan, the movies were taking back.[69] But just as surely, Murphy's billing was a warrant for the importance of strategy to the studio and, eventually, to its parent. The 1984 Gulf + Western annual report appeared just after *Best Defense* hit theaters, and it proclaimed that the conglomerate's recent restructuring had resulted in "a stronger, leaner, more profitable, more growth-oriented company." A year later "strategic planning" as such would occupy the center of the company's self-understanding. Strategy, like synergy, had found its home first at the studio and then at the parent company.

By tipping its hand in this way, Paramount invites a reading of Murphy's career not simply as its own creation but as its own self-mapping. At the smallest scale, Murphy's films nod toward their studio. Early in *48 Hrs.* Gans settles in to watch a Paramount cartoon, *Space Kid*, on television. (The juvenile alien silences a cop with his ray gun.) In *Trading Places*, the crop report that the Dukes intend to steal is being held under guard at the Department of Agriculture. At the time of the theft, the guard is conveniently watching the conclusion of *Sunset Blvd.*[70] In *Best Defense*, Kate Capshaw idly sings the *Raiders* theme as she waits in a car. That same summer she would star in *Temple of Doom*, co-written by *Best Defense* director Willard Huyck.

These bits of studio identity still seem contingent, mere inside jokes, even though they stake out the films as Paramount's territory. Yet at another scale, and like the popsicals, Murphy's story in these films parallels and anticipates Gulf + Western's. The climax of *48 Hrs.* occurs in a steamy, neon-lit, Chinatown alley in some unholy fusion of the studio's seventies narrative indeterminacy and its eighties stylishness. That backlit, industrial mise-en-scène is absent from *Trading Places*, which is nearly all woody luxe and slushy streetscapes. But what *Trading Places* gives up in style it gains in narrative explicitness. The money in *48 Hrs.* is just a duffle bag full of cash Hammond and Gans stole from "a dealer during a sale." The money in *Trading Places* comes, hyperexplicitly, from commodities. When Ameche and Bellamy sit Murphy down to explain what it is they do, they present him with what looks like an ordinary breakfast.

> BRV: No thanks, guys, I already had breakfast this morning.
>
> Mortimer: This is not a meal, Valentine. We are here to try to explain to you what it is we do here.
>
> Randolph: We are commodities brokers, William. Now, what are commodities? Commodities are agricultural products, like, coffee which you had for breakfast, wheat, which is used to make bread, pork bellies which is used to make bacon, which you might find in a bacon and lettuce and tomato sandwich.

At this point, Valentine cannot take it anymore and looks directly into the camera. Most critics have taken this to be one of director John Landis's trademarks, and it is; and it is something Murphy did as Buckwheat on *SNL*. Yet it is also a declaration: the studio (through its star) knows its way around the commodities markets. By that afternoon, Valentine is dispensing advice based on his (street-smart, authentic, urban, etc.) insight into investor psychology. For him, what matters are the feelings of the players in the game ("Christmas is around the corner and I ain't gonna have no money to buy my son the G.I. Joe with the kung-fu grip"), not the structure of the deal (certainly not agency-style commissions) and not the underlying phenomena of supply and demand.[71]

Like Bluhdorn, the Duke brothers attempt to increase their gains and remove the risk from their commodities portfolio through illicit activities, and like Bluhdorn, Randolph Duke will keel over when he realizes the extent of his losses. Randolph's fictional heart attack was filmed within a month of Bluhdorn's own.[72] "Fuck him!" shouts Mortimer, as much at Bluhdorn as his brother, for by the time the film was released, Martin Davis was already busy remaking the company, hastily shedding its commodities businesses and its investment portfolio to focus on high-profit, growth industries. The new Gulf + Western would cater to "the enduring human desire for something new, something fresh,"[73] rather than frozen, concentrated orange juice.

By late 1984 commodities had been squeezed out of Gulf + Western by entertainment and financial services. The Consumer and Industrial Products division would be the next major divestiture. As Murphy's Detective Axel Foley headed from Detroit to Beverly Hills in his iconic, weathered Mumford Phys. Ed. Dept. T-shirt and his beat-up Chevy Nova, Gulf + Western was arranging the sale of its apparel and auto parts subsidiaries.[74] With his arrival in Beverly Hills style returns to his films, but as the *genius loci* rather than as a hallmark of directorial authorship. The case will revolve around art, but art as a cover for illegal trade in bearer bonds and cocaine. And its crucial location will not be an alley or a trading floor but a warehouse.

Deep in the DVD commentary for *Beverly Hills Cop*, director Martin Brest sighs, "What is it about villains and warehouses?" And while warehouses might seem very unstylish (but also very Paramount, particularly in the wake of *Raiders*), *BHC* does its best to make them interesting by turning valuation into a problem of certification, that is, things matter in *BHC* to the extent that they can be branded. The film opens with Axel conducting a sting involving stolen cigarettes. What makes them special is that they already have the federal tax stamp. "You can't beat that; you can't get no cleaner than that." No grit. The crime in Beverly Hills is a more complicated version of the same. Art dealer Victor Maitland ("Art isn't the only thing he deals") is diverting newly arrived crates from the bonded warehouse before they can clear customs. Instead, they first go to *his* warehouse, where the smuggled bonds and drugs can be removed. It is, as a plot point, both deadly dull and absolutely necessary. As Brest put it, "I remember being in a fevered phone call with Don Simpson, rest his soul, about the expositional requirements for this area of the story and how much we should jam in and how much we shouldn't jam in and which story points we should hit."[75] And while one might object that Brest and Simpson failed to solve the intractable problem of villains and warehouses, they succeeded in making the warehouse something other than a place commodities are stored. In *BHC*, the warehouse is the place where authenticity is assured.

All this talk of bonds—"I could have twenty-five agents down here in fifteen minutes to march in here, snatch your bond from underneath you, and you guys would be out of business, permanently," Foley tells the employees of the warehouse at one point—raises questions of trust, of storytelling, and of fabulation. From the opening, when Foley proclaims, "I'm a business man, that's my thing. I'm doin' business here," he is both doing business and telling stories (about doing business). Midway through the film, attempting to deflect blame from himself and two officers in the police department, he spins a tale of the two "supercops" who foiled a robbery. They confess to the truth: "Detective Foley deserves all the credit"; but Foley is clear: "Before I go, I just want you two to know something. The supercops story . . . was working." By the end of the film, straight-laced Lieutenant Bogamil has learned how to tell a nearly believable, but, more important, effective story. "You expect me to believe that report?" asks the chief. "That's the report I'm filing." In Murphy, Paramount found—or made—a teller of tales whose insistence on exigency rather than truth rivaled the studio's own.

At this point in Murphy's career, though, it became difficult to know who was leading and who was following. Paramount might still believe the narrative that it had made Murphy a star, but in that narrative, the star had saved Paramount from itself. Murphy's next picture, *The Golden Child*, carried that tension to the verge of explicitness. As Murphy became a more expensive but more essential player, the studio looked to cut other parts of the film's budget. Dawn Steel, the last vestige of the Diller regime, suggested filming everything locally (not going to Katmandu) and "skimping on the special effects." Producer Edward Feldman, defending his film's budget, played his trump card: "Has anyone discussed this with Eddie Murphy?" to which Steel responded, "I want you to understand something once and for all, Ed. *Eddie Murphy does not run Paramount Pictures.*" "*Oh yes, he does.*"[76] That it was even an issue points to the conflations of power and identity between studio and star. Out of this dynamic, Feldman came up with the film's highly successful teaser trailer:

> It was a takeoff on that famous scene in *Lawrence of Arabia*, when a lone figure on a camel (Peter O'Toole as Lawrence) appears as a speck far off in the desert and then approaches the camera, becoming recognizable as he rides. Our teaser starts with a lone figure in the snow. . . . There is a voice-over by our villain. . . . "Every

hundred years a special person comes along" . . . And the figure is coming closer to the screen and he's on a yak. He's got all this snow gear on him. We realize it's Eddie Murphy. "And he is known as the Golden Child." And Murphy looks at the camera and says, "Sure, all these guys at Paramount are sitting in their warm offices and I'm freezing my ass off." When the teaser-trailer appeared on the screen, people went bananas. . . . I think we were the first ones to poke fun at studio executives.[77]

Feldman is historically wrong, but not terribly wrong. For what he is sensing here is that something was gathering. Not just a build-up of tension between studio and star—that is a baseline condition of the Hollywood system in all its modes—but a build-up of tension that might be released for the audience as a whole. The corporate design of these films could come to the fore without risking the films behind them. Story and backstory had become continuous enough to exploit the identity between them. And to the extent that this balance could be maintained, the system had found its footing at last.

High Concept and the Story of Story

But that balance was always in flux. The mutual dependence of studio and star threatened to come undone in *Buchwald v. Paramount*. The case required an intensive investigation of Hollywood authorship as it was understood, as it was practiced, and as it was controlled. In Buchwald's version of events, argued by Pierce O'Donnell in court and recounted in *Fatal Subtraction*, he had sold an idea to Paramount that became the Eddie Murphy vehicle *Coming to America* (Landis, 1989). The conflict was not, though, a battle over credit. Buchwald had only discovered the similarities between his treatment (begun as *It's a Crude, Crude World* but quickly changed to *King for a Day* when Paramount, yet again, spotted it in turnaround) and *Coming to America* after the film was in distribution. Had Buchwald been interested in credit, the best he might have hoped for was that the Writers Guild of America (WGA) would support him in his lawsuit, issue sanctions against the studio, and guarantee that future releases of the film include a line that the film was "based on" his work.

Instead of pursuing his claim through the guild, he sued. If he could prove that the film was in fact "based on" his story, then he would be entitled to 19 percent of the net profits. Buchwald routinely described what occurred as "theft," but it was a particularly difficult sort of theft to pin down. At issue was not the unattributed use of particular lines or even scenes but an alienation of his idea within what the studio called "the continuity of creative management."[78] After initially developing *King for a Day*, Paramount had let it languish. Then, somehow—and this process lay at the center of the trial of fact—the studio and Eddie Murphy Productions developed what became *Coming to America.* Was there continuity between the two projects? Were they, in fact, the same project? While the wholesale changes in Paramount's executive corps after Bluhdorn's death made the notion that there were, in fact, two different projects with the same conceit at their core plausible, the fact that these projects existed at the same studio in temporal proximity seemed to the plaintiffs, and most others, prima facie evidence that they were the same project. There was also evidence that Murphy had heard the *King for a Day* pitch, that various members of his production company had access to the treatment and early scripts for that film, and that certain (potentially) telling elements found their way into *Coming to America.*

Buchwald's lawsuit, then, was the operationalization of high concept: you know a high concept truly exists when it can be stolen. O'Donnell put it this way: "What Buchwald sold Paramount was an idea, I acknowledged, but ideas were the lifeblood of Hollywood. Paramount itself conceded that point in a philosophy paper Katzenberg wrote and distributed to the studio's inner circle in June 1982. . . . 'Idea is King and material is Queen. . . . Essence lies in the way it is new, unique, different, or in some way imaginative and exciting.'"[79] Judge Harvey Schneider found for the plaintiffs. Interestingly, he avoided relying on any of the expert testimony from movie industry players regarding what "based on" meant. Instead, he turned to precedents in the area of copyright infringement, which this case was not (it was a breach of contract). For copyrights, a two-part test ruled: Did the defendants have access? And is there similarity between the two works? Crucially, "Where there is strong evidence of access, less proof of similarity may suffice."[80] And given that in *Buchwald v. Paramount* access was a given, the proof of similarity could be tenuous. Hence the ease with which Schneider reached a decision on the merits.

More important to those who want to understand the operation of the contemporary studio system would be the question of motivation: Why would the studio exclude Buchwald? The plaintiffs offered two reasons. First, Paramount did it simply to avoid paying Buchwald and his producing partner, Alain Bernheim. This may have been true, but the amount of money at stake was, in the overall revenue stream of the film, relatively small if it existed at all. The studio's accounting showed that *Coming to America* had not reached the point when it would have generated "net profits" for those participants; O'Donnell professed to be shocked that this had occurred, but the traditions of such accounting were venerable. Even after a clear victory on the merits of the case, and a rather stunning repudiation by the judge of the studio's contractual boilerplate that determined net profits, Buchwald and Bernheim were still awarded less than $1 million, certainly far less than Paramount's legal expenses.

More central to the narrative of *Fatal Subtraction*, the plaintiffs also believed that Paramount did whatever it did to "keep Eddie happy." The studio's desire on this point was also not financially driven—Murphy was a gross profit participant; Buchwald's net would not have affected the star's earnings. Instead, in this theory, Paramount cut Buchwald out in order to preserve the notion that *Coming to America* was Murphy's story. O'Donnell and Buchwald assume that Murphy's importance to Paramount required the studio to provide more than millions of dollars up front, overhead for his production company, and luxurious trappings for himself and his entourage on set. Having given him all these things, all that remained was writing credit. As O'Donnell argued in his opening statement, Murphy served as the corporate author:

> Eddie calls the shots. Whatever Eddie wants, Eddie gets. If he wants Paramount to put its name on vulgar movies like *Raw*, okay, Eddie. If he wants a scene shot his way, he summons the president of the studio, Ned Tanen, to the set. Okay, Eddie. And if he tells the president of the studio, Ned Tanen, that he's conceived a movie idea strikingly similar to Buchwald's original idea, okay, Eddie.[81]

Paramount's attorney Robert Draper highlighted the problems with both aspects of the theory. "The idea that somehow Eddie Murphy, this bad Eddie Murphy, this dumb Eddie Murphy is such a force at Paramount that it's an incentive for them to be un-nice to Mr. Buchwald and Mr. Bernheim and not pay them $250,000, I don't think stands up."[82]

Yet if one eliminates the executive toadying and conspiracy mongering of O'Donnell's narrative, there is something fitting about this story. Certainly Murphy's interest in his own authorship was long-standing. He had effectively gone on strike at *Saturday Night Live* in order to secure writing credit. (The policy on the show was that performers received such credit only if they wrote for skits they were not in.)[83] As soon as he was able, Murphy set up his own production company. Little more than a year later, he talked about his ambitions to *Newsweek*: "I want to direct and write and score and produce—like Chaplin used to do. Nobody does that anymore."[84] After writing credits on *SNL* and the concert film *Delirious*, Murphy received his first story credit for *Beverly Hills Cop II*. That had gone to WGA arbitration, but Murphy and his manager, Bob Wachs, had prevailed over novelist-sportswriters (and fellow ICM clients) Dan Jenkins and Bud Shrake. They retained "story" credit, while screenplay credit went to Larry Ferguson and Warren Skaaren.[85] *Coming to America* would be Murphy's second story credit. At the same time, Murphy's stardom and ego were at their peak. Both director John Landis and producer George Folsey thought that "Eddie was a different Eddie Murphy on *Coming to America* than he was on *Trading Places*" (Folsey); "He was a very different guy than the guy I had made *Trading Places* with" (Landis). "He once said to me," Landis recounted, "'You treat me like you treat everybody else.' I thought, 'Isn't that a good thing?' And then I realized maybe he meant I wasn't obsequious enough or something."[86] As in the teaser trailer for *The Golden Child*, *Coming to America* ironizes Murphy's imperiousness, with Murphy surrounded by kowtowing subjects and yearning for the freedom of anonymity.

A crucial question is whether Murphy would have received credit if Buchwald had. The answer is unclear. Landis says that Murphy called him and said, "'I have an idea for a movie,' and he pitched it to me, and the idea was essentially *Cinderella*."[87] The credited screenwriters attest that he gave them Act I and the idea for what would follow, and that after the script was ready, he altered the plot and invented much of the dialogue. Had it gone before the WGA, he might have found himself in the same situation he had been in at *SNL*. By assuring that Murphy was credited—either by losing the trail of attribution in the fog of development hell (as the studio contended) or intentionally obfuscating it (as the plaintiffs argued)—Paramount hewed to its role as the author of authorship. Lynn Roth, one of the plaintiffs' experts, put it bluntly: "Paramount is a signatory to the Writers Guild, so the Writers Guild would say Paramount has no power to determine any kind of credit whatsoever."[88] In fighting *Buchwald v. Paramount*, the studio was defending its system-setting power more than its bottom line.

How is credit allocated in *Coming to America*? Certainly Murphy receives a lot of it: "Paramount presents an Eddie Murphy Production"; his is the only name above the title; and he receives sole story credit. In the closing credits, he and Arsenio Hall are given additional credits for each of the roles they played in heavy makeup. This credit story enters the film's narrative via the logo bleed. *Coming to America* features the relatively novel computer-generated mountain leader that the studio debuted in 1986. Gone was the transition from the painterly, realist mountain to the stark, almost Saul Bassian, logo of the seventies. Instead, all sorts of new, photoreal effects appeared: stars began to pivot and have heft; the mountain was reflected in a lake in front of it; and the whole leader seemed to draw the viewer into the Paramount world. In *Coming to America*, the camera continues to push in, past the mountain, into a low-level flyover of just the sort pioneered in *Star Trek II*'s "Genesis" sequence. Off in the distance lies the palace of the Kingdom of Zamunda. Not yet the country's ruler, Murphy's Akeem is, at least, the face of its currency.

Figure 5.8. Passage to Zamunda. *Coming to America* (John Landis, Paramount, 1988)

Once in America, Akeem's working-class masquerade will meet its corporate complement. His love interest is the daughter of what one might call a counterfeit restaurateur. Everything about his fast-food enterprise is lifted from McDonald's—the trade dress, the menu, even its operations manual. But what elevates him is his commitment to design. Not only do he and McDowell's employees wear tartan; so does his sofa and, in the best touch, so do the travesties of French paintings he has hung on his walls. (The tartan is Royal Stewart, not McDowell.) To pull this off, though, the producers had to get McDonald's approval, and that created a pathway from the film's backstory to its plot, as Landis explained: "It was a very complicated thing to create a faux McDonald's and not get sued by McDonald's. It was very much like it is in the movie." Someone at "the studio" told producer George Folsey that McDonald's would never agree. "They have kind of a lock on that Mc, M-c derivatives." Yet, as David Sheffield described it, "To our amazement they said okay. Because they like the fact that we were pointing out that the McDonald's guys were after [McDowell], trying to enforce their copyright."[89]

Whether we understand the film's intense interest in copyright and trademark claims as simply ironic or as the projections of Paramount's guilty conscience matters very little. In light of *Buchwald v. Paramount* the question seems no longer to be one of *whether* the film allegorizes its studio's operations but only of *how*. Pragmatic, modal questions have replaced existential ones. The full armature is in place: the logo bleed at the opening, the easy ironies of Murphy-

Figure 5.9. Trade dress as travesty. *Coming to America* (Landis, Paramount, 1988)

as-money (and later of Murphy as Martin Luther King), the self-quotation when Ameche and Bellamy reprise their roles as the Duke brothers, now homeless bums grateful when Murphy gives them several thousand dollars. The rules Judge Schneider adopted have become the guidelines of the modern studio as auteur: Do they have access to their own story, and is there similarity between story and backstory? Whether Paramount was being run by Murphy or not remained an open question, and the stories on-screen remained contingent. As the studio fought to defend its authority and its author in court, the relationship between them entered a new phase. Schneider found in favor of Buchwald in January 1990 and again in December; he awarded the plaintiffs $150,000 in March 1992. In September 1991, Paramount re-signed Murphy to a four-picture deal worth at least $12 million per picture; a month later Disney announced that Murphy would star in his first non-Paramount movie, *The Distinguished Gentleman.*

The Studio after the Studio (after the Studio)

At Paramount 1985 was a tough year; the studio had only one film, *Witness*, finish in the top 30 domestically. But it recovered in 1986, dominating the top 10: #1 (*Top Gun*), #2 (*Crocodile Dundee*), #5 (*Star Trek IV*), #8 (*The Golden Child*), and #10 (*Ferris Bueller's Day Off*). (The rebound appears as a spike in income in 1986 and 1987.) The dip and recovery at the studio followed a pattern typical of executive transitions. As Bruckheimer described it, "As soon as new management comes in, usually they strip everything and start their own development.

We were very fortunate, we had lunch with Ned Tanen who came in and re-placed Jeffrey [Katzenberg] and Michael [Eisner], and at lunch he said, 'Whad-dya have? We got nothing to make, we want to make some movies.'"[90] In the transition, Simpson and Bruckheimer's long-gestating and nearly dead *Top Gun* project was revived. According to Bruckheimer, Tanen green-lit the film with-out having read it, as long as it could be made cheaply enough (budgeted at $14 to $15 million, completed, according to director Tony Scott, at $16.6). The film's production story seems tailor-made for the post-studio era, where "Para-mount" survives only as a financier and distributor, and where films gestate outside any overarching or unique vision that might shape their identity. What-ever *Top Gun* was about, it would not be about the studio's or the conglomer-ate's twists and turns.

But at Paramount, that free-floating state of affairs amounted to a dras-tic reversal. Earlier in *Top Gun*'s development, the studio threatened to put it in turnaround but relented when Bruckheimer and Simpson begged them to allow development to go ahead. "Don got to a point where he actually got on his knees and begged Michael not to put the picture in turnaround. Michael looked at Jeffrey and said, 'We gotta let 'em keep developing the project, they're this passionate about it, we can't turn 'em down.'"[91] (The producers believed in the film, certainly, but they were also exclusive to Paramount and would not have been able to travel with the property had it been picked up elsewhere.) Passion, happening—the Diller system was still in place at that point, and the reasoning behind Eisner's decision was the polar opposite of Tanen's. Does the film bear the traces of this story—that is, does it tell the story, somehow, of the studio's loss (and recovery) of identity, or does it exist within a space where identity is so contingent that it cannot be thought of as won or lost? If the neoclassical system is as firmly established at Paramount in 1985 as I have been arguing, then a film this particular to its studio should not be able to avoid reckoning with that corporate vacancy, or, if it does manage to be a movie driven by its own internal forces, then those forces should offer the studio a way out of its temporary lull—must suggest that the lull is necessarily temporary. What is the real story of *Top Gun*?

Plot-wise, the film tells the story of a maverick called Maverick, a pilot who has to prove himself to everyone—to his commanding officers, his fellow pilots (the one with the most sangfroid is called Iceman), and his ghost of a father. Yet even one of its co-writers, Jack Epps, could not defend the film's story: "It was not a plot movie; it was not a movie about the mission."[92] Still, one could cer-tainly read that plot as an allegory of the battle for the soul of the industry be-tween the "textbook maneuvers" of someone like Iceman and the "real genius" of Maverick. Dangerous, but successful, Maverick's tactics cannot be replicated: "The encounter was a victory, but I think we've shown it as an example of what not to do." In the climactic battle, it will be Maverick, held in reserve, who will take Hollywood's place: "Wood's been hit. We've lost Hollywood. Repeat, we've lost Hollywood." He and Iceman together will fight off a squadron of MiGs. The entente between the two schools is clear: "You're still dangerous," Iceman says, "but you can be my wingman anytime." "Bullshit," Maverick responds. "You can be mine." For Don Simpson, who prided himself on macho risk taking yet who was bound to a major studio, this would be the model of his own relationship to authority, a tale in which the studio could locate its need for innovative rebels. One story of *Top Gun*, then, is simply that of the mutual dependence between studio and producer.

In *Sleep with Me* (Rory Kelly, UA, 1994), emerging auteur Quentin Tarantino offers a rather different reading of the film, a routine that he and then-writing partner Roger Avary had been doing at Hollywood parties. The bit is an extended interpretation of *Top Gun* as "the story of a man's struggle with his own homosexuality," in which Tom Cruise has to decide whether he will be with Kelly McGillis or "go the gay way." After ticking off the major plot points, now reread, we reach the "real ending" of the film, in which Val Kilmer (Iceman) offers to let Tom Cruise (Maverick) "ride my tail" and Cruise responds that "you can ride mine." (The line is misremembered, but the point is only slightly dulled.) Tarantino's on-screen audience is a newly successful screenwriter who initially derides *Top Gun* as "a bunch of guys waving their dicks around." Five minutes later, having thoroughly succumbed to Tarantino's version of the film, he and Tarantino are grabbing their crotches yelling, "Sword fight! Sword fight!" The circle is complete, and now *Sleep with Me* is a movie about a bunch of guys emulating *Top Gun*. But the point of the rereading is not to upend the writer's initial opinion, which was correct; much less is it to enlist him in Tarantino's vision of screenwriting: "The whole idea is subversion. You want subversion on a massive level." Instead, Tarantino sets up an economy of moviemaking and interpretation in which taking pleasure in the mainstream film would consist in reveling in the thoroughness with which it grounds our first impressions and the pleasure of the indieWood feature would lie in making the subversive or subtextual explicit.

This economy proved to be both relatively stable and readily amenable to the major studios, who spawned or bought their own indie divisions in order to capture and capitalize on this market segmentation. Yet the cleverness of Tarantino's reading and the pathetic masculine displays at the Hollywood party have obscured the basis for the routine in the first place: the assumption that mainstream movies can be "fucking brilliant" or, in my terms, that they often know what they are about. He is utterly sincere in his admiration, while his audience attributes the cleverness of the reading to Tarantino's film buffery or to *Top Gun*'s own unconscious. *Top Gun*'s creators are left out of this loop, blindly managing to build a relentlessly homoerotic film in the guise of hypernationalist war porn. If the film's politics are shot through with sexuality, nevertheless it maintained its balance between the obvious (masculine competition) and the implicit (one man's struggle with his homosexuality). *Top Gun* remained deniable; "right on the fucking line," as Tarantino would have it, yet to understand the subtext of the film, all one had to do was settle down to read it.

Such a reinterpretive project is made easier because *Top Gun*'s images are models of classical balance, nearly Davidian in their evocations of the ideal male body, and rigorously balanced. In this shot from the locker room—the essential site for the assertion of the fighter jock ethos—the display could hardly be more candid. The space is relatively deep and recedes rapidly, but our three central figures are all downstage. The pronounced perspective of the room conveyed by the tops of the lockers and horizontal pipes along the ceiling draws the viewer to the center of the image, Anthony Daniels's (Goose's) waist. He stands, still in his flight suit, along the central axis of the shot, positioned between the upthrust knees of another pilot in T-shirt and boxer briefs while a third, to his right, wears only a towel, his dog tags, and his slicked-back, freshly showered hair. (True to neoclassical form, the lower edge of the image serves almost as a pediment.) The three figures are sniping at one another's prowess, but they are also versions of one another, rotated around the void along the left aisle. (The right aisle is blocked by a partial replication of our group: a second man in a flight suit (Tom Cruise's "Maverick") and a second man in a towel (Sundown, the African

Figure 5.10. A model of classical balance. *Top Gun* (Scott, Paramount, 1986)

American who will temporarily serve as Maverick's radar intercept officer when Goose dies). The whole image is framed internally, with rough concrete pillars marking off dark spaces on the outer edges, in effect masking down the shot. On each pillar, naturally enough, hangs a perfectly broken-in pair of blue jeans and an equally casual yet equally perfect shirt. Among the beiges and olives of the rows of lockers, the blue of the jeans (and a helmet), the red of the locker doors, and the white of the towel and underwear stand out. A crisp, cream cowboy hat lies just so on the bench; the nationalist archetype is complete.

The legibility of the frame extends to the ultra-clean-cut look of the men. Much of what gave Tarantino's reading its purchase, and which has spawned cult screenings of the film, was this queer look. Scott is explicit about its source and its power:

> One of my favorite books that I stole from in terms of looks of male models that I was shooting in commercials was Bruce Weber. He had this book of all these guys, just great looking guys, and the centerfold in this book had these three guys and they're sitting inside this Chevy and they're all no shirts on and haircuts. And one of them looked just like Tom, and one looked just like Val, and the other one in the background was this jock who looked like Rick Rossovich. I took that into Paramount and they went [mouth agape, eyes bulging]. They saw this book, and they thought I was going to take too big a leaf out of that book for this movie. That really became the look of the movie, the look of the actors.[93]

What Paramount feared was that the film would be undeniably, insistently gay, and not covertly (or "subversively") so: "They got a bit scared because it was infamous in terms of the gay community, this book; that's where all these haircuts came from and this sort of hard-edged military look." Still, Scott stuck with it, most notoriously in the volleyball scene backed by Kenny Loggins's "Playin' with the Boys." It "became a favorite with the women as well as the guys, especially the San Francisco guys."[94] Early on, Maverick's commanding officer explains to him (not for the last time) that the airplanes he flies are expensive. "Your ego is writing checks your body can't cash." Scott hoped that by lifting Weber's aesthetic, the male bodies might have sufficient reserves to cash those checks.

Weber's pictures were black and white (or black and white washed with a particular tone), so Scott was compelled to invent a color palette for the film. The interior design of *Top Gun* is supremely consistent: olive/beige/white on the men, red/white/blue on flags behind them. The exteriors are nearly as consistent, and consistent with Scott's vision: "It wasn't *Apocalypse Now*, it was a definite popcorn movie, but it was the rock'n'roll stars of the sky, so I saw these great looking guys—actors—fighter pilots against blue-black skies in silver jets and rock'n'roll music."[95] When the skies aren't blue-black, they are a complementary orange, and they are always roiled with jetwash.

The jetwash in the skies is the technological equivalent of the fine beads of water or sweat that seem always to coat the men, whether in the heat of the classroom or the cockpit, emerging from the shower or standing on the deck of a carrier in the Indian Ocean. This moisture is a mist of narcissism that holds the other men at bay, and when Maverick and Iceman overcome that barrier at last, it feels like "the real ending" of the film, according to Tarantino. If he is right and the ending on the carrier deck is the "real" ending of the film, then Maverick's reunion with Charlie is compromised. And in their final shot together, after he has explained that things will be complicated, and after he has smiled the Tom Cruise smile while wearing his clean, white, pocket T-shirt while standing in front of a flag and a throwback Wurlitzer jukebox on which the Righteous Brothers' "You've Lost That Lovin' Feelin'" is playing—after all that, we are ready for the final clinch. But it never happens; something has come between them. Tarantino would say that something was Maverick's desire for Iceman. Looking at the screen, that something is a neon sign for Pepsi (see second image in Chapter 3).

The Pepsi ending was the third one they shot. In two previous versions, Maverick and Charlie had met on the runway. Now they were inside, backlit, in front of more of the film's ubiquitous venetian blinds. The Pepsi sign that replaces the patriotic red and blue of the flags is incongruously hung so that it reads the right way from inside the barbecue joint. (Other signs in the film face outward and are only re-reversed when we see their reflections.) The color coding and strongly centered compositions of the film's interiors have been training the viewer for just this moment. There have also been earlier Pepsi appearances. Maverick, Slider, and Sundown are all drinking it from cans while they study. And when the officer in charge of the control tower gets doused with coffee for a second time, the petty officer is carrying the mugs on a Pepsi tray that conveniently faces the camera when the two collide. (The film's spirit of comedy, the control officer can harmlessly give voice to the film's otherwise deniable desires. "I want some butts!" he shouts, twice.)

During their extensive discussions of the film's genesis and production, neither Bruckheimer nor Scott mentions Pepsi's product placement. Synergy-obsessed Gulf + Western did, though, in their 1987 annual report:

> *Top Gun*, the top box office hit of 1986, debuted on video-cassette in March 1987 at $26.95, the lowest introductory price for any new film video, because of an

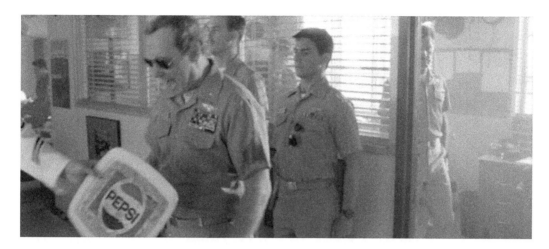

Figure 5.11. "I want some butts!" *Top Gun* (Scott, Paramount, 1986)

innovative promotional tie-in with Pepsi-Cola. The tie-in included a promotional campaign by Diet Pepsi featuring a *Top Gun* theme and a 60-second Diet Pepsi commercial on each *Top Gun* cassette. Nearly three million units have been sold.[96]

Downstream revenues were driven, in part, by the film's ability to serve as an extension of the sponsor's promotional campaign. Yet that campaign was utterly, organically tied in to the film's design. The overt Pepsi ad at the beginning of the videotape functions as a training exercise for viewers in how to see and read and feel design. Intense pictorialism had been a hallmark of Bruckheimer productions from *American Gigolo* on, and the albatross of Tony Scott's career. Talking about Bruckheimer and Simpson, Scott is effusive: "These two guys they had a vision about bringing a new look to movies, and Jerry was the one who was out there saying, 'I like what commercial directors are doing, rock video directors. So that's why he gave Adrian Lyne his first crack at *Flashdance*, and he gave me my first crack at *Top Gun*. . . . They were the only guys that had the courage after *The Hunger* to reemploy me."[97] But *Top Gun* is not *The Keep*. Its story was direct to the point of becoming an allegory of itself. Cinematography and production design opened it up for reading; the limited repletion of its story charged that reading, directing it toward the subversive. The frame became maximally legible, and audiences in the video era found themselves with the time (and energy) to search it for meaning. The overarching combination of cleanliness and paranoia allows it to sell almost anything. It is (certainly) an advertisement for danger, for the US Navy, for Pepsi. More than that, though, it is an advertisement for the Paramount way: the classic fashions and spontaneous musicality of *Footloose*, the pictorial sense of *American Gigolo*, the narrative of contained rebellion of *Beverly Hills Cop*. Even Kelly McGillis's car is a Paramount icon. It is the same car that belongs to Reggie Hammond in *48 Hrs.*;

its stunt double will be blown up in the sequel; and it will magically reappear in *Beverly Hills Cop 3*. True to Paramount's heritage, true to the ersatzishness of the neoclassical era, the car looks like a Porsche 356A but is an Italian replica.[98]

Top Gun was last of the real Killer Diller productions. But even as Paramount's executive corps could (and did) take over control of other studios—Diller went to Fox; Eisner, Katzenberg, and Mestres went to Disney; Steel, to Columbia—the studio was no longer in the business of asserting its own control but rather of controlling the assertions of its leading talent. Simpson and Bruckheimer received more credit than Paramount for *Top Gun*'s success, just as Murphy would demand and get more credit than the studio for his. The new Paramount, with its "low-key, team-oriented approach,"[99] rode the first film to great success and rode Murphy's career to great legal peril. The studio that had reinvented the look of Hollywood motion pictures and had transformed their ability to sell was, if not left behind, then, let us say, debranding.

Let's Make the Weather
Chaos Comes to Hollywood

Let's make the weather
Let's pull the stars closer in . . .

"Make the Weather," The Waitresses

Relevance

The ad campaign for the 1995 Honda Civic was an unqualified success. It not only won the Clio for best campaign—the equivalent of the Best Picture Oscar—it was ripped off by Isuzu for its Rodeo and Toyota for its Camry. The ads, narrated by Jack Lemmon, told strange little stories about art and the weather and your car.

> It's 10:15 in the Amazon and a butterfly flaps its wings, which spreads pollen and causes a Caribou to sneeze igniting a massive stampede, which adds wind to a mounting storm, which alters the global pattern of weather and creates a downpour that knocks out the electricity so you couldn't blow dry your hair. With all that can go wrong in your day, isn't it nice to know you can rely on your Honda Civic?

> It's 1954 at the university of Milan and a young man gets a C in mathematics, which causes him to lose his scholarship and take up sidewalk drawing, which spawns a worldwide movement in art that inspires a burgeoning painter, which leads to the opening at the museum that caused the traffic jam that's making you late for work. With all that can go wrong in your day, isn't it nice to know you can depend on your Honda Civic?

As Greg Hahn, the creative director behind the campaign put it, the ads "start off completely disconnected from you, something small and insignificant, then move up to some big thing and then back down to some insignificant thing that affects you."[1] From a C in math to a worldwide art movement to a traffic jam. From a butterfly flapping its wings to a bad hair day. (In the print ads, these connections are figured in propagating ovals and a quasi time line.)

These are stories of complicated, unexpected chains of events that start small and somehow get out of control. In the Honda ads, though, you get control back. Everything blows up, but your car still works. The childlike (or Bressonian) fascination with things such as the circulation of an individual coin

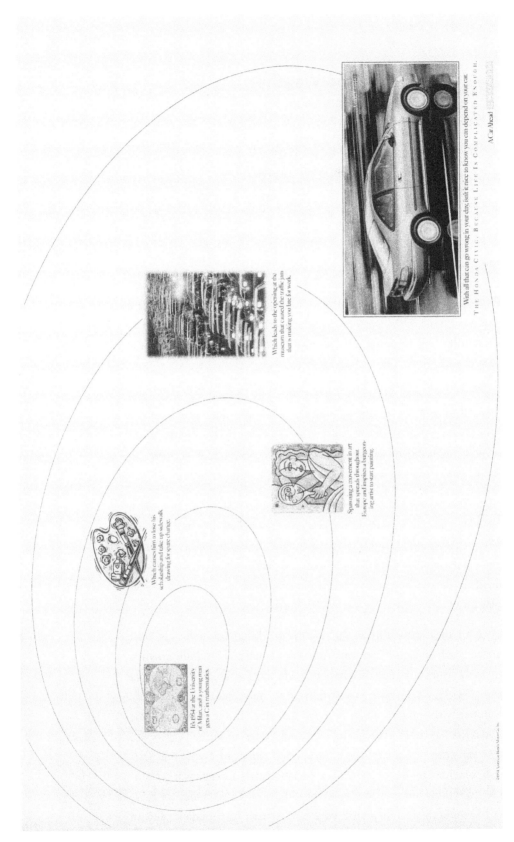

Figure 6.1. The 1995 Honda campaign. Source: American Honda Motor Company, courtesy Ruben Postaer

or "For want of a nail" stories is a large part of why the campaign, like the car, works. But the other part of the campaign's success is its pop version of "chaos theory," specifically what is more technically known as "sensitive dependence on initial conditions," but which is usually called, after the popular example, the butterfly effect.

In order to spare consumers the burden of tackling the math that would demonstrate why it is that weather exhibits sensitive dependence, the popular science writer offers narratives and examples that are more portable. In the Honda case there is a direct link from James Gleick's *Chaos: The Making of a New Science* (1987) to Philip Goldberg's *The Babinsky Reflex: And 70 Other Useful and Amusing Metaphors* (1990) to Greg Hahn. By converting math into metaphor, popular science paves the way for the metaphor to continue on its course until it reaches its logical end point, advertising. Here, the second spot is a tidy emblem for the trajectories of both chaos theory and its consumer: from a failure to understand math, to aesthetic revolution, to a traffic jam (the proliferation of cars, ideally, Hondas). From the language of nature to its metaphorical displacement and back to physical phenomena.

Hahn's pitch to Honda was that the butterfly effect "made reliability relevant." In the print ads, relevance—the link between the consumer and the bad math student—is embodied in the linking lines radiating out from the initial event. In the TV spots, relevance is embodied in the single tracking shot. A sweeping camera takes the viewer from the butterfly in the grass—an emblem of the actual Amazonian butterfly—out onto the driveway, to the woman having the bad hair day.

The scientific name for this link is "strange attractor," and it gets used in disconcertingly Chomskian sentences like "A strange attractor is a communicating channel between scales."[2] What that means and how it means for someone who knows chaos math is difficult to say; what it means for a reader of Gleick's book is easy. Just as John Hollander was able to write a poem ("Coiled Alizarine") that ended with Chomsky's semi-grammatical sentence "Colorless green ideas sleep furiously," so an aestheticizing, and literalizing, reading of chaos theory made ideas like "strange attractor" and "communicating channel" broadly available by rewriting them into the discourses of romance and social theory. *Chaos* was a huge best seller for a popular science book in 1987 and again in paperback, when it was a Book of the Month Club selection. Of those millions of copies of a book that took the math and turned it into a story—the story of the making of a science—many landed in Hollywood. Gleick made the butterfly effect part of casual studio conversation. The history of Hollywood ideas that follows explains why chaos was so readily assimilated, provides some evidence for the creation of an industry-wide mini-genre, and shows how an idea could be deployed in complex studio situations. But more than that, it shows how chaos's particular account of intentionality might come to the rescue of filmmakers and executives during a period of dramatic change. As the industry was roiling under new management and running headlong into the digital era, chaos theory promised to explain how particular forms of labor might be transformed.

Chaos, the book, seemed packed with images that were ready for the camera: flapping flags and trailing cigarette smoke, fractal images in which every part was like every other part ("self-similar"), and graphs of strange attractors in which the loops looked—to the scientists involved—like "the wings of a butterfly."[3] Self-similarity is the metaphor for self-similarity, as the butterfly is the metaphor for the butterfly or the poster inside the museum is the smaller-scale version of the poster outside the museum.

In addition to images, there were stories, three in particular. First, the story of Edward Lorenz, the theoretical meteorologist who coined the phrase "butterfly effect" and first distilled the butterfly-to-hurricane link. In his story, a fortunate mistake—the reentry of data that he did not know had been rounded—allowed him to rediscover sensitive dependence, something computer theorist Alan Turing had described a quarter century earlier. Second, there was the story of Mitchell Feigenbaum, a theoretical physicist experimenting with living thirty-hour days and thinking about clouds so much that he lost his flying privileges. And there was the story, no doubt dear to the studio executives' hearts, of a California science collective trying to break the bank in Vegas at the roulette wheel. But what had to be most heartening to Hollywood types was the concentration on movies. "For years," Gleick wrote, "no single object would inspire more illustrations, even motion pictures, than the mysterious curve" of the Lorenz attractor. Scientists made movies to solve chaos problems such as the strange persistence of Jupiter's Great Red Spot. And these movies were remarkably successful pitches: they got people grants. As Robert Shaw of UC Santa Cruz put it: "Audiovisual aids gave us an edge. We could hypnotize them with flashing lights."[4] Imagistic storytelling to solve problems and make money: the Hollywood system in a nutshell.

The Honda story is a reminder that although advertising is designed to get the consumer to think and feel and eventually do something, advertising campaigns are not pitched to the consumer. They are pitched to the company; that is, they are bought by the producer. Agencies sell campaigns to advertisers before advertising sells products to consumers. As Hollywood has become more pitch-driven, though, most commentators have seen it as less producer-specific. Yet this makes little sense: Every ad pitch is tailored to the advertiser; every story pitch is tailored to the producer. To say that marketing has come to dominate Hollywood production ordinarily is taken to mean marketing at the expense of story or vision or art or something valuable. Implicit in that narrative of loss has been the notion that when marketing triumphs, studio identity fades. Though many factors have chipped away at the old studio brands, this should not necessarily be among them. To the extent that a film is pitched, both the pitcher and the catcher may appeal to a contingent image of the studio; and to the extent that the films that emerge have been pitched and approved, they constitute, willy-nilly or intentionally, a reservoir of possible studio identities. The advertising model suggests that each side in the pitch meeting has an interest in appealing not only to what will move the eventual consumer (the audience) but to what might best motivate this interstitial consumer (the exec, or her boss, or the studio or conglomerate head) to green-light the film.

In the case of the Honda ads, though, while the allegorical stories were reassuring consumers about the car, the agency was reassuring the client about the effectiveness of the advertising. One might think of these commercials as the eruption and containment of what advertising ordinarily represses—namely, the terrible knowledge that the consequences of any campaign are impossible to judge in advance. When chaos theory arrives in an industry where unreliability, unpredictability, and the alibi are essential, where, as William Goldman put it at the dawn of the neoclassical era, "Nobody knows anything," the idea begins to have strange consequences. Chaos theory provided a way to think about the general situation of the contemporary studio, yet however widely it might be applied, each instance would take on some of the unique coloring of the studio responsible for the reflection. Sometimes, chaos theory appears to impart occult knowledge to its initiates, the way Sun Tzu's *Art of War* did in the eighties. But in other instances, this science of natural recursion seemed ready to guide Hollywood studios through a thicket of indeterminacy back toward the actualities of filmmaking, back, in other words, toward the sort of literalism Hollywood does so well.

The Talent

The earliest significant chaos film is *Groundhog Day* (Ramis, Columbia, 1993). Initially, the film jumps from the Columbia logo into time-lapse images of Mitchell Feigenbaum's clouds, with credits over. That superimposition is among the most conventional pieces of Hollywood arbitrariness, and no viewer would be expected to notice it.[5] Yet the viewer should notice when the film dissolves from the blue sky to the blue of Phil Connors's (Bill Murray's) chromakey. His hand is laid out across it as Phil narrates an imaginary dialogue in which he explains that if he could be anywhere in the world, he would be "[h]ere, in Elko, Nevada." The unreality of Elko intensifies the flicker of oddity one feels upon seeing the disembodied hand, a hand that suggests a perverse understanding of philosopher G. E. Moore's declaration, "Here is one hand." Whatever this hand is doing, it is being fetishized as an equivalent of the film's other potential authors—the studio, the director, and the others in the credits.

If this were a Derek Jarman film, the play of surfaces might be frozen here, but in Hollywood, the ambiguity is quickly resolved: The hand belongs to a weatherman who is talking about an image he can see on the monitor to the side of the blue screen, a composed image that puts his hand against a different picture of the sky. When the film cuts to the monitor view and resolves the ambiguity, Phil will quickly make two jokes about this composed image. The jokes are immediate reminders of the slight tension the viewer might have felt faced with the uncertain hand. First, he asks of a certain meteorological pattern, "What's that gonna mean for us in the Three Rivers area? One of these big blue things." This is literalism, and it pokes at the Moorean or even Tarskian common sense the viewer might have had recourse to.[6] (The blue thing means that it will snow, not that there will be a big blue thing in the sky.) Second, when Phil puts the satellite images in motion, he blows the cloud front across the screen. This is godlike, to be sure, and subtly introduces the byplay of power and arrogance that will surround Phil throughout the film. Still, he is not just any god,

Figure 6.2.
Groundhog Day's logorrhea begins with Phil's forecast and culminates in Rita's goofing around (see Figure II.1). (Ramis, Columbia, 1993)

but Zephyr, the West Wind, and if one had the mythology at one's fingertips, one would see him as the messenger of spring, already an appropriate match for his eventual groundhog sidekick.

In the rush toward the deeper meaning of the film, we should pause to notice that, like the films that led with logo bleeds I discussed in the first chapter, *Groundhog Day* quickly thematizes the trick. Indeed, it is *about* explicating the apparently arbitrary, and the logo trick is no cheaper than any of the other video tricks in the sequence. The seemingly arbitrary cuts have the same effect as the seamless shot in the Honda commercial; they draw attention to themselves. These revelations of the device integrate story and product, story and studio. Part of the strategy of the film is to promote the instance—a cheap set—into a philosophical problem: How do we know what something or someone is worth?[7]

Already implied in that conversion from instance to system is the idea of "scale" I am (saying the film and the commercials are) taking from chaos theory. What is true of the cut is true of the character, is true of the film, is true of the studio, may be true of us. This remarkable functionality and unexpected profundity is one characteristic of a classical style. When the philosopher Stanley Cavell was asked by the *New York Times Magazine* to pick a contemporary film of enduring significance, he chose *Groundhog Day*. For him it "ask[s] how, surrounded by conventions we do not exactly believe in, we sometimes find it in ourselves to enter into what Emerson thought of as a new day."[8] Cavell excavates the profundity the film had literalized by trapping Phil Connors in the same day, day after day.

Seen in this scalar way, being "surrounded by conventions we do not exactly believe in" is the plight not only of Emersonian man but the very particular problem of the Hollywood screenwriter. And while screenwriters might successfully aspire to ask and answer Cavellian questions, they are more often mired in problems of function. How do you make a movie work? The answer has long been to think of it in terms of acts (usually three). But if the movie is built around acts, how to build each scene? The same way. In *Cast Away* (Robert Zemeckis, DreamWorks, 1997), Tom Hanks's character was required to learn several new survival skills: how to build a fire, open a coconut, or bury a body. Each of these scenes is "based on a three-act dramatic structure," according to Zemeckis.[9] As screenwriter John Rogers put it in a review of Jeff Kitchen's *Writing a Great Movie*,

> The second tool is something I find fascinating—for lack of a better term it's *fractal plotting*. He establishes, for the entire script, a series of inciting incidents, reactions, resolutions. Then he backs up one level, and applies the same method to each act.

> Then to each sequence. Then to each scene. So, by the end of the process, absolutely every level of the script is based around some conflict, driving you ever forward in both the immediate and the meta.[10]

There are myriad ways to write Hollywood films and nearly as many ways to describe the process of writing them. The chaos film finds its writerly theorization in the fractal plot. When we see a film work across levels or scales, we should not be entirely surprised. That possibility is evidence of the professionalism of the writers who have worked on it. *Deus ex regula.*

To return to the opening sequence: Phil's mock apotheosis does not end the play of TV image and film shot. He then goes and sits in front of a then-standard, TV-news-set photo of the Pittsburgh skyline, framed as if it were a window. Once he leaves the set, he catches Rita (Andie MacDowell) playing in front of the blue screen in her blue coat. The blue coat disappears in the chromakey, and on the monitor she appears to be a disembodied head and hands. (See the first image at the beginning of Part II.) She is now standing in for the lady with the lamp; as Phil's fill-in comments on her at this moment, "I think she's gonna be a great producer." But in place of the castrating figure with a torch, she is, as Phil was, castrated and fractured, an object lesson in Mulveyite visuality. "Not my kind of fun," Phil says and leaves.

The monitor view then shows a helicopter shot of the actual Pittsburgh skyline (the news-set photo is in motion). From there, we cut to the comparatively lush, wide-screen, filmed "original" of the helicopter shot, which then shows the WPBH truck on its way to Punxsutawney. As with the climax of *Tootsie*, the opening sequence of *Groundhog Day* foregrounds the techniques of (cheap) video production and turns to (expensive) film as a way to show video technique. And as it typically does, Hollywood substitutes technology and practice for materiality and essence—the movie as movie for the film as film.

The rest of the movie, in which Bill Murray is forced to relive Groundhog Day over and over, continues this project and extends it. But rather than reveal the technology behind the image, it reveals the technique behind the film. *Groundhog Day* is about acting. Each day is a new take on the same material, and each day, each line reading, each performance is slightly different. Phil tries to plan the perfect day so he can get Rita into bed, and his planning takes the form of repeated takes of the same scene. But the moment he has everything perfectly planned, his timing becomes slightly off, and he is rejected. The small change blows up in his face in a montage of slaps.

The film is thus deeply about chaos. Its formal center, the process of multiple-take, discontinuous Hollywood acting, is a phenomenon susceptible to the butterfly effect. And its protagonist is both Edward Lorenz, a weatherman with bad predictions, and Mitchell Feigenbaum, a man who has slipped out of phase with everyone else. Weather forecasting itself is a strange attractor that allows communication between Phil Connors's human scale and Punxsutawney Phil's rodent scale. And the self-similarity of those scales (weatherman to weather-hog; Phil to Phil) can happen only on a scalar day—February 2. The strange attractor is also the spirit of comedy.

Groundhog Day has swiftly acquired classic status. For Kristin Thompson, the film lends further support to the notion that Hollywood has remained clas-sical since it first classicized in the 1920s. *Groundhog Day*'s "only real departure from tradition—admittedly a striking one—is the failure to motivate or ex-plain the plot's sudden move into an impossible situation." *It's a Wonderful Life* has Clarence, *Back to the Future* has its DeLorean, but "Groundhog Day gives no explanation as to what force causes the same day to repeat for the protago-nist and for no other character. By the end, however, there is some suggestion that a supernatural agency of some sort has intervened in Phil's life."[11] Here again, the hypothesis that Hollywood operates in an allegorical mode where individuals and individual films can have systematic effects—where "the im-mediate" and "the meta" are the same—suggests that we actually follow the "suggestion" of "a supernatural agency of some sort." It might plausibly have been Mike Ovitz's CAA, of which Murray and Ramis were clients, or the Second City comedy troupe, where Murray, Ramis, and several other performers in the film were trained. But in this case, it was the studio. As Thompson describes in her footnote to this very passage, "At one point, the producers wanted to add motivation to the film. . . . 'As Ramis related, "The problem was that any ex-planation seemed completely arbitrary."' [Screenwriter Danny Rubin proposed that Murray be cursed by a gypsy. His] 'famous "gypsy curse" scene was cut only after a new studio head, Mark Canton, came on board while the film was in development, and remarked after reading the script, "You don't need this curse thing, do you?"'[12] Chaos classicizes the abstraction at the heart of high-concept filmmaking.

Once there was a gypsy; then there was Mark Canton; then there was no gypsy anymore. Why? In 1992, as the film was in production, Sony Pictures Entertainment (SPE) was deep in the throes of its synergy malaise. Having spent $5 billion for Columbia, Sony had seen nothing come of its promise of hardware/software magic. At first, from roughly 1989 to 1991, the *Boyz n the Hood* era, Sony was committed to spending unbelievable amounts of money on its new studio. Now, in 1992, mired in a *hardware* recession, Sony began to look more closely at the bloated overhead of SPE.[13]

This legacy became Mark Canton's problem. Having got the job in part because of his working relationship with Peter Guber, Canton was a fully enrolled member of the party of excess. But in the new Columbia context, Canton was compelled to square off against "the beast," Jon Dolgen, a man Barry Diller called "an impossible person, but his impossibleness is somewhat loveable." Dolgen was charged with taking money out of already budgeted projects, driving down marketing costs, and slashing overhead. Dolgenomics "was like going from *The Age of Innocence* to *City of Joy* in one step," said a studio executive. "It's amazing how tight those budgets were."[14] Canton's job was to manage the boundaries of Columbia Pictures. Inside Columbia, Canton had to struggle against Dolgen's austerity, particularly a collapse in development funding that drove a wedge between the studio and both outside talent (e.g., CAA) and inside producers. Outside Columbia, Canton fought a public battle for credit on films he had inherited from Frank Price at one stage or another—constantly asking to be thanked, telling reporters of his contributions to films, and so on.

Yet a more complicated scenario than the "I did it," "No, I did" press battle was taking shape inside Columbia. As Nancy Griffin and Kim Masters noted in *Hit and Run*,

> [S]ome Columbia executives noticed that [Frank] Price's pictures seemed to perform better when Price wasn't around. One . . . conclud[ed] that Price and Canton— inadvertently paired on these films—worked well together. "Frank Price is the guy to have when you want to pick the movies," says this high-level executive. "But Frank Price couldn't finish a movie and market it to save his life. That's all Mark is good at. The irony is, all those movies Frank greenlit, Mark edited and marketed. That's a hell of a team."[15]

Groundhog Day was the last of the partnership films to hit the screen before the Canton-only era arrived. That new era would be marked by the debut of a new studio logo. In the Columbia logo that opens *Groundhog Day*, and unlike the credit sequence, the clouds do not roll. But they would. In March 1992, Columbia debuted a new leader at the ShoWest exhibitors convention. As part of Canton's desire to dynamize the studio's identity, the lady with the torch stood among billowing clouds. *Groundhog Day* was one of the last Columbia films to carry the old logo; *Last Action Hero* would be the first of the new. Indeed, the centerpiece of Columbia's dynamic identity was *supposed* to be *Last Action Hero*, a film that bore all the hallmarks of the Guber-Peters-Canton heritage: self-conscious franchise building through star-driven, big-budget, "knowing" action films. It was the film that would "make or break" Canton, he thought.[16]

But before the make-or-break, *Groundhog Day* would have the chance to be surprising, to sneak up on the studio, and, it turned out, to mark precisely this moment in corporate history. (Part of what makes the film—not the characters, but the film—something to root for is its resigned confidence. Throughout, it projects a belief that the filmmakers have made this thing, together, despite. Despite what? Despite it all.) Canton needed to justify his extravagant production decisions in the era of budgetary constraint. In March, as Columbia was pushing *Groundhog Day* into more theaters and before *Last Action Hero* hit the fans, Canton summarized the transition this way: "We used to say 'We want it, no matter how much it costs.' Now we've adopted the mantra of all well run businesses: 'We want it, but only if the price is right—or if Arnold is in it.'"[17]

Here the shift from video to film comes to Canton's rescue. Video, in *Groundhog Day*, is about technology, and that is a bounded, framed artifact—a budgetable enterprise. Film, though, is about technique, which depends on talent and craft. These forces are as natural and unpredictable as the weather or love—things supposedly beyond money. "Talent" is one of the film's running gags, from Chris Elliott's joke that the only network interested in Phil is the Home Shopping Network to Phil's unknowing remark that Rita's job as producer is to "keep the talent happy." "Did he just refer to himself as 'the talent'?" Chris laughs. It is only after Phil has taken the time and spent the money (one thousand dollars per lesson) to acquire a new talent—the piano—and displayed it for free at the town dance that he becomes "the talent." Rita, who stood in for Columbia in the opening sequence, stands in for the studio again when she cleans out her checkbook—$339.88—to buy a date with him at the bachelor auction. The economy of all this rests on the belief that talent can and should be bought even if it is vastly expensive. This is Canton's economy, Guber's economy, the economy Sony wanted to believe in when it bought Columbia, an economy now threatened. The Punxsutawney dance hall in which producers buy talent for love not money is Sony's fantasy of vertical integration: the conglomerate as community. *Groundhog Day* is one last justification of Guber's vision to Sony, one last reassurance to the creative community, the talent pool.

The merger of producers and talent comes when Rita buys Phil and helps him from the stage. Phil's talent, though, is not his—it, too, is bought and paid for. In the story, we see Bill Murray play the piano and we see Andie MacDowell buy him. In the credits, though, we see that Bill Murray's hands and the piano solo were provided by Terry Fryer, veteran music producer, authority on digital sampling, and longtime keyboardist for a number of Columbia Records acts. Where video divorced Andie MacDowell's hands from her head, film unites Bill Murray's head with someone else's hands and unites his hand with hers as she helps him from the stage. Video divides; film unites. Video is the claustrophobic society of the Thalberg building on Columbia's new lot; film is the integrating world of synergy.

Now integrated, Phil returns to phase. In what Thompson calls "one of the subtlest cues in recent Hollywood cinema, the change in causality is signaled by the fact that a slightly different passage from 'I Got You, Babe' starts on the radio."[18] Her note says that, appropriately, the passage is now "Hey, I got you babe" and no longer, "Then put your little hand in mine." Having solved the Producer/Talent problem, overcome Phil's castration anxiety, and unconsciously acknowledged Frank Price's contribution, Rita, Phil, and Mark Canton face the new day. "Why am I here?" Phil asks. "I bought you. I own you," she answers. "Why are you here?" "You said stay and I stayed." At this point, though, the radio is playing, "They say our love won't pay the rent, before it's earned, our money's all been spent." It nearly has: she has cleaned out her checkbook; he has paid one thousand dollars for a piano lesson and purchased, as Thompson notes, every conceivable insurance policy. Rita hits the snooze button. With her hand. The world of impending financial constraint lies just outside the bed-and-breakfast. As they scamper down the walk, Phil tells Rita they should live in Punxsutawney, but, "we'll rent to start."

Chaoticians

Groundhog Day was the first fully formed chaos film to appear in Hollywood, but it was followed only a few months later by *Jurassic Park* (Spielberg, Universal, 1993), which is still the biggest. *Groundhog Day*'s chaos theory supplies a motiveless motive to its time-warp narrative. The film plays on the romantic resonances of notions such as "sensitive dependence," "strange attraction," and "communicating channels." *Jurassic Park*'s version of chaos is more malign. If the romantic comedy took chaos as a metaphor, novelist Michael Crichton had looked to one of chaos theory's disciplinary homes, biology, where it could provide a high-falutin' substitute for Murphy's Law.

Crichton's overriding moral, that life will find a way, and its corollary, that it's not nice to fool with Mother Nature, find their mouthpiece in Ian Malcolm. Malcolm, a rock-star mathematician—"Chaotician. Chaotician," he objects—knows from the outset that the life-forms in the park will overcome whatever control measures have been put in place to contain them. In addition, it falls to him to explain (or, rather, to assert that chaos explains) why. His riffs on chaos theory topics are delivered with Jeff Goldblum's characteristic syncopation and speed. When Drs. Grant (Sam Neill) and Sattler (Laura Dern) look at him uncomprehendingly, he resorts to metaphor. "Strange attractors? Dr. Sattler,

I refuse to believe that you are unfamiliar with the concept of attraction." Yet unlike *Groundhog Day*, this change of register constitutes no real commitment to romance on the part of the film (or the novel). Instead, and as is frequently the case, explicit thematic use seems to strip an idea or an event of its narrative power. In *Jurassic Park*, chaos names, and contains, industrial indeterminacy even as it points to the absolutely uncontainable.

To explain chaos theory, Malcolm gives the briefest sketch of the butterfly effect—"A butterfly can flap its wings in Peking and in Central Park you get rain instead of sunshine." When that does not work, he takes up Dr. Sattler's hand to perform a small experiment. He takes a cup of water to put a drop of water on the back of her hand and asks which way she thinks it will roll off. She guesses. He repeats the process, only now the drop rolls another way. "Tiny variations in the orientation of the hairs on your hands, the amount of blood distending your vessels, imperfections in the skin . . . never repeat and vastly affect the outcome." "Unpredictability." The water may behave unpredictably on her hand, but in the plastic cup it will be the great emblem of the film, the emblem of suspense. It vibrates with contained indeterminacy. And when a tropical downpour fills the T-Rex's footprints, there too the water will ripple with anticipation, distorting Malcolm's reflection in the process. If the protruding fin in *Jaws* allegorized neoclassical control over the balance between narrative surface and depth, *Jurassic Park* can eliminate the fin and leave only the frame. Now the allegorical emblem consists of the perturbation of a framed surface, the water in the glass or the puddle. Chaos obviates classical motive here as well.

Figure 6.3.
Contained indeterminacy.
Jurassic Park
(Spielberg, Universal, 1993)

As is usually the case in a Spielberg film, the distinction between what we might call the production narrative and the exhibition narrative collapses. The behind the scenes becomes "the scenes" with beneficial effects. The making of *Jurassic Park* reset the balance of labor in the world of special effects, nearly wiping out model animators in favor of CGI teams at Industrial Light and Magic. Phil Tippett, who had dramatically advanced stop-motion animation technique, was stunned when he saw the first CGI of a hunting T-Rex. The motion was so lifelike, and the scale so believable, he recognized at once that the number of model shots would be slashed. "The change was devastating. I had different concessions . . . and all of a sudden, the plug was pulled." Or, as he put it to Spielberg, "I think I'm extinct." In the film, as Spielberg notes, that was the situation of the paleontologists. "Looks like we're out of a job," Dr. Grant says. Malcolm responds, puckishly, "Don't you mean extinct?" "I kind of rubbed it in by using it in the film itself," Spielberg grinned.[19] But it remained (on the surface) a joke between friends because Tippett's animation crew found their way into the CGI process. They still manipulated articulated forms, but they reconceived their product. Instead of producing camera-ready poses, they generated data points that the CGI animators would then flesh out and render.

Again, scale proves crucial. Spielberg initially wanted to rely on full-scale models for *all* the dinosaurs. Later, he opted for a hybrid approach: full-scale models for shots in which the dinosaurs interacted with humans, Tippett's go-motion for wide shots, and CGI to blend them. Still later, he eliminated the go-motion, leaving only full-scale models and virtual dinosaurs. And for the final sequence, shot at the end of production when the full power of the CGI effects could be seen, he decided to use CGI dinosaurs even though they would be interacting closely with human characters. *Jurassic Park* thus contains within itself the history of the move from traditional to digital effects, even as it was responsible for that history. If Malcolm's distorted reflection in the rain-filled footprint was the film's emblem for on-screen suspense, its other emblematic reflection captured the off-screen story from Tippett's point of view.

Thrown away in Malcolm's water-rolling experiment is his opening line: "Put your hand flat, like a hieroglyphic." He likely means for her to stiffly extend her hand in a way reminiscent of an ancient Egyptian painting or relief. But to call it a hieroglyphic identifies it with a system of ancient and illegible picture writing. In *Jurassic Park*, that system is the DNA of the dinosaurs. The film, of course, makes a great deal of the illegibility and partiality of dino DNA, but at the core of its imagination is the supposition that we cannot read it not simply because it is old or complex or fragmentary but because there is too much of it. One could never read an entire DNA sequence just as one could never debug two million lines of code (something conspiratorial computer programmer Dennis Nedry [Wayne Knight] counts on). What is required, then, is a complete "system reset," a way of turning the genetic sequence into a programming sequence. In the film, that method appears most dramatically in a scene in which the letters of the DNA bases are projected onto the skin of a marauding dinosaur. W. J. T. Mitchell identified that image as heralding the age of biocybernetic reproduction. The computed "biological" letters can stand in for the graphical computation required to render the virtual velociraptor.[20] Production designer Rick Carter confirmed that that identification was his intention when he imagined the shot. DNA may be unpredictable, but computers, at least in *Jurassic Park*, always follow instructions. The emblem for that boundedness is the grid. Crichton's novels are filled with such grids, nearly inscrutable quasi reproductions of computer screens that invite the reader to participate alongside the characters in the search for a solution. Armed with both chaos theory and computers, the filmmakers position themselves within a bounded unpredictability, a space marked out for invention, but an invention that will, ideally, always be contained.

If Malcolm's main point about chaos theory is that the future is unpredictable, his secondary point is that it will be self-reflexive. "See, here I am now by myself talking to myself. That's, that's chaos theory." Self-absorbed discourse not only typifies chaos theory but also constitutes neoclassical Hollywood's aspiration. Many audience members have noticed the similarities between the on-screen tour of Jurassic Park and the Universal Studios theme park ride; others have remarked on the convergence of souvenir merchandise. *Jurassic Park* seems to anticipate, even relish, its downstream uses and ancillary revenue channels. It reflects on that anticipation, too, at both the macro and micro levels. At the grand scale, the entire film occurs within a necessary test-run of the park done solely to appease the insurers, while at the scale of the individual element, a book called *The Making of Jurassic Park* by Don Shay and Jody Duncan appears in the Jurassic Park store. Shay and Duncan are the real authors of the making-of book for the film.

Two pieces of the surrounding narrative clarify the seriousness of the film's self-regard here. The sequence in the Jurassic Park store begins with a low-angle shot of an inflatable brachiosaur. In the previous shot, Dr. Grant has thrown aside his fossil velociraptor claw—it is a souvenir that has poked him in the rear end one too many times. For Grant, the real fossil is no longer necessary now that actual raptors exist. But, as the cut makes clear, the effect of Jurassic Park the park is not to replace an inadequate embodiment of realism (the metonym) with an adequate one (the animal). Rather, it is to replace a *real* fossil with a *fake* dinosaur. And at some level the filmmakers know this. Yet at the same time, the montage (claw to inflatable dino) suggests the opposite, that the metonymic relic has the power to deflate the child's knickknack. For Dr. Grant, throwing away the claw amounts to the final casting aside of childish things—he had previously used it to threaten and impress a young boy at his dig site—and the taking up of his deferred paternal responsibilities.[21] Both claw and dino are compensatory: the claw for an unrealizable power and a "lost world"; the dino for an unportable experience.

The second narrative element in this tour of self-regard begins with park impresario John Hammond sitting at a candlelit table eating ice cream. It is all melting anyway. Where Grant has thrown away his fetish, Hammond is seemingly unable to restrain his inner child. Joined by Dr. Sattler, he tells her the story of his flea circus—a triumph of mechanical ersatz over perception—and of his resolve to do a better job of planning the next time around. She responds with a Malcolm-esque bit of faux chaos: "Control *is* the illusion," one the childlike Hammond persists in. (Later, when the kids are back in the visitor center, they, too, will gorge themselves on the spoiling desserts.) *Jurassic Park* heaps culpability on Hammond, crushing any remnants of ambivalence. When we rack focus from the making-of book to Hammond eating, he inherits the blame for the film's product autoplacement as well. The answers to moral questions become increasingly trivial. Yet if the film seems smugly aware of where the moral lines ought to be drawn, that assuredness masks an aggression directed at both the audience and, to a lesser extent, at Spielberg himself. He is, he implies, a showman suffering from the compulsion to delude. His audience, though, exhibits both a desperate willingness to be deluded and a need to be reassured that they are not. The smugness, in other words, marks Spielberg's resistance to the pandering he imagines his audience demands. Such cynicism suffuses the project: Everyone will be back for the sequel.

That cynicism—Ian Malcolm's wan declaration that he is tired of being right all the time—mobilizes the film's marketing. Knowing that the reassertion of moral rigor will accompany the unjustifiably enjoyable paleo-havoc, the *Jurassic Park* series sells itself as a symptom that must be reindulged because it cannot be cured. The store in *Jurassic Park* binds consumption to responsibility, knowing that no amount of moralizing can blunt the attractiveness of the scale-shifting commodity. Still, the central communication between Hollywood scales lies between a film and its trailer, and one of the characteristic pleasures of a good trailer is hearing a line that clearly means one thing in the film now being used to sell the film. But with the existence of Jeff Goldblum's on-screen chorus, there is no repurposing involved. In the trailer for *The Lost*

World, one of his new comrades will gawp at a herd of stegosaurs, and Gold-blum will respond, "Ooh, ahh, that's how it always starts but then later there's running and then screaming." The running and screaming quickly follow—as he (and Spielberg, and the audience) knew they would.

"Both is happening at the same time"

Chaos-influenced screenwriting transmutes the relationship between the story and the marketing campaign. If the conventional worry is that the nefarious forces of marketing have somehow infiltrated the sacred realm of coherent story-telling, fractal plotting and scale-shifting dialogue recast the opposition of art and commerce as a potentially utopian continuity. Out of that immanent linkage precipitates what passes for pure art and pure commerce. The commerce side consists of prominent product placements. And the metonym for artistic purity is the extended tracking shot.

The notion that a movie, and in particular a continuous shot, can best communicate the passage from one scale to another is an older idea. It goes back at least to Charles and Ray Eames's *Powers of Ten*, which they worked on throughout the seventies. In that film, the camera pulls back and pushes in one power of ten meters every ten seconds (and then every one second) moving through the ear of a sleeping man to intergalactic and microscopic scales. As in the Honda commercials, the Eameses set out to bridge otherwise disparate events through continuity.

In Hollywood, that logarithmic journey meets up with a more native tradition, the long tracking shot—usually the opening shot—that models the central social mechanism of the film that follows. The most famous instance of this is the opening of Orson Welles's *Touch of Evil* (Universal, 1958); the most famous recent instance, in large part because it insistently comments on its own length and purpose, is the opening shot of Robert Altman's *The Player* (Fine Line, 1993). Like the openings of *Touch of Evil* and *Absolute Beginners* (to which it refers), *Boogie Nights* and *Snake Eyes* (which both followed), and the opening of the grand ball scene in Martin Scorsese's *Age of Innocence* (Columbia, 1993), the opening shot of *The Player* is an almost ethnographic attempt to make sensible the web of social connections of its setting, a setting that revolves around a central, governing institution that will be the object of investigation. The studio lot thus joins the border town, 1958 SoHo, 1977 disco, fight night, and Gilded Age New York high society. All these shots, however different, evince a conviction that the mere stipulation of social connections would be insufficient to convey the dawning recognition that those relationships cumulate into a coherent or even systemic whole. Out of such doubts, filmmakers produce the effect of coherence by speeding up the pace with which one would have to reckon with phenomena to such a degree that the spectator must admit that only a native could grapple with the network of conventions.

Unlike the opening of, say, *The Player*, which redoubles its self-presentation through dialogue and obvious points of focus, the opening of David Koepp's *The Trigger Effect* (Amblin/Gramercy, 1996), moves rather slowly to show how a simple accident radiates outward to affect our hero. This is perhaps the most banal example of the application of chaos theory to Hollywood production: mining the science for stories that can be used in the service of the conventional "dangerous Los Angeles" narrative. But even here, there is the assumption that the effect comes to a head in the movie theater, an acknowledgment of the intellectual heritage of the shot. That Koepp wrote and directed *The Trigger Effect* was no accident. He was the screenwriter with Crichton on *Jurassic Park*. It was his job to turn Ian Malcolm from a Brit who would say, "I do maths," into someone who would say, "Chaotician. Chaotician." After *Trigger Effect*, he would go on to write De Palma's *Snake Eyes* with its then-record twenty-minute opening shot.

The egregiously long tracking shot compensates in part for the industry-wide acceleration in editing. Average Shot Length is a crude measure of the pace of a film, but however crude, ASL has been decreasing.[22] "Cut, cut, cut," as the head of studio security puts it in *The Player*. Still, an extended shot can prove just as sensorily assaultive as the most rapid-fire scene in a Tony Scott film. In these cases, the relevant metric would not be ASL but something like "potentially focal objects"—those people and things that might (one cannot be certain) attract the viewer's eye. In both sorts of sequences, redundancy will be built in, often through music or the rhetoric of the image. When Welles and cinematographer Gregg Toland first built an aesthetic around long takes in "deep focus," André Bazin remarked that they had arrived at an aesthetic in which "reality has the same density everywhere." Whether this was "real" or not, Bazin was certainly correct to note that the number of sites for audience attention had increased. Such multiplication is implied in speaking of "density." Density amalgamates the effects of depth of field, a cluttered or bustling mise-en-scène, and a restless camera. But with the nearly complete disappearance of deep focus—something Rick Altman has called "a labor-intensive flourish or ornament"—and the attenuation of the average depth of field in contemporary Hollywood, it may very well be that the number of potential focal objects has not kept pace with the proliferation of shots.[23] Whatever the measurements might show, the stylistic consequences of these dynamics—duration and density—might be mapped in a two-by-two matrix. The Wellesian quadrant would be + + while the Tony Scott quadrant would be − −. The − + quadrant (rapid-fire deep-focus) would be nearly unoccupied by Hollywood filmmakers except in certain moments of narrative extremity or as part of genres that aim to instill a particular disquiet or investigative mood in the audience. This leaves + –, the region of extended shots of almost gaseous density, and there is no better emblem for this quadrant than the opening of *Forrest Gump*.

The drifting feather that lands at Forrest's soiled Nikes, that just barely material sign of fated randomness, the embodiment of his gift for being in the right place at the right time, follows a pattern the animators took from chaos models of turbulence—the trailing smoke of a cigarette. Motive has been sublimed. We might historicize that process by saying that in 1985, Zemeckis needs a DeLorean to motivate the time shift, to make the system concrete (*Back to the Future*), but in 1995 he needs only a feather, the intimation of materiality, to emblematize the *question* of motivation, not motivation itself.

That *Forrest Gump* extends the feather's turbulent path into its story is not, by itself, illegitimate. Chaos problems were never confined to the merely scientific or the merely corporate. Even in Gleick's book, the scientists reach outward from their mathematical conclusions to "the problems of philosophy." As Doyne Farmer, a member of the Santa Cruz Dynamical Systems Collective, told Gleick, "On a philosophical level, it struck me as an operational way to define free will, in a way that allowed you to reconcile free will with determinism. The system is deterministic, but you [meaning everyone up to and including God] can't say what it's going to do next."[24] Forrest's graveside meditation is the Hollywood translation: "Jenny, I don't know if Momma was right or if, if it's Lieutenant Dan. I don't know if we each have a destiny, or if we're all just floating around, accidental-like on a breeze, but I, I think maybe it's both. Maybe both is happening at the same time."

William Empson identified the "child cult" of modernism as a version of pastoral, and *Gump*, with its cultural-political picaresque, makes that insight trivial through comprehensive repetition.[25] Like the ancient shepherd, the child (or the mentally childlike narrator) stands outside the corruptions of the world in order to comment on them. That commentary, however pointed, ultimately confirms the audience in two beliefs: First, that however corrupt the world is, those corruptions might be diagnosed even by the simplest among us; and second, that however corrupt the world is, that corruption has neither reached this audience nor prevented it from diagnosing the situation. Pastoral is a conservative discourse. But in his ironically "correct" ungrammatical formation, Forrest offers more than a stumblingly apt undoing of a knotty philosophical problem. He embodies and guides the inscription of neoclassical principles in form and narrative.

"Both is happening at the same time": This is the New Classical approach to destiny. The system has to be determined—Paramount will not throw money away for nothing—*and* unpredictable—in Paramount's case, *The Phantom* and *The Ghost and the Darkness* happen. In the classical era, Gump's destiny would have been in the hands of blind luck (at MGM) or God (at Universal) or an angel or an insurance company (both at Warners). Here, his destiny and our own are figured in the drifting feather, as producer Wendy Finerman notes. Chaos gives studios in the New Hollywood more than stories; it gives them alibis—stories about the success and failure of the studios themselves.

That said, I want to look at a film that is an alibi not of success but of failure—Disney's *Pocahontas* (1995). In part because Disney from its founding moments has articulated a pro-American winner's mentality, and in part because between the arrival of Eisner and Katzenberg in 1984 and Frank Wells's death and Katzenberg's departure in 1994, the studio was imagined as the studio that could not fail. Disney has always been more anxious about failure than success.

Disney has long been thought of as a studio that foregrounds its own problems. In 1941's *Dumbo*, for example, the production number "Hit the Big Boss (for a Raise)" contains caricatures of striking Disney cartoonists. Several commentators have seen allusions to Disney's failed plans to build Disney's America, a historical theme park in Virginia, in *Pocahontas*. In that fiasco, Disney had purchased three thousand acres of land near Haymarket. But a coalition of wealthy hunt-country estate owners, environmental groups, the *Washington Post*, and several prominent, popular historians opposed what they regarded as Disney's conversion of real history—some of the land they bought included Civil War sites, and the Manassas Battlefield was nearby—into Disney history, or Distory as Stephen Fjellman calls it.[26] It did not help matters that documentarian Ken Burns, whose *The Civil War* had become PBS's most successful broadcast ever, was a leading voice in the opposition. After several million dollars of design work and schmoozing, and after successfully lobbying for infrastructural improvements, Disney backed out in September 1994.

That is the story behind the story of *Pocahontas*, which premiered in New York's Central Park and not in Virginia. In the ideological production number "Mine," Governor Ratcliffe, dreaming of gold, sings to the troops, "Dig, dig, with all that's in ya, boys / Dig, dig, dig up Virginia, boys." The self-incrimination of Ratcliffe's possessiveness is also Eisner's mea culpa. As he put it in *Work in Progress*:

> Our first important misstep was the decision to call the park "Disney's America." "Disney" and "America" just seemed to slide off the tongue together easily and naturally. Frank [Wells] and I both liked associating Disney with America and America

with Disney. But the name would prove to be a disaster. Disney's America implied ownership of the country's history, which only antagonized our critics. That was unfortunate because we were never interested in a park that merely reflected a Disneyesque view of history.[27]

So the film is a confession of hubris; Ratcliffe (the bad mouse) will be carted back to England.

It would be a mistake, though, to see *Pocahontas* as simply confessional, to see Disney only in Governor Ratcliffe and not throughout the film. Even in the song "Mine," we are offered the alternative of the Mel Gibson–voiced John Smith, who imagines the country is his to claim in the sense that the adventures he can have in it will be his. This is seemingly more acceptable, and we are obviously to take it as such, but Smith is still guilty of imagining that he is bringing civilization to the savage natives. (He will be upbraided.) Here, then, the problem is not ownership; it is content. In the story of Disney's America, this colonial encounter corresponds to the phase when Disney invited its historian-critics to Epcot Center. During that process, they were shown, as Eisner described it,

> *American Adventure*, a twenty-five minute Audio-Animatronics presentation that recounts the story of the founding of the country. . . . The gathered group turned out to be highly critical of *American Adventure*. . . . "My general impression is that it's not the America I know, neither from the scholarship nor from my own perspective," said George Sanchez, a history professor at the University of Michigan. "There's way too much that's ignored about American history." . . . Others echoed his comments. . . . More broadly, they voiced a criticism that we'd heard frequently in recent months. Disney, they argued, couldn't be trusted to depict American history in ways that were sufficiently complex, subtle and inclusive. I was surprised by the intensity of their reaction, but not upset by it. Disney's America remained very much in the early planning stages, and the whole purpose of this meeting was to solicit more input and make it better.[28]

This is a process that Disney, in its book on *Hercules*, calls "The Chaos of Creation."

The process of incorporating criticism—the voices and echoes of the historians—is precisely what *Pocahontas* and Pocahontas are all about. She wants John Smith to "sing with all the voices of the mountain" and "paint with all the colors of the wind." She is the philosopher of possibility. Powhatan tells her that rivers take the easiest course; she says, à la Heraclitus (or *Hercules*, whatever), that she never steps (or missteps) in the same river twice. She is also the embodiment of chaos theory. She regularly appears wind-whipped, with trailing hair, and pursued by a stream of leaves that follows classically chaotic forms of turbulence. In "Colors of the Wind," we even see a burst of Edward Lorenzian butterflies. Finally, the trickiness of the lyrics—"You think the only people who are people / Are people who look and think like you / But if you walk the footsteps of a stranger / You'll learn things you never knew you never knew"—like the trickiness of the puns and feminine rhymes in "Mine, Mine, Mine" is not merely Disney magic; it is also the song's version of chaos theory's "scalar incorporation." "People who are people / Are people who" and "You never knew you never knew" are not repetitions but instances of lyrical self-similarity that deftly convey the passage from redundant, identitarian thinking to something intuitive yet so unthought it has been unthinkable.

Pocahontas does not merely represent the voices of the historians; she represents the chaos theory of the creative process that Eisner and Disney want to defend, that they had failed to defend in the case of Disney's America. "We also left ourselves vulnerable to the claim that any changes we subsequently made were a response to outside pressures rather than a natural part of our own creative process and our commitment to excellence."[29] Disney's psycho-characterological splitting allowed them to identify with the villain, the hero, and the heroine as necessary. If the male guises of Ratcliffe and Smith are unacceptable—Smith, too, is taken back to Europe at the end of the film—Pocahontas remains. And it is through her lecture-song to Smith that Disney advances its claim of being

Figure 6.4.
Butterflies in effect. *Pocahontas* (Mike Gabriel and Eric Goldberg, Disney, 1995)

able to "paint with all the colors of the wind"—as in, "You can own the earth but still / all you'll own is earth until / you can paint with all the colors of the wind." In Virginia reality, as Eisner put it, "[t]he revised economic projections took the last bit of wind out of our sails. . . . Having decided to give up the ship, we turned our attention to withdrawing in a way that avoided creating more ill will and left the door open to eventually building the park elsewhere."[30] In the film, Pocahontas's maternal wind-stream pushes the sail-clouds of John Smith's ship back to England.

By 1998, when Eisner wrote *Work in Progress*, Disney had recovered enough to imagine, through Pocahontas in *Pocahontas II*, that it was time to stop "listening to the spirits with your heart" and time to more directly "listen to your heart." This turn to a solitary inwardness leaves behind the collective nature of the first film. In Parliament, which one might take to be the locus of democratic speech, Pocahontas tells King James, "[T]here are many voices around you, but you must listen to your heart." The natural, spectral democracy of the "voices of the mountain" will find its best defender in the divine right of a king. The worry about outer forces is foreclosed, and the problems of Disney become internal problems—their own missteps, as Eisner routinely calls them.

Bifurcation Points

If metaphoric extensions of chaos theory had been used by Hollywood studios to explain essentially everything, from personal to corporate to national destiny, by 1995 decidedly nonmetaphorical uses of chaos theory were beginning to impinge upon the relatively free incorporative rein Hollywood had enjoyed until then. It would not be out of place to call this year, the year of the Honda campaign, a bifurcation point. *Groundhog Day*, *Jurassic Park*, and *Pocahontas* put chaos theory to work to solve problems—*Groundhog Day* to reckon with the formal problems of integrity, motivation, and value; *Jurassic Park* to rebroker the interplay between technology, labor, and predictability; *Pocahontas* to recover for Disney a national role that would not be tainted by its imperial designs. But from 1995 on, literal references to chaos theory will seem increasingly old hat. Like Jeff Goldblum in the trailer for *The Lost World*, the audience, particularly the internal, industrial audience, has seen this before. Chaos becomes a theme, no longer a node of energetic new relating among the scales of the system. This is one path. Down the other, one finds chaos still doing work, but it is work that will bring decreasing returns. Doubtless the self-representing imperatives of the Hollywood system encourage animators, effects artists, and their professional colleagues to find ways of displaying their work in films such as *Twister*, *The Avengers*, *Frequency*, and *The Butterfly Effect*.

The routinization or domestication of chaos theory obviates the need for inventive storytelling around the moment of incorporation. If neoclassicism is an aesthetic founded on aspiration, then such moments of domestication are ultimately more threatening to the system than the novelties that precede them. Hollywood filmmakers know how to convert crises into interesting stories; the neoclassic era was founded on precisely that knowledge. But left to generate its own creative forces, Hollywood in its classicist mode is bound to flounder. In 1993, chaos looked like a way to cement labor to studio aims. After 1995, those two grow apart even as they can be more decisively described by chaos theory. In one direction, animators yoke chaos to a realist aesthetic and a defense of craft. In the other, executives who had premised their status and control on a superior knowledge of economics and the market are forced to entertain the possibility that such knowledge would completely deligitimize their place in the corporate hierarchy.

Unlike other Disney animated features, *Pocahontas* originated with a song, in this case, "Colors of the Wind." The animation team members *heard* the film before they saw it. And what they created to go with the song perfectly matched the state of their art to the story. *Pocahontas* was the first Disney feature to use significant CGI in an effort to link features to the environment in a more natural way. "The trick is to get the three-dimensional elements to 'marry' with the rest of the two-dimensional world of the film," said Steve Goldberg, head of the CGI department.[31]

Jeffrey Katzenberg called this hybrid form "tradigital" animation. *Beauty and the Beast* (Gary Trousdale and Kirk Wise, Disney, 1991) thematized the marriage in the dance between Belle and the Beast. This nuptial rehearsal pairs the "now" of a completely digitally rendered set against a "then" of hand-drawn 2-D characters. Yet this chronological fusion was itself classicized by Mrs. Potts's song. She turns a moment of industrial novelty into a balanced "Tale as old as time / Song as old as rhyme / Beauty and the Beast." In any case, the successful marriage of character and set purposely bracketed the much more challenging problem of relying on computer models to animate natural phenomena. In 1991, computer animation makes hard-surface reflections much simpler, it opens up the possibility of dramatic camera moves, and it smooths particular sorts of textural motion. This last is particularly true of Grandmother Willow in *Pocahontas*. Her face is hand-drawn, but her bark is CG. If Mrs. Potts's singing nostalgized the scene before her, old Grandmother Willow's sagacity effaces the novelty of her own existence.

This convoluted idea is not as implausible as it might sound. The willow-as-character entered the story process rather late. As producer James Pentecost explained, animator Joe Grant's initial idea was that an old oak stump (with consciousness) would be the vehicle for our traveling back in time. "Oh, yeah, Pocahontas. Four hundred years ago. I remember . . . " Since it had "not enough shape or persona," they created "an offshoot." That is, the new character that was not only an offshoot of Grant's conception and part of the chaos of creation but also a literal offshoot of the ur-willow. In its hybrid form, Grandmother could be both stump and tree, dead and alive. First she conjures the naturally turbulent spirit of Pocahontas's dead mother. She follows that by goading Pocahontas to climb to the top of her branches and report what she sees. Pocahontas looks out at the sails of the arriving British ship and calls them "Clouds." The sails, though, are old-fashioned 2-D animation; the chaos techniques that might allow for realistic clouds are being used in the ancient tree itself.

The animations that chaos scientists produced in order to solve their problems have become central in this era of special effects– and animation-led studios. Fractals in particular are the everyday stock-in-trade of the computer animator; they are what make surfaces "real," by giving them a feeling of scalable texture. To take an exemplary case, as DreamWorks geared up its animation division, it needed to produce certain pieces of software from scratch, particularly those that would render complex systems. Indeed, a trifecta of the most notorious problems in animation—representing gold, fire, and flowing water—were first successfully tackled in DreamWorks's *Prince of Egypt* (Brenda Chapman, Steve Hickner, Simon Wells, 1998) by applying nonlinear dynamics.

Figure 6.5. Grandmother Willow, dead and alive. *Pocahontas* (Gabriel and Goldberg, Disney, 1995)

DreamWorks hired Patrick Witting as part of the team, who had written his dissertation at Stanford on the "Numerical Investigation of Stratus Cloud Layer Breakup by Cloud Top Instabilities" (1995). He was, in other words, the inheritor of the Lorenz–Feigenbaum–Phil Connors tradition. After his work on *Prince of Egypt* was complete, he presented a paper at SIGGRAPH, the flagship conference for the profession, precisely on the tradigital moment, "Computational Fluid Dynamics in a Traditional Animation Environment."[32] "The style of the smoke was established by my simulations. Where hand-drawn stuff had to match to it, my stuff was used as a reference. That's the beauty of paper and pencil: you can draw anything you want—matching a particular style poses no problems."[33] By 1998, then, the situation for CGI had turned nearly 180 degrees from *Jurassic Park*. For Tippett's animators, computer rendering was making them obsolete; they found a solution in becoming the choreographers of natural phenomena. But on *The Prince of Egypt*, the crucial phenomena could not be modeled by hand but only by computer. Witting's simulations could then serve as models for hand-drawn animation. Chaos theory, once an explanation for tremendous changes in the division of labor, now seemed to provide an explanation for the temporary jurisdictional solution. It had been thoroughly domesticated.

The domestication of chaos theory had a second aspect, though, and in this guise, it affected not simply the division of labor but the very idea of executive labor. By 1996, economists Arthur De Vany and W. David Walls had come to the conclusion that movie revenues followed a particularly chaotic pattern, and that while there were of course groups of movies with similar earnings, one would not be able to predict those similarities in advance. Perhaps the best way to reckon with this randomness was one the industry had already found: Relatively "inflexible admission prices lead to a pure quantity signal," which allows theaters to pull a film when it no longer attracts a sufficient audience.[34] Very quickly, their conclusions reached a popular audience when De Vany was the subject of a *New Yorker* piece, "Chaos in Hollywood." The battle line was drawn between De Vany, who contended that "[n]one of them know what they are doing. . . . There is no formula, no way of predicting how a film will do. The studios are kidding themselves," and executives, typified by Frank Biondi, who put the studio case strongly: "There is a distribution of success in the movie business that can be impacted by management."[35]

Indeed, Biondi's position is not simply what one would expect but rather what the system would require. For De Vany's claim is impossible for a producer (or director, or screenwriter, or actor, or animator, or, I would argue, any creative member of an organization) to hold. How could one reasonably imagine ongoing professional activity in the absence of a belief that skill or competence correlated with outcomes? Or, less speculatively but more foundationally, if there is no link between labor and output, how can one be certain there was labor in the first place? This, ultimately, is the shadow corollary to John Kenneth Galbraith's point that "belief in the purposes of the corporation" is more important than the money the corporation pays its executives.[36] Galbraith was weighing money against purpose and found purpose to be greater. Behind that balancing act lies the possibility that only *belief* in the purposes of the corporation could sustain it since there may be no relationship between one's *actions* and the corporate results.

In a particular sense, how one sees the economics of Hollywood depends on how seriously one takes Goldman's law. For Richard Caves, the idea that "nobody knows anything" has given rise to a regime of option contracts that reduces the scale of each decision. At each point in a film's career, the relevant question is not whether the whole project might be worth it (might be successful) but whether it is worth paying an incremental amount to reach the next decision point. The option contract should, in this model, constrain the level of risk for the relevant decision maker. Nobody may know anything about whether a given idea will make a hit movie, but, Caves contends, the option contract makes the relevant question smaller: Do executives know something about films at this particular juncture? De Vany takes the position that they do not. Indeed, he takes the stronger position that they cannot because the ultimate financial fate of a film depends not only on the film's internal qualities but also on the competition week in and week out during its release.

It may be the economically correct position for a studio to take, but the lessons of chaos theory, particularly as they were extended into Hollywood narrative, make it a more difficult position to take. The integration of the Hollywood studio and the studios' elevation of that search for coherence into the neoclassical aesthetic depend on communication between scales. Here is De Vany's version of that process: "The choices inside the studio tend to be driven by playing out alternative movies as scenarios. This is story-telling, not good decision logic, and it is prone to errors of all sorts."[37] He suggests that instead of storytelling studios move toward green-lighting portfolios of movies and, ideally, securitizing the revenue streams of those films.

Hollywood's aggressive importation of chaos models is built on a neoclassical, perhaps even postmodern, presumption that there is no inconsistency between adaptive reuse and unique authorship (between what is yours and what is "Mine"). The industry assumes, in other words, that credit for these innovations belongs to the one who claims it. However radically the indeterminacy spins out of control, the films conclude in a way that might be called stable. That word, as used by De Vany, "refers to the fact that the process retains its structure on all scales."[38] He is looking at Hollywood from the outside, but if we follow Hollywood's tendency to internalize such characterizations, then he seems to be describing contemporary narrative as much as contemporary economics, even as he would like to divorce economics from narrative. The "happy" endings of classical Hollywood have given way to "stable" endings that demonstrate self-similarity at all scales. The consequences are far-ranging. Where the happy ending seemed forced—as in a Douglas Sirk melodrama, a film noir, or even a Preston Sturges comedy—it encouraged an oppositional or even subversive reading. But the stable ending seems tentative and encourages elaboration. To imagine a sequel, one need only imagine the expansion of a single scale—a character, a setting, a plot point. *Jurassic Park* projects to *The Lost World* (Spielberg, Universal, 1997) by reversing the scalar relationship between the finished product and the prototype (or pitch), while *The Bourne Ultimatum* (Paul Greengrass, Universal, 2007) nests most of its action within the space of a cut in *The Bourne Supremacy* (Greengrass, Universal, 2004). Narrative closure yields pride of place to the introjection of downstream revenues, and the movies become advertisements for themselves.

Part III

Hollywood the Day after Tomorrow
Neoclassical Endings?

George (Jay Sanders) is hanging from the roof of a mall somewhere in New Jersey. "I just dropped in to do a little shopping." No one thinks it funny; no one is supposed to. Midway through *The Day after Tomorrow* (Roland Emmerich, Centropolis/Fox, 2004) massive storms are bringing a new ice age to much of the northern hemisphere. Jack Hall (Dennis Quaid) and two of his colleagues are trekking north to New York to rescue Jack's son, Sam (Jake Gyllenhaal). So much snow has already fallen that the men have unknowingly wandered onto the glass roof of the mall.

George's reflexive bit of snark sounds more like a line from a movie than actual faux bravado. But perhaps we all would say things that sound like lines from movies in such a case. ("In such a case" meaning the case in which we had been walking across New Jersey during a superstorm and were now dangling from the ceiling of an abandoned mall.) Regardless, the line is of a piece with the production design. Below George, one sign reads "Inventory Blowout," capturing precisely the unfunniness of his remark. It hangs next to a Verizon storefront, one of the film's glaring product placements. Placements like that

Figure PIII.1. *The Day after Tomorrow* (Roland Emmerich, Centropolis/Fox, 2004)

one recast the signs and symbols of collapsing capitalism as audience impressions that may be sold to advertisers. Yet beyond the do-si-do of end times advertising, the film displays Emmerich's penchant for autoplacement. Fox News is the TV channel of choice, and, slightly more cannily, the mall is named the Sky Galleria. (News Corp's satellite systems included BSkyB, Sky Global, ISkyB in India, and so on.)

In editing the sequence, David Brenner said they faced a classic choice between the Hitchcock alternatives: surprise and suspense. Following the script's painful literalism, they went with suspense. To be sure, this is a behind-the-scenes joke as well. Describing the auction process for the film, Emmerich's agent Michael Winer noted that prospective studios would be able to see that "this is not a cast-dependent movie." George makes that clear enough when he cuts himself loose in order to save Jack and Jason.

He will drop all the way in, but we will not see or (more surprisingly) hear him land. Instead, we will see Jack watching him, doubly mediated by his goggles and a glass panel of the roof. Still, there is no doubt about George's fall. We have seen an almost exactly parallel scene early in the film; we have seen what happens to the sled George cuts loose to lighten the load on his end; and we see Jack's reaction. George's death follows the Hollywood rule of three. So will *The Studios after the Studios.*

The end of an aesthetic is more elusive than the end of a minor character in an action spectacular. When we try to pin down a period, our usual recourse is to go hunting in some exogenous field for a cause so supererogatory that no contemporary aesthetic formation might have survived it unscathed. In the case of filmgoing, Hollywood studios content themselves that nothing short of ecological catastrophe or the collapse of capitalism as a whole would prevent audiences from turning up. Yet since these events have not yet occurred, Hollywood turns to its projective oracles. In the case of *The Day after Tomorrow*, Dennis Quaid delivers the essential quote: "It's every disaster flick you've ever seen all rolled into one giant nonstop global meteorological cataclysm."[1]

Not every example of Hollywood losing its neoclassical momentum and balance need be a summa-meta-disaster movie. It might be a heist film, an old-fashioned sea yarn, a throwback story of the individual fighting the system, or a peplum-clad epic. These are, of course, still Hollywood movies, but they are subtly different movies from those of the high neoclassical period that precedes them. They are drifting away from a confident belief that the competing forces besetting the studio or the system might be brokered in individual films or even individual images. Instead, romantic confrontations of the micro and the macro abound. The sublime intrudes. The ocean—or a man who is an

Ocean—and the empire—or a man more powerful than an emperor—are the proper subjects. The neoclassical film elides the tension between its ideal and the ideals of the organization behind it, whether that organization is the studio, the synergistic conglomerate, or the entertainment industry. In this emerging period, even the most outsized films with the largest budgets often vouch for nothing beyond themselves. Because they cannot or because they will not? For now, Hollywood sidesteps such formal or psychological questions. Its grand productions may owe their existence to correlatively large organizations, but they acknowledge that lien only long enough to escape.

That Oceanic Feeling
One Merger Too Many

I can say that I am profoundly "religious"—without this constant state (like a sheet of water which I feel flushing under the bark) affecting in any way my critical faculties and my freedom to exercise them). . . . I may add that this "oceanic" sentiment has nothing to do with my personal yearnings. . . . [T]the sentiment I experience is imposed on me as a fact. It is a *contact*.

Romain Rolland to Sigmund Freud, 1927[1]

Saturation

At the end of the nineties, Universal escaped its legendary flop *Waterworld* and its indifferent owners Matsushita and washed up on Seagram's shores. No sooner was it dry than it rushed to catch up with newly merged AOL Time-Warner by joining with Vivendi—a merger that surrounded and mimicked the plot of the World War II submarine movie *U-571*. At the same time, AOL Time-Warner was crafting elaborate self-advertisements in films such as *You've Got Mail* and *Batman Begins*.[2] Both megacorporations, though, quickly foundered. Vivendi Universal registered the largest loss in European history and announced its breakup within eighteen months of its formation; TimeWarner dropped the AOL from its name in 2003 after taking the largest write-down in world history.

Yet if the films that accompanied these ownership changes and strategic reprioritizations continued to perform the same sort of corporate conceptual work that they had since the eighties, then they would seem to constitute a warrant against the larger historical narrative that I have been laying out. If conglomerate implosion does not threaten neoclassical allegories, what could? And what work could a movie usefully do in the face of such meltdowns? At the same time, one might object that while Universal, Focus Features, Warner Bros., and New Line would have to come to terms with the end of an era, the system circa 2000 remained remarkably consistent with the one that had been built over the previous decades. In that case, the persistence of the same allegorical tendencies would argue for an industrial rather than a corporate basis for the order of composition, and my overarching story would be weakened in another way. Yet each objection is slightly off target. The first misreads the historical break because it looks for a homology between corporate and narrative *forms* rather than a match between corporate *aspiration* and narrative form. Still, the line between form and aspiration is not obvious, and it bears looking for. The second

247

objection is more to the point, since inside jokes and logorrhea are everywhere a decade hence. In this view, particular allegorical instances, however corporate, would only be tokens of obeisance while the film's real fealty was to an industry or a mode that found temporary incarnation only in a particular corporation.

How would we decide whether Hollywood neoclassicism had been a matter of industrial self-reflection all along or whether the system was losing its corporate neoclassical balance? Where would we spot a new relation between allegory and underwriter? The claim has been that neoclassical Hollywood depends on a structure where players in the system project a tiered collection of self-understandings, and that collection requires and reinforces a (merely) heuristic distance between the system and the reading of it. What announces the end of that relationship of mutual implication would not be the collapse of a given conglomerate but the completion of its possibilities, the saturation of the corporation by its reading, the collapse of distance between model and mode. If the allegories remain the same, of the same intensity, and with the same role, then we would conclude that they had their source in the industry itself. If, though, the office of the allegory attenuates, it may do so because the order of composition has altered internally, and we would find our evidence within the formation. This is treacherous ground for at least two reasons. First, it is practically so since to say that a corporation's possibilities are saturated does not seem to be an accurate description of any corporation's position, particularly in a period of massive technological upheaval. Second, it is theoretically so since, as Stanley Cavell says of genre, "There is no way to know when the state of saturation, completeness of expression, has been reached."[3]

The difficulty lurking in the concept of saturation runs parallel to the problem of deniability I addressed in the opening chapter. In that account, the decisive difference between classical and a neoclassical Hollywood lies in the level at which deniability operates. As deniability migrates up the ladder from the project to the contract, logorrhea and allusion drive it back down through the story. When films bleed their logos into their stories, our problem is no longer that we don't know which companies are claiming them but that we won't pay attention. The system seemingly runs greater risks because the links to its productions become more contingent and tenuous, and in compensation we find a heightened explicitness about those links. What was an ontological problem (is this film the studio?) becomes an aesthetic and epistemological problem (how can we recognize this film?). It becomes a problem of balance.

Cavell's elaboration of genre began with his study of the remarriage comedies. There, he put his notion of genre-as-medium up against a more structural version in which "the members of a genre share the inheritance of certain conditions, procedures, and subjects and goals of composition" and in which each member "represents a study of these conditions." The consequence of such an account, for him, is that there is "nothing one is tempted to call *the* features of a genre which all its members have in common."[4] What they share, instead, is an inheritance and a hermeneutic. In contrast, Cavellian genres *do* share all their features in common, and when they do not, they take up a determined relationship to those features—a member either compensates for its missing feature and so contests and elaborates the very underpinnings of the genre or it negates that feature and proffers an "adjacent" genre. By this logic the "melodrama of the unknown woman" lies adjacent to the remarriage comedy.

While it is difficult to see the difference between "studying the conditions" of a genre and "investigating the myth" that underlies it, that distinction sufficed until Cavell turned to "The Fact of Television" in 1982. In this new context, genre-as-medium found itself opposed to genre-as-cycle. In the latter, he contended, every instance "is a perfect exemplification of the format, as each solution of an equation . . . is a perfect instance of the formula that 'generates' it."[5] Whereas a film could fail to belong to its Cavellian genre, an instance in a genre-as-cycle could not. We might be tempted to view this theoretical distinction as a fig leaf for a difference between good and bad objects—films versus TV shows, and further, to think that the competing notions of genre are a way of expressing a preference for a world where instances (and criticism) matter. But rather than determine the utility of these ideas of genre in the service of some elaborate critical sorting operation, I want to turn to the image of system that each implies.

The genre system that envelops a Cavellian genre-as-medium is replete. A particular genre-as-medium is saturable because the genre system itself is saturated. "If genres form a system (which is part of the faith that for me keeps alive an interest in the concept), then in principle it would seem possible to be able to move by negation from one genre through adjacent genres, until all the genres of film are derived."[6] Put another way, genre-as-medium is a way of preserving the (faith in the) genre system. In contrast, the instances of genre-as-cycle are distributed evenly, hence unsystematically, across the surface of possibility. "The instances do not compete with one another for depth of participation . . . and whether an instance 'belongs' to the formula is as settled by the formula as is the identity of the instance."[7] This genre is an algorithm.

What does a particular problem in the theory of genre have to do with the saturation of conglomerate possibilities at Vivendi Universal or AOL TimeWarner? The conceptual drift that accompanies Cavell's shift in subject from (classical) Hollywood cinema to (broadcast) television in other critics accompanies the historical shift from classical to postclassical systems. His classical genres are fundamentally about belonging and contestation; his postclassical television is uninterested in such a process: "Belonging has to be won, earned, as by an argument of the members with one another; as adjacency of genre must be proved, something irrelevant to the existence of multiple series, which, further, raise no issue of the definition and refinement a genre undergoes."[8] Cavell further specifies that this sentence ("Belonging has to be won, as by an argument") "is an allegory of the relation of the principal pair in such comedies," which implies that forms allegorize instances (and, perhaps, vice versa), and which suggests that this chain might be extended to other levels.

A classical synchronism of the kind implied by Cavell's genre system depends for its realization on "the details of the working out," the "investigation, or generation" of the formula "by the instances," that is, the system as allegory depends on its inductive base.[9] The further we force this account to come to terms with broader historical changes, the more important the reestablishment of studio allegory in Hollywood becomes as a marker of systemic change. That is, what appeared to be an instance in the history of criticism—Cavell's foray into television—maps an instance in the history of media systems—the apparent loss of classical allegory. (It would be too far afield to do more than suggest that the New Hollywood era represented the triumph of genre-as-cycle thinking within Hollywood, particularly since the landmark films of that era seem to make so much of their status as films-not-television.) Once concepts are made available to history, they can both exhibit a sort of pendular pattern in which classical allegories appear, then dry up, then come back, and be aestheticized or made immanent, as when the "features" of the classical system are neoclassicized, compensated, or negated.

How does that system break apart? The burden of this chapter and the next will be to illustrate how such a rupture becomes possible through a loss of faith in the instance or in the system. For now, I want to point toward a convergence that Cavell puts into play in his account of the (potential) saturation of a genre. On the one hand, he will say that it is impossible to know when a genre is saturated. On the other hand, he will say that when we cease to believe in the genre's myth, it "dies." Both statements are in keeping with the logic of the saturated genre system. There cannot be a migration from one genre to another through a patch of insignificance or meaninglessness because the relations between member films are *always* determined (as compensation, negation, etc.). Within such a system, a genre can only live or die, and that death is, again, based on "belief." Step out of the genre, though, and we find an allegory of that belief, its critical echo, when Cavell refers to his "faith" in the idea of a system, a faith that keeps his interest in the concept of genre "alive." It may be impossible to know when a genre is saturated; it would be decidedly easier to know when someone had lost interest in a critical concept.

And this is where the detour through form returns to the history of the studios after the studios. Neoclassical Hollywood aestheticizes its own systematicity. When it "loses faith" in that system, its interest in systemic allegory dies. The allegories may go on (they do), but the system falls out of self-saturation, leaving not genre-as-cycle but studio-as-cycle. Such an event only compounds our questions. What does it mean for a corporation to lose faith in the system? And if that loss of faith amounts to a history, how is that history not the most naïve idealism? Finally, what does this loss of faith have to do with oceans?

The Enigma of Distribution

There are not many opportunities for product placement in World War II movies, Coke bottles excepted. For *U-571*, Universal found a way around that by casting Island recording artist Jon Bon Jovi who, not uncoincidentally, released his first Bon Jovi album in five years (*Crush*) alongside the film. The joint appearance of the actor in his first big studio movie and the album attracted everyone from *Entertainment Tonight* to *Access Hollywood* to ESPN, which put Bon Jovi in a Jersey-themed SportsCenter commercial. The singer did his best to play along. Doing double publicity for the film and the album, he made the movie seem like the road not taken. Growing up in Sayreville, New Jersey, he told the *Bergen Record* that "there were four of us who hung out. . . . My three buddies joined the Navy. I was silly enough to stick with the music."[10]

For that "slippery when wet" story line to exist, all Bon Jovi needed to do was appear in the film—he didn't have to do anything, and in *U-571* he doesn't do much. One of the biggest rock stars in the world gets blown off the top of the sub without a second thought. The mismatch between Bon Jovi's music stardom and his role duplicates the predicament of his corporate owner, Universal. He is the poster boy for an impossible synergy between the recording goliath and its problematic motion picture arm. The story of *U-571*—the story behind it and the story it tells—is a remarkably detailed reckoning with the management problems of media conglomerates: corporate control, project finance, value chains, and synergies. Bon Jovi is only the most obvious instance of corporate cross-promotion in a film that is a relentless product placement for its studio.

Seagram, which owned Universal at the time, got Bon Jovi and the rest of Island when it bought Polygram in May 1998. That was what it wanted, but the deal seemed cursed. The culture clash between music labels was violent, and

Edgar Bronfman Jr. ("Effer") pushed through a brutal restructuring in order to achieve the $300 million in cost savings he had promised Wall Street. Morale was low. Agents threatened to withhold material from Universal labels if the company couldn't guarantee the distribution systems would mesh in time.

To finance the deal, Seagram sold Tropicana, and Moody's promptly downgraded its debt, making the deal that much more expensive. The stock remained flat. That was bad enough. But along with Polygram's record companies, Seagram also got Polygram Filmed Entertainment (PFE), which it didn't need and didn't really want. Philips, Polygram's Dutch parent, had pumped $1.25 billion into PFE, underwriting its films, building up a distribution network that Universal already had and a library that was not particularly profitable (a big chunk of it was old British television shows, hardly the Turner treasure trove).

As thorny as the integration of the record labels looked to be, it was PFE that proved the biggest problem. Seagram wanted to realize most of Philips's investment by selling the unit off as a whole. To do so, they had to move quickly. The film industry, even more than music, is one where distribution cred is central. A delay in the sale would mean a gap in Polygram releases, which would mean higher overhead charges for each film, crippling the company and forcing Universal to hold on to a progressively worthless mini-major. When Seagram put the unit up for auction, no one came close to the bid it wanted. Months passed, and eventually Seagram divvied PFE up in several ways: the film library went to MGM ($250 million); the TV library, to Carlton ($135 million); the distribution networks—October Films and Gramercy—went to Barry Diller's USA to become USA Films ($200–$300 million). A quick loss of $500 million.[11]

But the key piece of the Polygram protectorate was Working Title films, the most successful European production shingle of the nineties. Inside Universal, there was pressure on Effer to retain Working Title, even if the rest of Polygram were to be let go. Working Title, headed by Tim Bevan and Eric Fellner, had the usual stable of long-term relationships—in their case, with the Coen brothers, Stephen Frears, Hanif Kureishi, Tim Robbins, and Richard Curtis. The marquee pictures—the Curtis films—typically involved significant UK/US interchange (*The Tall Guy*, *Four Weddings*, *Notting Hill*, *Bridget Jones's Diary*), which made them more marketable and let them serve as think pieces for the transatlantic studio's identity. Even when Curtis was not involved, Working Title maintained that balance by putting American stars in the British Isles: Ted Danson in *Loch Ness* (1995), Janeane Garofalo in *The Matchmaker* (1997), John Goodman in *The Borrowers* (1997), Lucas Haas in *Long Time Dead* (2001).

Within Working Title, the Polygram sale brought new pressures. It had looked as though the production company would be the launch point for a successful British invasion of the major studios' ranks. But with Polygram folded into Universal, Working Title found itself underwritten by an American, or, rather, Canadian company, one that was already desperate for cash. There would be no more hymns to British nationalism like *Elizabeth* (1998) or the more allegorically freighted *Plunkett & Macleane* (1999), where the baddies bear the names of Arsenal defenders. At the same time Bevan and Fellner's contracts were coming up. Their years of critical and box-office success had not translated into great profits for them—they were essentially salaried. Now, though, they were looking to cash in, "finally being recompensed as proper Hollywood producers," as Fellner put it.[12]

On the other side of the ocean, Universal went on the block in early 1999. In January, the week before *U-571* began shooting in Rome, *Variety* published a long account of the studio's troubles—"It's truly Bosnia over here," one producer said—and its desire to find a financing partner for the sub film.[13] Universal needed Working Title in order to sell itself, to head off arguments that it let its most valuable assets get away, and to maintain its standing in the creative community. But it also needed the cash to make that commitment real. Universal then tied the financing of *U-571* to the Working Title slate: only someone willing to bankroll Working Title would share in the submarine film. U re-signed the Working Title duo in March 1999. With the leadership in place, it inked a cofinancing deal at Cannes in May with Canal+, the media arm of the giant French utility company, Vivendi.

Vivendi had its own story. When Jean-Marie Messier became the chair of Compagnie Generale des Eaux (CGE) in 1996, he wanted to transform the monopoly-with-a-market-face into a global media power. There were few opportunities for the old-line national utility to become an integrated industrial "solutions provider" as so many privatized entities had tried, and real future profits would come through other pipelines. At the same time, he could not simply divest the utility side. Barred from ordinary capital markets by French law and European tradition, CGE required the steady cash flow of the utility in order to finance Messier's acquisitions. The collapse of socialism had turned CGE loose, rich and hungry. Messier went after Havas, the French media conglomerate, and changed his company's name from CGE to Vivendi.

Vivendi already owned just under half of Canal+. Buying more would have triggered a financially disastrous sell-off of the waterworks because French law bars horizontal combinations between industrial corporations and media outlets of the GE–NBC kind for fear of polluted news. Through Canal+ and its film arm StudioCanal, Vivendi formed a number of joint ventures with well-established media conglomerates. They owned 25 percent of News Corp's BSkyB, half of AOL France, and half of Vizzavi (an Internet portal with Vodafone AG) before they entered into the cofinancing arrangement with Universal.

What this corporate backstory drives home is the importance of fit. In order to make mergers tax free, they have to be stock based, not cash. Thus, fit is important, because companies have to work for or own the other side; they can't take the money and run. Companies look for fit all the time—Lew Wasserman's MCA talent agency spent years farming out its players to Universal before taking it over. Seagram was looking for fit when it sought a partner for *U-571* and Working Title—a cash partner first, a stock partner later. That probe led directly to the meeting between Bronfman and Messier that raised the possibility of merger. One particular film was at the center of the corporate transaction.

We might approach this moment in another way. At the same time Universal was shopping the Working Title slate, it was also looking for partners for *Erin Brockovich*. Now, which movie looks like a better sell to a giant French water company—the one that features the largest rainstorm in film history; the one that reaches its climax when a sailor sacrifices his life to close a valve; or the one in which an intrepid investigator makes a giant American utility company pay millions for polluting the groundwater? Universal sold half of *Erin Brockovich* to Columbia (Sony). When the Vivendi-Universal merger was announced, the *Los Angeles Times* described the fit as "Bourbon and Water."[14]

But the story of *U-571* is not simply the story of how the film was deployed by the company. There is also a bottom-up story, a story of surfacing, in which the film tells the company a story it wants to hear. This is the single most important consideration in the pitching of a motion picture: Will the studio like it? As writer/director Jonathan Mostow described it, "When we sold the script to Universal I said, 'If you liked the end of *Breakdown*, where Kurt Russell and Kathleen Quinlan were in a pick-up truck being crushed in a metal container, now I'm going to take this group of actors, put them in a submerged sardine can and crush them underwater!'"[15] (hence the title of the Bon Jovi album). Always responsive to his patrons' desires, Mostow (and his co-writers and production designers and actors and costumers, etc., etc.) fashioned *U-571* into an allegory of the corporate dealings in Cannes, the same way that the plays-within-the-films of *Shakespeare in Love* or *Moulin Rouge* tell the story of their own production.

For any reader of the industry trades, U simply means Universal, the way the Lion means MGM and prexy means president. The sub simply *is* the corporation. But *U-571* tells two stories to two corporate audiences. The two stories are "the mission"—stealing the Enigma without the Germans' knowing—and "the professional"—testing Executive Officer (XO) Matthew McConaughey's fitness for command. In a mission film, there are two factions: the "mechanics" who do their usual job and the "intelligence" who have temporary control— "He's the boss. Whatever he wants, he gets," the pooh-bah will say. There is mutual mistrust, some tense moments when the mechanics act smart and the intelligence guys act brave, and then mutual respect. This nifty crisscross makes the mission film ideal for thinking about changes in ownership and control.

But in *U-571*, Mostow says, the real spine of the film is McConaughey's maturation. The underlying structure of that plot is that someone wants to be in charge but is held back. (Psychologically, this justifies the underling's repressed violence early in the story, repression that usually shows up as drinking.) A convenient emergency puts him in charge, and he muddles his way into deserving the accidental rank. The fit-to-command plot is ideal for thinking about corporate survival.

The Effer story is the maturation one. Derided by the *Wall Street Journal* as a "starstruck whiskey king" from the day he bought MCA (Universal), Bronfman had just cleaned house, firing both Universal CEO Frank Biondi and Universal Pictures CEO Casey Silver in less than two weeks.[16] The *Variety* headline must have screamed at Mostow and Ayer as they were rewriting the script: "With Biondi out, pressure's on Bronfman to turn U around." The trade paper went on, barely disguising its doubts: "Bronfman said he had 'learned a lot' in the 3 years since Seagram acquired a majority stake in Universal and felt able to do the job himself."[17]

On the DVD, Mostow says that he rewrote McConaughey's entrance after the actor was cast. Originally, Lieutenant Tyler was supposed to arrive drunk and with "a floozie" on his arm, but to capture McConaughey's "inherent nobility," Mostow gave him a stag entrance. "That's not like you," his captain's wife chides. (Bronfman Sr. had famously asked his son if Seagram was buying MGM stock "just so you can get laid"; Effer responded that it didn't cost $40 million to get laid.)[18] After discovering that Bill Paxton has "torpedoed" his bid for a command of his own, the XO heads out on the porch, where he drinks—not the beer he has promised to have with the enlisted men but a bottle of Seagram's VO (VO was, uncoincidentally, the company's stock ticker symbol.) The last-minute rewrite motivated the on-screen drinking that made the studio product placement possible.

In the climactic scene, McConaughey/Tyler/Bronfman will turn the *U-571* around, firing the aft torpedo and sinking the German destroyer. Paternal Paxton "shit-cans" McConaughey; McConaughey's sardine can shits on the Germans. (Mostow has said that the film embodies the "American can-do spirit.") McConaughey grows up, proving, as Barry Diller once challenged

Figure 7.1. The XO
drinks VO. *U-571*
(Jonathan Mostow,
Universal, 2000)

Effer to prove, that he isn't "a third-generation bimbo."[19] The "professional"
plot, like Bon Jovi's appearance, is calculated for maximum obviousness. (The
iron law of Hollywood psychoanalysis also dictates that the repressed violence
McConaughey feels toward Paxton be displaced and legitimized. In the film, the
German U-boat captain bangs out a coded message on the sub's pipes to let his
countrymen know that *U-571* has been captured. The usurped German stands
in for the dead Paxton. Lieutenant Hirsch [Jake Weber]—the intelligence officer in charge of the mission, here McConaughey's counterpart—bashes in his
face with a wrench.)

Canning puns aside, the mission plot of the film hinges on two questions:
Can the Americans operate the captured German U-boat? Can they get the
Enigma machine back to base without the Germans knowing? The first is a
question of translation, which in the Hollywood context is the inveterate question: Can the foreigners run a studio? It's something we know the Japanese
parents had failed to do; something Canadian Seagram was failing to do. The
second is a question of secrecy, of hiding the coding machine.

When they first board the U-boat, Seaman Bill Wentz (Jake Noseworthy)—Mostow calls him his on-screen persona—runs around the control
room, translating the names of the Vivendi-esque valves. Noseworthy's ultra-
competent Wentz is the place where the two mission teams—the two media
conglomerates—cross. He is "half-German," a human coproduction. He is the
radioman, which means he turns words into beeps and beeps into words, a
human translation machine. (His German counterpart is the one who operates the Enigma machine in the opening scene.) When the boarding party
arrives at the U-boat, Noseworthy shouts (*auf Deutsch*): "We're all mechanics.
And we're all very skilled." There is no tension between the intelligence guys

and the submariners. Once the Americans know what the valves are for, they can spin them.

The overriding visual motif of *U-571* is these spinning valves. There are gears and levers and gauges as well, but there are dozens and dozens of valves, which must be spun, usually in pairs. Every couple minutes or so in the sub control room, an actor will grab a pair of bright red valves and spin like mad. This frantic synchronized spinning is yet another Hollywood version of baring the device, an instance where the movie-ness of the movie is put on display. The spinning valves echo the old-fashioned process of editing on a Moviola or KEM table. There is even a shot in the "on location" documentary in which valves from the sub are nearly indistinguishable from film cans.

This may seem like so much undecipherable code. But the movie, of course, is about encryption. And while the encryption device, the Enigma machine, looks like a typewriter—a nostalgic script-generator—the guts of it are a series of unseen rotors, the invisible echoes of the spinning valves. Encrypted encryption. The message the *U-571* sends out on the Enigma is "Send help." That one is translated for Effer's benefit. From his point of view, help comes in the form of McConaughey's command. But the coded message of *U-571* is that there is nothing so different about plumbing and running a Hollywood studio.

If we follow the auteur for a moment here, we see just how far-reaching this attempt to appeal to Vivendi—the water company on the way to being a media conglomerate with its own Hollywood studio—is. The original Universal/Canal+ deal to cofinance *U-571* also bankrolled the great British hope Working Title. In the sub film, the elimination of things British was systematic. *U-571* begins by giving the Americans credit for something the Royal Navy had done even before American entry into the war. It was originally to end with a kind of

Figure 7.2. Men among valves. *U-571* (Mostow, Universal, 2000)

symbolic payback when the raft of survivors catches sight of the English coast. But Mostow went back into the computer months later and substituted a twin-engine US Navy seaplane. (He has even been meticulous about the markings, which include a red circle in the center of the National Aircraft insignia and red and white tail stripes. Both of those elements would be eliminated on May 15, 1942.)[20] He has replaced British terra firma with double spinning; sentimental insularity with big-time American production values.

Shortly after *U-571* opened, Vivendi and Universal officially merged. Vivendi also agreed to buy out the rest of Canal+, which meant it would have to spin off its waterworks. To finance the deal and maintain a media focus, Vivendi Universal also sold off the Seagram's drinks business. The corporate equivalent of "bourbon and water" produced neither. Instead, it joined the tradition of the wettest Hollywood studio, the one engineered into a colossus by Lew *Wasser*man; the one built around the ritual floods of the Universal Studio tour, the success of *Jaws*, and the failure of *Waterworld*.

When the new Vivendi Universal executive team met at the Deauville (i.e., Watertown) Festival of American Film in September 2000, they screened *U-571*. To Alain Terzian, *U-571* producer Dino De Laurentiis was proof "that a European can succeed in America" and a good example for Vivendi to follow. Laurentiis did not attribute his success to translation: "I left Europe 30 years ago with no good English. And still, no good English."[21] Universal Studios president Ron Meyer "confessed to knowing no French," but his new boss, Canal+'s Pierre Lescure, knew enough English to send his own coded message. When Seagram bought PFE in 1998, Lescure declared "with classic Gallic bravado," "Anything that can prevent PolyGram films from falling under American control is worth backing."[22] Two years later, he was all intimation: "Why meet in Deauville? I would simply say that the opportunity to get to know each other in our universe is essential."[23] Their universe indeed.

Frictionless Worlds

Vivendi's plunge into media conglomeration occurred with such speed and so thoroughly that it would have been difficult for anyone to keep up. In this case as in others, instead of a perfect tracking of story and backstory, we find that each phase of a project can only sketch out ways a particular corporate story might evolve, hoping that the eventual convergence or conceptual synergy will codify that intention. Yet the tension-filled whirl that surrounds projects at the center of a corporate imaginary may suddenly go slack or find itself yanked into an alternative orbit. In such cases, what the projects leave behind is not the successful articulation of corporate and creative aims but a history of failed sync. What remains when prophecy and planning fail is a particular gap in the company's self-narrative. At Vivendi, that gap is occupied by Curious George.

The original Curious George Goes to . . . series had ended at seven installments, but in the late nineties, the publisher had been issuing new adventures at quite a clip, "illustrated in the style of H. A. Rey by Vipah Interactive" they all proclaimed. In 2000, Curious George was the spine of the children's fiction list at Houghton, and the company was attempting to keep George ubiquitous and relevant. Following Margret Rey's death in 1996, Houghton sold the rights to merchandise the monkey to Universal Studios Consumer Products.[24] It was a sensible decision given that the film rights to the series were held by Imagine Entertainment, the Ron Howard/Brian Grazer shingle that was set up at the studio. When (or if) the film was finally produced, the merchandising would be consolidated.

Despite much ballyhoo surrounding the rights transfer in 1997, Imagine continued to struggle with its live-action-with-CGI-monkeyface *Curious George* project. In 1999, they changed tack and brought in Brad Bird to direct.[25] That project stalled as well, until in July 2001 the newly merged Vivendi Universal announced that it would be acquiring Houghton Mifflin for $2.2 billion. By adding another huge asset to its publishing portfolio, Vivendi hoped to extend its transmedia brands. On the one hand, owning a major educational publisher would allow the studio (and, shortly, the cable networks) to gain access to youth markets. On the other hand, certain underexposed properties could be revitalized through movies and television series. Imagine's film version was now back on the fast track.

Messier had already fashioned himself a world-historical figure, referring to himself in the third-person cybernetic as "J6M," that is, "Jean-Marie Messier, moi-même, maître du monde." His imperial aims were thoroughly consonant with both halves of the Curious George story. He was both the Man with the Yellow Hat and the inquisitive monkey in a happy little story about the great white father who captures the little brown scamp and takes him away from home to a land of modernity and adventure.

In full-page ads announcing the closure of VU's offer for Houghton, Messier himself promoted the idea that Curious George would be the company's new mascot, the Mickey Mouse to its Disney. "Curious George goes to Vivendi Universal," the ads proclaimed. "Soon, George will be able to feed his curiosity by tapping into Vivendi Universal's incredible content and distribution network." George is consuming content from "five Vivendi businesses: publishing, music, television and film, the internet and interactive games and telecommunications," according to Bloomberg News.[26] "Curious George is a

Curious George
goes to
Vivendi Universal

Dear shareholders,

It is with great pleasure that I announce our pending acquisition of Houghton Mifflin, one of the oldest and most respected publishers in the United States.

Vivendi Universal's offer of $60 per share, net to the seller in cash, represents a fair and full price.
The offer is scheduled to expire on Friday, July 6.

Soon, George will be able to feed his curiosity by tapping into Vivendi Universal's incredible content and distribution network. That network includes Universal Music, with the world's most extensive and prestigious catalog of music; Universal Studios and StudioCanal with their combined libraries of 9,000 movies; Vivendi Universal Publishing and its educational books and software, as well as education.com, Blizzard Entertainment, and flipside.com; plus numerous TV channels and European telecommunications activities.

With the addition of Houghton Mifflin and its impressive array of educational publishing and children's books, Vivendi Universal, a world leader in media and communications, will become number two worldwide in education.

With Houghton Mifflin, we will further reinforce our goal of becoming the world's preferred creator and provider of personalized information, education and entertainment across all distribution platforms and devices.

Welcome George. Here's to your insatiable curiosity.

Sincerely,

Jean-Marie Messier
Chairman and Chief Executive Officer
Vivendi Universal

VIVENDI
UNIVERSAL

www.vivendiuniversal.com

Figure 7.3. Multimedia monkey mascot. Source: Reprinted with permission of Vivendi

great character and we are interested in leveraging the character all through our different businesses," Messier told the *New York Post* while relaxing at the Allen & Co. summer retreat for media barons. Incorporating the monkey in VU's corporate advertising was "one way to convey a message that Vivendi Universal is dedicated to education and entertainment and that we want to capitalize on wonderful characters."[27]

Had Messier survived the company's disastrous earnings reports later that year, and had Brad Bird's version of *Curious George* gone into production, the monkey might indeed have become a functional corporate mascot. Instead, both Bird's version of the film and Messier's conglomerate fell apart. A year later, Messier was forced out, and his replacement, Jean-René Fourtou, conducted a fire sale of assets, including Houghton. Vivendi lost $23 billion in 2002. Asked what his "long-term plans" were, Messier declared, "I will stay [in America]. I have some unbelievable stories and one day I will tell them."[28]

The studio was the site within Vivendi Universal where the various parts of the far-flung conglomerate would find articulation. That union would be supported by narration (movies) and marketing (consumer products), that is, by the corporate unit that married the two. But as the disarticulation proceeded, the corporation's stories became, as Messier put it, "unbelievable." Vivendi no longer required a fantasy consumer/producer in the form of a mascot, an idol, or a master. Whatever would hold the conglomerate together would no longer aspire to representability: a unit's contribution would be, first and last, financial. The continuity of the corporate surface—that sheet of water flushing under the bark—came apart.

The Vivendi collapse did not quite take Curious George with it. The books continued to sell. The film was scaled back and, as Houghton might have put it, "executed in a classic 2-D cell-animation style." It finally reached theaters in early 2006 where it did not perform particularly well. In this incarnation, the Man with the Yellow Hat is desperate to save a failing natural history museum. His plan to draw crowds with an African idol fails (the idol is tiny), but George, eventually, reanimates the museum. (Fox's parallel adaptation, *Night at the Museum*, was released later that year to tremendous business.) The monkey also starred in a longer-lived PBS series, which blended George's cartoon adventures with live-action segments of children being curious. Capitalizing on the movie's museum-centered plot and backstopping the TV series was a traveling children's museum exhibit, *Curious George: Let's Get Curious!*, which appeared in Boston, Chicago, Seattle, Atlanta, and other cities. By mid-decade, Curious George was a brand being managed across several companies and different platforms. He was, himself, a master of media, mascot of none.

Domestic Distribution

Steven Soderbergh had a banner 2000, culminating in a double nomination for the Academy Award for Best Director. *Erin Brockovich* was released early in the year; *Traffic*, at the end. The first film was developed and domestically distributed by Universal; the second, by USA Films, the mini-major that had been created out of the disposal of PFE after Universal acquired it. *Brockovich* and *Traffic* constitute two pinnacles of Hollywood neoclassicism, and they are, as it happens, films about domestic distribution. For while each of them approaches a somatic issue—the effects of industrial pollution and drugs—each is preoccupied with the interlocking systems that render the somatic social, and vice versa. Through intense interest in the social mechanisms behind a mass individual-action lawsuit and international drug interdiction efforts, both films become elaborate allegories of their own interleaving of labor, law, and organization.

Not content to merely display those connections, both movies feature characters in the process of *finding* them. In *Brockovich*, there are two phases. In the first, she has to find the link between the power plant's leaching ponds and the genetic maladies of the plant's neighbors—this is the story of "the plume" and occupies the first two-thirds of the film. In the second search, she has to hold more than six hundred plaintiffs together while she finds the link between the PG&E plant and what the film calls "PG&E corporate." That link comes from a man who awkwardly stalks Brockovich, finally approaching her with lines like, "I think you're someone I could really talk to." He explains that he was supposed to shred some documents, but, "as it turns out, I wasn't a very good employee." He comes "out of the blue" Erin tells her boss, Ed Masry. A rogue employee, the entirely fictional character of Charles Embry is an apparently unmotivated coincidence, a weak point in the plotting. Yet Embry is played by veteran character actor Tracey Walter, whose most famous bit of dialogue comes from the cult classic *Repo Man* (Alex Cox, Universal, 1984), where he details the "lattice of coincidence that lays on top of everything": "Say you're thinking about a plate of shrimp, and someone says 'plate' or 'shrimp' or 'plate of shrimp.' Out of the blue." He isn't a coincidence; he is the spirit of coincidence, a transfilmic concept, and he pops up in *Erin Brockovich* to make the link between the plume and the corporation real.

In *Erin Brockovich*, though, Universal—or Soderbergh—was not about to leave the "link to corporate" to coincidence. The film opens with Erin explaining to a doctor that, despite her lack of education, she could be a medical assistant because she becomes passionate about her work. Previously she worked for an oil company, and she "fell in love with geology." The doctor, of course, thinks she's nutty for talking about her previous job that way, but the film makes it clear that her love of geology and her desire to work in medicine can and must come together as she tracks hexavalent chromium into the water and then into the bodies of the power plant's neighbors. In its final step, the screenplay converts geology to document production when Masry compliments Brockovich on "everything you've dug up."

Not content with a thematic payoff from its subterranean interests, the film turns the link between archeology and DNA into a product placement. Erin's son is going through his "dinosaur phase." He watches *Land before Time* (Bluth, Universal, 1988) and sleeps in dino sheets. But most important, he has a poster for *Jurassic Park* on the door to his room. In three shots. In another, though, that poster has been moved to the wall of his room so that it can be seen even when Erin holds open the door. The product placement for a product that needs no placement (for a product that began as a placement for itself) stands more as a reminder of corporate parentage than an instance of hidden persuasion. The universality of Universal.

What *Brockovich* adds to the Spielberg story is a newly sentimental motherly gaze. Spielberg's dinos are all female, yet they evolve into a parthenogenetic nightmare. *Brockovich*'s mothers are all concerned. When she persuades one that the chemical threat in the water is real, it is the mother's gaze that carries the sense of recognition and mounting fear as she watches her children play in the backyard pool. When Brockovich meets with a family whose daughter is slowly dying of a combination of maladies, a set of increasingly tight shot/reverse-shot pairs will vouch for her commitment to the cause. And when she finally convinces Pamela Duncan to join the suit, it will be because Brockovich has brought her own children along. Distribution is what *befalls* the children who are PG&E's victims, and because the threat is invisible, only a particularly motivated gaze can see it.

In *Traffic*, Catherine Zeta-Jones's Helena carries the investigative/maternal story line. Left alone, outcast, and pregnant when her husband is arrested, she is at a loss. Only after her son's life is threatened does she begin to piece together her husband's languishing network. A "mama bear protecting her cubs" writer Stephen Gaghan calls her.[29] Once she has most of the pieces put back together, and once she has resolved to save herself and her family at the world's expense, she travels to Mexico to confront the head of the cartel. He explains that with her husband in jail, "[p]erhaps it is time for me to deal with other distributors in California." "I don't think you're going to do that," she counters, because that would entail missing out on a revolutionary new modality of distribution, "the project for the children." They will use dolls to deliver the cocaine—

not by secreting the drugs inside but by crafting the doll itself out of odorless, "high impact, pressure molded cocaine." "The doll is cocaine," she explains, but "Spastic Jack" ("Espastico Jacobo") is also an upcoming movie, bruited on the side of a delivery truck an hour earlier in the film.[30]

The late return of Spastic Jack to the narrative confirms that *Traffic* is, as its title declares, a film about distribution *as such*: packaging, shipping, warehousing, marketing, and selling. When *Brockovich* was rolling into theaters, though, *Traffic* was still finding its way. Initially developed at Fox 2000, it went into turn-around in late 1999 when its budget grew. USA Films and 50 Cannon picked it up. In February 2000, Michael Douglas dropped out and Harrison Ford came on board. That switch constituted a "change of elements" in the project that allowed Fox to swoop back in, this time as Fox Searchlight.[31] Fox's return, though, was brief, and by the time the cameras rolled that spring, USA Films was set to distribute in the United States. The studio that Diller had stumbled into now had stumbled into its own allegory.

At the heart of *Traffic* is a problem of blurred boundaries—who controls what where—hence the film's fascination with the mechanics of the San Ysidro border crossing and the El Paso Intelligence Center. There are different ways of dealing with such complexities. Helena's growing maternal ruthlessness is one; it finds its complement in what we might call the paternal glare. Both the gaze and the glare are forms of recognition, but the latter brings silence. As Michael Douglas and Topher Grace wait in a car, Grace explains the demand-side forces that turn black ghettoes into drug zones. Douglas stares him down.

Figure 7.4. The project for the children. *Traffic* (Steven Soderbergh, USAFilms, 2000)

There is, at this moment, no discourse that can meaningfully connect the story of his lost daughter with the overarching narratives both he and Grace deliver so glibly. The glare, then, reestablishes paternal authority at moments of particular threat—when the mismatch between the somatic and the social becomes too great, when an interest in distribution occludes an interest in consumption. In a parallel Mexican scene, Benicio Del Toro suspects that his young partner will attempt to profit by playing one cartel against another. He pulls the car over and demands that his young partner remove his glasses and "show me your eyes": "We're going to keep our mouths shut." It is the same look; only here Del Toro is attempting to somatize their professional relationship. Douglas's drug czar character early on wonders "why there isn't anyone from treatment on this plane," when that is the point: there is no place for "treatment" in the militarized world of drug policy. His character arc requires that he break his fascination with interdiction and replace it with a real desire "to support" his daughter and "to listen." Similarly, the interdiction agents played by Del Toro and Don Cheadle come to terms with the futility of their actions by finding a way to focus on consumption. Del Toro convinces the DEA to pay for lights for a little league baseball stadium, where kids can play and where he can watch with a spectator's eye, not a father's glare. Cheadle walks, uninvited, into Helena's house to pick a fight and plant a surveillance bug. The fight may be an excuse, but his dialogue is groping toward a critique of consumption: "You got nice shit. Drug money buys a lot of nice shit." Ultimately, he wants to domesticate their distribution business: "Is that what you wanted? A nice little bedtime story, Helena? You tell him how you murdered my partner!" At this point, though, she is beyond reach. "What's his problem?" her husband asks. She answers, by not answering, "The carpet, sweetheart."[32]

Are You In or Out? Analog Players in a Digital World

Soderbergh's career after 2000 maintained its general one-for-them/one-for-me alternation. Now, though, his principal address would be at Warners, and the ones-for-them would be the series of *Ocean's* films. Yet even the ones-for-him would often find a place at the studio. As part of Warners' attempt to locate that difficult market niche between the art house and the mainstream, the studio backed Soderbergh and Clooney's Section Eight Productions in 2000 and set up its own "classics" distributor, Warner Independent Pictures, in 2003.[33] In short, the studio's commitment to the indieWood sector was intense, largely because it continued to believe that it could turn the directors and other creative workers behind indie films into teams that could refresh the franchises in its tent pole–heavy production slate. The model had its successes: it was through Section Eight's production of *Insomnia* that Christopher Nolan came to Warners, and from there he would direct *Batman Begins.*

In February 2001, still in the first flush of his double Best Director nomination, Soderbergh sat down with the *New York Times* for an installment in their series "Watching Movies with . . ." He chose *All the President's Men* (Alan Pakula, Warner Bros., 1976) because he thought it "one of the better examples of a movie that managed to have a sociopolitical quotient and still be incredibly entertaining. It's my sense that you can balance those things, and that the audience will sit still for it, even today's audience, if they feel there is some real connection between the political content of the film and their lives." It sounded like the recipe for *Brockovich* and *Traffic.* "I took my cue from *All the President's Men* in finding oblique ways to handle important issues while still making a film that is satisfying on a pure entertainment level." The *Ocean's* films are free of this sort of social conscience—Soderbergh called the first installment "sparkly"—and seem to constitute a rejection of the political entertainments that had proven so successful. Why bother with the heist films?[34]

The answer lies in Soderbergh's particular understanding of explication. "I like scenes like this in movies where things are explained," he says about the scene in *Ocean's 11* in which Clooney details the layers of security they will have to penetrate during the robbery. Yet it is an odd thing to say about a movie that leaves as much unexplained as *Ocean's 11* does, and odder about a scene that leaves the audience utterly in the dark about how the heist will work. But this sort of concentrated misdirection is in keeping with the film's habit of explaining a process in voice-over while flashing forward to its (false) actualization. The *Ocean's* films are what Bordwell would call narrationally overt—they perpetually announce the stories they are about to tell; they perpetually don't tell us the stories we need to know.

In short, the *Ocean's* films, like all good confidence game films, make a fetish of the management of audience expectations. Soderbergh has elevated this into an aesthetic: "I've come to believe that a large part of a movie is about transitions, literally transitions from one scene to another—whether you're able to make transitions that are not only successful creatively but are emotionally successful for the audience in terms of rhythm and release and the suppression of certain information to keep them interested but not irritated."[35] But as we should expect, the management of expectations on the micro-level resonates throughout the genre, the studio, the system. Confidence films breezily advertise their overtness, and in so doing, they provide an alibi for the intense project management exercises they actually are—Soderbergh calls them "mousetraps."[36] For it is as problems of project management that the *Ocean's* films are of a piece with *Brockovich*, *Traffic*, and *Syriana*. All the narratives move along several paths at once. There are a dozen (give or take) main roles that require attention, and the director has "to service everybody's character."[37] Nearly all of these roles are filled with stars who, presumably, come with strings attached. Can they be appeased? Will their roles be sufficient to them? How will they all be paid?

The original *Ocean's 11* (Lewis Milestone, Warner Bros., 1960) was about surplus. Here was a group of guys who had time on their hands—Frank Sinatra, Dean Martin, Sammy Davis Jr., Joey Bishop, Peter Lawford; they worked nights and their days were free. And what they did together on any given day was interesting enough that they lived in a perpetual backstory. The genius of the original film was to take that situation and make it a mode of production: turn the Rat Pack's empty days into a movie. It was a scheme more elegant than the heist they devise in the film.

The heist was bold enough: rob three casinos at once. The vision required even to imagine such a caper is Sinatra-esque. Warner Bros. was interested in acquiring Sinatra's Reprise record label and was willing to back his films in order to get closer to him. It worked, but there were strings attached. When the deal for Reprise was finally made in 1963, Sinatra ended up owning a third of Warner Bros. Records and holding a veto over any change in Warners' ownership; he cashed out for $22.5 million when Steve Ross acquired the company.[38]

The remake of *Ocean's 11* approached the talent problem from the opposite side. If in 1960, the talent was already on the scene and only required an excuse to move into action, by 2000, the trick would be assembling the talent in the first place and managing the location. This fell to producer Jerry Weintraub and, through Section Eight, Soderbergh and Clooney. "The feat of a project like this is casting, getting huge stars . . . to appear and mesh on the same set," according to Weintraub. "Soderbergh and Clooney had everything to do with pulling this off. They contacted the actors and explained the beauty of the project—this is as close as you can get to old Sinatra days. In was important that Clooney made the calls because he got people to take less money and less back end because it was an ensemble piece."[39]

But if the film testifies to the producers' powers of assembly, it suggests something very different about the conglomerate as a whole. *Ocean's 11* premiered in Los Angeles on the evening of December 5, 2001. As soon as it was over, Weintraub and the stars left L.A. for an airbase in Turkey, where they would show the film to members of the US armed forces.[40] In the wake of the 9/11 attacks and the launch of Operation "Enduring Freedom," the sparkly heist film might have seemed out of step with the times—Warner Bros. had already delayed the

Schwarzenegger film *Collateral Damage* (Andrew Davis) from October to February 2002. By turning the stars of *Ocean's 11* into the equivalent of a USO show, the film could testify to the importance of "pure entertainment" in wartime.

Earlier that day, at a hastily scheduled 8:00 a.m. board meeting of AOL TimeWarner, CEO Gerald Levin unexpectedly resigned.[41] Levin appeared on Lou Dobbs's *Moneyline* on CNNfn that evening at 6:00 p.m.. Following a report from Afghanistan detailing shelling in Tora Bora, and an interview with former Secretary of Defense William Cohen, Levin came on to discuss his departure from the troubled conglomerate. After taking credit for the TimeWarner merger and the purchase of TBS ("That's how we got you, Lou"), and after being given credit by Dobbs for having a "steel spine" and for being right even when he was "pretty much alone in [his] judgment," Levin explained that he was "no longer a suit" and that he intended to devote himself to "moral and social issues." "It's an intensely personal decision. I'm taking a risk, because tomorrow nobody will return my calls."[42] He was righter than he knew.

Halfway through *Ocean's 11*, casino owner Terry Benedict (Andy Garcia) is preparing to host a heavyweight title fight at the MGM Grand. Speaking into a phone while practicing his putting, he says, "Well then inform Mr. Levin that he'll be better off watching the fight in front of his television at home. Surely he must have HBO." "The only time this scene got a huge laugh was at the premiere," according to screenwriter Ted Griffin. Soderbergh added, "Now it's even funnier, because now nobody wants to help him." "I do," Griffin mocked. "He calls. I pick up."[43]

Unspooling mere hours after Levin announced his resignation, *Ocean's 11* was able to be the first post-Levin film in part because the film studio had been against the merger from the beginning. Warner Bros.' executives had never been happy with the forced integration with AOL. They had resisted using the system for e-mail, they had balked at demands that the Harry Potter website be migrated to AOL, and they had refused to force the Wachowskis (and their producers) to accept a $70 million deal with Nokia for product placement in the sequels to *The Matrix* because "You don't fuck with vision."[44] The studio wanted synergy on their terms, synergy that would testify to the labor involved in the assembly of the particular package and not to the digital flow within the megacorporate assembly they were now part of. But more to the point, the film was able to be a post-Levin film because its joke was both *projective* and *deniable*. Had Levin pulled off a palace coup as he had before and forced Chairman Steve Case and disgruntled board member Ted Turner to leave, then the line would have pointed up Benedict's egotism. Within *11*, then, the inside joke functions according to the film's own version of narrative overtness: it is the unreliable voice-over to its own future actualization that is being presented simultaneously.

Ultimately, it was not the film studio that led the charge against Steve Case but HBO's Jeff Bewkes. Bewkes had been given the go-ahead by new CEO Dick Parsons, and in a 2002 board meeting he confronted the AOLer: "I'm tired of this. . . . This is bullshit. The only division that's not performing is yours. Every one of us is growing, making the numbers. The only problem in this construct is AOL.'"[45] A year later, Alan Horn, the head of the film studio,

> expressed a desire to lop the AOL clean off the company name. . . . Horn was soon
> enough lecturing the group on how it should be an honor to have your name on
> a corporation, and how he didn't think AOL's name was appropriate. This struck
> many present as absurd, considering the thuggish and excessive reputations of many
> in Hollywood. As AOL's vice chairman Ted Leonsis put it, "I found it ironic to have a
> movie studio executive talking to me about integrity, honesty, and lifestyle."[46]

It may have been ironic, but Horn got his wish. "AOL" came off the company name in October, and when the new headquarters building opened the next month, it was the TimeWarner Center.

At just that moment, Soderbergh and Clooney debuted *K Street*, a short-run television series about political insiders for HBO. (It ran for ten Sundays from September 14 to November 16, 2003.) The series was an experiment that set actors John Slattery and Mary McCormick, playing seasoned DC hands, alongside husband-and-wife partners James Carville and Mary Matalin, playing fictionalized versions of themselves (versions of themselves intent on cashing in as lobbyists). Their fictional firm fictionally represented real clients and held fictional meetings with actual politicians, reporters, lobbyists, and security consultants. It was a technique that had worked wonderfully in a Georgetown cocktail party scene in *Traffic*, but once it was turned into the premise of a weekly series, critics found the Hollywood-on-the-Potomac frisson smug and unsatisfying, and ratings remained low (2–3 million viewers).[47] Still, the conceit of nesting the fiction within the fact often succeeded formally. The snappiest moment in the series came in the first episode when Carville, playing at prepping presidential candidate Howard Dean for an upcoming debate, used a line that Dean subsequently repeated in the actual debate: "Well if the percent of minorities that's in your state had anything to do with how you can connect with African American voters, then Trent Lott would be Martin Luther King." The episode was able to show Carville give the line, Dean deliver it, Carville and Slattery hear him deliver at the debate, and, best of all, Matalin at home to both hear Dean deliver the line and realize that it must have come from Carville.

K Street assumed that if its docudrama were going to be topically charged, it would have to exist in the pressures of the present. To stay as current as possible, episodes were shot and edited in a week. Such a crushing workload would have been unsustainable, so two "flashback" episodes shot and set in July and August were dropped into the story as episodes 4 and 9. That involuted backstory meant that whenever the tide of events might alter the narrative that fall, the fictional would still have to take precedence or be abandoned: the flywheel of every major subplot had been set in motion over the summer. Nevertheless, everyone showed a remarkable ability to adjust to changing circumstances. Midway through the shoot, the unfolding scandal over the leak of CIA agent Valerie Plame's name mushroomed, and Matalin was named as a possible suspect. The (fake) lobbyists worry that the FBI intends to investigate the firm over the (real) leak, but their worry (which might have been real for Matalin and Carville) is repurposed as a narrative misdirection. The real (fake) FBI investigation of the firm will be over its fake client, the Committee for Middle East Progress (CMEP).

Or, rather, its imaginary client. In *K Street* CMEP is the brainchild of the fictional lobbying firm's absentee owner, Richard Bergstrom, played by an Elliott Gould still occupying his producer's role from *Ocean's 11*. "They have jobs to do. I employ them." Bergstrom appears only in the flashback episodes, a hypochondriac agoraphobic with a penchant for mystery mongering and an obsession with *Mildred Pierce*. (That Warner classic would appear as a Todd Haynes HBO miniseries in 2011.) The overarching scheme in the series, in which Bergstrom places a mole named Francisco Dupré (played with superb intensity by Roger Guenveur Smith) into his own firm, is a way of restoring his interest in the game. But it will also be a way of completing the debasement of AOL. Late in episode 10, FBI agents corral Dupré outside a Washington Wizards basketball game.[48] As they deliver their warning—"At this stage of the game, buddy, the ship is going down"—they seem to be both addressing the mole and speaking about the glowing American Online sign behind him. (However hastily the series was put together, it retains Soderbergh's interest in signage and semitransparency. As an accommodation to the guerrilla-style shooting, *K Street*'s establishing shots are almost always low-angle close-ups of window signs. More important, Slattery's plotline turns on half-reflections and a dumb show shot through a streetside window.) At the conclusion of this final episode, in a coda titled "tomorrow," Bergstrom emerges from the flashbacks into the present. He arrives at DC's Reagan National Airport, cleaned up and whistling. His waiting driver holds a sign reading "M. Pierce." The producer, the puppeteer, the studio, has had its revenge.

Figure 7.5. The ship is going down. *K Street* (Soderbergh, HBO, 2003)

Seen one way, *K Street* is Clooney and Soderbergh's attempt to maintain contact with the political fiction of *Traffic* in the wake of *Ocean's 11*. But to the extent that its politics are a simulation of politics, the series opens itself up as an arena for allegorical investigation. It brings together film and television in order to see, anew, what that merger will be like. At the plot's smallest scale, the results look like ordinary (if sped-up) procedural television: the day's events chewed over for story points. (Comparisons to *The West Wing* were common.) At the largest scale the results are old-fashioned—the return of the political veteran and forties melodrama—and decidedly unserious: Bergstrom's lobbying firm is essentially an *Ocean*ic long con. Film and television converge only when Bergstrom's *Mildred Pierce* obsession becomes a model for multimedia success. "That's Eve Arden. She did a really successful television series, *Our Miss Brooks*. She was a star." As the center of gravity within ~~AOL~~ TimeWarner reverted to entertainment, albeit to entertainment now driven as much by HBO and cable as by Warner Bros. and cinema, Section Eight attempted to prove useful to the new order. By that measure, *K Street* failed.

The following spring, Soderbergh and George Nolfi repurposed the latter's script *Honor among Thieves* as an *Ocean's* sequel. Soderbergh was adamant that the serial impulse came from him: "To be clear, nobody was asking for a sequel, the studio wasn't asking for a sequel, none of the actors were asking for a sequel, this is something that I generated, and then you can absolutely be sure that after *12* nobody was asking for another one."[49] *Ocean's 12* is the slightly-too-on-the-nose, slightly-too-twee follow-up. Instead of unexpected allusions to the French New Wave, we have extended homages (beginning with the opening scene's Brazilian pop sound track and its supersaturated, Coultardian look). Mostly, though, its excessiveness appears as a problem of number. In *11*, Clooney has a wonderful bit of dialogue with Pitt. They are at a bar, and Clooney's Ocean gives off the nervousness he is only comfortable showing around Pitt's Ryan. Pitt is facing the other way entirely and doesn't react; he need only wait for Clooney to come to the right conclusion. "Ten oughtta do it don't you think? You think we need one more? You think we need one more. Alright, we'll get one more." Given that we *know* they are assembling eleven, we read Pitt's impassiveness as both a sign of their long acquaintance and as a sign of his familiarity with the film's plot. Eleven it must be. In *12*, though, the idea of a dozen has led to the idea of eggs, which has given us both the object (the Fabergé Coronation Egg: "this is the most appropriate thing for us to steal") and a host of winking allusions. (Rusty can't go back to a favorite café, not because it reminds him of his girlfriend but because "[t]hey did something to the eggs.")[50] In the first film, the gang constructs a duplicate vault in order to record a fake robbery that they will use to convince Benedict that he has really been robbed. In the second film, they will use a fake Julia Roberts (played by the real Julia Roberts) to stage a fake robbery (fake because they will have already committed the real robbery) in order to be captured so that they can convince a competing thief that he has won their contest. Rather than leave the entire process tacit, the film can only flailingly ridicule its flimflammery. Early on, Damon asks Pitt, "Did you ever notice that Tess looks exactly like—" but is cut off before he can say "Julia Roberts." Pitt interrupts defensively: "Look, it's not in my nature to be mysterious, but I can't talk about it and I can't talk about why," and Damon responds, mockingly, "Ooooo!" The capper of this nudging duplication comes when Bruce Willis appears as himself and snipes at audiences who claim to have figured out the twist ending of *The Sixth Sense* (and, by implication, *Ocean's 11* or *12*): "Everybody's so freakin' smart. How come the movie did $675 million worldwide?"

Ocean's 11 made $451 million; *Ocean's 12* made less, $363 million. A further contrast might better explain how the sequel slips, and why. At the conclusion of *11*, Tess realizes that the entire scam has been performed for her benefit and that she belongs with Danny. This realization happens over the course of a long tracking close-up designed to allow Roberts to register her conviction. "It's one of things that films do so well that you don't get to see very often which is show people thinking, showing them come to some realization." For Soderbergh, it amounts to a genre switch: "[T]he film goes back into the thirties and forties, what I consider to be classic, studio romantic movies."[51] The third-act conceit of *12* has the same source, but now it is being used as justification. Where the studio had worried that the "Julia-as-Julia thing" "was going to open up a vortex that would swallow everything and everyone," that it was "too inside," "too self-referential," and that it was "going to antagonize more people than it's going to please," Soderbergh again drew on the classics:

> And the justification that I used to the studio was that in point of fact this is not a new idea, at all, and not destructive, that there's a very famous line/situation in *His Girl Friday* when Cary Grant is telling someone to do a number on this guy that's waiting outside his office and the guy says, well, what does he look like, and Cary Grant says, "He looks like that actor, what's his name, Ralph Bellamy." And of course *it is* Ralph Bellamy. This is a movie that was made in 1940. That's a pretty crazy joke to throw in—it totally works, it's one of the biggest laughs in the movie, and it convinced me that—

At this point, writer George Nolfi jumped in: "We can do a whole third act," joking about the obvious difference in scale between a "pretty crazy joke" and the narrative premise of the action climax.[52] How did the film (the series of films) lose the balance between the tacit and the overt? It did so in two ways, strategically and conceptually. The strategic source of the problem is the attempt to invent a sequel that is countably one more that *Ocean's 11* while it is serially simply the second. In medial terms, films have sequels but television series have episodes, and *12* seems to be an episodic number. At a dozen, it becomes difficult to know who the twelve are—the eleven from *11* plus Tess (Roberts) seem to have been joined by several others from the plan's inception. The conceptual source of the problem is that at no point (in the commentary) do Soderbergh and Nolfi consider the problem with the self-impersonation: Tess has no desire to be Julia Roberts, so there is no way for Roberts to perform into the role without appearing self-loathing—the audience's antagonism begins on-screen.

And the reason that self-loathing is as prominent as it is in the second *Ocean's* film lies in the premise. Where *11* told a story of success marred by (what will be recognized as) romantic misunderstanding, *12* is a "180-degree flip" from that, according to Nolfi. Soderbergh elaborated: "They had to fail throughout the movie, and only in the last couple of minutes do they succeed . . . [T]he movie was really about failure and how do you deal with failure and people's expectations and I don't know, that seemed like a fun sort of spine to hang all this stuff on." Their failure has its complement in the failure-in-success story line of Catherine Zeta-Jones's Isabel, a Europol detective who will not acknowledge the thievery in her blood and who, when she finally understands her failings, regains both her boyfriend (Brad Pitt's Rusty) and her long-lost father (Albert Finney's master thief,

LeMarc). This latter story is the film's emotional heart. It makes *12* "ultimately, about a character that isn't part of the group and isn't part of the first movie."[53] It makes it hard to think of the film as a sequel except in managerial terms.

We can understand the commitment to inverting the narrative premises of the first film (winning/losing, Danny/Rusty, Vegas/Europe) as part of its attempt to grapple with the weight of precedence in a sequel. This inversion extends to its corporate underside. Where the first film brings the gang together in a parody of synergy, "Did you guys get a group rate or something?," the second immediately has them squabbling about the form of the organization:

> Frank: You told me that your wife said that [Benedict] called it "Ocean's 11." Now who decided that? I'm a private contractor.
>
> Livingston: It was a collaboration. That moniker? Is insulting.
>
> Turk: I mean, Danny, it was one job that we all did together. I don't know where this proprietary stance comes from.
>
> Linus: One could make the argument that because it was in fact Danny's idea that maybe—
>
> Basher: We all had our own areas of expertise. Without us, it don't leave your head, mate.
>
> Virgil: It just *hurts*, you know? Because it seemed like we all agreed to call it "The Benedict Job." That's what we called it when we were doing it. If you wanted to call it something else all along, then—
>
> Linus: Wait. When you have a problem who do you go to?
>
> All: Rusty.[54]

Yet it does not matter what sort of "organization" they are; they still have to come up with $190 million to pay off Terry Benedict. Had they invested wisely, they would be able to cover their debts. As Reuben puts it, "What? You think the stock market's some great mystery beyond the realm of human understanding? Didn't you see the signs? I saw the signs."[55] They did not; they remain, as *Ocean's 13* puts it, "analog players in a digital world." What they understand is materiality, and as a sort of material penance, their first target is the "first" stock certificate, one from the Dutch East India Company.

By the time *12* shot, the office of the motion picture within the conglomerate had narrowed. Soderbergh retained his belief in insistent, neoclassical constraint, but that belief no longer extended to the utility of the films for the company as a whole. He could continue to assert, "Good decisions create solutions for other problems." They hire Vincent Cassel as the antagonist; Cassel suggests to Soderbergh that he watch *Sheitan*, a horror film he had starred in; Soderbergh sees that the film is shot with a highly distorting 9mm lens and then decides that lens is the right one for a fight scene staged on a train. But those limitations were now of Soderbergh's own choosing. Now this would be the fundamental question:

> What's the best way to accomplish this, given the general aesthetic that I've established for the movie? Usually for me it's less about what you're allowed to do and more about what you shouldn't do, what kind of shots you're not allowed to do, what kind of equipment you're not allowed to use, giving yourself very specific parameters, being disciplined about "this is how we're doing this."[56]

Here, Soderbergh's thinned-out Dogme 95 principles might still have lent their support to a corporate imaginary. The studio, though, did not ask for the sequel and put almost no constraints on it. "You know, one of the things I like about Warners is they let you muck around with their logo, which I like to do." It may have been because the studio trusted Soderbergh; it may have been because they no longer cared. With its "loops within loops within flashbacks," *Ocean's 12* had spun so far inside itself that it would have been impossible for the studio to know its own mind. "I was trying to send a message here with this logo treatment . . . that it was going to be sort of psychedelic. I don't know that it came across that way, but that was my intent."[57]

Everything Is Disconnected

Syriana and *Traffic* may seem like twin tales of addiction. Yet the best way to understand the differences between the complicated narconarrative in *Traffic* and the complicated petronarrative in *Syriana* is as twin tragedies of distribution. In *Traffic*, demand in the United States is so high that the distribution system becomes robust enough to weather any level of interdiction. The aesthetic is entrepreneurial ("In Mexico, law enforcement is an entrepreneurial activity"), and the commodity is uniquely dependent on marketing (the Spastic Jack doll), yet there is a supreme confidence that nothing can stop the drugs from getting to the people who want them. It's a USA Films film; it's a Diller film. In contrast, *Syriana* works through the problems besetting an overextended oligopolist; the aesthetic is corporate seigneurial, and the commodity is almost unbrandable. Instead of confidence, there is an underlying fear that no matter what forces conspire to keep oil flowing, the system remains vulnerable to disruption and shortsightedness. It's a TimeWarner film.

Syriana ends with the radicalized young Pakistani laborer ramming the side of an enormous US-bound LNG tanker, a tanker that constitutes the first installment in the predatory American oil company's fresh deal with the new emir. The explosive will be the missile the CIA agent lost track of in the opening scenes in Iran, a tidy instance of geopolitical blowback. This literalization of more complex processes enforces, as much as it is evidence for, the film's tagline, "Everything is connected." That assertion in turn suggests that it will be through montage that the film will register its beliefs. And those political and social beliefs remain, even at this comparatively late date in the history of neoclassicism, intimately bound up with Hollywood business.

Within the film's imaginary emirate, there is a good brother, who wants to build a modern, diverse economy even if it means selling oil to the Chinese, and a bad, dissolute brother, who wants to lead a life of Western degeneracy. When the pro-Western prince is made emir, his older brother gathers the tribal elders and generals to launch a coup. His pitch concludes: "When a country has five percent of the world's population but does fifty percent of its military spending, then the persuasive powers of that country are in decline." His gestures sell the argument. He begins with a lecturing index finger as he lays out the statistic, segues to an upturned palm to demonstrate "persuasive powers," and finishes with a perfect move in which he turns his hand palm down, giving just enough momentum to it that he can appear to be wiping the United States off the table. But there is no effort to the movement; it is not the *prince* who is doing this but history. The decline belongs to the United States, and it is a reassuring rhetorical move given that Prince Nazim is trying to persuade his audience to back him on a project of national renewal. He is making it clear that if they do not seize the moment, they will be, as Matt Damon put it earlier, "out here in tents in the desert chopping each others' heads off."

From Nazim's palace outside the capital we cut to a close-up of a woman's hand as she slides a movie ticket and some change across the counter of the box office. The cut is punctuated by the satisfying chunk of the automatic ticket dispenser. Since we are watching hands closely here, we may notice the woman's manicure, but we will surely notice the Band-Aids that wrap the tips of all of Clooney's fingers. (He's had his nails ripped out with pliers.) He gingerly picks up the ticket and change ($4.50; his matinee ticket is only $5.50) and walks off. He is going to see *8 Legged Freaks* (Ellory Elkayem, Warners, 2002), but the theater is simply a place for him and a former agent played by William Hurt to discuss the agency's evolving investigation of his activities. The connection between this scene at a Baltimore multiplex and the one before it in an imaginary emirate is one of scale: the prince has his eye on the big picture; the internecine conflict in the US intelligence community is all byplay.

Yet the jump, as usual in these multiplexed narratives, suggests a more fundamental identity: the powers of persuasion that the United States is losing are cultural as much as they are diplomatic. For *Syriana*, the increasingly manic, increasingly corrupt, and increasingly barbarous methods the United States uses to secure its oil supply are necessary because it has lost faith in its institutions of persuasion, in this case, Hollywood. "Corruption is why we win," Danny Dalton (Tim Blake Nelson) says. He is describing the oil industry, but "corruption" would exist whenever persuasion gives way to the material, whenever specific projects, even Spastic Jack, are converted into indistinguishable commodities, like liquid natural gas. If war is politics by other means, cinema is politics as such.

The film's nefarious oil company, Connex Killen, has merged only to gain access to fresh supplies. Cartels and monopolies have been a staple of Hollywood's industrial imaginary, stretching as far back as Griffith's *A Corner in Wheat* (1909) and reaching a peak in *Gilda*'s fascination with tungsten (Charles Vidor, Columbia, 1946). Still recovering from its disastrous merger with AOL, TimeWarner in 2005 is losing its transactional aesthetic. Where *Ocean's 11* flaunted the filmmakers' ability to successfully manage so ungainly a project, *Ocean's 12* collected its stars only to bring them together in a jail cell. Soderbergh was aware that "we've set up a situation in which two of our lead characters are not involved in the physical plot climax of the movie," "which most people would say is a totally stupid thing to do," Nolfi added.[58] *Syriana* drives the point home: In *Ocean's 12*, stars are simply a resource, and Warner Bros. (and Jerry Weintraub, and Soderbergh) are the emirs who must modernize or find themselves back in the desert.

While the Leibnizian tagline to Gaghan's film—"Everything is connected"—offers an audience the ultimate in paranoid spectatorship, it is also a line that would prove reassuring to a corporation under increasing pressure to justify its multimedia conglomerate status. As Carl Icahn and other TimeWarner shareholders pushed the company to spin off its profitable cable TV operations, or to break up as Vivendi Universal and Viacom were doing, it could only resist that pressure by successfully arguing that the pieces did, in fact, make a system. And it remained the case that the only places that system could be made visible were in stories such as *Syriana*.

Between Gaghan's *Syriana* and his own *Ocean's 13* Soderbergh directed two wildly different films that functioned as radical experiments in directorial restraint. The first was *Bubble*, a micro-budgeted feature shot digitally and with a cast of nonprofessionals for a budget of around $1 million. More important than its technical limitations, though, was its distribution. The film was backed by 2929 Productions, the Mark Cuban–owned company that also owned the Magnolia chain of indie multiplexes and the HDNet cable channel. As a synergistic independent with little capital at stake, Cuban's company was free to release the film in theaters, on DVD, and on television simultaneously. Trade publications quickly dubbed this new strategy "bubble releasing," turning the project into an eponym, a literalist allegory of its own production. (Bubble releases pop all at once.) Soderbergh's next project was his most technologically restrictive, forties-throwback film of all, *The Good German*. Filmed only on backlots and around Los Angeles, recorded only with an overhead boom, released in black and white, and marketed with a *Casablanca*-esque poster, the film made a fetish of its classicism. Soderbergh shot it in the fall of 2005, just as *Bubble* was headed to theaters. If *Bubble*'s murder mystery set in a doll factory was hyperreal and hyperindie at the same time, *The Good German* was studio hyperstyle. It, too, proved to be financially unsuccessful, yet it, too, was allegorically astute. By the time it premiered in late 2006, TimeWarner had weathered the assault led by Icahn and Lazard Frères CEO Bruce Wasserstein, who hoped to break up the conglomerate and buy back $20 billion in stock. In place of an integrated mono-lith, there would be the cable system, the film and TV operations, the group of magazines, and AOL. More than a little, the four resulting companies resemble the four sectors of Berlin (and Germany as a whole) that would emerge from the Potsdam Conference that was *The Good German*'s background.

Although it did not break up, at least not right away, TimeWarner agreed to much of the stock buyback and to $1 billion in administrative cuts. Management "ridiculed" Icahn's plan, then "quietly implement[ed] something similar."[59] It had sold the Warner Music Group, its book publishing arm, and its half of Comedy Central; it would eventually spin off the cable operation (the Rus-sian sector?). Yet what was left no longer had a guiding purpose. In June 2006, Bewkes told the *Wall Street Journal* that synergy was "bullshit," and he meant it. But where other media companies had fragmented, TimeWarner had appar-ently fought off the breakup artists. The studio had argued against "forced co-operation" since the AOL merger, and now the company as a whole had acceded. Yet without a belief in synergy what kept the company together? And what gave movies pride of place in the new arrangement? The new rationale looked more like an anti-rationale: "instead of 'synergies' managers speak of 'adjacencies.'" Organizationally unmotivated, TimeWarner would look to profitability as its lodestar. "This is pure business," said Bewkes.[60]

Diller had, as usual, foreseen the industry's turn away from synergy and had rationalized it best:

> Look, we have hundreds of millions of dollars created in the spaces between our businesses. But we don't have an organizing reason, aside from what you could call natural law. I hate synergy, but a natural relationship is valid. . . . "Synergy" requires discipline. Everything has to be hand-wired. There's no scalability. If the opportu-

nistic gene is the biggest part of you it conflicts with this executional, rationalized, one-company approach. Synergy is too constraining.[61]

Where synergy in its ideal form flowed through a company, drawing every part closer, making each part a potential emblem of the whole, saturating it, adjacency looked "opportunistically" to spaces between and alongside units. What remained of the synergistic company became something like a map of the market. "Its breadth gives management a bird's-eye view of the industry's shifting landscape."[62] In the prior era, the difficulty and "discipline" of "hand-wiring" a company together had been part of synergy's appeal: this was the sort of corporation-as-medium thinking that treated questions of culture and belonging as important. That aspiration had, by mid-decade, fallen by the way-side. "These days, as TimeWarner's various divisions pull in different directions, it's not clear what, if any, corporate solidarity remains."[63]

Ocean's 13 is a film about corporate solidarity in a world (a city, an industry) where that virtue seems as inherently ironic as having "a movie studio executive talking to [Ted Leonsis] about integrity, honesty, and lifestyle." The trick of the heist movie is to turn the irony (the comeuppance) inside out so that the underlying honor among the thieves serves as an alibi for the audience's apparently venal rooting interest in their material success. In the first film, the aim of the heist was ostensibly financial but was actually romantic. The second film compounded that misdirection by turning the actual heist into a mere contest to determine who the world's greatest thief might be and by turning the romance toward the father-daughter reunion. In the final installment, the financial payoff is initially incidental. "It's a reverse big score—" "It doesn't matter if we win—" "As long as the casino loses." The scam is squarely aimed at demonstrating loyalty to producer-figure Reuben Tishkoff and exacting punishment. And that punishment is utterly indirect. The target, malign casino owner Willie Bank, will suffer not because he has lost money ("You don't even know where my soft targets are") but because his new hotel will receive a lousy rating and because the outside directors on his board will give him the boot. The aim of the con is to "make Reuben whole" again, and one would expect the compounding difficulty (the Act II midpoint shift) to add to the problem, to deepen it somehow. Yet when the gang is forced to go to old nemesis Terry Benedict for more money (to pay for the setup), the only deepening effect is to make them care about the "big score" for themselves and to expand the heist to include Bank's diamonds (because Benedict wants Bank "to lose what matters most to him"). Moreover, Reuben is healthy enough to join in the climactic scam; he is emotionally if not financially whole even before they have won a dollar. All that remains is the winning montage, and that felt awkward to Soderbergh. "Do you want to make a movie where people are so excited about cash? Where that's presented as the ultimate in happiness? . . . I guess our feeling was, they're beating Willy Bank."[64] He could hope that the overriding impulse shone through, but the design of the crowd shots in the montage belied that deeper purpose. Garishly colored, pseudo-digital totals float over the heads of joyous winners. The palette recalls both the saturated and striated logo play that opens the film and the credits that end it. This look is the movie's heart, and it is filled with money.

Ocean's 13 imagines a world in which the Icahn/Wasserstein uprising has succeeded and the Warner loyalists are called upon to defend the vision of the integrated company from the usurpers. Bank has betrayed one of the gang— Elliott Gould's Reuben—and must pay for it. At the same time, Bank has fallen prey to the sort of delusions that Icahn accused Parsons of. At his major presentation to investors in February 2006, Icahn cast Parsons's continued faith in the conglomerate as an architectural obsession. "Dick Parsons is not a bad man," Icahn said. "He is in love, really, with the building at Columbus Circle." At the time, Icahn owned the tallest building in Vegas, the Stratosphere, an icon that appears in half a dozen shots in *Ocean's 13*. Bank is similarly tower-obsessed ("Bank fired Gehry, Gwathmey, Meier, and four others just so he could say he designed the hotel himself," Pitt explains in the film), and he gets his comeuppance in the form of a con game they call an "Irwin Allen." Allen, of course, was the producer of disaster movies like *The Towering Inferno* and a pioneer of the sort of cater-casting that *Ocean's 11* turned into a narrative strategy. (In the film,

Figure 7.6.
The color of
money. *Ocean's 13*
(Soderbergh, Warner
Bros., 2007)

Bank's building is three-stranded, not the "two towers" of the TimeWarner Center or *The Lord of the Rings*.) The *Ocean's* gang has brought in the drill that

dug the Chunnel, which they will bore toward Bank's tower until they hit the foundations. There, the drill will turn at the tower's "resonant frequency" and induce an earthquake. The earthquake is the gang's exit strategy from the con, but it is also a handy emblem of the compounding effects synergy was supposed to bring. As a result of Bank's architectural arrogance, the tower has "no unified set of plans," but confronted with the possibility of a devastating earthquake, Bank does draws up a unified evacuation plan. When that plan is put into effect, the hotel's super-high-rollers—what the film calls "whales"—will scatter to the desert.

At the end of *Ocean's 13*, Pitt and Clooney joke with each other. "Next time, try to keep the weight off in between," Pitt says, reminding the audience that Clooney had gained thirty-five pounds for his role in *Syriana*. "You should settle down. Have a couple of kids," Clooney responds, reminding the audience that between *Ocean's 12* and *13* Pitt had adopted two children, fathered a third, and was about to adopt a fourth. Their chatter confirmed the retreat from the studio-shaping aspirations of the series. All that is left is a final con in which a rigged slot machine will pay out. Clooney: "So I guess it's just the Susan B. Anthony. Again." Pitt: "I never get tired of it." Early on, Don Cheadle (Basher) had explained, "You don't run the same gag twice; you do the next gag." But there they are, running the same gag. What makes it enjoyable for Pitt is that the winners are truly deserving. And while the film might try to disguise its cash obsession by casting it as a charitable impulse—Oprah's "Angel Network" makes two crucial appearances—the truth of the matter is that the film and the studio have fallen out of saturation. The belief in an endlessly creative, improvisational, synergistic corporation has drained away, leaving the punctuated cycles of progressive slots.

8. The Anxious Epic and the Qualms of Empire
Conglomerate Overstretch

A new empire in rags

The truth in one free afternoon

"My Rights versus Yours," The New Pornographers

Brows and Furrows, Folds and Wrinkles

Writing about the Romans on film sixty years ago, Roland Barthes saw in their sweaty brows the mythology of "man thinking." Along with the "insistent fringes" of the conspirators' haircuts and the bedhead of their wives, the sweating brows of Joseph L. Mankiewicz's *Julius Caesar* (MGM, 1953) were signs passing themselves off as nature. Barthes found them indefensible. In their place, he proposed that signs either be completely conventional—like Chinese theater, he thought, or "all-in" wrestling—or spontaneous expressions, produced anew each time. Against mythology, then, he proposed an "ethic of signs."

Brando's version of the funeral oration does not sit easily on Barthes's continuum. On the one hand, the rhetoric of Method acting that surrounded his stardom told the audience to expect that the emotions one saw were the ones he felt at the time. On the other hand, the funeral oration in particular is no spontaneous outpouring of grief. The high irony in close-up solicits a doubled performance that the movie audience might doubly read, indeed, would necessarily have to read to make sense of the desires that drive the film's politics. Brando must give some sign that he is playing the crowd. On top of this, and to maintain the balance between the off-screen world of Method acting and the on-screen formal rhetoric, he must authentically manipulate.

Yet that is not what he does. Instead, Brando will let us in on Antony's double game only to show it slipping away from him. The irony will inhere in the words but leech away from the delivery. He will feel the betrayal, even as he crafts the phrases that will make his audience feel with him. In the moment, his emotions will overrun his cynical aim and congeal in an authentic sign—an extra finger wag, the mounting liquid behind the word "honorable." Yet this wavering of control poses no threat to his aim of riling up the crowd; it is as though Antony knows himself better than he can control himself. And the audience will follow him as he loses his way. His strategy calls upon their mimetic desires, conscious or not, not litotes, paralepsis, or anaphora.

283

Figure 8.1. The honorable method. *Julius Caesar* (Joseph Mankiewicz, MGM, 1953)

In place of Barthes's ethic of signs, the best moments of *Julius Caesar* offer us a more complicated frisson of signification. In Barthes's account, signs are strung between the "intentional and irrepressible, artificial and natural, manufactured and discovered."[1] Barthes values texts (and films) that segregate these aspects of the sign, yet he is just as often taken by moments of semiotic convergence. We might divide these mergers into two classes. One occurs in, and defines, the texts Barthes calls "classical" or "readerly." In the American midcentury of *Julius Caesar*, the term of art was "middlebrow," and however diagnostic that might have been about a particular audience (or the sweaty foreheads of the conspirators), it was also a term that implied a kind of narrative closure or repletion. Or, to put it in Brandonian terms, readerly texts control themselves better than they know themselves.

The other class emerges when the conceptual seams become too insistent to ignore, when the obviousness of the balancing act points up the bad faith of the middlebrow, as something like its guilty formal conscience. Against the overwhelming force of spectacle, epics loaded themselves down with starkly divergent interests in politics, religion, ethnicity, or the film industry itself. Producers hoped that these various centers might balance each other in a stew of equal parts edification and titillation. It rarely worked, and what these internal battles left behind was an inescapable sense of the genre's bad faith, one that Barthes, in turn, elevated into a semiotic theory.

"It is a good thing if a spectacle is created to make the world more explicit,"

Barthes wrote. But the "intermediate sign" "reveals a degraded spectacle."[2] What is worse, these naturalized signs were effective. Summing up the era of sword-and-sandalry still vibrant in 1962, Jacques Siclier, writing in *Cahiers du cinéma*, proclaimed it "the age of the peplum" (that one-shouldered toga): "Ancient, biblical, mythological subjects; increasingly numerous characters; land and sea battles; the sacking of conquered cities; banquets and orgies; catastrophes, circuses, colors, scope and what else? The superspectacle attracts crowds."[3] Brando's speech calls forth an individual mimesis, but his rabble rousing has a social corollary: Crowds attract crowds. And once attracted, those crowds are available for politicization. The spectacle is the come-on for the edifying interpellation.

The Brandonian voice of that social aspiration belongs to critics who find the convergence of on-screen epic and off-screen mass irresistible yet who, at the same time, find that convergence "degraded." Robert Burgoyne is more optimistic than most when he sees in the epic both "a long tradition of borrowing from the Roman past in order to crystallize and critique aspects of American national identity" and "a huge multi-faceted metaphor for Hollywood itself."[4] The politics of the epic fall on the good-spectacle side of Barthes's divide, but the Hollywood metaphor is limited by the industry's willingness to be self-critical in public. So while epics are "a mechanism for the display or interrogation of national identities," they are also "a mechanism for the display of cinema itself—its technical capacities and its cultural value."[5] Note that in the second, parallel clause, "interrogation" drops out, and what is left is cinematic capacity but not consciousness, that is, degraded spectacle. Thus, for Burgoyne, *Gladiator* (Ridley Scott, DreamWorks/Universal, 2000) begins with a Universal logo shifted into the black-and-gold palette of the rest of the film followed by an epigraph touting the span of the Roman Empire "stretching from the deserts of Africa to the borders of Northern England." Together, logo and empire "form a striking parallel construction: Hollywood and Rome both encircle the world; one empire ceaselessly flowing into the other"—and it is left to the critic to restore the political realities submerged by that allegory.[6]

Vivian Sobchack's "Surge and Splendor" follows this critical tradition, albeit in more nuanced and rigorous terms. For her, the epic form induces, even realizes, the broader consumer culture to which it belongs. The genre consists of films that bring together History and production history, and the result is something like the constructive interference of two waves:

> The genre *formally repeats* the surge, splendor, and extravagance, the human labor and capital cost entailed by its narrative's *historical content* in both its *production process* and its *modes of representation*. Through these means, the genre *allegorically*

and *carnally* inscribes on the model spectator a sense and meaning of being in time and human events exceeding any individual temporal construction or appropriation—and, most importantly, in a manner and at a magnitude that is *intelligible as excess* to lived-body subjects in a historically specific *consumer* culture.[7]

The link between the crowds on-screen and the crowds in theaters works two ways: phenomenologically and interpretively (allegorically). The management of these "inscriptions" points to the late fifties and early sixties cult of management as surely as *How to Steal a Million* points to the late-sixties emergence of the conglomerate.

Or, to put it another way, when Maximus, in *Gladiator*, barks to the crowd, "Are you not entertained?!," he is, as baldly as possible, installing the film's central theme. As James Russell puts it, "The film is focused on a ruler whose ultimate downfall is his heavy reliance on the distractions of the arena. It follows that *Gladiator* can be read as a defence of popular entertainment, especially epics. Critics of Hollywood have often dismissed epics as 'middlebrow,' thus culturally insignificant, forms of expression. *Gladiator* champions the middlebrow, the popular-yet-meaningful, as a vital medium of political and social expression."[8] Is the epic a vital medium of industrial expression as well? Or does it leave its criticism to critics? That is, if neoclassical Hollywood marked the triumphant incorporation of certain kinds of criticism within the system, does the epic maintain that capacity, or is it being lost? And how does the industrial history of this revivified genre interact with the political and social histories it assimilates in its efforts to entertain us?

The Epic Epoch

Gladiator relaunched the sword-and-sandal epic in Hollywood, and relaunched it as self-conscious allegory. Here is how screenwriter/producer David Franzoni described it: "The movie is about our culture, our society: promoter Proximo (Oliver Reed) is sort of a Mike Ovitz, and Commodus (Joaquin Phoenix) is sort of a Ted Turner. And Maximus (Russell Crowe) is the hero we all wish ourselves to be: the guy who can rise above the mess that is modern society."[9] Spielberg, clearly seeing himself as the guy rising above the mess, gave the film his blessing based on a ten-word exchange. Yet Franzoni's commitment to this vision of Rome-as-Hollywood was too intense for DreamWorks, which dialed back some of the more egregious moments. In one, Proximo suggests signing a deal with the "Golden Pompeii Olive Oil company." (Like DreamWorks, Golden Pompeii is "small, but profitable.") Maximus abjures, but for marketing reasons—"What would the poster say: '[Maximus] would kill for a taste'?"[10]

And though gladiatorial endorsements did exist, this overly insistent scene did not survive in John Logan's draft from that summer.[11] Rising above the mess was important, but striking a balance between the promoter and the emperor was just as necessary.

As the studio went through the process of bringing *Gladiator* to the screen, DreamWorks could look to the two principal sources of the film's story for guidance: Kirk Douglas's *Spartacus* (Stanley Kubrick [Anthony Mann], Bryna/Universal, 1960), the source of much of *Gladiator*'s combatants' ethos and a film that managed its political and industrial allegories in exemplary fashion; and *The Fall of the Roman Empire*, produced by Samuel Bronston at his gargantuan Roman studio lot in Spain and distributed by Paramount (Mann, 1964).[12] *The Fall* was the source of *Gladiator*'s political swirl, but just as important it was a $20 million flop that cost Bronston his studio. As a mini-major intent on achieving the size and status of its major competitors, indeed, as an aspiring studio in the throes of a convoluted pursuit of a lot to call its own, DreamWorks needed to pay close attention to the story of a failed indie. Moreover, *The Fall* came on the heels of *Cleopatra* (Joseph L. Mankiewicz, Fox, 1963), and the combination of the two all but killed off the big-budget ancient epic. If DreamWorks could make the genre profitable again, the studio would be positioned not simply as the industry's allegorical conscience but as its narrative and economic engine.

Why was it "the right time" to begin making epics again? As James Russell makes clear, *Gladiator* followed a host of director-driven historical epics such as *Dances with Wolves, Braveheart,* and *Titanic* in the decade before. Still, as he argues, there were two essential conditions for the return of the ancient epic. One was demographic. The central filmmakers (writers, producers, directors) came of age as audience members during the roadshow era, and with their ascent to positions of power, they were able to make the sorts of films they themselves enjoyed, regardless of industry wariness about the financial risks involved. The second condition was economic. The risks of big-budget films were mitigated by the possibility of further revenues downstream. In particular, the effulgent home-owner-DVD market allowed fans of a particular film to register their affection for it in a way that mimicked the high ticket prices paid for roadshow films; only in this new market, that price was spread across two platforms.[13] That economic rationale meshed with the boomer directors' narrative aims so completely that they could consider the theatrical releases mere warm-ups for the hyperextended multi-DVD versions. "Thank God for DVD," Ridley Scott says somewhere in the commentary track to the four-disc version of *Kingdom of Heaven* (Fox, 2005).

Despite *Gladiator*'s ostensibly precarious genre economics, and despite some rather daunting production problems (culminating in Oliver Reed's death before the end of the shoot), *Gladiator* is utterly self-assured. "Are you not entertained?!" is a taunt, but it is thoroughly rhetorical for all that. The film needs no momentum to build up the reservoir of references that might then be deployed against or for the studios. Franzoni (and Scott, and DreamWorks) can be confident that the audience speaks the language of entertainment. Why should that be the case? In part, certainly, it must be that the previous generation of epics was becoming more available, and those epics survived as backstories as much as anything. *Fall of the Roman Empire* was issued on LaserDisc in 1993 and again in 1997; *Cleopatra* appeared in 1990; and *Spartacus* had been reissued several times, including a Criterion Collection version in 1992 before debuting on DVD in March 1998.[14] That last version included a 1960 interview with Peter Ustinov (Batiatus) explaining how the film is "very different from the usual Roman film."[15] In *Spartacus* Ustinov plays the unctuous agent to the hilt (he won the Oscar for his performance). First he brags of the training Spartacus received at his school—"If it isn't too . . . subversive . . . to say so, I made him what he is today." Then, when pressed for a physical description of the rebel, Batiatus agrees on the condition that when the defeated slaves are auctioned, he will be the middleman. "Could not the agent for that sale be he who shares this tiny moment of history with your honor?" Industrial allegory was the subversion that made the politics of the late epic go.

Spartacus was the most politically ambitious of that wave of imperial epics. Star/producer Kirk Douglas chose most of the major players, including director Anthony Mann and Mann's replacement, Kubrick. Along the way, he helped break the blacklist by securing on-screen credit for writer Dalton Trumbo. In Trumbo's hands, Howard Fast's novel of ancient class warfare became an allegory of resistance to the House Un-American Activities Committee (HUAC). Asked to name Spartacus, the entire surviving army steps forward—"I am Spartacus." They are all subsequently crucified, and their crosses line the Via Appia like telephone poles.

Gladiator was a self-conscious return to *Spartacus*'s political epic making. But where Spartacus drew on his gladiatorial-managerial skills to forge a slave army with remarkable speed, Maximus (Russell Crowe) could draw on his actual battlefield skills to turn the gladiators into a unified force *in* the arena. In *Spartacus*, the "surplus value" of gladiatorial entertainment is institutional—it teaches you to lead men; in *Gladiator*, the surplus value of leadership is thrilling display. When Spartacus fights an impossible opponent, it is the Roman legions near Brundisium; when Maximus does, it is Tigris of Gaul and his attendant tigers, playing the role of the lions that ate the Christians.

Gladiator takes this insistence on theater one step further. What makes Maximus indispensable to the empire is not his leadership but his entertainment value, his cultural capital. "I saw a slave become more powerful than the emperor of Rome." Without HUAC to combat, *Gladiator* turns even further inward for its allegory. Franzoni elaborated: "When I saw Commodus, I thought, *Here we have Ted Turner*, a man who can combine politics and entertainment to create a power base."[16] Initially contrived as a way of containing political unrest and centralizing power, the gladiatorial arena has come to substitute for politics, and the central power it yields up as politics reaches the arena's event horizon is not the awesome majesty of the emperor's thumb but of Russell Crowe's body.

Franzoni and the others did not need to lean on the audience's past as the sole support for their allegorical architecture. For the new sword-and-sandal epic could imagine itself as the summa of the allegorical education of the past quarter century. The epics reconfigure not simply their generic predecessors but the entire industry as something very like a training ground. On the studio-as-school model of *Gladiator*, the practice arena segues into the great arenas of the empire—the Colosseum or the battlefield. This emblem will recur in the Warners epics *Troy* (Wolfgang Petersen, 2004), *Alexander* (Oliver Stone, 2004), and *300* (Zach Snyder, 2007), and in the European entry *Agora* (Alejandro Amenábar, Fox/Lionsgate, 2009), in part because ancient Greece on-screen tends inexorably toward the academic and in part because Warners has been thoroughly bound up with a notion of education. The latter is both a legacy of the educational efforts that the studio undertook around Stone's *JFK* and its tendency to grow tent-pole directors in-house, as it has done with Christopher Nolan and Zack Snyder.[17] The studio-school is an essential topos of neoclassicism, one the epics share with films as different as *Taps*, *X-Men*, and *Police Academy*. In this recursive emblem, a film finds an audience, a studio discovers its conditions, and an industry rebalances the relationship between inside and outside.

Alongside this educational model, we find a second essential analog—the studio-as-outpost—in *King Arthur* (Antoine Fuqua, Touchstone, 2004), *Kingdom of Heaven* (Ridley Scott, Fox, 2005), and the subsequent indie epics *The Last Legion* (Doug Lefler, De Laurentiis/Weinstein, 2007), *Centurion* (Neil Marshal, Pathé/Magnet, 2010), and *The Eagle* (Kevin MacDonald, Focus, 2011). The outpost film turns the narrative directly to questions of strategy and values-in-practice. Its essential question is whether there is any value to the empire's ethos, and the way it answers that question is to strip its heroes of the overwhelming might and inevitability of the imperial. *Gladiator* mounts a similar ethical test in its North African section.

In either case, outpost or school, a small group of trainees or occupiers will be scaled up by orders of magnitude on-screen before being further scaled up when the film is released. Education comes to an end, and when it does, the stakes will be higher and there will be thousands of witnesses either in the form of an audience to be entertained or in the form of troops to be led. The outpost is always under threat from a barbarian horde that must come to be respected and that must come to distinguish between the empire and its virtues. By 2000 these scalar shifts within the narrative are interleaved with the "tradigital" technologies of the time. That is, the changes in magnitude are as much digital as they are actual. Where the sixties epics enlisted thousands of extras, the 2000s versions rely on hordes of digital replicants. Every collector's edition DVD will feature its clichéd extra feature showing the cast of mere hundreds of Irish or Bulgarian or Mexican extras, dragooned onto the sands of Malta or Morocco or Cabo San Lucas to be drilled into a makeshift ancient army in a matter of weeks. Later, in post-production, the hundreds will be cloned into thousands. As a result of this analog/virtual combination, these films are epics of a particular sort of synthetic endurance. Their battles are always metonyms for their staging, and the ground of that metonymy is the ready deployability of both capital and martial bodies.

The concentrated martial body—the corporeal reminder of the effort that has gone into sculpting it—at the heart of *Gladiator* allows it to unite the roadshow epics *Spartacus* and *The Fall of the Roman Empire* with the tradition of much lower-budget, body-building spectaculars (the "peplum" films). This narrative union casts an industrial shadow since each source had a distinct cinematic legacy. The indie producer Bronston had lost his studio when he attempted to make the former sort of film, but Joseph Levine parlayed the downmarket *Hercules* films into a durable mini-major (Embassy Pictures) that would release major hits *The Graduate* and *The Lion in Winter*. *Gladiator* accrues much of its generic dominance from its successful synthesis of these sources and their institutions. Indeed, more than any other film in its renascent genre, *Gladiator* works through metonymy. It is maximized; it contains multitudes.

Thus, when Peter W. Rose says that *The Fall of the Roman Empire* "is the more explicit and ambitious work," he is only partially correct. *Gladiator* may be "reluctant to raise explicit questions about [the] global system," but we might read that reluctance as confidence: there is no reason to question the empire as such because there is no gap between it and the imperial corporation that is its analog.[18] "Hollywood and Rome both encircle the world; one empire seamlessly flowing into the other," as Burgoyne put it. In the late nineties, the immanent allegories of the film are enough to justify it.

Our Genre Is Crisis

As an allegory of its studio's position within the industry, *Gladiator* captures the precession of causality at a moment of standstill: there is promotion; there is agency; there is the man who rises above the mess. This triad is a particularly useful dialectical image since any film, just by making it to the screen, can become the hero of its own narrative. "A Hero Will Rise" in *Gladiator*; "Rule Your Destiny" in *King Arthur*; "Arise a Knight and Baron of Ibelin" in *Kingdom of Heaven*; "Fortune Favors the Bold" in *Alexander*; "Rise and Rise Again," says Russell Crowe in *Robin Hood* (Scott, 2010). All the preparation, of both the audience and the film, culminates in this one, great theatrical burst, the filmmakers' anxious version of Maximus's question: Are you not entertained? More than other genres the epic belongs to a culture of poses.

Such a culture shapes the epic both internally and externally, rendering each instance an emblem of both current politics and the current state of the industry. In order to understand *Gladiator*'s legacy comprehensively, we will have to account for the histories of both aspects. It might seem that the immanent reading of the genre would suffice because awaiting us within that interpretation is the requirement that we attend to contemporary politics. As Sobchack argued, the auto-allegorical, formal configuration of the epic captures the situation of the postwar consumer under capitalism. But the evolution of that configuration occurs along both formal and thematic lines, even if, in the major instances, the film aims to restore the underlying balance between them. As the examples pile up, the work of the individual film becomes more intense as each holds back the deluge of set pieces and spectacles that it conjures.

A sense of this stalled accumulation informs Gilles Deleuze's reading of the ancient epic in its midcentury heyday. For him, the genre brings together all three strands of Nietzsche's historicism. It is monumental, in that it works by analogies; it is antiquarian, in that it obsesses over accurate details; and it is critical, or ethical, in that it sorts the good from the bad, over and over. What is more—and here Deleuze draws closer to Robert Warshow and Stanley Cavell—"the American cinema constantly shoots and reshoots a single fundamental film, which is the birth of a nation-civilisation." Its "ethical judgement must condemn the injustice of 'things,' bring compassion, herald the new civilisation on the march, in short, constantly rediscover America."[19] Burgoyne, in his analysis of *Gladiator*, takes Deleuze as his model only to find that the film is not a celebration of founding (or founding as refinding) but an expression of "a contemporary sense of foreboding and crisis." Stepping out from the model in which epic films stand as critiques of the present, Burgoyne feels that *Gladiator* "seems to foreshadow the crisis of national identity and modern social structures catalyzed by the events of 9/11."[20] Or, to put it slightly differently: despite dwelling in an endless present, the contemporary epic (at least *Gladiator*) looks into an uncertain future.

It would be simple enough to say that in *Gladiator* the nation is founded on foreboding and crisis and thus, dialectically, preserves both the Deleuzean model of the epic and Burgoyne's description of *Gladiator*'s tone. Instead, I want to suggest that this real sense of foreboding—Proximo's vision of "shadows and dust"—is neither simply part of the film's predictive carapace nor some mystical premonition but a claim-staking move. The films that follow *Gladiator* will have to work to reinvent its peculiarly blended temporality. And that work will show in the successors' flat-footedness. *Gladiator* bequeaths a double legacy of conscience and capacity, foreboding about the future and confidence in the present. And that legacy will seem definitive to its followers.

Gladiator seems predictive of 9/11 for two principal reasons. First, because the later entries in the genre will in fact be attempts to grapple with both the attacks and the subsequent wars in Afghanistan and Iraq. Second, because the attacks and the wars effected a remarkable cultural erasure, one that vacated *Gladiator*'s own political context, a context that did not require the sort of prophetic reading that came to dominate the genre.

Earlier, I said that *Gladiator* relaunched the sword-and-sandal film, and that was certainly true from the industry's perspective. Yet five months earlier, Julie Taymor's *Titus* (First Look, 1999) premiered. Despite its tale of a victorious Roman grappling with the political and familial consequences of the empire, *Titus* plays almost no role in histories of the recent epic turn. Doubtless it seems to be already spoken for as an instance of Shakespeare-on-film. It also conforms to a particular mode of independent filmmaking and makes clear how that mode depends on a dramaturgical conception of narrative: *Titus* presumes that the story is familiar and that what will count as a successful production will depend on the staging, not the story. Taymor's film is, like other epics of ancient Rome, a transtemporal clash. But that clash is not something held in the wings. It is not deniable, and it does not require the audience *notice* it in order to come into existence. Everything about *Titus*—the opening scene in which young Lucius plays with toy soldiers, the costumes, the architecture—declares that this past and our present are connected. The illustrated screenplay is clear: "We could be in Brooklyn or Sarajevo." *"All of the buildings in the film are present-day ruins of the ancient Roman empire. Time is blended. In costume as well. It is simultaneously ancient Rome and the second half of the twentieth century."*[21] Where at least some of the excitement of *Gladiator* lies in making this initial connection ("It's *really* about *us*"), the pleasure of *Titus* lies in sizing up the interpretation of that connection. We might make a comparative evaluation: Does Taymor's version of *Titus* accord with our own, or with other versions we know? Or we might make an immanent evaluation: Does Taymor's version revivify the moral problems of the play for us? In either case, the interpretive work of the audio-viewer is compounded: Taymor and her cast and crew have interpreted the text, and we are to come to terms with that interpretation. What is it?

On the one hand, Taymor understood the film as a media critique in much the same way Franzoni did. She wanted to adapt the play

> speaking directly to our times, a time whose audience feeds daily on tabloid sex scandals, teenage gang rape, high school gun sprees and the private details of a celebrity murder trial. And equally a time when racism, ethnic cleansing and genocide have almost ceased to shock by being so commonplace and seemingly inevitable. Our entertainment industry thrives on the graphic details of murders, rapes and villainy, yet it is rare to find a film or play that not only reflects the dark events but turns them inside out, probing and challenging our fundamental beliefs on morality and justice.[22]

In short, *Titus* is not only a Shakespeare film but one about Kosovo. Its Colosseum is not the Roman version—which was "off-limits" to filming—but one in Pula, Croatia. "We shot the opening and closing scenes for the film in the winter of 1998. Two months later, with the war in Kosovo, this would have been impossible. The irony of shooting these scenes in the Balkans lay heavily upon us."[23] Upon them and, one would add, upon the audience as well.

Gladiator wears its Kosovar context much more deniably, yet it lurks in the images of a multinational fighting force and in the threat of inveterate ethnic clashes. Its foreboding comes not in the post-9/11 forms of a bolt-from-the-blue attack or some long-delayed revenge but from a sense of the grinding military work required to hold the empire together. (Hollywood's UN films are more common than one might expect. DreamWorks's first feature had been a Balkans political thriller, *The Peacemaker* [Mimi Leder, 1997]; Scott followed *Gladiator* with *Black Hawk Down* [Revolution/Columbia, 2001]; Universal released Sydney Pollack's *The Interpreter* in 2005.) The combination of foreboding and confidence—conscience and capacity—is the clearest representation of the late Clintonian affect. Only later does the multilateral doctrine that resulted in UN intervention in Kosovo give way to a more cynical diagnosis that the nation and its military aims are based on a fundamental manipulation. Only later will the Clintonites build an industry on synthetic anxiety. "Our brand is crisis," Clinton advisers Stan Greenberg and James Carville declare in Rachel

Boynton's documentary about the 2002 Bolivian presidential election, and with that declaration they are moving into a post–Iraq invasion, pre–*K Street* understanding of American political culture.[24] The country will follow suit.

Hollywood Chases Itself

However manipulative they might have been, the Clintonites were still attempting to export (moderately) participatory democratic politics in 2002. That strategy had come apart by the beginning of 2003 when protests reignited against the Bolivian government and turned into violent clashes; by that October, their candidate had been driven from office via a popular uprising led by Evo Morales. In the meantime, the Bush administration had opted for militarized regime change and occupation in Iraq. The speed of the political transformation would be ratcheted up: two weeks from "shock and awe" to the capture of Baghdad, and less than a month from then to Bush's aircraft carrier landing and "Mission Accomplished" speech. The subsequent years of insurgency and government by crisis inspired dozens of films and television series, from the landmark documentaries *Gunner Palace* and *Taxi to the Dark Side* to the sustained allegories of the third season of *The Wire* and *Battlestar Galactica*. It was also a fertile ground for epic reflection, and each of the major studio epics took on Iraq in a particular way.

In order to understand the political commitments of the neo-epics, it is necessary to ask the sorts of questions I raised in the previous chapter. Do these movies constitute a Cavellian genre or a genre-as-cycle (an epicycle)? What would mark the genre's end? At the heart of those reflections lay the peculiarly convoluted temporality of the Iraq War. On the ground, the standstill persisted, and the grinding work of occupation lay ahead indefinitely. Yet the speed of the initial military success after the long build-up made the situation seem prone to sudden reversals. Overlying both was the odd declaration of an end to something obviously not over.

If, in retrospect, it only makes sense that a group of filmmakers raised on roadshows would be able to capitalize on a new, technologically driven revenue stream, that convergence was not obvious when *Gladiator* was green-lit. A genre and a market niche were born together. The new epic thus seems to be an instance of Cavell's genre-as-medium. It emerges "full-blown, in a particular instance first (or set of them if they are simultaneous), and then works out its internal consequences in further instances."[25] *Gladiator* is the particular instance, and the subsequent films (*Troy, Alexander, King Arthur, Kingdom of Heaven*, and *300* are the ones I will examine) are the potential members. Yet these followers are also market strategies, tests of the exploitability of different combinations of talent and story within the niche opened by *Gladiator*. This latter description of a genre-in-the-making follows Rick Altman's "producer's game." Nestled inside an evolving industry, producers place bets on particular elements (narratives, techniques, stars) on the assumption that this particular mix will duplicate the success (or correct the faults) of a prior movie while at the same time provide sufficient distance between the new film and earlier instances. The great advantage of the producer's game is that it offers a rationale for the mad copycat rush of filmmaking while it still leaves space for innovation and, just possibly, aesthetic achievement. Thus, while it is undeniably true that generic films are, before they are anything else, instances of the art of assembly, they might be more.

Gladiator knew the risks and rewards of its marketplace, the perils and possibilities of its allegories, and it appeared at precisely the moment that would allow it to balance those in such a way that the studio's commitment to the film could only be read as a commitment to its own judgment. A film built on poses and frozen moments incorporates both the stasis of Deleuze's account of the epic and the foreboding that the equilibrium is always threatened, always evolving. *Gladiator* derived its central political figures from *The Fall of the Roman Empire*, but it maintained its equipoise by ignoring the fall altogether. The earlier film had explained that the fall "was not an event, but a process, spread over 300 years. Some nations have not lasted as long as Rome fell." And as *Gladiator* became a process and not an event—that is, as it became a genre—it was burdened with the knowledge that as a genre it was doomed. These neoclassical classical epics took that knowledge and internalized it, made it the condition of their narrative; they became, to use Cavell's term, "absolutely explicit" about their generic status, saturated. *Gladiator* alone ends with a moment of deferral when Djimon Hounsou promises to join Maximus, only "not yet." Only there is the stalled temporality insistent.

What would follow it? While directors and writers might have used their clout to secure financing for long-gestating dream projects or to veer off in a new direction, the major players on *Gladiator* all quickly returned to the genre, largely because such projects were now much easier to fund. Logan worked on other DreamWorks films and a *Star Trek* installment before *The Last Samurai* shot. Fox canceled Scott's Barbary Pirate epic *Tripoli* just before production was to begin, but they willingly backed the Crusades epic *Kingdom of Heaven*. Franzoni was adamant that after *Gladiator* he would choose his own path.

> I don't pay attention to the shit that's going on here [in Hollywood]. Because if you do, you'll start doing what they want you to do, and it's always wrong. It's always wrong. . . . I'm sitting with Ridley watching the final mix [of *Gladiator*] and Ridley

goes, "You know, Franzoni, you've got to do another one, because Jesus Christ, it's hot now. Michael Mann is developing *Gates of Fire* and *Julius Caesar*." I said, "Ridley, we're here because I wasn't chasing somebody else before. Do you think now I'm going to start chasing myself?"[26]

Yet like Scott and Logan, Franzoni chased himself. He would write *King Arthur* and an unproduced script for *Hannibal the Conqueror*.

The genre economics had already shifted. Where *Gladiator* earned 41 percent of its gross domestically and 59 percent abroad ($188 million vs. $270 million), the films that followed succeeded when they did only because international audiences turned modest domestic disappointments into hits. Foreign box office averaged three times the domestic take for *The Last Samurai* ($111 million/$346 million, a 24/76 split); *Troy* ($133 million/$364 million, a 27/73 split); *King Arthur* ($52 million/$152 million, a 25/75 split); *Alexander* ($34 million/$133 million, a 21/79 split); and *Kingdom of Heaven* ($47 million/$164 million, a 22/78 split). The only exception to this pattern was Gibson's independently produced *The Passion of the Christ*, which earned $371 million domestically against $241 million abroad, a 61/39 split. Even the indie epics, which began with *The Last Legion* (Doug Lefler, Weinstein, 2007; $6 million/$19 million, 23/77), maintained this pattern; although they dwell not in epic grandeur but in a downscaled world where production tax credits, UK Lottery funding, and other budget-side elements could make the difference between profit and loss.

Gladiator originated a Cavellian genre, but its followers found themselves working in an Altmanian one. The initially balanced configuration of allegories—allegories of scale and technology, studio and audience, bodies and spectacles—depended on that founding moment of deferral. In what followed, the producer's worry that the genre-as-market-niche was exhausted converged with the critic's interest in whether the genre-as-medium was saturated. The ostensible difference between critics and producers comes down to a material interest in the outcome, one we might schematize this way: Where the critic can lose faith in an idea, a producer can also lose faith that the idea will pay off. A producer might head off a flop by canceling a project (although that is difficult for the reasons Richard Caves lays out) or by scaling it back (although that, too, is difficult when one of the principal attractions of the genre is the scale of its spectacles). But once a project is green-lit, producer and critic converge: The material commitment has largely been made; the loss of faith is now restricted to what transpires *on-screen*. For the moment, the screen becomes the only place left where the producer's faith can be realized or dashed. Grappling with that essentially critical assessment requires an ideological figure for the material. In the wake of *Gladiator*, imperial retreat became the sign of industrial retreat, a sign that couched itself as an omen of future decline but that was shot through by the anxiety that the rout of the genre was already on. In short, the major studio epics that followed *Gladiator* tell the story of the studios' retreat from the genre in the guise of stories of imperial retreat as such. And given their uncertainty about the success of the enterprise, they begin to fret over something supposedly more durable: the imperial legacy.

As the profitability of the genre became murkier, as the "fall" became a process, the process of filmmaking was extended beyond the first exhibition window into the home. The recent wave of epics came to theaters trailing longer versions of themselves, in some cases much longer. These directors' cuts had different motivations. For *King Arthur* it was the material that had been excised to make the movie they had shot as an R into a PG-13; the "unrated" DVD would restore that material, as much as possible. In *Troy*, the restored material added to the characterization of the leads, providing more domestic backdrop to the battle sequences. *Alexander* got reworked twice, once to slim it down and punch up the action ("The Director's Cut"), once to spread it out and shuffle the temporality ("The Final Cut"). *Kingdom of Heaven* was perhaps the most extreme case. Not only was the DVD forty-four minutes longer, but in those forty-four minutes, a whole swath of plot involving Eva Green's Sibylla and her son would be restored, as would dozens of graphic and thematic matches.

Why does this tendency toward bloat matter? At one level, it is of a piece with the unaccountable surplus of American culture. For if there's a movie that captures and skewers the psyche of America's inevitable but accidental empire, it is *Dodgeball* (Rawson Marshall Thurber, Fox, 2004), the *Why Are We in Vietnam* of the W era. A ragtag band of misfits comes together to defend their Average Joe's gym against the weenies across the street at Globo Gym America, Incorporated. Like the Bush administration, the movie does not really care about the reasons for intergym war. Our heroes come across as willing victims of their youthful indoctrination into the dodgeball ideology of "violence, exclusion, and degradation," on the one hand, and cultural surplus, on the other. The coach's mantra consists of the Five D's: "dodge, duck, dip, dive, and dodge"; the tournament is sanctioned by the American Dodgeball Association of America and telecast on "ESPN-8, 'The Ocho.'" All of these jokes are repeated without end as the film becomes a meditation on its own propaganda function, a meditation that culminates in the spectacle of the defeated Globo Gym owner White Goodman (Ben Stiller) attempting to drown his self-hatred in his own bloat. Of course it has a mock-ironic aesthetic corollary. Post-credits, Goodman returns to the screen to inveigh: "Good guy wins; bad guy loses. Big frigging surprise. I love happy endings. That's the problem with the American cinema. Can't handle any complexity. Don't make me think. I just want to be entertained."

Within the industry, these extended cuts on DVD mark a crucial moment when directors (including those with the contractual right to "final cut") would be willing to accede to studio demands that the release print conform to a particular notion of popularity (that it be playable under three hours, that it be PG-13, linear, causally motivated, that it move swiftly through the third act, etc.) because they always knew that another, longer version would be available in the aftermarket. Even as the post-production crew scaled *Kingdom of Heaven* back for theatrical release, Scott told Per Hallberg, the supervising sound editor, "Maybe we'll take this out now, but I'm gonna have that in the DVD version." This made Hallberg "believe, [Ridley's] already got a plan—surprise. He knew that there was a venue for this. And soon as the film was really done and released, work started pretty much immediately."[27] The promise of a more extensive version would entice fans of the film to purchase rather than rent, since the additions and special features made these epics the sorts of products one would have to return to, several times, if one was ever to watch all the material. That owners' market would ideally provide viewers with a version of the filmmakers' own experience. As Dody Dorn, editor on *Kingdom of Heaven*, put it, "The amazing experience that I had in dailies of watching every day, I felt like I was in a rocket ship being pressed back into my seat by the power of these images, and I think that it would be great for the enthusiasts of the film to get a chance to see more of that, because it's just absolutely thrilling material."[28] Being epics, the theatrical narratives of these films are already extensive, but as their on-screen stories are further elaborated and ultimately merge with their production histories, they reach another order of extension altogether. These stories are still "intelligible as excess," as Sobchack put it, but that excess is now nested in a rhythm of surplus and containment. If there was too much of *something* for the theater, it can be properly presented in the home version—whether in the fictional narrative or the production narrative makes little difference. And while filmmakers still evaluate the iterations of the film, the evaluations are less categorical. (Whatever the package says, Scott calls the extended *Kingdom of Heaven* not the "director's cut" or the "best version" but his "favorite version.") In short, the aspiration to an "ideal" or authoritative cut gives way to an aspiration to archive.[29]

While filmmakers are busy reinventing their stories as libraries, the audience is being segmented according to the depth of its involvement with the film's world. The theatrical releases play to an increasing preponderance of non-US theatergoers, while the dwindling US audience for epics might compensate for its relative weakness by increasing its investment in particular films (by being "enthusiasts"). I want to call this system "continuity marketing" because it links the various revenue streams in a way that provides the appearance of causal motivation all along the chain. These films are not "toyetic" superhero movies; their profit comes from the single narrative extended across a variety of platforms. It is this system that is peaking with the epic cycle. DVD revenues plateaued in 2005; no epic with a budget of more than $100 million was green-lit after.[30]

Three of the four films in the 2004–5 wavelet turn on the retreat from empire. *King Arthur* tells the story of the Roman abandonment of Hadrian's Wall; *Alexander* concludes with the disastrous retreat across the Makran desert; and *Kingdom of Heaven* culminates in the surrender of Jerusalem. Only *Troy* maintains a vision of empire, yet even that is deeply qualified: it kills off Menelaus and Agamemnon in Troy itself rather than allow them to return home. At one scale, the generic focus on retreat is a purely immanent form of reflection. The producers are asking: In making this film, have we taken the genre too far? What will its reception be around the globe, and how can that reception be crafted? A level higher, and imperial retreat is a corporate and industrial question: Has this company become too big? How will it be managed? What should be cut loose, and what should be retained? Finally, there is the level of actual geopolitics where the occupation of Iraq was always promised to be temporary. How might it end, and what would be left behind? The films that followed *Gladiator*, then, found themselves beset: However much the filmmakers might regard the American-led invasion of Iraq and the subsequent, disastrous occupation with horror, they were dependent on the rhetoric and some of the tools of empire for the success of their own outsized visions. These auteurs found themselves, really for the first time since the seventies, pitted against a system they needed. Critical and dependent, they were able to hold themselves in that fraught position, to the extent that they did, through a compensatory image of destiny. If Hollywood had based itself on the notion that movies could solve problems well outside the scale of their own enterprise, the later epics abandoned that sort of scalar aspiration. Rather than solve problems, moments of destiny made them vanish, leaving behind only the swirl of overwhelming forces that might look like politics, or economics, or religion. And whatever the directors might have believed about their own capacities became far less important than the story of their inevitable unimportance.

History's Actors

In the wake of *Gladiator*, most other major studios ventured into the genre. DreamWorks and Universal planned to team up again on Baz Luhrmann's *Cleopatra*. Disney distributed the Jerry Bruckheimer–produced *King Arthur*, Fox distributed *Kingdom of Heaven*, and Warner Bros. backed the Greek trilogy of *Troy*, *Alexander*, and *300*. Even the Weinstein Company gave it a shot with *The Last Legion*. Only Paramount and Columbia avoided sword-and-sandal films, although even they had epics of their own. Paramount, of course, had jumped into epic filmmaking earlier, with *Braveheart* and *Titanic*, and would again with *Beowulf*; Columbia had tried with *The Patriot* and developed another version of *Cleopatra*. Whether they made epics or not, after 2000, studios were required to answer the question of how they were going to follow *Gladiator*'s success. The balance had swung away from existential questions (should we or shouldn't we?) toward questions of modality (what kind?). What is striking is that despite the diversity of modes, the epic form was as consistent as it was in the ways it was across studio lines.

The Jerry Bruckheimer/Antoine Fuqua *King Arthur* casts its myth backward to the end of the fifth century in order to reinvent the chivalric romance as an outpost film. Arthur and the knights are Sarmatians forced into service at the Roman empire's northern frontier and then effectively stop-lossed. The Saxons are pouring into Britain, and the Romans are abandoning Hadrian's Wall. "Rome is dead. This place, this land is the last outpost of freedom, of everything you hold dear. These are your people," Guinevere tells Arthur. For Fuqua, the analogy between Rome and the United States was total: "Anyone they defeated was in Rome, I mean, Rome was America. It was the exact same place." But the interest of the film for him lay in a particular twist on the imperial analogy: "The idea of these young boys being . . . folded into the Roman military to fight against an enemy not of their own, reminded me a lot of my own culture, being African American."[31] Undercut by the imperial center, the knights now must choose to fight for the virtues the empire never demonstrated. The film thus transcends (or sidesteps) the problems of Roman imperialism by making them into the problems of *the end* of Roman imperialism. As Fuqua put it, describing the preparations for the film's version of Badon Hill,

> This section of the movie is important because you see Rome leaving the wall. Because this reminds me a lot of what's happening today, you know, with America in Iraq, and America was in Vietnam, and we fight these wars, you know, and we leave the land. And these people have to figure it out for themselves. . . . [W]e go into these places and we just, we leave. I mean, the Romans were there for two hundred years or more, and then they just . . . left. [It's] irresponsible behavior, because you can, because you're the most powerful and you can just leave. . . . What I'm talking about is the parallel and the lessons that we never seem to learn. Anybody in power, any leader, any group of people, who go into another country, and at some point, you gotta leave. What happens to the country?

The historical diagnosis that withdrawal is the height of imperial arrogance allows Fuqua (and the film) to be agnostic about the motives and means that made the empire possible. The best one can hope for is that the empire will show itself in retreat. Our hero rises above the mess by knowingly taking on his role as defender of an unjustifiable, even virtual empire. And in this self-consciousness lies his infinite capacity for surprise at the betrayals to come.

In *King Arthur*, Arthur isolates himself from the Roman hierarchy theologically by hewing to an anachronistic Pelagianism and then carries his belief in free will and universal salvation to its logical end, to the moment it forces his break from the (once-) universal empire. This isolation lies in Clive Owen's voice, a timbre that speaks of his shock that so reasonable a functionary as he might be being led by his better nature despite himself. (As a corollary, Owen's body is less important than those of the other epic heroes; in this he resembles Richard Burton, who compensated for his notional pecs by talking up a storm when he played Alexander the Great in Robert Rossen's 1956 version and Mark Antony in Mankiewicz's *Cleopatra* in 1963.)

The industrial betrayals were as inevitable as the political ones. Late in the process, the R-rated film was repositioned as a PG-13 movie. Fuqua discussed the resulting changes at length, and in the same terms and tones that Arthur uses.

> It was extremely difficult for me and the rest of my team, [editor] Conrad [Buff] and those guys, because they had to rethink everything—they had to rethink the tone, they had to rethink the scenes, restructure the battle scenes. That sort of thing just sends chaos throughout post-production. Because a director has a vision that he came in with, which is why all those people signed on to make the movie, and when it changes they have to now rethink everything, and restructure everything, and sometimes that's done without great passion. . . . It was very difficult for me to sit in a room with him, when I didn't have passion on days because my movie that I shot was being chipped away, as far as I was concerned. The tone of the movie, the ideas of the movie were all changed. And I spent a year and a half of my life, and I spent days out in the freezing cold and out in the mud and rain to create something, and now I'm sitting in a room and I have to be enthusiastic doing something that I don't want to do.[32]

Post-occupation and post-production amount to the same. They are zones of potential chaos where "people have to figure it out for themselves," "rethinking everything" now that the plan has changed. Mired in post-production, the director still has a number of options—hope for the best; commit himself to the new regime; abandon the project; subvert the imposed rating; and so on. Fuqua and his fellow directors fobbed off some of their disappointment on the longer or uncut versions. But for that economy to be convincing, the directorial vision had to be compelling enough to justify the new version. Something had to be lost for it to be found again. While the studio would gladly allow the secondary market to extend and intensify the audience's relationship to the film, such a marketing plan would only intensify the director's quandary: Why do this thing that you don't want to do?

The trick would be to turn the studio's loss of faith in the director's version as the theatrical version into a narrative of redemption. And the story here would not be figured as a contest of agendas (the venal and virtuous, for instance) but as the fulfillment of a destiny deferred. Late in the truncated battle of Badon Hill, in and among the heroic low angles and the Steadicam shots, there is a crane shot. The camera rises above the anonymous mass of combatants toward the wall. It is not a particularly spectacular image—certainly not as showy as the extended homage to *Alexander Nevsky*'s battle on ice—but for Fuqua, this is the angle of fate: "There's something about the angle for me that says Biblical, that is destiny, that is already written." What Fuqua wanted—indeed, what neoclassicism wanted—was a seamless integration of that sense of destiny with the Pelagian condemnation to free will, to people figuring it out for themselves. *King Arthur* thus manages to maintain a tenuous grasp on its politically critical position by joining critique to destiny in the most Deleuzean fashion: this story of the end of the Roman Empire is the story of the founding of modern Britain.

Troy demonstrated its commitment to something like free will by excising the gods from the tale. Screenwriter David Benioff made that choice initially, and director Wolfgang Petersen supported him. "Today, the first thing Homer would say would be 'Get rid of the gods.'" "Do you remember how Laurence Olivier as Zeus descended from the clouds in *Clash of the Titans*? Today's 16-year-old moviegoers would chuckle or yawn. They want to see how Brad Pitt takes his fate into his own hands, and when Orlando Bloom fights and runs away it's because he's a coward, not because the gods tell him to."[33] Yet within that world of self-determination and character testing, there are limits. Robert J. Rabel summarizes the mutual dependency at the heart of *Troy*'s politics: Agamemnon requires the services of Achilles in order to extend his empire first to Thessaly and then to Troy. Achilles needs Agamemnon's military resources to provide him with a theater of operations on a scale so vast and unprecedented that his glory will never be forgotten.[34] The relationship is, of course, an emblem of Petersen's relationship with Warner Bros. (He moved on to *Troy* after Warners "back-burnered" his version of *Batman vs. Superman*;

still, he explained, the battle between Hector and Achilles "closely parallels" the superhero clash he envisioned.)[35] And it is the sort of happy compromise that a neoclassical auteur such as Petersen was routinely willing to make. He had made both *Outbreak* and *The Perfect Storm* for the studio. After the latter, he signed a first-look deal and moved onto the lot.[36] *Troy* would be the first project under that deal.

Such a history makes it harder to claim, as Martin Winkler does, that *Troy* is "primarily" Petersen's film because he "is one of only a few filmmakers in Hollywood who have final cut." Initially, that is hard to credit because the theatrical cut was a half-hour shorter than the Blu-ray version—hardly a final cut. More important, from the beginning, *Troy* belonged to Warners (not Petersen's Radiance Productions) just as Batman and Superman did. To be sure, Warners relied on Petersen for all the reasons that Winkler wants to attribute the film to him, and more—that he was, in fact, classically trained, that he was bankable and stylish, and that he brought with him an enormous reputation in Germany. In the last case, the mesh between Petersen's own background and Germany's historic philhellenism would be an essential part of the marketing strategy for a film budgeted at nearly $200 million. Studio and auteur needed each other as much as empire builder and hero.

At least, that was the balance when the production began. The film would not take sides between Hector and Achilles, or, although this would be more difficult, between Achilles and Agamemnon. Petersen defended the movie's evenhandedness: "For a blockbuster, the characterizations are quite differentiated; there aren't good and evil. Even Agamemnon has, in his view, good reasons for his action. He wants to make Greece a modern state."[37] In the film, Agamemnon puts it this way, ranting: "I created a nation out of fire-worshipers and snake eaters." Yet as the Iraq War unfolded, the equation between studio and empire became unstable. The director might still have the unflagging support of his studio, but if Agamemnon became George W. Bush, then the empire of entertainment would need to be distinguished from the empire in Asia Minor. Moreover, the war altered the film not only tonally but materially. The scenes inside the reconstructed Troy were shot in Malta, which had become the go-to location for filmmakers looking to re-create the ancient Mediterranean. For the beaches, the production was to relocate to Morocco. "Then the whole political situation changed," according to Petersen.

> With the Iraq War we had to cancel that; we couldn't shoot there. The whole com-
> pany had to move then to Mexico instead, around Cabo San Lucas. And that was
> easier said than done, because there are not so many places with a really Mediter-

ranean look and feel to it where you can hire extras who from their skin tone and so forth would also look Mediterranean. Climate is okay, in that case also closer to Los Angeles and that helps with logistics and everything. . . . The problem with Mexico was we had not these enormous gigantic battlefields for a hundred thousand people doing a battle because it doesn't exist in Mexico.[38]

At the same time that the Iraq War was forcing the production to move halfway around the world, it was also forcing the filmmakers to rethink the central conflict. The project was initially developed out of the sense of Homer's eternal verity before becoming charged with contemporary imperial history, a "bonus," according to Petersen. "This direct connection between Bush's power politics and that of Agamemnon in the *Iliad*, this desire to rule the world, to trample everything underfoot, that became evident only during filming. Only gradually did we realize how important Homer still is today."[39]

To the filmmakers, Achilles's willingness to further Agamemnon's ends for his own glory looks like increasingly bad politics, whatever its accuracy. But what the film cannot deny politically, it might accomplish rhetorically. Odysseus, who had attempted to broker Achilles's return to battle ("You were born for this war"), delivers the final voice-over. "If they ever tell my story, let them say I walked with giants. Men rise and fall like the winter wheat, but these names will never die. Let them say I lived in the time of Hector, tamer of horses. Let them say I lived in the time of Achilles." Unmentioned, Agamemnon's name will not live on, and Odysseus's envoi is the first attempt at an erasure. Unmentioned, polytropic Odysseus's name *will* live on, as the teller of stories and the trickster behind the horse (he does not throw Astyanax from the walls). In such oblique ways, the film skirts the political dependence that made Achilles's eternal glory possible by splitting the material and narrative empires.

At every level of the production, from visual effects to production design to editing, people are working it out for themselves in a way that is also already written. The DVD and Blu-ray versions will reveal the artifice behind those elisions by oscillating between the contingent and the determined. That oscillation will itself resolve into the narrative empire now purged of its associations with the "actually existing" empire. Perhaps the most daunting visual-effects challenge of the film lay in scaling up the armies. Petersen's *In the Line of Fire* (Castle Rock/Columbia, 1993) had pioneered crowd cloning, but that was a much simpler task. Even in *Gladiator* only the audience needed to be cloned. But in *Troy*, there were thousands of soldiers to be rendered, and they had to do much more than stand and cheer. The solution was to create a "library of actions" in motion capture, then build an artificial intelligence that could render those actions in seamless sequence, thousands of times. Each of the virtual soldiers would be assigned an "aggression coefficient" that would determine both action and victor. "And then the software basically is able to blend all of those motion capture clips together, and it can do it within a few frames, and therefore your fifty thousand people are always individually different from each other. Because variation is the name of the game when you have fifty thousand people so that you don't end up getting repetition and replication because, unfortunately, that is what the eye immediately seeks out and finds."[40] The soldiers would appear to have free will, but their actions would be controlled overall.

Similarly, the design of the Trojan horse had to hew to pseudo-improvisational canons: it had to appear to be something the Greeks might have built in twelve days out materials they had on hand. Ultimately, the production gave the horse the look of being fashioned out of the wreckage of burned-out Greek ships. And while it only appeared to be built out of the ships, as Supervising Assistant Director Kevin Phipps explained, it actually had to be "dismantlable, to be transported from England [where it was built] to Malta and then be taken apart again and taken from Malta to Mexico," where it would be hauled through the gates. What was essential for the horse during the production became a "bonus" during distribution as it was hauled from one premiere to another. Petersen finishes the story: "So the horse we brought to Berlin for the world premiere of the film, we had to dismantle it, put it back together there, very, very big deal again . . . a great marketing tool. . . . I think we did the same then in Tokyo. . . . It ended up in Troy, in the real Troy in Turkey."[41] The Trojan Horse is the emblem of continuity marketing, the sort of internationally mobile production that mirrored, when it did not exemplify, the internationally mobile war machine Petersen abhorred.

The rendered soldiers and the peripatetic horse both retain the tension between "working it out" and hidden determination, but the union of virtual army and horse pulls that opposition into an image of destiny, a transcendent flow. It is a shot reminiscent of the biblical angle in *King Arthur*, but much closer to the traditional "God's-eye view." Once the Greeks have dropped out of the horse and killed the sleeping Trojan guards, they open the doors of the city. Thousands of their countrymen rush in, beginning on the beaches of Cabo San Lucas before passing through the gates and arriving in Malta. The entire charge appears as a single shot but is the merger of two wire-cam shots. One knows the scene is a moment of transcendence because the local sounds of the slaughter drop out almost entirely, smoothed over by wordless Enyan vocalizing. There is nothing heroic about this action. Indeed, the vague and unsettling sonic intimations of

Figure 8.2. The stars gather before the enormous prop assembled for the Berlin premiere. Director Petersen is the second from the left. Source: REUTERS/Fabrizio Bensch

the killing going on behind the score seem to insist upon the hard, narrative work of transcendence that the Greeks will perform in order to erase their butchery.

The wire-cam shot is the natural bookend to the film's remarkable opening, when Brad Pitt's pumped-up Achilles rushes into single combat against Boagrius, his Thessalian foe. Pitt moves impossibly fast, leaps with thoroughly unexpected grace, and delivers the killing blow in a single sword thrust. All the while, the sound track keeps us as close to Achilles as possible, insisting upon the humanity of the hero. He follows his sudden victory with a version of the Maximus taunt—"Is there no one else?!"—as though war might be converted into a long chain of metonymic one-on-ones. Yet single combat is outmoded by the time we reach the climactic sacking of Troy. The fight between Menelaus and Paris has come to almost nothing. Achilles has killed Hector and humiliated him (although his leaping thrust failed to find its mark). Yet the war goes on. The siege of Troy has become war-as-atrocity: Arrows are replacing swords; the victims are asleep or unprepared; the fight is between thousands; the victory secured through trickery. Deception runs throughout the film's efforts, baring its guilty conscience over its attempt to disavow Bush/Agamemnon's

Figure 8.3. In this split-screen image, the upper portion is taken from a Cablecam shot done in Malta (note the unfinished exterior wall of the city and the miscellaneous production junk piled around the gates). *Troy* (Petersen, Warner Bros., 2004)

Figure 8.4.
Achilles rises in
single combat. *Troy*
(Petersen, Warner
Bros., 2004)

imperial politics. The narrative center moves toward Odysseus when Achilles tells him, "Of all the kings of Greece, I respect you the most." It is an echo of Agamemnon's early line, "Of all the warlords loved by the gods, I hate him the most." The two statements are designed to push us first toward the hero and then toward his crafty, sometime ally. *Troy* is the story of an auteur finding a studio he can call home. Yet once the hero has made his (our) choice, he dies, passing into legend, leaving only the studio. The trouble is that the studio can no longer be the empire it aspired to be without, at the very least, guiltily confessing the costs of its imperial designs.

Oliver Stone's *Alexander* focuses the genre more directly on the destiny and legacy of the empire builder. Of the 2004–5 epics, it seems the closest to those films made to justify earlier imperial overreaching. Where *Arthur* borrowed from *Nevsky*, *Alexander* is far more indebted to *Ivan the Terrible, Part II*, particularly the famous color sequence in which the Oprichniki—Ivan's imperial guards—dance for him as he plots the death of the usurper Staritsky. Stone, though, had no real reason to fear that he might be sent to the Gulag. Instead, he seemed to regard Bush as a competitor. True, he described the president as a dangerous man, but the terms of that description were close to the terms he would use to describe his own work. He explained to *Rolling Stone*, "It's not just Iraq, it's the whole Bush adventure. It's a radical revolution in American thought and ideas—the notion that we are an empire, and that by setting the rules, we set reality. That is, to me, a complete perversion of natural law."[42] Here, Stone was reacting to an infamous article from the *New York Times Magazine* just before the election in which Karl Rove explained to Ron Suskind that "guys like [Suskind]" were "in what we call the reality-based community," people who "believe that solutions emerge from your judicious study of discernible reality." "That's not the way the world really works anymore," he continued. "We're an empire now, and when we act, we create our own reality. And while you're studying that reality—judiciously, as you will—we'll act again, creating other new realities, which you can study too, and that's how things will sort out. We're history's actors."[43] And as much as Stone regarded that arrogance as a "perversion," it was close to his own vision of Alexander. After the election, he seemed to have softened: "The thing about Bush—and we have to give him credit—he's a fighter. He has proved he had more guts than we thought. I mean, he went through a tremendous bashing. To be in his shoes, I would've destroyed myself with doubt. . . . I'm not going to belittle Bush. There might be something there that I didn't see."[44] (This was long before Stone committed to making his biopic *W*.)

Stone could not have known just how seriously the administration took its reality-creating powers when he was shooting *Alexander*, but he did give his hero heartfelt neocon set pieces to deliver. "These people want change; they need change," Alexander asserts. His mission is "to free the people of the world." "Populations will grow; people will mix." When his commanders question him, he is offended, not because of "your lack of respect for my judgment; it's your lack of respect for a civilization far older than ours." To be sure, the ironies are thick: after the first speech, Alexander's boyfriend Hephaistion changes the subject to his dreamy eyes. And during Alexander's second "major policy address" on the subject, Hephaistion is busy dying, flailing away out of focus in the background while Alex is enthusing about Babylon's "deep water port."

It would be impossible to determine just how much of Stone's interest in empire was owed to Bush and how much to the icon of imperial overstretch closest to his heart, TimeWarner—distributors of *Alexander* and before that his documentary on Fidel Castro, and *Any Given Sunday*, *Nixon*, and *JFK*. Given that there are limits to empire—to Alexander's or Gerald Levin's or the Bushes'—Stone understands that the great problem is knowing when to turn back and that the great rhetorical achievement lies in justifying the retreat. For imperial rhetoric is boundless and must be so—"we'll act again, creating new realities." The language is not founded on revenge or restoration, but on world remaking. *Alexander* explores both sides of the question of retreat. When a trusted commander complains that conquering all of Asia "was not your father's mission," Alexander responds, again à la W., "I am not my father." Another easy potshot at the president, but also a redemption since Alexander is resolving to pursue Persian emperor Darius up into the mountains until he is captured or killed—this amounts to finishing the job in Tora Bora. It is Alexander's "cabinet" who think the pursuit is useless now that Darius is out of power.

Why stop now? Why stop ever? One more month, Alexander tells his men in India. They speak of wanting to go home to see their wives and children; Alexander first apologizes for extending their tours—"I should have sent you veterans home sooner"—but then he reminds them of their mistresses and the libertinage of their time away from home. It is an unholy moment when a commander rallies his men by calling on their self-betrayals, the ease with which they might rediscover their inhuman capacity for violence. This is the great scene of the film, what gives it whatever toehold on immortality it may deserve. As more voices join the chorus against the campaign, Alexander wades into his men, seeking out the nascent traitors; he is lost in his need to refute and rebuke them, and they can do nothing but resist more openly. No outright mutiny erupts, but the film begins to look like its battle sequences. (These have a variety beyond those of other epic slaughters in the *Braveheart* line.) Stone here depicts what Anthony Hopkins's Ptolemy calls "the end of all reason." Cut to a tracking shot of corpses, stripped and splayed in Alexander's camp—the bodies of the men who thought they were debating policy with their commander-in-chief.

In the ensuing battle against the Indian army and its elephants, Alexander takes an arrow to the chest and is borne away on a shield to die. The image desaturates, the sky goes white, and the contrast pushes toward its maximum—Stone has shifted to infrared film stock to get this effect, driving home the uniqueness of the moment. Yet Alexander recovers from his seemingly fatal wounds and announces the retreat. The men receive the word as if it came from a god, and in a way it does. Not because he is divine but because there is no justification, save a theological one, for ending this or any other imperial drive. More lands exist to be assimilated, more treasure to be gained, more glory to be won, more people to be liberated from tyranny; yet here it stops. In his haste to return to Babylon, Alexander leads the men through the Makran desert, where untold thousands die. "It was the worst blunder of his life," Hopkins says. The problem with the rhetoric of empire, Stone finally seems to be saying, is not that it is false or ignoble but that it leaves you without an exit strategy. So empires retreat in a mix of denial, betrayal, irony, and gore.

What they leave behind are stories, and, clumsy as it is in all its versions, *Alexander*'s story is being narrated from the Library of Alexandria by Hopkins's Ptolemy. More clearly than the other epics, *Alexander* equates "everlasting glory" with library rights. Where *Troy* tried to avoid sullying its own expansive designs in the mire of America's new empire, *Alexander* was less possessed by the need to distinguish between the country and the conglomerate. No doubt Stone would argue that Alexander got "Phase IV" right—he always had a plan

for the aftermath: to build a city, educate the natives, and enlist the men to his cause. What the film makes clear is that in the contemporary context, with leaders utterly uninterested in those legacies, the job of winning the peace would fall to Warner Bros. *Alexander* and *Syriana* are both, ultimately, about the studio's persuasive powers.

Texture and Definition

By early 2005, studios were halting development on many of their epics, either because they were redundant (Baz Luhrmann's Alexander movie) or thought to be tricky (various Cleopatras) or simply too risky now that the box office had decisively shifted to a 3:1 split (Vin Diesel's Hannibal). Thus it fell to *Kingdom of Heaven* to revitalize the epic. Charles Gant captured the critical consensus leading up to its release: "The problem is that it is coming after *Troy*, which was camp and dull; *King Arthur*, which was boring; and *Alexander the Great*, which was an unmitigated disaster, so the genre is slightly tarnished."[45] Anthony Breznican was clearer: "Forget damsels—when this movie rides into theaters on May 6, it could single-handedly save a genre in distress."[46] *Kingdom of Heaven* did not restrict its interest in self-archiving to its own or its studio's narrative but extended that vision to the genre as a whole. In that expansion of its capacity it aspired to saturate the epic, and nearly managed it. From the beginning, the project was imagined as a niche-filling exercise. "One of the things that Ridley talked about was that if there was an era of epic making, the crusades would have to be covered," said Brendan Gleeson. (Gleeson himself was an integral part of that era, playing Reynald de Chatillon in *Kingdom of Heaven*, Menelaus in *Troy*, and Wiglaf in *Beowulf*.) And given that Scott's *Gladiator* had launched the genre, it was only logical that *Kingdom of Heaven* would contrast with it from beginning to end. *Gladiator* ends in deferral; *Kingdom of Heaven* ends with continuity—Richard the Lionheart is on his way to launch the third Crusade.[47] Maximus dies and is reunited with his family in an agricultural Elysium; Balian returns, alive, to his forge, with his new bride. *Gladiator* is black and gold; *Kingdom of Heaven* is presided over by the cornflower blue and silver of the Army of Jerusalem. "Kind of an Air Force blue," Scott explained.

The historical epic is strung between the demands of accuracy and narrative. The usual solution to that dilemma is to vouch for the intensity of the material detail against the liberties of plot, and the key notion is texture. Scott's costume designer, Janty Yates, said, "Ridley is always exciting to work with because he's such a textures man." She is referring to fabrics, but something else as well, something closer to world making. As Jeremy Irons, one of the film's stars, put it after attending the premiere: "We were constantly cutting, . . . but I was decently surprised by how much texture there still is. It's difficult for all of us to really provide texture. But nowadays people want lots of fighting and a love story, and I think Ridley found a very good balance."[48] Production designer Arthur Max touted the world-creating ambitions of such films in similar terms. "People spend their entire lives studying a very small part of the whole tableau, the tapestry, if you will, of that world, and we're given twenty-four weeks to create it all."[49] Finally, one of Fox's hired-gun historians, Nancy Caciola, felt the film did "a very, very good job of presenting the material texture and look of life in the Middle Ages."[50]

Why, though, does detail matter? Scott and his collaborators recognize that the interest in texture is of a piece with the unfolding economy of the genre and the concept of coverage. If one could "cover" the Crusades, that authority might extend to the film's politics more generally. This hope may seem a merely personal hallmark, but it can be understood much more broadly. In art historian Robert Rosenblum's account, neoclassicism shares with romanticism a foundational historicism. Texture emerges from the universal library. "From the late eighteenth century on, all times, all places, all peoples could be entered into an encyclopedic repository of knowledge and could be reconstructed with a growing precision of detail." The processes of excavation and archiving continued, culminating in the midcentury Hollywood epics.

> Historicism became more and more vulgarized until, in our own century [Rosenblum is writing in the mid-1960s] it reached its inevitable conclusion, the presentation of different historical milieux through animated photographic verisimilitude. The roster of popular historical films today offers the most restricted narrative

themes within the most unrestricted range of environments—the Ice Age, Ancient Troy, Imperial Rome, Renaissance France, Colonial America, the Third Reich— all carefully reconstructed in Technicolor by a learned staff of experts whose historical specialties may range from archeology and decorative arts to coiffures and ballistics.[51]

As the historicism industry has been rationalized and ramified, it has only undercut the initial impetus for neoclassicism. Where the artists of the late eighteenth century turned to the past for "new reformatory and propagandistic purposes," research into these "diverse milieux" has left them "flattened in value." Nietzsche blamed antiquarianism for that "leveling" objectivity; Rosenblum agrees, but adds the "familiar dramatic situation" and the "almost palpably real" setting to the list of culprits. When Monahan declared that "*Kingdom of Heaven* is probably the most accurate historical movie that's ever been made, in many, many ways, despite the liberties we took with Balian," he neatly captured the split between the palpable reality of the setting and the plot's romantic conventions.[52] At the same time, he expressed the hope that the genre might be revitalized through the cultivation of detail, by precisely the process that undercut the mode more generally.

The expertise that the crew brought to bear in the service of the film's political payoff proved to be too much. As a result, the details and the drama disarticulated. Irons was impressed by how much texture the theatrical version retained, but to editor Dorn, the two versions of *Kingdom of Heaven* "feel like two different films. The one film seems like an action-adventure, sword-and-sandal film, and the other film seems to me like a sophisticated historical epic."[53] If *Gladiator* redeemed the genre from its sword-and-sandal muscleman aspects by folding those into the larger political narrative, by *Kingdom of Heaven* those two subgenres were coming apart again. To bring them together, *Kingdom of Heaven* on DVD would be forced to redeem itself, and by redeeming itself, it would salvage the historicist project more generally: God would be in the details, somewhere. Discs 3 and 4 of the DVD set are "The Path to Redemption," and that narrative culminates in "Part VI: Sins and Absolution," including "Paradise Found: Creating the Director's Cut." The emblem of *Kingdom of Heaven* is the image of Dorn reediting the film.

The theatrical version peaks with a sequence that serves as a bridge between the images of destiny in *Arthur, Alexander,* and *Troy* and *300. Arthur*'s Badon Hill commences with a charge through a gate of Hadrian's Wall into the murk on the other side; Alexander is carried off on his shield in infrared; the Greeks take *Troy* by sneaking through the gates. In all three cases, the God's-eye view nudges the viewer toward a belief that this is History playing out on-screen. In *Kingdom of Heaven*, there are no gates to charge. Instead, the forces of Saladin pound their way through the walls of Jerusalem, and the battle takes place in the breach. The only aim is a holding action, a deferral until the Saracens offer terms. Yet the sequence carries the same import: the sounds of slaughter will be ducked under the chanting music; the camera will crane up. As Thompson describes it, "We see the fighters shrink and the horizon expand. It's as if we've taken God's point of view, from which it is a great deal harder—impossible, in fact—to justify the savagery below. 'That clearly speaks for itself, right?' Scott says." Scott was more graphic in his DVD commentary: "What [the shot] symbolizes of course is maggots consuming themselves, a morass of humanity eating itself up."

What Dorn restored to the director's cut, in contrast, was not an image of destiny but an allegory of her own work in the story of Eva Green's Sibylla. It is Sibylla who shuttles between the grand promises and the brutal politics of the Holy Land. While still married to the rapacious Guy du Lusignan, she billows into a romantic idyll with Orlando Bloom's Balian. When her brother, the leprous Baldwin IV, dies after brokering a tenuous peace, she finds herself effectively regent to her young son. As her son is sealing the proclamation that will maintain the peace, hot wax drips on his hand. He feels nothing, and she knows that he is afflicted as her brother was. At that moment she must act. Screenwriter Monahan lamented that in major films, the role of the leading woman is "to be an ear . . . to get the hero to talk about himself. If I can change one thing in film, it will be that."[54] The change is most ironically visible when Sibylla pours poison into her sleeping son's ear. This rather horrific act recalls both the vision of regicide in *Hamlet* and the political manipulation of Staritsky by his mother in *Ivan the Terrible* (earlier the boy-king has dangled his feet as the young Ivan did). And while we know she made her agonizing choice to save the boy from his uncle's fate, his death also leaves her queen of Jerusalem, free to choose Guy as her king. As she hardens her heart, her actions can seem a pure power play. "She's got more backbone than I do," says Reynald. Later, Balian will deliver a rousing speech in defense of a pluralist Jerusalem, and she will be moved toward redemption. Along that path she will trade her remarkable silks and her flowing locks for the coarse cloth and shorn hair of a nurse during the siege. "We are what we do," she asserts, bandaging up the wounded.

Kingdom of Heaven underperformed, but Warners' *300* was the runaway hit of early 2007. It found an almost *Gladiator*-ial balance between domestic and international box office, taking in $210 million in the United States and $245 million abroad. It also came in for a critical drubbing—of the sprayed-on

Figure 8.6. The porches of the ear in *Kingdom of Heaven* (Ridley Scott, Fox, 2004) and *Ivan the Terrible*, Part II (Sergei Eisenstein, Mosfilm, 1958).

abs, the quasi-fascist mythologizing, the casual homophobia (Leonidas calls Athenians "philosophers and boy-lovers"), and the clean line drawn between the white-skinned, body-hairless, heroically-not-quite-nude Spartans and the dusky "hundred nations" under Xerxes who oppose them.

So where is the subtlety? Or, if subtlety is impossible, where is the ambiguity? It might have been in the narration itself, which double-nests. The opening, hardest of hard-boiled accounts of Spartan childhood and Leonidas's victory over the wolf begins as exposition only to be revealed as Dilios's narration to the Spartan council, only to have that story conflate with his exhortation to the troops for the battle of Plataea. By giving the narrative to an obvious propagandist, the film is (apparently) searching for some deniability that it never finds. When Doug Wolk describes graphic novelist Frank Miller's "cheesecake, presented in a way that poses unconvincingly as a critique of cheesecake" or his "politics, posing as disgust with politics," he seems exactly right:[55] *300* is a film of unconvincing poses.

The internal narration simply could not create an escape big enough for the film to fit through, and the design seems only to have compounded the problem. Snyder remained faithful to Miller's representation of Xerxes as an enormous, multiply-pierced androgyne, and critics both popular and academic saw that as part and parcel of the Iran baiting of the late Bush administration. The film opened at the peak of US brinksmanship with Iran, and Iran appealed to UNESCO saying *300* was an insult to the Persian past.[56] Yet Snyder continued to believe that the film had nothing to do with contemporary politics. "That kind of debate is unavoidable right now. . . . People will say 'You made this because we are going to war with Iran.' I'll say, 'We are? Not if I have anything to do with it.'"[57] Even as he and Warners scrambled to put some distance between the film and contemporary politics, they also played to the gung-ho audience by commissioning an introduction to the reissue of the graphic novel from historian Victor Davis Hanson, one of the loudest proponents of the Iraq War and an armchair architect of the 2007 "surge."

What *300* does, and why Snyder calls it the "opera" of the Battle of Thermopylae, is highlight the extremity and incapacity of a culture of poses. When a head is severed, it falls in slow motion. The flesh at the back of the Über-Immortal's neck tears achingly as if it were intentionally holding on; when Artemis's son Astinos is decapitated, the body pauses, yearning to endure as a piece of sculpture. The tension in these shots—as in the adaptation of Miller's *Sin City* (Robert Rodriguez/Miller/Quentin Tarantino, Dimension, 2005)—lies between the relentless motion that the camera requires and the stillness of the original graphic to which it aspires. These images may seem like red vase painting (as Hanson claims), but they seem that way in utter bad faith. The design of the film is as unconvincing an alibi as the filmmakers' attempt to fob off the film's portrayal of the Persian army on Dilios's subjectivity.

But *300* freely acknowledges its debt to the recent cycle. It takes essential stylistic elements from *Gladiator*. The look is grain-flecked and dusty, overwhelmingly black and gold; Sparta is set in Elysian fields of wheat; its heroine is mature by Hollywood standards—she has borne a son; the dialogue routinely conjures with grand words taken from, or at least plausibly taken from, ancient sources. Yet whatever it owed to its predecessors, *300* amped up its generic claim by highlighting its own digital origins. Every piece of the production design that might have been an homage to *Gladiator* was cranked to the point where it looked just sufficiently fake.

The essence of its artifice was dimensional. At its simplest this was a matter of turning blood into ink. Snyder explained to *Wired* that "90 percent of the blood is 2D."[58] When Howard Kissel said that *The Hunger* was "really" about the beauty of blood splattering across a sheet of music, such criticism counted as an insight into the altered relationship of production design and narrative in mainstream Hollywood filmmaking. The surface had become a site of industrial contestation. But to say that *300* is "really" about the dimensionality and patterning of blood and mud would miss the sources of its balance. The trick of the 2-D blood was not that it played on the surface but that it installed the slightest dimensional wobble between the bodies and scenes located in a 3-D space and the explicitly graphic overlay. What was coming to the fore was the digital superfield as such.[59]

Rosenblum believed that historicism "flattened" the differences between epochs and milieux. The solution to that problem of historical evaluation lay in the counter-flatness of formal innovation. He begins his investigation of neoclassicism by aligning it with a general historicism; he ends by turning to drawings by William Blake and Ingres. Their "capacity to create an intensely personal spatial system that juggles traditional techniques with new goals of pictorial flatness appears to prophesy the conditions of twentieth century art."[60] The "goal" is "a continuous, pristine flatness" that will "accommodate the absolute flatness of the white paper."[61] For the late-epic director who discovers that historically saturated filmmaking can no longer salvage the genre, the best hope lies in the insistence upon flatness *within* the image, an insistence on space as *rendered*.

Where *Gladiator*, *Troy*, and *Kingdom of Heaven* blended practical and digital elements in an effort to achieve a certain scale economically, to stage the stage of the spectacle, *300* blended them in order to highlight the artifice of the image. (In this, it was a major-studio version of the indie graphic revolutions in the wake of nonlinear editing systems. Darren Aronofsky's *π* would be a useful touchstone of that history.) The audience's exceptional clarity about where in the dimensional superspace a particular element lies constitutes the visual equivalent of THX sound. As Michel Chion described the George Lucas–developed sonic standard, it possesses a "stable sound, extremely well defined in high frequencies" as well as a bass "clean of all distortion and secondary vibrations, even though very low sounds in the real world have the necessary consequence of causing small objects to vibrate."[62] That is, the images in *300* impress not via "fidelity" but through "definition."

Definition—of abs or spatters—is *300*'s stand-in for generic confidence and the reason it arrived in theaters looking both belated and prophetic. The film knew it was already too late to be the last of the great second wave of imperial films—the installments that have followed it are all indies—yet it had to find a way to augur something beyond itself. For the major studios, *Alexander* killed the genre; *300* aestheticizes that moment, an epicycle on the epic cycle.

The manic energy that collects around the film's narrative and design compensates for its comparatively small budget ($70 million). The hope is almost an indie hope that talent and technique will suffice as evidence of confidence. Yet the film's confidence is always undermined by its intensity: *this* is what it will take to preserve a genre built on a pose. And that is partly why the film deserves attention. Snyder knows, yet refuses, the links to contemporary politics. Miller knows his politics are what Wolk calls "infantile" or at least regrettable, yet he cannot stop himself. Warners clearly knew what it had on its hands yet could muster only the vaguest denials of the film's politics. Like Brando in *Julius Caesar*, they know themselves better than they can control themselves. There are venal reasons for all this bad faith, but venal reasons are usually obvious and lead to dismissal rather than sustained concern. Yet rather than brush any criticism away, the authors of *300* are fascinated by their own helplessness in the face of the consequences of their actions. The film is part of its culture surely because there are discourses that demonize Persia, political submission, bisexuality, and imperial rule in whatever combinations they might take. But *300* sharpens that culture's self-understanding by dwelling at the ambiguous point where consciousness and capacity part ways. It *entertains* the idea of deniability through subjective narration (Dilios) or fidelity to a source (Snyder, Hanson's "red vases") but knows that any accusation leveled against it is, as Snyder says, "unavoidable."

Just before Dilios turns the story of the death of the three hundred into the pep talk for Plataea, the film settles on its "biblical" angle, its image of destiny. Leonidas lies dead in the middle of the frame, pierced by innumerable Persian arrows, surrounded by the bodies of his private guard. However differentiated they may be, one from another, their bodies compose a nearly uniform, ultra-moderne pattern. The image is frozen, and it is clearly taken from the penultimate spread of Miller and Lynn Varney's graphic novel. Yet the angle has shifted from an oblique "crane shot" in the text (and in *King Arthur*) to a direct over-

Figure 8.7. "Here, by Spartan law, we lie." *300* (Zack Snyder, Warner Bros., 2007)

Figure 8.8. The graphic novel's oblique crane shot. Source: *300*™, © 1998, 1999, Frank Miller, Inc.

Figure 8.9.
Neoclassical
frontality. Source:
Jacques-Louis
David, *Leonidas at
Thermopylae*, 1814,
oil on canvas, 395 ×
531 cm. Photo: René-
Gabriel Ojéda. Musée
du Louvre © RMN-
Grand Palais / Art
Resource, NY

head in the film. That shift is slight, but it is enough to recompose the image as the x-ray of Jacques-Louis David's *Leonidas at Thermopylae* (1814). Where David's Leonidas gazes upward anticipating his death, Snyder's averts his eyes (the confrontation with virtue comes via Dilios's voice on the sound track). And where Leonidas's penis was ironically masked by his scabbard in the David, it is decorously flaunted in the Speedo at the dead center of Snyder's frame.[63] Uneasy with tragedy (and the phallus), *300* turns sacrifice into self-authorship almost immediately. Yet in its Davidian image, *300* reckons with the neoclassical legacy more directly than any other film in its genre. The major studios may have been done with ancient epics, but Snyder recognized that the body's only durable pose, that a culture's only lasting balance, comes in death. In exchange for that recognition, he was willing to trade the politically and aesthetically critical stances that Scott, Stone, Fuqua, and Petersen had adopted. To save the genre system, he declared the genre saturated, and he was not wrong.

Conclusion

Why do we need to ask and answer questions about studio authorship? At the most general level—and this would apply not simply to Hollywood studios but to the studios of painters or sculptors, to the studios of Gustave Courbet or Bruce Nauman, to recording studios and dance studios and TV studios—the studio is an intensified space of collective aesthetic endeavor, a workplace where we might fashion not only art but also a society in microcosm, arts and societies that we might export to other spaces to be consumed or bought or emulated or criticized or ignored. These studios have histories, and they might, together, have a shared history to which this volume might contribute.[1] There are strictly individual studios, and there are works that never leave a studio; these we might call "degenerate" cases. Yet even in those cases, our enduring fascination with the artist in his or her studio and with fleeting images of works in progress justifies the question of whether there is more to be learned from the making than the consumption, purchase, or criticism lets on. Our fascination suggests that we wish to see how far an individual might go toward fulfilling the aesthetic and political promises we have made to each other. And when that creation is collective, the group inside the studio and the group outside it are drawn into mutual reflection—not always and everywhere, but under the right conditions. Art that succeeds in taking those conditions of reflection seriously and making them real is formidable. Studio allegories are approaches to utopia.

In the Hollywood case, this general account is qualified in ways that may be more meaningful to us because the constraints of capital and labor, of mass production and the mass audience, force us to see the antinomy of individual and corporation starkly displayed and seamlessly resolved. "Film is the most collaborative of arts," one hears endlessly, but always slightly disingenuously. Does authorship or integrity or authenticity exist in such cases, and should that matter? Why do the hundreds who collect around a particular story devote themselves to it so intently? The major examples I have been discussing find these questions as natural and essential as questions of character motivation and narrative coherence, which is to say they find them natural or artificial by turns. How else do we find our artists and our societies?

Once the rock is turned over, collective aesthetic endeavor is almost everywhere in Hollywood movies: in a criminal band, a movie crew, a TV crew, a submarine crew; in a newsroom, a bachelor penthouse, a garage; on an archeological team or a dodgeball team; in a club of babysitters or first wives. What do they work on or work toward? What motivates them or keeps them in check? How does this come to us—as knowledge, humor, revelation, tragedy?

When studios deny their agency, we might take that as a reasonable qualification: their interests are always somewhere else. Profit today; utopia tomorrow. But it is a denial we—I—ultimately cannot countenance. The wager here is that the people who shape these stories—the people above and below the line, writers and designers and actors and directors, the distributors and marketers, the executives and CEOs—cannot meaningfully deny the emblematic virtue of their own efforts. "This is why I leave my kids," says Erin Brockovich.

At the dawn of the Hollywood New Wave, Stanley Cavell worried over the trappings of reflexivity. "If the presence of the camera is to be made known, it has to be acknowledged in the work it does. This is the seriousness of all the shakings and turnings and zoomings and reinings and unkind cuts to which it has lately been impelled."[2] Many of these tricks were frivolous, but some were serious, and by that he meant that film had discovered that it could no longer avoid (his word) the problems of modernism that had beset painting. These tricks and trappings persist; indeed, we see other examples in Bordwell's anatomy of "intensified continuity," and we hear others in Ben Burtt's soundscapes.[3] For Cavell, such devices open the text to us, compel us to acknowledge the presence of the camera. Yet at the same time Cavell takes issue with the vogue for the open artwork, asking "whether it is nice for aestheticians to speak of the re-creation of art as if that meant that we are to do the artist's work again."[4]

In this light, one of the emblematic virtues of classicism is that its relative closure maintains the artwork as a site of potential recuperation (and, by implication, as a site where that recuperation can be disrupted: it keeps the issue alive). Neoclassicism, by extension, might aspire to that sort of control, but its ordinary role is to investigate the rules for the achievement of that sort of balance. The behind the scenes that Hollywood has thrust before us for more than a century has always been a hybrid location where recuperation and labor coexist, happily or not as the case may be, but inextricably. The intensified production consciousness that has preoccupied the industry and that has reshaped its relationship to its audience threatens the balance between what the industry and its products sometimes call "real life" and "the job." Yet Hollywood takes that risk the way it took the risk of modernist self-consciousness: because the imagined gain seems worth it. What did we have to gain? It took time for Hollywood to figure that out with any precision, and it was a realization that proved evanescent when collective authorship was once again drained of confidence in its means and its aims. What audiences might have gained was a sense of enterprise and the individual in service to each other under conditions that would seem contingent or inherent, depending. The aesthetic terrain of neoclassical Hollywood was, it is true, delimited (but wider than its critics allowed) and practical (at least in its self-avowals). But however we qualify the achievement of the last thirty years of Hollywood filmmaking, it was, as it turned out, as close as American society came to self-justification and renewal.

Notes

Introduction

1. Peter Biskind, *Easy Riders, Raging Bulls* (New York: Simon & Schuster, 1999), 392.

2. The Towne draft is dated August 4, 1977. For a discussion of the original structure, see Elaine Lennon, *The Screenplays of Robert Towne, 1960–2000* (PhD diss., Dublin Institute of Technology, 2009), 317–37.

3. The story of Towne's troubles is available in Biskind, *Easy Riders*, and in a more lurid version in Tom King, *The Operator* (New York: Random House, 2000), 332–36.

4. Hugh Hudson, *Greystoke* DVD commentary.

5. Peter Wollen, *Singin' in the Rain* (London: BFI, 1992), 51.

6. This extended reading is Charles Dove's. Along with Kathy Kerr, he was part of the first generation of Christensen students to begin to explore the possibilities of corporate allegory in Hollywood cinema.

7. Paul Grainge, *Brand Hollywood: $elling Entertainment in a Global Media Age* (New York: Routledge, 2008), 16.

8. Thomas Elsaesser, *The Persistence of Hollywood* (New York: Routledge, 2012), 338.

9. Ibid., 337. Elsaesser is discussing Jerome Christensen's work and mine in this passage, including, most graciously, an unpublished version of the subsequent chapter. It is rare to find someone generous enough to tackle such work in draft form, much less someone willing to publish about it.

10. Vivian Sobchack, "'Surge and Splendor': A Phenomenology of the Hollywood Historical Epic," *Representations* 29 (1990): 24–49, quote on 29.

11. John Thornton Caldwell, *Production Culture: Industrial Reflexivity and Critical Practice in Film and Television* (Durham, NC: Duke University Press, 2008), 21, 20.

12. Jerome Christensen, *America's Corporate Art: The Studio Authorship of Hollywood Motion Pictures* (Stanford, CA: Stanford University Press, 2012).

13. Ibid., 15.

14. Stringer, interviewed for "The Monster That Ate Hollywood," *Frontline*, June 2001, http://www.pbs.org/wgbh/pages/frontline/shows/Hollywood/interviews/stringer.html.

15. Christensen, *America's Corporate Art*, 14.

16. Rick Altman, "Deep-Focus Sound: *Citizen Kane* and the Radio Aesthetic," in *Perspectives on* Citizen Kane, ed. R. Gottesman (Berkeley: University of California Press, 1996), 94–121, quote on 107.

17. Christensen, *America's Corporate Art*, 20, 21.

18. Aljean Harmetz, "Who Makes Disney Run?," *New York Times Magazine*, Feb. 7, 1988, 28–30, 49, 51; Robert La Franco, "The DreamWorks Machine," *Wired* 13:6 (June 2005), http://www.wired.com/wired/archive/13.06/dreamworks.html. The quotation from *Wired* is "With a legendary thirst for power, Katzenberg has developed DreamWorks into a high tech version of the old studio system, a centralized organization in which talent is kept under contract and often shuttled from project to project."

19. For an exception, see Christensen, "Saving Warner Bros.: *Bonnie & Clyde*, the Movements, and the Merger," in *America's Corporate Art*, 245–79.

20. Justin Wyatt, *High Concept* (Austin: University of Texas Press, 1994).

Chapter 1

1. Amiel quotes from the DVD commentary.

2. Amiel says nothing about this little pep talk or the vague financials of the opening scene.

3. The DVD may have made it profitable, but 2003 was a bad year for Paramount. See Dave McNary, "Par Swings for the Fences," *Variety*, March 15, 2004, 1, 58.

4. I owe this insight, and much else, to Tom Conley, one of the great logo readers. See his *Cartographic Cinema* (Minneapolis: University of Minnesota Press, 2007).

5. Author interview, August 11, 2004.

6. See Grainge, *Brand Hollywood*.

7. Marc Vernet, "The Filmic Transaction: On the Openings of Film Noirs," *Velvet Light Trap: A Critical Journal of Film and Television* 20 (Summer 1983): 2–9.

8. For an account of the Animaniacs and their relationship to the contemporary global labor economy of zaniness, see Sianne Ngai, *Our Aesthetic Categories* (Cambridge, MA: Harvard University Press, 2012).

9. Interview, "*Indiana Jones*: Making the Trilogy," *The Adventures of Indiana Jones* DVD set.

10. It also cuts Lucas out of the loop: director and studio, not director/producer/ studio. The tense relationship between Spielberg and Lucas is the great submerged theme of the *Indiana Jones* films. See Tom Shone, "Lucas vs. Spielberg: The Worst Best Friends in Hollywood," *Slate*, June 14, 2005, http://www.slate.com/articles/news_and_ politics/summer_movies/2005/06/lucas_vs_spielberg.html.

11. *X2* DVD commentary.

12. Max Horkheimer and Theodor Adorno, *The Dialectic of Enlightenment*, trans. Edmund Jephcott (Stanford, CA: Stanford University Press, 2002), 96, 97.

13. Ibid., 98, 99, 133.

14. Ibid., 99.

15. Ibid., 97.

16. David Bordwell, Janet Staiger, and Kristin Thompson, *The Classical Hollywood Cinema: Film Style and Mode of Production to 1960* (New York: Columbia, 1985), 4.

17. Ibid., xiii. The full sentence: "A mode of film practice is not reducible to an *oeuvre* (the films of Frank Capra), a genre (the Western), or an economic category (RKO films). It is an altogether different category, cutting across careers, genres, and studios. It is, most simply, a context." It is worth noting that despite the antitheoretical stance associated with Bordwell in particular, the next sentence amounts to an ex-

cessively debatable claim: "And we cannot arrive at this context simply by adding up all the histories of directors, genres, studios, producers, etc.; this would be, as George Kubler suggests, like trying to determine a country's network of railroads by studying the itinerary of every traveler." Actually, what Kubler says is that it would be like trying to study the railroads "in terms of the experiences of a *single traveler* on *several* of them. To describe the railroads accurately we are obliged to disregard persons and states, for the railroads are the elements of continuity, and not the travelers or the functionaries thereon" (*Shape of Time* [New Haven, CT: Yale University Press, 2008], 6, emphasis added). If we had the itinerary of every traveler and functionary (and parcel) on every railroad, what would we have if not the network? *Practically* it may seem impossible (or may have seemed so when Kubler published *Shape of Time* in 1962); *theoretically* we have something asymptotically close to the network that Bordwell envisions. Or to be more pointed still: What is the "neutral sample" but an attempt to operationalize the "every traveler" problem in a practical way? A style is a railroad only metaphorically. It can reify until it reaches a point where it might seem railroadlike, but surely the more important question for travelers and functionaries is the degree of reification of the system and style.

18. The consultant is Clotaire Rapaille, profiled in Jack Hitt, "Does the Smell of Coffee Brewing Remind You of Your Mother?," *New York Times*, May 7, 2000, SM71.

19. Tom Schatz, *The Genius of the System: Hollywood Filmmaking in the Studio Era* (New York: Pantheon, 1998), 12.

20. Douglas Gomery, "Hollywood as Industry," in *American Cinema and Hollywood: Critical Approaches*, ed. John Hill and Pamela Church Gibson (Oxford: Oxford University Press, 2000), 19–28, quotes on 24, 20.

21. For "youthquake," see Kristin Thompson, *Storytelling in the New Hollywood* (Cambridge, MA: Harvard University Press, 1999), 2, 365; for the walk back of the critique of high concept and for intensified continuity, see David Bordwell, *The Way Hollywood Tells It* (Berkeley: University of California Press, 2006).

22. Thompson, *Storytelling*, 10.

23. Steven Bach, *Final Cut: Art, Money, and Ego in the Making of* Heaven's Gate*, the Film that Sank United Artists* (New York: Newmarket, 1999), 49.

24. This is a recurring problem. In Bordwell, Staiger, and Thompson's *Classical Hollywood Cinema*, the unbiased sample of one hundred films is not corrected for studio representation (or for popularity, or breadth of distribution, etc.). For the period from 1929 to 1939, thirteen of thirty films are from Warner Bros. (43%). In this case, at least, the imbalance is noted. "The high . . . resulted from the fact that the studio's output for these years is completely preserved at three archives. . . . (It may also be relevant that between 1930 and 1937, Warner Bros. typically released more features than did any other studio)" (389). Depending on the degree of studio integrity in the crucial professions (writing, cinematography, editing), such an imbalance could certainly throw off our characterization of the period. The Warner Bros. reputation, from Schatz's general account, to Bergman's history of Depression genres, to Roddick's work on the interplay of genre and prestige, is remarkably consistent. Indeed, the discourse of the ordinary film seems to take much of its ideology (if not its formal apparatus) from the high-water mark of Depression-era Warners. The extended sample may correct much of this bias

in the thirties. Still, the principle—that studios qua studios do not deserve particular attention or accounting—holds across virtually all scales of analysis.

25. Richard Maltby, *The Hollywood Cinema*, 2nd ed. (New York: Wiley-Blackwell, 2003), 15, 16.

26. Ibid., xiii–xiv.

27. Again, see Caldwell, *Production Culture*.

28. Other critics have considered the period "neoclassical" on different grounds. For an early use, see Peter Krämer's discussion of Michael Pye and Linda Myles's *Movie Brats* (New York: Holt, Rinehart and Winston, 1979), where he summarized their argument thus: "[F]ollowing three decades of aesthetic and economic crisis and flux, the late 1970s saw a return to the stability, popularity, and high standards of the studio era. In this neo-classical Hollywood, auteurs had taken over the executive role of the moguls" ("Post-classical Hollywood," in Hill and Church Gibson, *American Cinema and Hollywood*, 62–83, quote on 78). Warren Buckland puts the birth of neoclassicism at the same point, but, again, for other reasons: "The year 1975 witnessed the phasing out of the New Hollywood in favor of the blockbuster era, a politically conservative, neoclassical style of filmmaking" (*Directed by Stephen Spielberg: The Poetics of the Contemporary Blockbuster* [New York: Continuum, 2006], 11).

29. Jean-Claude Lebensztejn, "Framing Classical Space," *Art Journal* (Spring 1988): 37–41, 37–38.

30. The proscenium, curtain, lighting shifts, and other elements of legitimate stagecraft are present, of course; I am only making a relative claim. For more on the lengths to which classical-era exhibitors went to experientialize moviegoing as a stage set (and thereby avoid the trompe l'oeil effect), see Maggie Valentine, *The Show Starts on the Sidewalk: An Architectural History of the Movie Theatre* (New Haven, CT: Yale University Press, 1994).

31. Maltby, *Hollywood Cinema*, 63.

32. Ruth Vasey, *The World According to Hollywood, 1918–1939* (Madison: University of Wisconsin Press, 1997), 107.

33. Maltby, *Hollywood Cinema*, 61.

34. Ibid., 65.

35. The notion here is that Stanley Cavell's *Pursuits of Happiness: The Hollywood Comedy of Remarriage* (Cambridge, MA: Harvard University Press, 1981) is not merely a collection of readings of films but a chronicle of a decisive episode in the history of the subject.

36. Michael Rogin, *Blackface, White Noise: Jewish Immigrants in the Hollywood Melting Pot* (Berkeley: University of California Press, 1998), 73–121.

37. Victor Navasky, *Naming Names* (New York: Hill & Wang), 2003.

38. Robert Sklar, "Empire to the West: *Red River*," in *Howard Hawks: American Artist*, ed. Jim Hillier and Peter Wollen (London: BFI, 1996), 152–61.

39. Maltby, *Hollywood Cinema*, 65.

40. Peter Krämer, *The New Hollywood: From* Bonnie and Clyde *to* Star Wars (London: Wallflower, 2003).

41. Maltby, *Hollywood Cinema*, 220.

42. Maltby credits Vasey with the introduction of the notion of deniability, and (in e-mail) she could not confirm that it was a conscious allusion; indeed, the term seemed

only a stopgap to her: "I suppose it was an oblique reference since the phrase was already in circulation, but if I had been able to come up with something that was more neatly descriptive of that kind of public self-absolution I would have used it." Furthermore, she suggested that Lea Jacobs was the originator of the notion (or at least the first to publish). Jacobs does not use the bureaucratese "deniability," though. For her, "denial" retains more of its psychoanalytic valence: "[T]he film sets up an interpretation in one scene that it denies in a later one. In negotiations with producers, the Production Code Administration insisted upon revisions which effectively insured this kind of open-ended treatment of potentially offensive sexual material" (Lea Jacobs, *The Wages of Sin: Censorship and the Fallen Woman Film* [Berkeley: University California Press, 1997], 112). In any case, Jacobs's more usual term is "ambiguity": "Even if such an interpretation makes sense in the context of the plot, a contrary reading always remains possible. This use of ambiguity, in which the spectator is not forced to make an inference about the omitted action, is typical of the later phase of censorship" (118). I will retain the more historically apposite term.

43. Noël Carroll, "The Future of Allusion: Hollywood in the Seventies (and Beyond)," in *Interpreting the Moving Image*, by Noël Carroll (Cambridge: Cambridge University Press, 1998), 244–45. The first quotation, from 244–45, is cited in part in Krämer, "Postclassical Hollywood," 79; the second appears on 258.

44. Lebensztejn, "Framing Classical Space," 40.

45. Susan Christopherson and Michael Storper, "The Effects of Flexible Specialization on Industrial Politics and the Labor Market: The Motion Picture Industry," *Industrial and Labor Relations Review* 42:3 (Apr. 1989): 331–47, quote on 340.

46. Ibid., 345. Christopherson and Storper's thesis has not been uncontroversial. Chief among the critics were Asu Aksoy and Kevin Robins, who felt the flexible specialization thesis was fatally blind to the power dynamics of image markets around the globe and the persistence of the dominant players in the Hollywood system ("Hollywood for the 21st Century: Global Competition for Critical Mass in Image Markets," *Cambridge Journal of Economics* 16:1 [1992]: 1–22). Storper's response was similarly pointed. "Aksoy and Robins' argument completely misses this central dynamic. The big studios, in spite of their enormous market power, are compelled to live with this situation (at least until a new kind of production process is invented permitting greater differentiation with re-integration of production). All the majors lament their impotence faced with such rising costs, and much of the benefit from these rising costs is going precisely to the independent producers who make films under contract to the majors" ("Flexible Specialization in Hollywood: A Response to Aksoy and Robins," *Cambridge Journal of Economics* 17:4 [1993]: 479–84, quote on 481). Whether one sees oligopolistic endurance as a mark of power (Aksoy and Robins) or powerlessness (Storper) matters less to me than the effects of that situation on the players involved.

47. Gomery, "Hollywood as Industry," 19.

48. Jerome Christensen, "Post-Warners Warners: *Batman* and *JFK; You've Got Mail*," in *America's Corporate Art*, 280–313.

Chapter 2

1. "Curbs on CIA Actions Urged," *Los Angeles Times* (hereafter *LAT*), June 5, 1973, A8.

2. Carl Gottlieb, *The* Jaws *Log* (New York: Newmarket, 2001), 61–62.

3. David Anthony Daly, *A Comparison of Exhibition and Distribution Patterns in Three Recent Feature Motion Pictures* (New York: Arno, 1980), 109–10.

4. Ibid., 126.

5. Ibid., 137–38.

6. John Getze, "*Jaws* Swims to Top in Ocean of Publicity: Huge Film Promotion Began before Book was Published," *LAT*, Sept. 28, 1975, G1–2, quote on G1; Daly, *Comparison*, 130.

7. Daly, *Comparison*, 137.

8. Fredric Jameson, "Reification and Utopia in Mass Culture," *Social Text* 1 (1979): 130–48, quote on 142.

9. Ted Morgan, "Sharks: . . . and Then, and Then, and Then . . . : The Making of a Best Seller," *New York Times Magazine*, Apr. 21, 1974, 10–11, 85–91, 95–96.

10. Getze, "*Jaws* Swims to Top."

11. Gottlieb, *The* Jaws *Log*, 186.

12. Ibid., 90.

13. Ibid., 89, 204–5, 204.

14. Getze, "*Jaws* Swims to Top," G1.

15. Vincent Canby, "Entrapped by *Jaws* of Fear," *New York Times* (hereafter *NYT*), June 21, 1975, 19.

16. Gottlieb, *The* Jaws *Log*, 52.

17. Ibid., 142.

18. Thompson, *Storytelling*, 35.

19. Ibid.

20. Daly, *Comparison*, 109.

21. Morgan, "Sharks," 90, 88.

22. DVD making-of featurette.

23. Antonia Quirke's marvelous entry in the BFI Modern Classics series pulls together many of the same formal and thematic elements that I do here. What I am calling the management of control, she sees as an "aggressive purposelessness." Quirke, *Jaws* (London: BFI, 2002), 69.

Chapter 3

1. For a summary, see Wyatt, *High Concept*. The quotation from Spielberg is on 13. The original is from J. Hoberman, "1975–1985: Ten Years That Shook the World," *American Film* (June 1985): 36.

2. Charles Sanders Peirce, "How to Make Our Ideas Clear," in *The Essential Peirce*, ed. Nathan Houser and Christian Kloesel (Bloomington: Indiana University Press, 1992), 1:124–41, quote on 132.

3. Wyatt, *High Concept*, 15, 65.

4. Thompson, *Storytelling*, 3; Bordwell, *The Way Hollywood Tells It*, 26, 188–89.

5. Wyatt, *High Concept*, 106–7.

6. Cited in ibid., 26.

7. Ibid., 61.

8. Kevin Heffernan, *Ghouls, Gimmicks, and Gold: Horror Films and the American Movie Business, 1953–1968* (Durham, NC: Duke University Press, 2004), 183.

9. Ibid., 190.

10. Robert Evans, *The Kid Stays in the Picture* (New York: Hyperion, 1994), 121.

11. To be more specific, they were typical of the Bill Bernbach–led revolution at the beginning of the decade. By the late sixties, design styles in consumer goods had radically changed. Yet film advertising was, more or less, the last to know. See Thomas Frank, *The Conquest of Cool: Business Culture, Counterculture, and the Rise of Hip Consumerism* (Chicago: University of Chicago Press, 1997).

12. Heffernan, *Ghouls, Gimmicks*, 61, 190.

13. Philip O. Dougherty, "Advertising: Creative Young Man at Y & R," *NYT*, Mar. 17, 1968, F17.

14. John Dempsey, "One-Sheet Wonder," *Variety*, July 21, 1997, 4.

15. Quoted in the anonymous profile of Frankfurt for the Art Directors Club Hall of Fame (1983), http://adcglobal.org/hall-of-fame/steve-frankfurt/, accessed June 4, 2014.

16. "*Rosemary's Baby*: A Retrospective," *Rosemary's Baby* DVD feature.

17. Evans, *The Kid*, 173.

18. Robert A. M. Stern, Thomas Mellins, and David Fishman, *New York 1960: Architecture and Urbanism between the Second World War and the Bicentennial* (New York: Monachelli Press, 1995), 722.

19. Evans, *The Kid*, 172.

20. This is a transcript of "The Film That Saved Paramount" from *The Kid Stays in the Picture* DVD extra features. Much of this material appears in slightly different form in the book version. I have opted for the film version even when it is less grammatical.

21. Peter Bart, "I Like It. I Want It. Let's Sew It Up," *NYT*, Aug. 7, 1966, 95.

22. David N. Eldridge, "'Dear Owen': The CIA, Luigi Luraschi and Hollywood, 1953," *Historical Journal of Film, Radio, and Television* 20:2 (2000): 149–96.

23. Bernard F. Dick, *Engulfed: The Death of Paramount Pictures and the Birth of Corporate Hollywood* (Lexington: University Press of Kentucky, 2001), 128–32.

24. Stephen Farber, "'The Conformist': Freud vs. Marx?," *NYT*, Apr. 11, 1971, D15.

25. *Italian Job* DVD commentary.

26. Scott Eyman, *Ernst Lubitsch: Laughter in Paradise* (New York: Simon & Schuster, 1993), 227.

27. Ethan Mordden, *The Hollywood Studios: Their Unique Styles during the Golden Age of Movies* (New York: Fireside, 1988), 23.

28. *Italian Job* DVD commentary.

29. Evans, *The Kid*, 226.

30. The shift in Michael's motives came relatively late to the process. In the screenplay's second draft (a draft that still retained the complex flashback structure in the early scenes), Michael delivers an impassioned speech on the endlessness of the personal as justification for killing Sollozzo and McCluskey: "It's all personal Sonny, every piece of dirt a man has to eat every day of his life is personal. You know where I learned that from? The Don. My old man. The Godfather. If a bolt of lightning hit a friend of his he would consider it personal. He took my enlisting in the Marines personal. He takes everything personal. That's what makes him great" (quoted in Jon Lewis, *The Godfather* [London: BFI, 2010], 79–80). This version is strikingly close to the novel.

31. Ibid., 19.

32. Ibid., 83–85.

33. William E. Farrell, "Colombo Shot, Gunman Slain at Columbus Circle Rally Site," *NYT*, June 29, 1971, 1, 20; Eric Pace, "Joe Gallo Is Shot to Death in Little Italy Restaurant," *NYT*, Apr. 8, 1972, 1, 34.

34. Gus Russo, *Supermob: How Sidney Korshak and His Criminal Associates Became America's Hidden Power Brokers* (New York: Bloomsbury, 2006), 386.

35. See Jon Lewis, *Whom God Wishes to Destroy: Francis Coppola and the New Hollywood* (Durham, NC: Duke University Press, 1995); Nick Tosches, *Power on Earth* (New York: Arbor House, 1986).

36. I am using the term "certification" in a somewhat technical sense, derived from Walker Percy's *The Moviegoer* (New York: Knopf, 1961), 9. In the novel, our narrator and his cousin/girlfriend emerge from a screening of *Panic in the Streets*, and she says, "Yes, it is certified now." The narrator explains: "Nowadays, when a person lives somewhere, in a neighborhood, the place is not certified for him. More than likely he will live there sadly and the emptiness which is inside him will expand until it evacuates the entire neighborhood. But if he sees a movie which shows his very neighborhood, it becomes possible for him to live, for a time at least, as a person who is Somewhere and not Anywhere." If the agency of the motion picture is to certify a place, the agency of the girlfriend/critic/moviegoer is to generate concepts such as certification.

37. The narrative of the Directors Company derives from materials in the William Friedkin Papers, Margaret Herrick Library, Academy of Motion Picture Arts and Sciences, Beverly Hills, CA.

38. "The Directors Company: Logo" folder, in ibid.

39. Memo from Edward Kessler and Robert Dalva, Nov. 4 (no year given; 1973), in ibid.

40. "A Legacy of Filmmakers: The Early Years of American Zoetrope," *THX-1138* extra feature.

41. Ibid.

42. Joan Didion, *Slouching towards Bethlehem* (New York: FSG, 1968), 100.

43. Fredric Jameson, *The Geopolitical Aesthetic: Cinema and Space in the World System* (Bloomington: Indiana University Press, 1992), 13–16.

44. *THX* DVD commentary. ARPANET went live in October 1969.

45. Ibid.

46. One might understand New York in the seventies as the last outpost of nostalgia for a future, hence the delay between *THX* and *Condor*.

47. *THX* DVD commentary.

48. Sean McCann and Michael Szalay, "Do You Believe in Magic? Literary Thinking after the New Left," *Yale Journal of Criticism* 18:2 (2005): 435–68.

49. *THX* DVD commentary.

50. Ibid.

51. Ibid.

52. Ibid.

53. Biskind, *Easy Riders*, 163.

54. For a press release announcing the fortieth anniversary of the program, see "Personalized License Plate Program Turns Forty on Saturday," California Department of Motor Vehicles, Aug. 19, 2010, http://dmv.ca.gov/pubs/newsrel/newsrel10/2010_24.htm.

55. *Conversation* DVD commentary.

56. The "field" is also the place where you "drop horseshit making lettuce grow."

57. Conversation: *Original Screenplay* (San Francisco: Directors Company, 1972), 9.

58. The scene functions as a foreshadowing of the concluding sequence. It begins with Harry placing a call to nowhere (his girlfriend has changed her number), it picks up with the argument between him and the secretary played by Harrison Ford, and in the midst of their discussion a man walks by carrying a saxophone.

59. Walter Murch, *Conversation* DVD commentary.

60. "The Beginning and the End," *Chinatown* DVD supplement.

61. Michael Eaton, *Chinatown* (London: BFI, 1997), 51.

62. Ibid., 12.

63. Rick Altman, "Sound Space," in *Sound Theory, Sound Practice*, ed. Rick Altman (New York: Routledge, 1992), 46–64, quote on 63.

64. Richard Keller Simon, "Between Capra and Adorno: West's *Day of the Locust* and the Movies of the 1930s," *Modern Language Quarterly* 54:4 (Dec. 1993): 513–34, quote on 527.

65. Robert von Dassanowsky, "'You Wouldn't Even Believe What Your Eyes Can See': Cinema's Messianism and Fascist Reflection in John Schlesinger's *The Day of the Locust*," *Senses of Cinema*, May 2006, http://sensesofcinema.com/2006/feature-articles/day_locust/.

66. Ibid.

67. Dick, *Engulfed*, 180.

68. Stephen Prince, *A New Pot of Gold: Hollywood under the Electronic Rainbow, 1980–1989* (Berkeley: University of California Press, 2000), 123–32; Geoff King, *New Hollywood Cinema: An Introduction* (New York: Columbia University Press, 2002), 224–56.

69. Carlo Rotella, "Grittiness," in *Good with Their Hands: Boxers, Bluesmen and Other Characters from the Rust Belt*, by Carlo Rotella (Berkeley: University of California Press, 2002), 105–66.

70. Nik Cohn, "Tribal Rites of the New Saturday Night," *New York*, June 7, 1976, http://nymag.com/nightlife/features/45933/.

71. Nigel Andrews, *Travolta: The Life* (London: Bloomsbury, 1998), 60.

72. Rotella, "Grittiness." This process continued in *The Eyes of Laura Mars* (Kirshner, Columbia, 1978).

73. "Catching the Fever: Platforms and Polyester," *Saturday Night Fever* DVD supplement.

74. Something similar is true of Karen Gorney. In the film she never wears the red dress she is wearing on the one-sheet. Instead, another woman wears it during this opening dance.

75. Andrews, *Travolta*, 75.

76. "Catching the Fever."

77. Derek Nystrom, *Hard Hats, Rednecks, and Macho Men: Class in 1970s American Cinema* (New York: Oxford University Press, 2009), 126.

78. Ibid., 110; for the urban background, see Richard Harris, "The Geography of Employment and Residence"; Steven Brint, "Upper Professionals: A High Command of Commerce, Culture, and Civic Regulation"; and Cynthia Fuchs Epstein and Stephen R. Duncombe, "Women Clerical Workers," all in *Dual City: Restructuring New York*, ed.

John Mollenkopf and Manuel Castells (New York: Russell Sage, 1991), 129–52, 155–76, 177–204.

79. Andrews, *Travolta*, 81.

80. Evans, *The Kid*, 293.

81. "Catching the Fever."

82. Aljean Harmetz, "Fever Redone for PG Rating," *NYT*, Jan. 11, 1979, C15; Gene Siskel, "'Saturday Night Fever' Is Cooled Down for PG Release," *Chicago Tribune*, Feb. 4, 1979, E2; Brandon Gray, "'Saturday Night Fever' Box Office Mystery Solved?," Box Office Mojo, June 20, 2002, http://boxofficemojo.com/news/?id=1204&p=s.htm.

83. Harmetz, "Fever Redone."

84. Ibid.

Chapter 4

1. Ingrid Sischy, "Interview with Armani," in *Giorgio Armani*, ed. Germano Celant and Harold Koda (New York: Guggenheim Museum, 2001), 2–19, quote on 13.

2. Book-length treatments of Ovitz include Stephen Singular, *Power to Burn: Michael Ovitz and the New Business of Show Business* (Secaucus, NJ: Birch Lane, 1996), and the more thorough and authoritative Robert Slater, *Ovitz: The Inside Story of Hollywood's Most Controversial Power Broker* (New York: McGraw-Hill, 1997). The material on CAA's client numbers is from Slater, 77, 201.

3. Ken Auletta, *Three Blind Mice: How the TV Networks Lost Their Way* (New York: Random House, 1991), 31; Harold Vogel, *Entertainment Industry Economics: A Guide for Financial Analysis*, 4th ed. (New York: Cambridge University Press, 2004), 481n57.

4. Singular, *Power to Burn*, 45; Vogel, *Entertainment Industry Economics*, 459n3, puts CAA's rate at 3-3-10 in the 1990s.

5. Slater, *Ovitz*, 62; Singular, *Power to Burn*, 45.

6. Slater, *Ovitz*, 87.

7. It was a coproduction between Asahi Television and Toho in Japan and Paramount in the United States. Those ratings make it the fourth highest-rated miniseries of all time, behind *Roots*, *The Thorn Birds*, and *The Winds of War*.

8. The quotes are taken, respectively, from John J. O'Connor, "'Shōgun,' Englishman's Adventures in Japan,' *NYT*, Sept. 15, 1980, C22; Tom Shales, "Shōgun: The Bravado and Blunders of NBC's 12-Hour Samurai Saga," *Washington Post*, Sept. 14, 1980, G1, 6–7, quote on 7; and Arthur Unger, "'Shōgun'—an Oriental 'Gone with the Wind'?," *Christian Science Monitor*, Sept. 11, 1980, 19. One major exception was Marilynn Preston writing in the *Chicago Tribune* ("Richard Chamberlain: 'Shogun' Warrior," Sept. 11, 1980, A1, 12): "I almost hesitate to mention it because if you allow yourself to get swept up in the easy flow of the story and stay in touch with the action as seen through Blackthorne's dreamy eyes (Chamberlain is very good!), I don't think you'll have a problem understanding one bit of the action."

9. Paul J. Scalise, "Sisyphus, the Japan Specialist," Japantoday.com, Jan. 12, 2001, http://www.japanreview.net/review_is_japan.htm,.

10. "Total quality management (TQM) is "a term initially coined by the Naval Air Systems Command to describe its Japanese style management approach to quality improvement." Definition at ASQ, Six Sigma Forum, http://asq.org/sixsigma/quality-infor mation/termst-sixsigma.html, accessed June 14, 2014.

11. Peter Drucker, *Management: Tasks, Responsibilities, Practices* (Woburn, MA: Butterworth Heinemann, 2003), 25–26.

12. Richard T. Athos and Anthony G. Pascale, *The Art of Japanese Management: Applications for American Executives* (New York: Simon & Schuster, 1981), 201.

13. Henry Smith, "James Clavell and the Legend of the British Samurai," in *Learning from Shōgun*, ed. Henry Smith (New York: Japan Society, 1980), 1–19, quote on 18.

14. Henry Smith, "Postscript: The TV Transformation," in Smith, *Learning from Shōgun*, 161–63, quote on 161.

15. Shales, "Shōgun," G6.

16. Jerry London, "The Director's View of Shōgun," *American Cinematographer*, Sept. 1980, 900–901, 940–43, quote on 942. Cinematographer Andrew Laszlo put it this way: "One also had to consider that this particular subject was shot primarily for television. When the average television receiver reproduces this image, any softness photographed into the image is magnified and sometimes becomes detrimental to the overall effect." "Shooting *Shōgun* on an Epic Scale," in ibid., 890–91, 961–70, quote on 969.

17. Biskind, *Easy Riders*, 377, from an interview with John Milius.

18. "Dressing Down in Sloppy Chic: The Rumpled, Crumpled, Wrinkled, Crinkled Look, *Time*, July 3, 1978, 68.

19. Stella Bruzzi calls this "a bland pop music track," which it is not (*Undressing Cinema* [New York: Routledge, 1997], 26). First, the song is a notable departure from the Teutonic Giorgio Moroder accompaniment we hear in so many scenes. Second, Robinson's extreme falsetto (and Gere's decision to sing along in his normal voice) adds to the anxiety about sexuality that runs through the film.

20. Germano Celant, "Giorgio Armani: Toward the Mass Dandy," in Celant and Koda, *Giorgio Armani*, xiv–xxiii, xiv.

21. Ibid., xvii.

22. Pauline Kael, "Why Are Movies So Bad?," *New Yorker*, June 23, 1980, 85.

23. *American Gigolo*, like much of the Movie Brat corpus, vests its misogyny in the conversation of gay or bisexual men; this may be the most extreme example.

24. Biskind, *Easy Riders*, 162. "In the case of *The Godfather*, Yablans says he got an unprecedented $25 to $30 million from the chains before the picture even opened, and a 90/10 split (in favor of Paramount) for the first twelve weeks."

25. Celant, "Giorgio Armani," xxi, citing "Armani Disarmed," *Emporio Armani Magazine* 14 (Sept.–Feb. 1995–96): 7.

26. Sischy, "Interview with Armani," 13. *Kagemusha* is something of a touchstone of overreaching: Francis Ford Coppola and George Lucas convinced Fox to partner with Toho in exchange for rights to the American release. Not only did the Americans re-edit the film but Coppola served as its presenter.

27. James Clavell, "Foreword," in *The Art of War*, by Sun Tzu (New York: Delacorte Press, 1983), 8.

28. Slater, *Ovitz*, 65.

29. Ibid., 69.

30. Vogel, *Entertainment Industry Economics*, 154.

31. Screenwriter John Rogers summarizes the difference: "An agent helps your *CAREER*. A manager helps *YOUR* career." For his description of his relationship with his CAA agents

and his manager Will Mercer, see Kung Fu Monkey, "Writing: Agents & Managers," Aug. 17, 2005, http://kfmonkey.blogspot.com/2005/08/writing-agents-managers.html.

32. William Goldman, *Adventures in the Screen Trade* (New York: Warner Books, 1983), 39, 43.

33. Frank Rose, *The Agency: William Morris and the Hidden History of Show Business* (New York: Harper Business, 1995), 388.

34. Slater, *Ovitz*, 78.

35. Michael Eisner, with Tony Schwartz, *Work in Progress* (New York: Hyperion, 1998), 160.

36. Roger Ebert, "3 Men and a Cradle," May 2, 1986, Rogerebert.com, http://www.rogerebert.com/reviews/3-men-and-a-cradle-1986.

37. Eisner, *Work in Progress*, 156.

38. Ibid., 159, 158.

39. Roger Ebert, "Three Men and a Baby," Nov. 25, 1987, Rogerebert.com, http://www.rogerebert.com/reviews/three-men-and-a-baby-1987.

40. Harmetz, "Who Makes Disney Run?," 30. A title like that was bound to upset Eisner.

41. Donald Trump, with Tony Schwartz, *Trump: The Art of the Deal* (New York: Ballantine, 1987), 1. Schwartz would ghostwrite Eisner's autobiography, *Work in Progress*, a decade later.

42. Stone notes that there are actually three fathers in the film: Martin Sheen (who plays and is Charlie's biological father), Hal Holbrook (who plays a version of Stone's own father, the righteous Wall Street trader), and Michael Douglas (the bad father). He leaves Wildman out.

43. Otto Friedrich, "The Lucky Gambler: Sir James Goldsmith Is a Billionaire Buccaneer," *Time*, Nov. 23, 1987, http://www.time.com/time/magazine/article/0,9171,966046-1,00.html.

44. William Shawcross, *Murdoch* (London: Chatto & Windus, 1992), 235.

45. Ibid., 249.

46. *Wall Street* DVD commentary.

47. Shawcross, *Murdoch*, 218.

48. Both remarks from Levinson's *Rain Man* DVD commentary. As Faulkner's Benjy in *The Sound and the Fury* is an emblem of modernism, so Raymond is the privileged perceiver of high concept.

49. Hoffman and Cruise, "Original Featurette," *Rain Man* DVD supplement.

50. Johnson, in ibid.

51. L. J. Davis, "Hollywood's Most Secret Agent," *New York Times Magazine*, July 9, 1989, 24–27, 51–54, 74–75.

52. The Eszterhas story is a complicated tale of innuendo, leaking, and self-serving revision. Slater rehearses it in *Ovitz*, 210–16.

53. Davis, "Hollywood's Most Secret Agent," 53.

Part II

1. In *The Last Dinosaur Book* (Chicago: University of Chicago Press, 1998), W. J. T. Mitchell notices this same equivalence. When Rick Carter, the production designer for *Jurassic Park*, visited my class in the spring of 2005, he caught sight of this image as it

appears in Mitchell's book. "That's my shot!" he said and went on to explain that while there is no source for the projection we see on the dinosaur, he felt the image would be striking, precisely because it suggested the relationship between DNA and digital coding. After reading Mitchell's chapter, Carter agreed with virtually all of it.

Chapter 5

1. Horkheimer and Adorno, *Dialectic of Enlightenment*, 99.

2. Biskind, *Easy Riders*, 377, quoting John Milius.

3. Bordwell, *The Way Hollywood Tells It*, 115.

4. Actually it was set up through Film Properties International, N.V., which was a one-off, likely a subsidiary of CIC. (Whatever the actual structure, it was CIC that handled the accounting and the dispersal of revenues, based on the income statements in the Friedkin archive at the Herrick library.) In 2012, Friedkin sued both Universal and Paramount, ostensibly for royalties, but in reality to clarify the ownership situation in order to make a re-release of *Sorcerer* possible.

5. Diller quote and Barron estimate from interviews cited by Connie Bruck, *When Hollywood Had a King* (New York: Random House, 2003), 347–48.

6. Seymour Hersh, "S.E.C. Presses Wide Investigation of Gulf and Western Conglomerate," *NYT*, July 24, 1977, 1, 34; "Gulf and Western's Relationship with Banks Is Issue in S.E.C. Study," *NYT*, July 25, 1977, 1, 35; "Gulf and Western Tax Practices Coming under Wide Investigation," *NYT*, July 26, 1977, L1, 43. The lawsuit itself also received front-page coverage: Clyde H. Farnsworth, "S.E.C. Suing Gulf and Western, Charging Impropriety and Fraud," *NYT*, Nov. 27, 1979, A1, D15; Larry Kramer, "G&W Accused of Securities Fraud," *Washington Post*, Nov. 27, 1979, A1, 12. For the settlement, see "Gulf and Western Agrees to Settlement with S.E.C." *LAT*, Oct. 29, 1981, H1.

7. Biskind, *Easy Riders*, 312.

8. Vincent Canby, "*Sorcerer*: Action Movie Set in Latin America," *NYT*, June 25, 1977, 11.

9. Biskind, *Easy Riders*, 310; the final quote is from Nat Segaloff, *Hurricane Billy* (New York: Morrow, 1990), 164. Like the story of Bluhdorn's picture, the story of Friedkin's insolence is likely exaggerated. It culminates with the director passing out cold when Sheinberg "show[s] him an ad line the studio had prepared," but neither the poster nor the trailer has an ad line at all.

10. Universal handled domestic distribution.

11. The film's newspaper advertising did, at times, include insets of the four men: *NYT*, June 24, 1977, 55.

12. Tony Schwartz, "Hollywood's Hottest Stars," *New York Magazine*, July 30, 1984, 24–33, quote on 33.

13. Ibid., 27.

14. Dawn Steel, *They Can Kill You but They Can't Eat You* (New York: Pocket Books, 1994), 142–43.

15. Mark Litwak, *Reel Power: The Struggle for Influence and Success in the New Hollywood* (New York: New American Library, 1987), 44; quoted in part in Prince, *New Pot of Gold*, 168.

16. The phrase was pervasive, but I first encountered it in William Goldman's novel *Marathon Man* (New York: Ballantine 2001), 53. (Charlie, the Roy Scheider character,

will "luckily" raise his hand to block an assassin's garrote before his throat can be cut. The garroting survived the transition to the screen; the allusion to Rickey did not.) The first printed source for Rickey's slogan is in Dan Daniel, "Deviltry Denounced at Dodger Tech," *Sporting News*, Feb. 21, 1946, 10, where it is part of a parody of a Rickey lecture, indicating that the motto was already firmly associated with the skipper. The "Tenth Manager" responds pragmatically: "If that ain't double talk, I never heard none. Luck is what you ain't got when you lose."

17. Schwartz, "Hollywood's Hottest Stars," 32.

18. Steel, *They Can Kill You*, 140.

19. "*Flashdance*: The Choreography," *Flashdance* DVD supplement.

20. Ibid.

21. Ibid.

22. Wyatt, *High Concept*, 28.

23. "*Flashdance*: The Choreography." The quotation is from Deborah Caulfield, "Doing a Dancing Double Take," *LAT*, Apr. 20, 1983, G1, 4. The follow-up article is Deborah Caulfield, "OK, Jennifer, Who Did the Dancing?," *LAT*, Apr. 22, 1983, I1, 15.

24. Dale Pollock, "Flashfight," *LAT*, July 10, 1983, U1, 18–19, 32–35, quote on 18.

25. Pollock, "Flashfight," 35.

26. Caulfield, "OK, Jennifer," 15.

27. Tom Shales, "Commentary," *LAT*, June 26, 1983, N6.

28. Pollock, "Flashfight," 34.

29. "*Flashdance*: The Choreography."

30. Steel, *They Can Kill You*, 142.

31. Schwartz, "Hollywood's Hottest Stars," 28.

32. *Footloose* DVD, Craig Zadan/Dean Pitchford commentary.

33. *Footloose* DVD, Kevin Bacon commentary.

34. Arthur Lubow, "*Footloose* Fever," *People*, Apr. 2, 1984, 88, 95.

35. Frank Stallone, Mickey Gilley, and other musicians do, but only in the context of the narrative.

36. "*Footloose*: Songs That Tell a Story," *Footloose* DVD supplement.

37. Jeff Smith, *The Sounds of Commerce: Marketing Popular Film Music* (New York: Columbia, 1998), 158.

38. "*Footloose*: Songs That Tell a Story."

39. Smith, *Sounds of Commerce*, 164.

40. Larry Rohter, "In Movies, a Formula Is Born: Hitching One's Star to a Song," *NYT*, July 8, 1991, C11; Smith, *Sounds of Commerce*, 206.

41. *Footloose* DVD, Craig Zadan/Dean Pitchford commentary.

42. *Gulf + Western Annual Report*, 1985, 3.

43. *Gulf + Western Annual Report*, 1983, 10.

44. J. Fred Weston, *The Case for the Multinational Corporation*, ed. Carl H. Madden (New York: Praeger, 1977); J. Fred Weston, ed., *Large Corporations in a Changing Society* (New York: NYU Press, 1975); J. Fred Weston, Harvey J. Goldschmid, and H. Michael Mann, eds., *Industrial Concentration: The New Learning* (Boston: Little, Brown, 1974); H. Igor Ansoff, *Corporate Strategy: An Analytic Approach to Business Policy for Growth and Expansion* (New York: McGraw-Hill, 1965). The crucial chapter in that book, for my

purposes, is "Synergy and Structure," which Ansoff indicates is based on a paper written with Weston, "Merger Objectives and Organizational Structure," *Quarterly Review of Economics and Business* (Aug. 1962): 49–58.

45. Ansoff, *Corporate Strategy*, 110.

46. "Rage word": Arelo Sederberg, "Wasserman of MCA: Show Biz Conservative," *LAT*, Apr. 7, 1969, F8, 10, quote on F8; "basic buzzwords": Jerry Knight and James L. Rowe Jr., "Sears Is Building a Tower to Carry Out New Strategy," *Washington Post*, Oct. 11, 1985, G1, 4, quote on G4.

47. Anthony J. Parisi, "Management: GE's Search for Synergy," *NYT*, Apr. 16, 1978, D1, 4, quote on D1.

48. *Gulf + Western Annual Report*, 1985, 4.

49. Pollock, "Flashfight," 18.

50. Laura Landro, "Paramount Pursues New Markets As Change Confronts Movie Firms," *Wall Street Journal* (hereafter *WSJ*), May 25, 1983, 33.

51. Dale Pollock, "Davis Seeks Greater Synergy in Firm," *LAT*, Oct. 9, 1984, E1, 13, quote on E1.

52. Laura Landro, "G&W's Group President Arthur Barron Draws Entertainment Units Together," *WSJ*, Oct. 8, 1984, 20.

53. Harlan Kennedy, "Castle 'Keep': Michael Mann Interviewed by Harlan Kennedy," *Film Comment* 19:6 (Nov./Dec. 1983): 16–19, quote on 16.

54. F. Paul Wilson, *The Keep* (New York: Tor Books, 2000), 2–3.

55. *Thief* DVD commentary.

56. Ibid.

57. We may now distinguish several forms of nostalgia spanning the period from *Bonnie and Clyde* through *Raiders. Bonnie and Clyde* (and *Butch Cassidy and the Sundance Kid*, and the dance sequence in *Heaven's Gate*) was built around the idea of nostalgia as a form of passing, of love for "things that fade," of "capture." A second form would include *American Graffiti* and would aim at reimmersion, usually with the aim of recapitulating certain crucial moments of general experience. And the third form would be that of *Raiders, Pennies from Heaven*, and *Bugsy Malone*, in which the stylization of the period and the stylization of the overall effect would cohere, usually too explicitly, usually with the effect of winking pastiche. A 2 × 2 matrix would adequately capture much of this work, with one axis being overtness or knowingness and the other being stylistic coherence. So: Raiders is + +, *Bonnie* would be + –, and Graffiti would be – –. The missing quadrant, – +, that is, immersive coherence, would be occupied by Peter Bogdanovich.

58. Kennedy, "Castle 'Keep,'" 18.

59. Ibid., 18, 19.

60. Dick, *Engulfed*, 187.

61. Kennedy, "Castle 'Keep,'" 19.

62. Schwartz, "Hollywood's Hottest Stars," 27.

63. Paul Attanasio, "Getting a Percentage of Hollywood's Action: Jim Wiatt, Who Puts Reel Deals Together," *Washington Post*, May 26, 1985, D1, 2.

64. Justin Wyatt, "Independents, Packaging, and Inflationary Pressure in 1980s Hollywood," in *A New Pot of Gold*, ed. Stephen Prince (Berkeley: University of California Press, 2000), 142–59.

65. See the discussion of "the producer's game" in Rick Altman, *Film/Genre* (London: BFI, 1999), 38–48.

66. The underlying novel, Robert Grossbach's *Easy and Hard Ways Out* (New York: Harper's Magazine Press, 1975), also cuts between the defense contractors and combat. The film updates the book by shifting the conflict from Vietnam to an Iraqi invasion of Kuwait and changes the mode of combat from the aerial bombardment to ground warfare, likely due to scandalous cost overruns on the M-1 tank.

67. Laurie Deans, "Where Has All the Action Gone?," *Toronto Globe and Mail*, Oct. 28, 1983, E5; "I knew the script for *Best Defense* was horrible, but I got talked into the movie by Paramount [Pictures]. They started offering me all of this money. I was 21 years old. I said to hell with it and went for it. It was a mistake, but we all make mistakes in our careers" ("*Ebony* Interview with Eddie Murphy," *Ebony*, July 1985, 42–48, quote on 44).

68. Steven R. Weisman, "Reagan Proposes U.S. Seek New Way to Block Missiles," *NYT*, Mar. 25, 1983, 1.

69. Michael Rogin, *Ronald Reagan: The Movie* (Berkeley: University of California Press, 1987), 1–43.

70. The scene was cut from the release print of the film but is available as a deleted scene on the DVD.

71. Valentine's insight sounds naïve, but it is supported by the text on his Telerate Terminal. Below the rolling prices for feeder cattle and pork bellies is the following news report: "Holiday purchasing expectations indicate tightening of investment capital. . . . Year-end cashflow curtailed in anticipation." The Christmas Eve *Financial Journal* we see later only reinforces the theory. One headline: "*Just Looking*: Many Consumers Shop for Christmas Presents with Tightwad Touch." (That article actually ran in the *WSJ* on Dec. 2, 1982.)

72. The CEO had died from complications from lymphoma, but the company announced the cause of death as cardiac arrest.

73. *Gulf + Western Annual Report*, 1984, 4.

74. Axel's look is the urban version of *Footloose*'s "classic": a gray sweatshirt thrown over his T-shirt, Levi's, white Adidas with black stripes. The first time he walks down a Beverly Hills street and encounters two guys in Michael Jackson–style leather suits, he can't help laughing. Of course, Murphy had worn precisely that for his 1983 concert film *Delirious*.

75. *Beverly Hills Cop* DVD commentary.

76. Edward Feldman, *Tell Me How You Love the Picture* (New York: St. Martin's, 2005), 152–53.

77. Ibid., 186–87. Doubtless this is only a partial story, but Dawn Steel does not mention the production of *The Golden Child* in her memoir.

78. Pierce O'Donnell and Dennis McDougal, *Fatal Subtraction: How Hollywood Really Does Business* (New York: Dove, 1996). The profits figures are available on 60; the formulation, on 52.

79. Ibid., 237.

80. Citing Golding v. RKO Pictures, Inc., 35 Cal 2d 690, 695 (1950).

81. O'Donnell and McDougal, *Fatal Subtraction*, 237–38.

82. Ibid., 240.

83. Frank Sanello, *Eddie Murphy: The Life and Times of a Comic on the Edge* (New York: Birch Lane, 1997), 49.

84. Gene Lyons and Peter McAlevey, "Crazy Eddie," *Newsweek*, Jan. 7, 1985, 48–55, quote on 55, quoted in part in O'Donnell and McDougal, *Fatal Subtraction*, 34.

85. O'Donnell and McDougal, *Fatal Subtraction*, 159.

86. "Prince-ipal Photography: The Coming Together of America," *Coming to America* DVD supplement.

87. "Prince-ipal Photography."

88. O'Donnell and McDougall, *Fatal Subtraction*, 223.

89. "Prince-ipal Photography."

90. "Danger Zone: Making of *Top Gun*," *Top Gun* DVD supplement.

91. Ibid.

92. Structurally, the film is utterly clear: An opening altercation in the Indian Ocean (15:44) pairs off with the closing battle (15:25). When the scene shifts to Miramar, the first 14:03 minutes either continue the opening act or constitute a new exposition, culminating in Iceman's statement of the problem: that Maverick left his wingman. The next 43:04 minutes chart Maverick's rise and fall at Top Gun. Despite his continued refusal to fly by the rules, his romance develops and he manages to create a surrogate family (the "Great Balls of Fire" sequence). The rising action occupies 19:57 minutes. The next day, Goose will die in an accident. Maverick, though exonerated, will lose his "edge" and quit, only to be brought back. The falling action takes 23:07 minutes. After the final battle, an epilogue (2:05) puts him back at Top Gun to be reunited with Charlie.

93. "Danger Zone."

94. *Top Gun* DVD commentary.

95. "Danger Zone."

96. *Paramount Annual Report*, 1987, 21.

97. "Danger Zone."

98. The Internet Movie Cars Database has some of the details: imcdb.org, accessed June 14, 2014.

99. *Paramount Annual Report*, 1987, 7.

Chapter 6

1. Author interview with Greg Hahn, March 1995.

2. James Gleick, *Chaos: The Making of a New Science* (New York: Viking, 1987), 261.

3. Ibid., 29.

4. Ibid., 269.

5. Ryan Gilbey notices it in the BFI guide only to deride it as "bad news." Gilbey, *Groundhog Day* (London: BFI, 2004). "The first few seconds of the picture seem to bear out Danny Rubin's concern that his extraordinary premise was having the magic squeezed out of it" (24).

6. Moore's paradox is usually framed as "It is raining but I do not believe it." He called this lack of belief in the state of things "absurd." When Phil jumps out of the van, he explains that it cannot be snowing as he shivers in the middle of a blizzard. Whatever

Wittgenstein might have said about Moore's paradox, we would be more likely to say about Phil that *he knows better*. Why should Moore's paradox appear in a movie? When Moore adumbrated the paradox in "A Reply to My Critics" (*The Philosophy of G. E. Moore*, ed. Philip A. Schlipp [Evanston, IL: Northwestern University Press, 1942], 535–677), he was not talking about unbelievable weather. "I went to the pictures Tuesday, but I don't believe that I did" (543). Logically, both contexts are "p, I do not believe p," but the cinematic version seems far less absurd on its face than the meteorological one.

7. This is the second of at least three moments that might allude to Moore, here in his claim that value is not subject to analysis. (The third moment is Phil enacting Moore's paradox outside Punxsutawney.) Is this film *really* alluding to Moore? It seems unlikely, but perhaps no more so than the claims I will make about its references to chaos theory. What one might say is that *Groundhog Day* is about as astute as it is possible to be in running through the consequences, paradoxes, and affective complications of its commitment to supernatural realism. It should not be surprising, then, if it encounters skepticism (Here is one hand), problems of value (What am I bid?), and madness (It isn't snowing) along the way and that those encounters will have resolutions that look eerily Moorean.

8. Cited in William Rothman, ed., *Cavell on Film* (Albany: SUNY Press, 2005), 222.

9. *Cast Away* DVD commentary.

10. John Rogers, "Writing: Writing a Great Movie—Book Review," Kung Fu Monkey, May 30, 2007, http://kfmonkey.blogspot.com/2007/05/writing-writing-great-movie-book-review.html.

11. Thompson, *Storytelling*, 132.

12. Ibid., 378n1.

13. The lineaments of this account come from Nancy Griffin and Kim Masters, *Hit and Run* (New York: Simon & Schuster, 1996).

14. Ibid., 338, 339.

15. Ibid., 348.

16. Ibid., 362.

17. Ibid., 367.

18. Thompson, *Storytelling*, 150.

19. "The Making of *Jurassic Park*," *Jurassic Park* DVD supplement.

20. W. J. T. Mitchell, *The Last Dinosaur Book* (Chicago: University of Chicago Press, 1998), 214.

21. Ibid., 225.

22. Bordwell, *The Way Hollywood Tells It*, 121–38.

23. Rick Altman, "Deep-Focus Sound: *Citizen Kane* and the Radio Aesthetic," in *Perspectives on Citizen Kane*, ed. R. Gottesman (Berkeley: University of California Press, 1996), 94–121, quote on 113.

24. Gleick, *Chaos*, 251.

25. William Empson, *Some Versions of Pastoral* (New York: New Directions, 1974), 253–94.

26. Stephen Fjellman, *Vinyl Leaves: Walt Disney World and America* (Boulder, CO: Westview Press, 1992), 64–86.

27. Eisner, *Work in Progress*, 336. The most shocking aspect of Eisner's remark is the

casual slagging of a "Disneyesque view of history"—when even the CEO believes the brand is incompatible with objectivity, the project is in trouble.

28. Ibid., 329–30.

29. Ibid., 324–25.

30. Ibid., 337.

31. Stephen Rebello, *The Art of Pocahontas* (New York: Hyperion, 1995), 174.

32. International Conference on Computer Graphics and Interactive Techniques, *Proceedings of the 26th Annual Conference on Computer Graphics and Interactive Techniques* (New York: ACM Press, 1999), 129–36.

33. Charles Solomon, *The Prince of Egypt: A New Vision of Animation* (New York: Harry N. Abrams, 1998), 177.

34. Arthur De Vany and W. David Walls, "Bose-Einstein Dynamics and Adaptive Contracting in the Motion Picture Industry," in *Hollywood Economics: How Extreme Uncertainty Shapes the Motion Picture Industry*, by Arthur De Vany (New York: Rutgers University Press, 2004), 28–47, 46.

35. John Cassidy, "Chaos in Hollywood," *New Yorker*, Mar. 31, 1997, 36–44 quotes on 37, 43.

36. John Kenneth Galbraith, *The Anatomy of Power* (Boston: Houghton Mifflin, 1983), 59; cited in Steven Bach, *Final Cut*, 17.

37. De Vany, *Hollywood Economics*, 269.

38. Ibid., 2.

Part III

1. *The Day after Tomorrow*, DVD insert, n.p. [3].

Chapter 7

1. Cited in William B. Parsons, "The Oceanic Feeling Revisited," *Journal of Religion* 78:4 (Oct. 1998): 501–23, quote on 503. Emphasis in original.

2. Jerome Christensen tells the story of *You've Got Mail* in *America's Corporate Art*, 302–13.

3. Cavell, *Pursuits of Happiness*, 30.

4. Ibid., 28.

5. Stanley Cavell, "The Fact of Television," *Daedalus* 111:4 (Fall 1982): 75–96, quote on 82. Reprinted in William Rothman, ed., *Cavell on Film* (Albany: SUNY Press, 2005), 59–86, quote on 68.

6. Ibid., 81/67.

7. Ibid., 82/68.

8. Ibid., 82–83/68.

9. Cavell, *Pursuits of Happiness*, 248.

10. Amy Longsdorf, "Slippery When Wet; With His First Big-Budget Action Film, Jon Bon Jovi's Career Takes a U-Turn," *Bergen Record*, Apr. 16, 2000, Y1.

11. The account of the Polygram merger derives from numerous sources: *WSJ*, *Business Week*, and *Variety*. The loss on the deal is hard to figure without access to the corporate books. At the time of the announcement, Philips had put $1.25 billion into PFE, but Universal had to invest $150 million to keep it up and running. Universal wanted the

buyer to pay $750 million and absorb $300 million in debt. The best offer it got was from Artisan ($400 million + $300 million in debt = $700 million, or a $700 million write-off). Universal received between $585 million and $685 million in cash; it kept Working Title and absorbed pieces of the distribution network. My figure of $500 million loss is an exceedingly rough estimate. See Martin Peers and Benedict Carver, "Barry Bags a Bundle," *Variety*, Apr. 8, 1999, 1; Richard Siklos and Ron Glover, "When Will Bronfman Have to Face the Music?," *Business Week*, Nov. 9, 1998, 148–50; Bruce Orwall and Eben Shapiro, "Seagram Is Closer to Deal for PolyGram, but Concerns Haggle over Movie Assets," *WSJ*, May 18, 1998, B6; Eben Shapiro, "Unhappy with PolyGram Film Offers, Seagram May Ask Bidders to Try Again," *WSJ*, Oct. 5, 1998, B6; Bruce Orwall, "Seagram to Absorb Most of Film Unit of PolyGram NV," *WSJ*, Dec. 11, 1998, B8; Bruce Orwall, "MGM to Acquire 1,300 PolyGram Films from Canada's Seagram for $235 Million," *WSJ*, Oct. 23, 1998, B7; Eben Shapiro and Bruce Orwall, "Entertainment: Bronfman Takes the Reins at Universal," *WSJ*, Nov. 17, 1998, B1.

12. "Two Producers and a Deal," *LAT*, Mar. 26, 1999, C1.

13. Dan Cox, "U Passing the Hat," *Variety*, Jan. 18, 1999, 1.

14. James Bates, Sallie Hofmeister, and Claudia Eller, "Company Town: Seagram-Vivendi Acquisition Talks a Long Time Coming," *LAT*, June 15, 2000, C1.

15. Alan Jones, "Above the Waves," *Preview*, https://web.archive.org/web/20010802032 837/http://www.preview-online.com/march_april/feature_articles/u-571/, accessed 6/4/14.

16. Peter Howell, "Young Bronfman, the Man Who Would Be King of All Media," *Toronto Star*, Nov. 7, 1998, M1.

17. Martin Peers and Dan Cox, "Edgar at the Wheel: With Biondi Out, Pressure's on Bronfman to Turn U Around," *Daily Variety*, Nov. 17, 1999, 1.

18. Howell, "Young Bronfman."

19. Ibid.

20. Naval History and Heritage Command, "Frequently Asked Questions," http://www.history.navy.mil/faqs/faq2-1.htm, accessed Nov. 5, 2014.

21. Alison James and Lisa Nesselson, "Bonhomie in Deauville," *Variety*, Sept. 11, 2000, 6.

22. Hilary Clarke, "Saved by a French Connection: The Emergence of Canal Plus as a Buyer for PolyGram's Film Unit Has Given the Industry Fresh Hope," *The Independent*, May 24, 1998, Business 3.

23. James and Nesselson, "Bonhomie in Deauville," 6.

24. Gregg Kilday, "Curious Saga of George's Screen Gig," *Hollywood Reporter*, Feb. 3, 2006 (nexis).

25. Chris Petrikin, "Imagine, Helmer Bird Set to Monkey Around," *Variety*, Nov. 1, 1999, 1 (nexis).

26. David Evans, "Coming Soon: Curious George on Film: Vivendi Universal Hopes Monkey Will Raise Company's Profile in U.S.," *Ottawa Citizen*, July 17, 2001, B5.

27. Keith J. Kelly, "Monkeyshines for Messier," *New York Post*, July 16, 2001, 29 (nexis). A slightly different version of the quotation appears in Evans, "Coming Soon."

28. Vicky Ward, "Enemies in the Boardroom," *Vanity Fair*, Oct. 2002, 194, 198, 205–6, 208–10, 212–13, quote on 212.

29. *Traffic* DVD commentary.

30. Soderbergh ultimately cut two other references—a meeting between Helena and an assassin at a children's "Fun Zone" featuring a large Spastic Jack standee, and a trip to the empty factory where the coke dolls were being made. That is, he cut exhibition and production to focus on distribution.

31. Dana Harris and Claude Brodesser, "Fox Traffic Jams: Ford, Zeta-Jones Onboard for Soderbergh Pic," *Variety*, Feb. 16, 2000, 5.

32. The screenplay is clearer about the domestication: "You didn't win, Helena. You lost everything," Cheadle's character says. And once outside, we would have seen Helena's son playing with a Spastic Jack doll. The screenplay did not include the line about the carpet (*http://www.awesomefilm.com/script/traffic.txt*, accessed June 4, 2014).

33. Michael Fleming, "Par's 'Jacket' Fits Clooney-Soderbergh," *Variety*, June 29, 2000, 3; Jonathan Bing and Cathy Dunkley, "Boutique Chic," *Variety*, Aug. 11, 2003, 5.

34. Peter Biskind's *Down and Dirty Pictures* (New York: Simon & Schuster, 2004), 207–9, tells the story of Soderbergh's walk back from *Schizopolis* through the eyes of USAFilms' predicament. However contingent his situation might have been *before Brockovich* and *Traffic*, his options had dramatically increased. Still, there is evidence that Soderbergh's fascination with the con goes back a decade or more. While serving on the Sundance jury the year after winning for *sex, lies and videotape*, he lobbied the jury to give the prize to *Chameleon Street* (Wendell B. Harris): "[W]hen I was on the jury at Sundance in 1990, I refused to leave the room unless we gave the Grand Prize to *Chameleon Street*. Before you leap to the conclusion that this was a heroic act on my part, you should be aware that this situation arose only because the Festival had made the mistake of selecting an even number of Jurors without designating someone as Jury President" (Soderbergh, *Getting Away with It: Or, The Further Adventures of the Luckiest Bastard You Ever Saw* [London: Faber & Faber, 1999], 9).

35. *Ocean's 11* Blu-ray commentary.

36. Ibid.

37. Ibid.

38. Connie Bruck, *Master of the Game* (New York: Simon & Schuster, 1994), 50–51.

39. Jerry Weintraub, *When I Stop Talking, You'll Know I'm Dead* (New York: Twelve, 2010), 258.

40. *Ocean's 11* Blu-ray commentary.

41. The account of the AOL TimeWarner debacle is drawn from Alec Klein, *Stealing Time: Steve Case, Jerry Levin, and the Collapse of AOL TimeWarner* (New York: Simon & Schuster, 2003); Nina Munk, *Fools Rush In: Steve Case, Jerry Levin, and the Unmaking of AOL TimeWarner* (New York: HarperCollins, 2004); and Kara Swisher (with Lisa Dickey), *There Must Be a Pony in Here Somewhere* (New York: Crown Business, 2003).

42. Transcript, Lou Dobbs, *Moneyline*, CNN, December 5, 2001 (LexisNexis Academic, transcript no. 120500CN.V19).

43. *Ocean's 11* Blu-ray commentary. Andrew deWaard and R. Colin Tait mention the line about Levin in their excellent *The Cinema of Steven Soderbergh* as part of their discussion of Soderbergh's industrial reflexivity, but don't link it to their reading of the film as an allegory of capital later on (London: Wallflower, 2013, 31).

44. Klein, *Stealing Time*, 226, quoting Neil Davis, who was then a senior vice president at AOL.

45. Ibid., 2.

46. Swisher, *There Must Be a Pony*, 266.

47. Bill Carter, "Two HBO Shows Lose Viewers after Starting Strong," *NYT*, Oct. 13, 2003, *http://www.nytimes.com/2003/10/13/business/media-talk-two-hbo-shows-lose-viewers-after-starting-strong.html*.

48. The game was played on Nov. 11; the episode aired Nov. 16. Smith repeatedly announces that Allen Iverson scored forty points; Iverson did. See Basketball-Reference.com, Nov. 11, 2003, *http://www.basketball-reference.com/boxscores/200311110WAS.html*.

49. *Ocean's 12* Blu-ray commentary.

50. Soderbergh says in his Blu-ray commentary that the choice of the Coronation Egg was his doing: "I have to take the heat for coming up with this—I don't know why; I'm obsessed with these Faberge eggs. . . . I'm fascinated by Russia; I'm certainly fascinated by the Romanov family."

51. *Ocean's 11* Blu-ray commentary.

52. *Ocean's 12* Blu-ray commentary.

53. Ibid.

54. Soderbergh staged the scene to recall the first meet-up: "In this case I was consciously re-creating a compositional style and cutting pattern that we used at Reuben's house in the first film when they're setting up the plan and Danny's in front of the screen" (Blu-ray commentary). In both cases, he allowed actors to group as they wished and shot with a 27mm lens.

55. This line is an echo of Maureen Stapleton's line in *You've Got Mail*, when she explains to Meg Ryan that "[i]f you need more, ask me, I'm very rich. I bought Intel at 6."

56. *Ocean's 13* Blu-ray commentary.

57. *Ocean's 12* Blu-ray commentary.

58. Ibid.

59. Matthew Karnitschnig, "That's All Folks: After Years of Pushing Synergy, Time Warner Inc. Says Enough," *WSJ*, June 2, 2006, A1.

60. Ibid.

61. John Battelle, "Diller's Next Act: Synergy—Who Needs It?," *Business 2.0*, CNN Money, Mar. 1, 2005, *http://money.cnn.com/magazines/business2/business2_archive/2005/03/01/8253087/index.htm*.

62. Karnitschnig, "That's All Folks."

63. Ibid.

64. *Ocean's 13* Blu-ray commentary.

Chapter 8

1. Roland Barthes, *Mythologies*, trans. Annette Lavers (New York: Noonday, 1972), 26–28, quote on 28.

2. Ibid., 28.

3. Jacques Siclier, "L'age du peplum," *Cahiers du cinéma* 22:131 (May 1962): 26–38, quote on 26.

4. Robert Burgoyne, *The Hollywood Historical Film* (Malden, MA: Blackwell, 2008), 15, 76, citing Michael Wood, *America in the Movies: Or, "Santa Maria It Had Slipped My Mind"* (New York: Basic Books, 1975), 173.

5. Burgoyne, *The Hollywood Industrial Film*, 76.

6. Ibid., 81. Burgoyne neglects to mention the DreamWorks logo.

7. Sobchack, "'Surge and Splendor,'" 29.

8. James Russell, *The Historical Epic and Contemporary Hollywood: From* Dances with Wolves *to* Gladiator (London: Continuum, 2007), 170.

9. John Soriano, interview with David Franzoni, cited by Jon Solomon, "*Gladiator* from Screenplay to Screen," in Gladiator: *Film and History*, ed. Martin Winkler (Malden, MA: Blackwell, 2004), 1–15, quote on 4. Solomon's source, a Writers Guild of America interview with Franzoni, is available through the Internet Archive: http://web.archive .org/web/20011107224337/www.wga.org/craft/interviews/franzoni2001.html, accessed June 4, 2014.

10. David Franzoni, *Gladiator*, first draft, rev. Apr. 4, 1998, *http://www.hundland.org/ scripts/Gladiator_FirstDraft.txt*. In this draft, Maximus is called Narcissus; I have altered it in order to keep the character name consistent.

11. The second draft, Oct. 22, 1998, is available at http://www.hundland.org/scripts/ Gladiator_SecondDraft.txt.

12. Winkler, *Gladiator*.

13. Russell does not describe the system in precisely these terms.

14. Information on release dates from the LaserDisc Database, *www.lddb.com*. While filmmakers would have had access to archival prints, and casual viewers might have seen these titles and many others on television or in VHS versions, the existence of LaserDiscs vouches for a videophile audience for these films. This audience, multiplied several times over, would become the crucial backstop for the financial success of the imperial epic in the 2000s. See Russell, *Historical Epic*, 173–80.

15. These interviews are included in the Criterion DVD reissue from 2001. In his 1992 interview on the same disc, Ustinov clarifies the differences. First, *Spartacus* was "the first secular Roman film," that is, the first one where Christianity played no important part in the agon. Second, it was an independent film "even if it was shot by a major studio."

16. David S. Cohen, "'Get a Life!' *Gladiator*, David Franzoni," in *Screen Plays: How 25 Screenplays Made It to a Theater near You—for Better or Worse* (New York: Harper, 2008), 19–36, quote on 26.

17. For the account of Warner Bros.' educational efforts surrounding *JFK*, see Christensen, *America's Corporate Art*, 299.

18. Peter Rose, "The Politics of *Gladiator*," in Winkler, *Gladiator*, 150–72, quotes on 171.

19. Gilles Deleuze, *Cinema 1: The Time-Image* (Minneapolis: University of Minnesota Press, 1986), 148, 151.

20. Burgoyne, *Hollywood Historical Film*, 82.

21. Julie Taymor, *Titus: The Illustrated Screenplay* (New York: Newmarket, 2000), 19, 20. "Instead of re-creating Rome, 400 A.D., the locations of the film would include the ruins of Hadrian's villa, the baths of Caracalla, the Colosseum, etc., as they are today, with all their corroded beauty, centuries of graffiti and ghastly, ghostly history" (178). "As in the production design, the blend of styles inspired from three select eras (ancient Rome, the 1930s and the present) was a meticulous procedure on the part of Milena Canonero, the costume designer" (180).

22. Ibid., 174.

23. Ibid., 182.

24. As Carville puts it, "Always remember this: Every movie starts out, and there's a setup, then there's a conflict, and at the end there's a resolution." The crucial ads in that film end with, "Sí, se puede," the slogan that would become Obama's in 2008.

25. Cavell, *Pursuits of Happiness*, 27–28.

26. Cohen, "'Get a Life!,'" 25.

27. *Kingdom of Heaven: The Path to Redemption* (Disc 4).

28. Ibid.

29. I discuss the library and the archive in much greater detail in "The Biggest Independent Pictures Ever Made: Industrial Reflexivity Today," in *The Wiley-Blackwell History of American Film*, vol. 4, *1976–Present*, ed. Roy Grundmann, Cindy Lucia, and Art Simon (New York: Wiley-Blackwell, 2011), 517–41.

30. The exception to this rule is Robert Zemeckis's *Beowulf* (Paramount, 2007).

31. *King Arthur* DVD commentary.

32. Ibid.

33. The first sentence from Peter Zander, "Deutscher Härtetest," *Berliner Morgenpost*, dated June 10, 2008; actually May 12, 2004, http://www.morgenpost.de/printarchiv/kultur/article398994/Deutscher-Haertetest.html. The remainder from Frank Arnold, "Wolfgang Petersen: Keine Welt in Schwarz und Weiß," *Kölner Stadt-Anzeiger*, May 13, 2004, http://www.ksta.de/kultur/wolfgang-petersen—keine-welt-in-schwarz-und-weiss,15189520,14068132.html. Translations mine. Both articles are cited and excerpted in Winkler, *Gladiator*, who offers a very useful roundup of the German press coverage of *Troy*.

34. Robert J. Rabel, "The Realist Politics of *Troy*," in Winkler, *Gladiator*, 186–201, quote on 199.

35. M. E. Russell, "Helmer of Troy," *In Focus* 4:5 (May 2004), https://web.archive.org/web/20090101065158/http://www.natoonline.org/infocus/04may/petersenuncut.htm.

36. Michael Fleming, "Petersen Hits Beach at WB," *Variety*, Jan. 11, 2001, http://variety.com/2001/film/news/petersen-hits-beach-at-wb-1117791718/.

37. Arnold, "Wolfgang Petersen."

38. "From Ruins to Reality," *Troy* DVD supplement.

39. "Bonus" from Zander, "Deutscher Härtetest"; the remainder of the quote from Winkler, *Gladiator*, 8, quoting Tobias Wiethoff, "Interview mit dem Regisseur Wolfgang Petersen: 'Ich gehe dahin, wo der Stoff ist,'" *Westdeutsche Zeitung*, May 7, 2004. Winkler's original link is no longer live. As is usually the case, the director gave several very similar accounts of his aims and methods during the pre-release publicity. He told Zander, for example, "It didn't begin with us saying 'Let's make a film about American politics,' but with Homer's epic. But while we worked, we realized that the parallels to outside events were obvious."

40. "*Troy*: An Effects Odyssey," *Troy* DVD supplements.

41. Ibid.

42. John Colapinto, "Stoned Again," *Rolling Stone*, Dec. 9, 2004, 52–53.

43. Ron Suskind, "Without a Doubt," *New York Times Magazine*, Oct. 17, 2004, 44–51, quote on 51. Rove is anonymously quoted as a "senior aide" in the piece, although numerous sources since have attributed the remarks to him.

44. Colapinto, "Stoned Again."

45. Quoted in Simon Edge, "A Crusade Too Far? Panned by Critics, Savaged by Academics and Attacked by Religious Groups, Ridley Scott's Latest Film, *Kingdom of Heaven*, Is an Attempt to Heal a Divide That Has Festered for 900 Years," *The Express* May 4, 2005, 31 (nexis).

46. Anthony Breznican, "Epics Struggle," *USA Today*, Apr. 20, 2005, 1D, http://usatoday30.usatoday.com/life/movies/news/2005-04-19-epics_x.htm.

47. His return in disgrace opens Scott's *Robin Hood* (2010).

48. Alan Riding, "The Crusades as a Lesson in Harmony?," *NYT*, Apr. 24, 2005, B11.

49. "Faith and Courage," *Kingdom of Heaven* DVD supplement.

50. Caciola from Bob Thompson, "Hollywood on Crusade: With His Historical Epic, Ridley Scott Hurtles into Vexing, Volatile Territory," *Washington Post*, May 1, 2005, Arts 1.

51. Robert Rosenblum, *Transformations in Late Eighteenth Century Art* (Princeton, NJ: Princeton University Press, 1974), 59.

52. *Kingdom of Heaven* DVD commentary.

53. "The Path to Redemption," *Kingdom of Heaven* DVD supplement.

54. *Kingdom of Heaven* DVD commentary.

55. Douglas Wolk, *Reading Comics: How Graphic Novels Work and What They Mean* (Cambridge, MA: Da Capo, 2007), 188, 189.

56. Michael Gordon's reporting in the *NYT* served as an important channel for the administration's case against Iran. See "Deadliest Bomb in Iraq Is Made in Iran," *NYT*, Feb. 20, 2007, 1; Michael Gordon and Scott Shane, "U.S. Long Worried That Iran Supplied Arms to Iraq," *NYT*, Mar. 27, 2007. Seymour Hersh presented the most sustained analysis of the ratcheting up of the possible new front in "The Redirection," *New Yorker*, Mar. 5, 2007, http://www.newyorker.com/reporting/2007/03/05/070305fa_fact_hersh.

57. Jason Silverman, "*300* Brings History to Bloody Life," *Wired*, Feb 2007, http://archive.wired.com/culture/lifestyle/news/2007/02/72775.

58. Ibid.

59. "Superfield" is Claudia Gorbman's rendering of Michel Chion's term "superchamp," in his *Audio-Vision: Sound on Screen* (New York: Columbia University Press, 1994), 69. For him, Dolby Surround is the crucial technical leap. It "creates a space with fluid borders, a sort of superscreen enveloping the screen—the superfield."

60. Rosenblum, *Transformations*, 191.

61. Ibid., 190.

62. Chion, *Audio-Vision*, 100.

63. The scabbard was added after the preliminary sketch, where Leonidas's penis was visible.

Conclusion

1. Only the most fragmentary bibliography can be offered here. For the creation of the studio, see Michael Cole and Mary Pardo, eds., *Inventions of the Studio* (Chapel Hill: University of North Carolina Press, 2005). For Courbet, see Michael Fried, *Courbet's Realism* (Chicago: University of Chicago Press, 1990). For Nauman, see Constance Lewallen, *A Rose Has No Teeth: Bruce Nauman in the 1960s* (Berkeley: University of Cali-

fornia Press, 2007). For American modernism more generally, see Caroline Jones, *The Machine in the Studio: Constructing the Postwar American Artist* (Chicago: University of Chicago Press, 1996). For the Actors Studio, see Lee Strasberg, *A Dream of Passion: The Development of the Method* (New York: Penguin, 1987). For music studios, see Susan Schmidt Horning, *Chasing Sound: Technology, Culture, and the Art of the Studio Recording from Edison to the LP* (Baltimore: Johns Hopkins University Press, 2013).

2. Stanley Cavell, *The World Viewed: Reflections on the Ontology of Film*, enl. ed. (Cambridge, MA: Harvard University Press, 1979), 128.

3. Bordwell, *The Way Hollywood Tells It*, 121–38.

4. Cavell, *The World Viewed*, 121.

Index

Note: Page numbers in italic type indicate illustrations.

Lightning Source UK Ltd.
Milton Keynes UK
UKHW051031031221
394935UK00001B/32